Date Due

JUL   2000

		JUN	2004
		JUN 09	
		JUL X X 2015	

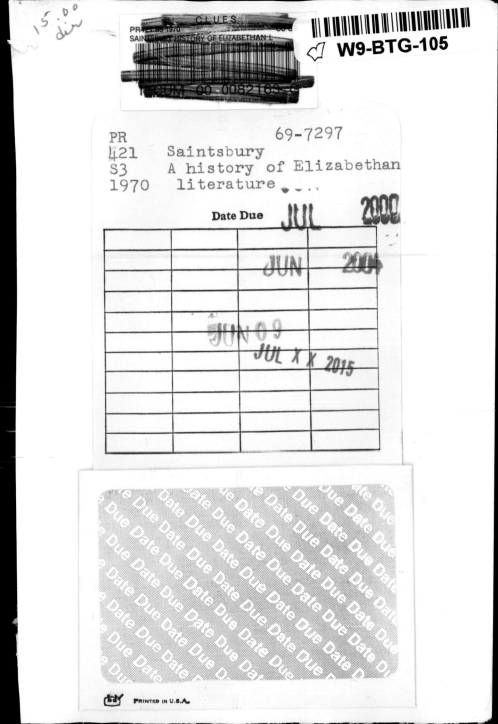

HISTORY OF ENGLISH LITERATURE

ELIZABETHAN LITERATURE

A HISTORY

OF

ELIZABETHAN LITERATURE

BY

GEORGE SAINTSBURY

NEW YORK / RUSSELL & RUSSELL

FIRST PUBLISHED IN 1887
REPRODUCED FROM THE 9TH EDITION OF 1907
AND REISSUED, 1970, BY RUSSELL & RUSSELL
A DIVISION OF ATHENEUM PUBLISHERS, INC.
BY ARRANGEMENT WITH THE ESTATE OF GEORGE SAINTSBURY
L. C. CATALOG CARD NO: 79-83853
PRINTED IN THE UNITED STATES OF AMERICA

PREFACE TO NINTH EDITION

As was explained in the Note to the Preface of the previous editions and impressions of this book, after the first, hardly one of them appeared without careful revision, and the insertion of a more or less considerable number of additions and corrections. I found, indeed, few errors of a kind that need have seemed serious except to Momus or Zoilus. But in the enormous number of statements of fact which literary history of the more exact kind requires, minor blunders, be they more or fewer, are sure to creep in. No writer, again, who endeavours constantly to keep up and extend his knowledge of such a subject as Elizabethan literature, can fail to have something new to say from time to time. And though no one who is competent originally for his task ought to experience any violent changes of view, any one's views may undergo modification. In particular, he may find that readers have misunderstood him, and that alterations of expression are desirable. For all these reasons and others I have not spared trouble in the various revisions referred to ; I think the book has been kept by them

fairly abreast of its author's knowledge, and I hope it is
not too far behind that of others.

It will, however, almost inevitably happen that a long
series of piecemeal corrections and codicils somewhat
disfigures the character of the composition as a whole.
And after nearly the full score of years, and not much
less than half a score of re-appearances, it has seemed to
me desirable to make a somewhat more thorough, minute,
and above all connected revision than I have ever made
before.   And so, my publishers falling in with this view,
the present edition represents the result.   I do not think
it necessary to reprint the original preface.   When I
wrote it I had already had some, and since I wrote it
I have had much more, experience in writing literary
history.   I have never seen reason to alter the opinion
that, to make such history of any value at all, the critical
judgments and descriptions must represent direct, original,
and first-hand reading and thought ; and that in these
critical judgments and descriptions the value of it consists.
Even summaries and analyses of the matter of books,
except in so far as they are necessary to criticism, come
far second ; while biographical and bibliographical details
are of much less importance, and may (as indeed in
one way or another they generally must) be taken at
second hand.   The completion of the *Dictionary of
National Biography* has at once facilitated the task of the
writer, and to a great extent disarmed the candid critic

who delights, in cases of disputed date, to assume that the date which his author chooses is the wrong one. And I have in the main adjusted the dates in this book (where necessary) accordingly. The bibliographical additions which have been made to the Index will be found not inconsiderable.

I believe that, in my present plan, there is no author of importance omitted (there were not many even in the first edition), and that I have been able somewhat to improve the book from the results of twenty years' additional study, twelve of which have been mainly devoted to English literature. How far it must still be from being worthy of its subject, nobody can know better than I do. But I know also, and I am very happy to know, that, as an Elizabethan himself might have said, my unworthiness has guided many worthy ones to something like knowledge, and to what is more important than knowledge, love, of a subject so fascinating and so magnificent. And that the book may still have the chance of doing this, I hope to spare no trouble upon it as often as the opportunity presents itself. [1]

EDINBURGH, *January 30,* 1907.

---

[1] In the last (eleventh) re-impression no alterations seemed necessary. In this, one or two bibliographical matters may call for notice. Every student of Donne should now consult Professor Grierson's edition of the *Poems* (2 vols., Oxford, 1912), and as inquiries have been made as to the third volume of my own *Caroline Poets* (see Index), containing Cleveland, King, Stanley, and some less known authors, I may be permitted to say that it has been in the press for years, and a large part of it is completed. But various stoppages, in no case due to neglect, and latterly made absolute by the war, have prevented its appearance.—BATH, October 8, 1918.

CONTENTS

CHAPTER I

FROM TOTTEL'S MISCELLANY TO SPENSER

CHAPTER II

EARLY ELIZABETHAN PROSE

CHAPTER III

THE FIRST DRAMATIC PERIOD

CHAPTER IV

"THE FAËRIE QUEENE" AND ITS GROUP

CHAPTER V

THE SECOND DRAMATIC PERIOD—SHAKESPERE

CHAPTER VI

LATER ELIZABETHAN AND JACOBEAN PROSE

CHAPTER VII

THE THIRD DRAMATIC PERIOD

CHAPTER VIII

THE SCHOOL OF SPENSER AND THE TRIBE OF BEN

CHAPTER IX

MILTON, TAYLOR, CLARENDON, BROWNE, HOBBES

CHAPTER X

CAROLINE POETRY

CHAPTER XI

THE FOURTH DRAMATIC PERIOD

CHAPTER XII

MINOR CAROLINE PROSE

CHAPTER I

IN a work like the present, forming part of a larger whole and preceded by another part, the writer has the advantage of being almost wholly free from a difficulty which often presses on historians of a limited and definite period, whether of literary or of any other history. That difficulty lies in the discussion and decision of the question of origins—in the allotment of sufficient, and not more than sufficient, space to a preliminary recapitulation of the causes and circumstances of the actual events to be related. Here there is no need for any but the very briefest references of the kind to connect the present volume with its forerunner, or rather to indicate the connection of the two.

There has been little difference of opinion as to the long dead-season of English poetry, broken chiefly, if not wholly, by poets Scottish rather than English, which lasted through almost the whole of the fifteenth and the first half of the sixteenth centuries. There has also been little difference in regarding the remarkable work (known as Tottel's *Miscellany*, but more properly called *Songs and Sonnets, written by the Right Honourable Lord Henry Howard, late Earl of Surrey, and other*) which was published by Richard Tottel in 1557, and which went through two editions in the summer of that year, as marking the

dawn of the new period.   The book is, indeed, remarkable in
many ways.   The first thing, probably, which strikes the modern
reader about it is the fact that great part of its contents is anonymous and only conjecturally to be attributed, while as to the part
which is more certainly known to be the work of several authors,
most of those authors were either dead or had written long
before.   Mr. Arber's remarks in his introduction (which, though
I have rather an objection to putting mere citations before the
public, I am glad here to quote as a testimony in the forefront
of this book to the excellent deserts of one who by himself has
done as much as any living man to facilitate the study of Elizabethan literature) are entirely to the point—how entirely to the
point only students of foreign as well as of English literature
know.   "The poets of that age," says Mr. Arber, "wrote for
their own delectation and for that of their friends, and not for
the general public.   They generally had the greatest aversion to
their works appearing in print."   This aversion, which continued
in France till the end of the seventeenth century, if not later, had
been somewhat broken down in England by the middle of the
sixteenth, though vestiges of it long survived, and in the form of
a reluctance to be known to write for money, may be found even
within the confines of the nineteenth.   The humbler means and
lesser public of the English booksellers have saved English literature from the bewildering multitude of pirated editions, printed
from private and not always faithful manuscript copies, which
were for so long the despair of the editors of many French
classics.   But the manuscript copies themselves survive to a
certain extent, and in the more sumptuous and elaborate editions
of our poets (such as, for instance, Dr. Grosart's *Donne*) what
they have yielded may be studied with some interest.   Moreover,
they have occasionally preserved for us work nowhere else to be
obtained, as, for instance, in the remarkable folio which has
supplied Mr. Bullen with so much of his invaluable collection of
Old Plays.   At the early period of Tottel's *Miscellany* it would
appear that the very idea of publication in print had hardly

occurred to many writers' minds. When the book appeared, both
its main contributors, Surrey and Wyatt, had been long dead, as
well as others (Sir Francis Bryan and Anne Boleyn's unlucky
brother, George Lord Rochford) who are supposed to be represented. The short Printer's Address to the Reader gives absolutely no intelligence as to the circumstances of the publication,
the person responsible for the editing, or the authority which the
editor and printer may have had for their inclusion of different
authors' work. It is only a theory, though a sufficiently plausible
one, that the editor was Nicholas Grimald, chaplain to Bishop
Thirlby of Ely, a Cambridge man who some ten years before had
been incorporated at Oxford and had been elected to a Fellowship at Merton College. In Grimald's or Grimoald's connection
with the book there was certainly something peculiar, for the first
edition contains forty poems contributed by him and signed with
his name, while in the second the full name is replaced by " N.
G.," and a considerable number of his poems give way to others.
More than one construction might, no doubt, be placed on this
curious fact ; but hardly any construction can be placed on it
which does not in some way connect Grimald with the publication. It may be added that, while his, Surrey's, and Wyatt's contributions are substantive and known—the numbers of separate
poems contributed being respectively forty for Surrey, the same for
Grimald, and ninety-six for Wyatt—no less than one hundred and
thirty-four poems, reckoning the contents of the first and second
editions together, are attributed to " other " or " uncertain "
authors. And of these, though it is pretty positively known
that certain writers did contribute to the book, only four
poems have been even conjecturally traced to particular authors.
The most interesting of these by far is the poem attributed,
with that which immediately precedes it, to Lord Vaux, and
containing the verses " For age with stealing steps," known to
every one from the gravedigger in *Hamlet*. Nor is this the
only connection of Tottel's *Miscellany* with Shakespere, for there
is no reasonable doubt that the " Book of Songs and Sonnets,"

to the absence of which Slender so pathetically refers in *The Merry Wives of Windsor*, is Tottel's, which, as the first to use the title, long retained it by right of precedence. Indeed, one of its authors, Churchyard, who, though not in his first youth at its appearance, survived into the reign of James, quotes it as such, and so does Drayton even later. No sonnets had been seen in England before, nor was the whole style of the verse which it contained less novel than this particular form.

As is the case with many if not most of the authors of our period, a rather unnecessary amount of ink has been spilt on questions very distantly connected with the question of the abso- lute and relative merit of Surrey and Wyatt in English poetry. In particular, the influence of the one poet on the other, and the consequent degree of originality to be assigned to each, have been much discussed. A very few dates and facts will supply most of the information necessary to enable the reader to decide this and other questions for himself. Sir Thomas Wyatt, son of Sir Henry Wyatt of Allington, Kent, was born in 1503, entered St. John's College, Cambridge, in 1515, became a favourite of Henry VIII., received important diplomatic appointments, and died in 1542. Lord Henry Howard was born (as is supposed) in 1517, and became Earl of Surrey by courtesy (he was not, the account of his judicial murder says, a lord of Parliament) at eight years old. Very little is really known of his life, and his love for "Geraldine" was made the basis of a series of fictions by Nash half a century after his death. He cannot have been more than thirty when, in the Reign of Terror towards the close of Henry VIII.'s life, he was arrested on frivolous charges, the gravest being the assumption of the royal arms, found guilty of treason, and beheaded on Tower Hill on 19th January 1547. Thus it will be seen that Wyatt was at Cambridge before Surrey was born, and died five years before him ; to which it need only be added that Surrey has an epitaph on Wyatt which clearly expresses the relation of disciple to master. Yet despite this relation and the community of influences which acted on both, their characteristics are markedly different, and each is of the greatest importance in English poetical history.

In order to appreciate exactly what this importance is we must remember in what state Wyatt and Surrey found the art which they practised and in which they made a new start. Speaking roughly but with sufficient accuracy for the purpose, that state is typically exhibited in two writers, Hawes and Skelton. The former represents the last phase of the Chaucerian school, weakened not merely by the absence of men of great talent during more than a century, but by the continual imitation during that period of weaker and ever weaker French models—the last faint echoes of the *Roman de la Rose* and the first extravagances of the *Rhétoriqueurs.* Skelton, on the other hand, with all his vigour, represents the English tendency to prosaic doggerel. Whether Wyatt and his younger companion deliberately had recourse to Italian example in order to avoid these two dangers it would be impossible to say. But the example was evidently before them, and the result is certainly such an avoidance. Nevertheless both, and especially Wyatt, had a great deal to learn. It is perfectly evident that neither had any theory of English prosody before him. Wyatt's first sonnet displays the completest indifference to quantity, not merely scanning " harber," " banner," and " suffer " as iambs (which might admit of some defence), but making a rhyme of " feareth " and " appeareth," not on the penultimates, but on the mere " eth." In the following poems even worse liberties are found, and the strange turns and twists which the poet gives to his decasyllables suggest either a total want of ear or such a study in foreign languages that the student had actually forgotten the intonation and cadences of his own tongue. So stumbling and knock-kneed is his verse that any one who remembers the admirable versification of Chaucer may now and then be inclined to think that Wyatt had much better have left his innovations alone. But this petulance is soon rebuked by the appearance of such a sonnet as this :—

(*The lover having dreamed enjoying of his love complaineth that the dream is not either longer or truer.*)

> " Unstable dream, according to the place
>   Be steadfast once, or else at least be true.
>   By tasted sweetness, make me not to rue
> The sudden loss of thy false feigned grace.
> By good respect in such a dangerous case
>   Thou brought'st not her into these tossing seas
>   But mad'st my sprite to live, my care to increase,[1]
> My body in tempest her delight to embrace.
> The body dead, the sprite had his desire :
>   Painless was th' one, the other in delight.
>   Why then, alas ! did it not keep it right,
> But thus return to leap into the fire ?
> And where it was at wish, could not remain ?
> Such mocks of dreams do turn to deadly pain."

Wyatt's awkwardness is not limited to the decasyllable, but some of his short poems in short lines recover rhythmical grace very remarkably, and set a great example.

Surrey is a far superior metrist.   Neither in his sonnets, nor in his various stanzas composed of heroics, nor in what may be called his doggerel metres—the fatally fluent Alexandrines, fourteeners, and admixtures of both, which dominated English poetry from his time to Spenser's, and were never quite rejected during the Elizabethan period—do we find evidence of the want of ear, or the want of command of language, which makes Wyatt's versification frequently disgusting.   Surrey has even no small mastery of what may be called the architecture of verse, the valuing of cadence in successive lines so as to produce a concerted piece and not a mere reduplication of the same notes.   And in his translations of the *Æneid* (not published in Tottel's *Miscellany*) he has the great honour of being the originator of blank verse, and blank verse of by no means a bad pattern.   The following

---

[1] In original "tencrease," and below "timbrace." This substitution of elision for slur or hiatus (found in Chaucerian MSS.) passed later into the t' and th' of the seventeenth and eighteenth centuries.

sonnet, combined Alexandrine and fourteener, and blank verse extract, may be useful :—

(Complaint that his lady after she knew of his love kept her face alway hidden from him.)

> " I never saw my lady lay apart
> Her cornet black, in cold nor yet in heat,
> Sith first she knew my grief was grown so great ;
> Which other fancies driveth from my heart,
> That to myself I do the thought reserve,
> The which unwares did wound my woeful breast.
> But on her face mine eyes mought never rest
> Yet, since she knew I did her love, and serve
> Her golden tresses clad alway with black,
> Her smiling looks that hid[es] thus evermore
> And that restrains which I desire so sore.
> So doth this cornet govern me, alack !
> In summer sun, in winter's breath, a frost
> Whereby the lights of her fair looks I lost." [1]

(Complaint of the absence of her lover being upon the sea.)

> " Good ladies, ye that have your pleasures in exile,
> Step in your foot, come take a place, and mourn with me a while.
> And such as by their lords do set but little price,
> Let them sit still : it skills them not what chance come on the dice.
> But ye whom love hath bound by order of desire,
> To love your lords whose good deserts none other would require,
> Come ye yet once again and set your foot by mine,
> Whose woeful plight and sorrows great, no tongue can well define." [2]

---

[1] As printed exactly in both first and second editions this sonnet is evidently corrupt, and the variations between the two are additional evidence of this. I have ventured to change "hid" to "hides" in line 10, and to alter the punctuation in line 13. If the reader takes "that" in line 5 as = "so that," "that" in line 10 as = "which" (*i.e.* "black"), and "that" in line 11 with "which," he will now, I think, find it intelligible. Line 13 is usually printed :

> "In summer, sun : in winter's breath, a frost."

Now no one would compare a black silk hood to the sun, and a reference to line 2 will show the real meaning. The hood is a frost which lasts through summer and winter alike.

[2] In reading these combinations it must be remembered that is there always a strong cæsura in the midst of the first and Alexandrine line. It is the Alexandrine which Mr. Browning has imitated in *Fifine*, not that of Drayton, or of the various practitioners of the Spenserian stanza from Spenser himself downwards.

"It was the (n)[1] night ; the sound and quiet sleep
Had through the earth the weary bodies caught,
The woods, the raging seas, were fallen to rest,
When that the stars had half their course declined.
The fields whist : beasts and fowls of divers hue,
And what so that in the broad lakes remained,
Or yet among the bushy thicks [2] of briar,
Laid down to sleep by silence of the night,
'Gan swage their cares, mindless of travails past.
Not so the spirit of this Phenician.
Unhappy she that on no sleep could chance,
Nor yet night's rest enter in eye or breast.
Her cares redouble : love doth rise and rage again,[3]
And overflows with swelling storms of wrath."

The "other" or "uncertain" authors, though interesting
enough for purposes of literary comparison, are very inferior to
Wyatt and Surrey. Grimald, the supposed editor, though his
verse must not, of course, be judged with reference to a more
advanced state of things than his own, is but a journeyman verse-
smith.

"Sith, Blackwood, you have mind to take a wife,
I pray you tell wherefore you like that life,"

is a kind of foretaste of Crabbe in its bland ignoring of the
formal graces of poetry. He acquits himself tolerably in the
combinations of Alexandrines and fourteeners noticed above
(the "poulter's measure," as Gascoigne was to call it later), nor
does he ever fall into the worst kind of jog-trot. His epitaphs and
elegies are his best work, and the best of them is that on his
mother. Very much the same may be said of the strictly miscellaneous part of the *Miscellany*. The greater part of the
Uncertain Authors are less ambitious, but also less irregular than
Wyatt, while they fall far short of Surrey in every respect. Sometimes, as in the famous "I loath that I did love," both syntax

---

[1] In these extracts ( ) signifies that something found in text seems better
away ; [ ] that something wanting in text has been conjecturally supplied.

[2] Thickets.

[3] This Alexandrine is not common, and is probably a mere oversight.

and prosody hardly show the reform at all ; they recall the ruder snatches of an earlier time. But, on the whole, the characteristics of these poets, both in matter and form, are sufficiently uniform and sufficiently interesting. Metrically, they show, on the one side, a desire to use a rejuvenated heroic, either in couplets or in various combined forms, the simplest of which is the elegiac quatrain of alternately rhyming lines, and the most complicated the sonnet ; while between them various stanzas more or less suggested by Italian are to be ranked. Of this thing there has been and will be no end as long as English poetry lasts. The attempt to arrange the old and apparently almost indigenous "eights and sixes" into fourteener lines and into alternate fourteeners and Alexandrines, seems to have commended itself even more to contemporary taste, and, as we have seen and shall see, it was eagerly followed for more than half a century. But it was not destined to succeed. These long lines, unless very sparingly used, or with the ground-foot changed from the iambus to the anapæst or the trochee, are not in keeping with the genius of English poetry, as even the great examples of Chapman's *Homer* and the *Polyolbion* may be said to have shown once for all. In the hands, moreover, of the poets of this particular time, whether they were printed at length or cut up into eights and sixes, they had an almost irresistible tendency to degenerate into a kind of lolloping amble which is inexpressibly monotonous. Even when the spur of a really poetical inspiration excites this amble into something more fiery (the best example existing is probably Southwell's wonderful "Burning Babe"), the sensitive ear feels that there is constant danger of a relapse, and at the worst the thing becomes mere doggerel. Yet for about a quarter of a century these overgrown lines held the field in verse and drama alike, and the encouragement of them must be counted as a certain drawback to the benefits which Surrey, Wyatt, and the other contributors of the *Miscellany* conferred on English literature by their exercises, here and elsewhere, in the blank verse decasyllable, the couplet, the stanza, and, above all, the sonnet.

It remains to say something of the matter as distinguished from the form of this poetry, and for once the form is of hardly superior importance to the matter. It is a question of some interest, though unfortunately one wholly incapable of solution, whether the change in the character of poetical thought and theme which Wyatt and Surrey wrought was accidental, and consequent merely on their choice of models, and especially of Petrarch, or essential and deliberate. If it was accidental, there is no greater accident in the history of literature. The absence of the personal note in mediæval poetry is a commonplace, and nowhere had that absence been more marked than in England. With Wyatt and Surrey English poetry became at a bound the most personal (and in a rather bad but unavoidable word) the most "introspective" in Europe. There had of course been love poetry before, but its convention had been a convention of impersonality. It now became exactly the reverse. The lover sang less his joys than his sorrows, and he tried to express those sorrows and their effect on him in the most personal way he could. Although allegory still retained a strong hold on the national taste, and was yet to receive its greatest poetical expression in *The Faërie Queene*, it was allegory of quite a different kind from that which in the *Roman de la Rose* had taken Europe captive, and had since dominated European poetry in all departments, and especially in the department of love-making. " Dangier " and his fellow-phantoms fled before the dawn of the new poetry in England, and the depressing influences of a common form—a conventional stock of images, personages, and almost language—disappeared. No doubt there was conventionality enough in the following of the Petrarchian model, but it was a less stiff and uniform conventionality ; it allowed and indeed invited the individual to wear his rue with a difference, and to avail himself at least of the almost infinite diversity of circumstance and feeling which the life of the actual man affords, instead of reducing everything to the moods and forms of an already generalised and allegorised experience. With the new theme to handle and the new forms ready as tools for the handler, with the general ferment of European spirits, it might readily have been supposed that a remarkable out-turn of work would be the certain and immediate result.

The result in fact may have been certain but it was not immediate, being delayed for nearly a quarter of a century; and the next remarkable piece of work done in English poetry after Tottel's *Miscellany*—a piece of work of greater actual poetical merit than anything in that *Miscellany* itself—was in the old forms, and showed little if any influence of the new poetical learning. This was the famous *Mirror for Magistrates*, or rather that part of it contributed by Thomas Sackville, Lord Buckhurst. *The Mirror* as a whole has bibliographical and prosodic rather than literary interest. It was certainly planned as early as 1555 by way of a supplement to Lydgate's translation of Boccaccio's *Fall of Princes*. It was at first edited by a certain William Baldwin, and for nearly half a century it received additions and alterations from various respectable hacks of letters; but the "Induction" and the "Complaint of Buckingham" which Sackville furnished to it in 1559, though they were not published till four years later, completely outweigh all the rest in value. To my own fancy the fact that Sackville was (in what proportion is disputed) also author of *Gorboduc* (see Chapter III.) adds but little to its interest. His contributions to *The Mirror for Magistrates* contain the best poetry written in the English language between Chaucer and Spenser, and are most certainly the originals or at least the models of some of Spenser's finest work. He has had but faint praise of late years. According to the late Professor Minto, he "affords abundant traces of the influence of Wyatt and Surrey." I do not know what the traces are, and I should say myself that few contemporary or nearly contemporary efforts are more distinct. Dean Church says that we see in him a faint anticipation of Spenser. My estimate of Spenser, as I hope to show, is not below that of any living critic; but considerations of bulk being allowed, and it being fully granted that Sackville had nothing like

Spenser's magnificent range, I cannot see any "faintness" in the case. If the "Induction" had not been written it is at least possible that the "Cave of Despair" would never have enriched English poetry.

Thomas Sackville was born at Buckhurst in Sussex, in the year 1536, of a family which was of the most ancient extraction and the most honourable standing. He was educated at Oxford, at the now extinct Hart Hall, whence, according to a practice as common then as it is uncommon now (except in the cases of royal princes and a few persons of difficult and inconstant taste), he moved to Cambridge. Then he entered the Inner Temple, married early, travelled, became noted in literature, was made Lord Buckhurst at the age of thirty-one, was for many years one of Elizabeth's chief councillors and officers, was promoted to the Earldom of Dorset at the accession of James I., and died, it is said, at the Council table on the 19th of April 1608.

We shall deal with *Gorboduc* hereafter : the two contributions to *The Mirror for Magistrates* concern us here. And I have little hesitation in saying that no more astonishing contribution to English poetry, when the due reservations of that historical criticism which is the life of all criticism are made, is to be found anywhere. The bulk is not great : twelve or fifteen hundred lines must cover the whole of it. The form is not new, being merely the seven-line stanza already familiar in Chaucer. The arrangement is in no way novel, combining as it does the allegorical presentment of embodied virtues, vices, and qualities with the melancholy narrative common in poets for many years before. But the poetical value of the whole is extraordinary. The two constituents of that value, the formal and the material, are represented with a singular equality of development. There is nothing here of Wyatt's floundering prosody, nothing of the well-intentioned doggerel in which Surrey himself indulges and in which his pupils simply revel. The cadences of the verse are perfect, the imagery fresh and sharp, the presentation of nature singularly original, when it is compared with the battered copies of the poets with whom Sackville must have been most familiar, the followers of Chaucer from Occleve to Hawes. Even the general plan of the poem—the weakest part of nearly all poems of this time—is extraordinarily effective and makes one sincerely sorry that Sackville's taste, or his other occupations, did not permit him to carry out the whole scheme on his own account. The "Induction," in which the author is brought face to face with Sorrow, and the central passages of the "Complaint of Buckingham," have a depth and fulness of poetical sound and sense for which we must look backwards a hundred and fifty years, or forwards nearly five and twenty. Take, for instance, these stanzas :—

> " Thence come we to the horror and the hell,
>   The large great kingdoms, and the dreadful reign
> Of Pluto in his throne where he did dwell,
> The wide waste places, and the hugy plain,
> The wailings, shrieks, and sundry sorts of pain,
>   The sighs,the sobs, the deep and deadly groan ;
>   Earth, air, and all, resounding plaint and moan.

> " Here puled the babes, and here the maids unwed
> With folded hands their sorry chance bewailed,
> Here wept the guiltless slain, and lovers dead,
> That slew themselves when nothing else availed ;
> A thousand sorts of sorrows here, that wailed
>   With sighs and tears, sobs, shrieks, and all yfere
>   That oh, alas ! it was a hell to hear.
>   .   .   .   .

> " *Lo here*, quoth Sorrow, princes of renown,
> That whilom sat on top of fortune's wheel,
> Now laid full low ; like wretches whirled down,
> Ev'n with one frown, that stayed but with a smile :
> And now behold the thing that thou, erewhile,
>   Saw only in thought : and what thou now shalt hear,
>   Recount the same to kesar, king, and peer." [1]

---

[1] The precedent descriptions of Sorrow herself, of Misery, and of Old Age, are even finer than the above, which, however, I have preferred for three reasons. ·First, it has been less often quoted ; secondly, its subject is a kind of commonplace, and, therefore, shows the poet's strength of handling ; thirdly, because of the singular and characteristic majesty of the opening lines.

It is perhaps well, in an early passage of a book which will have much to do with the criticism of poetry, to dwell a little on what seems to the critic to be the root of that matter. In the first place, I must entirely differ with those persons who have sought to create an independent prosody for English verse under the head of "beats" or "accents" or something of that sort. *Every English metre since Chaucer at least can be scanned, within the proper limits, according to the strictest rules of classical prosody: and while all good English metre comes out scatheless from the application of those rules, nothing exhibits the badness of bad English metre so well as that application.* It is, alongside of their great merits, the distinguishing fault of Wyatt eminently, of Surrey to a less degree, and of all the new school up to Spenser more or less, that they neglect the quantity test too freely ; it is the merit of Sackville that, holding on in this respect to the good school of Chaucer, he observes it. You will find no "jawbreakers" in Sackville, no attempts to adjust English words on a Procrustean bed of independent quantification. He has not indeed the manifold music of Spenser—it would be unreasonable to expect that he should have it. But his stanzas, as the foregoing examples will show, are of remarkable melody, and they have about them a command, a completeness of accomplishment within the writer's intentions, which is very noteworthy in so young a man. The extraordinary richness and stateliness of the measure has escaped no critic. There is indeed a certain one-sidedness about it, and a devil's advocate might urge that a long poem couched in verse (let alone the subject) of such unbroken gloom would be intolerable. But Sackville did not write a long poem, and his complete command within his limits of the effect at which he evidently aimed is most remarkable.

The second thing to note about the poem is the extraordinary freshness and truth of its imagery. From a young poet we always expect second-hand presentations of nature, and in Sackville's day second-hand presentation of nature had been elevated to the rank of a science. Here the new school—Surrey, Wyatt, and

their followers—even if he had studied them, could have given
him little or no help, for great as are the merits of Tottel's
Miscellany, no one would go to it for representations of nature.
Among his predecessors in his own style he had to go back to
Chaucer (putting the Scotch school out of the question) before he
could find anything original. Yet it may be questioned whether
the sketches of external scenery in these brief essays of his, or
the embodiments of internal thought in the pictures of Sorrow
and the other allegorical wights, are most striking. It is perfectly
clear that Thomas Sackville had, in the first place, a poetical eye
to see, within as well as without, the objects of poetical presentment ; in the second place, a poetical vocabulary in which to clothe
the results of his seeing ; and in the third place, a poetical ear by
aid of which to arrange his language in the musical co-ordination
necessary to poetry. Wyatt had been too much to seek in the
last ; Surrey had not been very obviously furnished with the first ;
and all three were not to be possessed by any one else till
Edmund Spenser arose to put Sackville's lessons in practice on
a wider scale, and with a less monotonous lyre. It is possible
that Sackville's claims in drama may have been exaggerated—
they have of late years rather been undervalued : but his claims in
poetry proper can only be overlooked by those who decline to
consider the most important part of poetry. In the subject of
even his part of *The Mirror* there is nothing new : there is only a
following of Chaucer, and Gower, and Occleve, and Lydgate, and
Hawes, and many others. But in the handling there is one
novelty which makes all others of no effect or interest. It is the
novelty of a new poetry.

It has already been remarked that these two important books
were not immediately followed by any others in poetry corresponding to their importance. The poetry of the first half of
Elizabeth's reign is as mediocre as the poetry of the last half of
her reign is magnificent. Although it had taken some hints from
Wyatt and Surrey it had not taken the best ; and the inexplicable
devotion of most of the versifiers of the time to the doggerel

metres already referred to seems to have prevented them from cultivating anything better.   Yet the pains which were spent upon translation during this time were considerable, and undoubtedly had much to do with strengthening and improving the language.   The formal part of poetry became for the first time a subject of study resulting in the *Instructions* of Gascoigne, and in the noteworthy critical works which will be mentioned in the next chapter ; while the popularity of poetical miscellanies showed the audience that existed for verse.   The translators and the miscellanists will each call for some brief notice; but first it is necessary to mention some individual, and in their way, original writers who, though not possessing merit at all equal to that of Wyatt, Surrey, and Sackville, yet deserve to be singled from the crowd. These are Gascoigne, Churchyard, Turberville, Googe, and Tusser.

The poetaster and literary hack, Whetstone, who wrote a poetical memoir of George Gascoigne after his death, entitles it a remembrance of " the well employed life and godly end " of his hero.   It is not necessary to dispute that Gascoigne's end was godly ; but except for the fact that he was for some years a diligent and not unmeritorious writer, it is not so certain that his life was well employed.   At any rate he does not seem to have thought so himself.   The date of his birth has been put as early as 1525 and as late as 1536 : he certainly died in 1577. His father, a knight of good family and estate in Essex, disinherited him ; but he was educated at Cambridge, if not at both universities, was twice elected to Parliament, travelled and fought abroad, and took part in the famous festival at Kenilworth.   His work is, as has been said, considerable, and is remarkable for the number of first attempts in English which it contains.   It has at least been claimed for him (though careful students of literary history know that these attributions are always rather hazardous) that he wrote the first English prose comedy (*The Supposes*, a version of Ariosto), the first regular verse satire (*The Steel Glass*), the first prose tale (a version from Bandello), the first translation from Greek tragedy (*Jocasta*), and the first critical essay (the above-mentioned *Notes of Instruction*). Most of these things, it will be seen, were merely adaptations of foreign originals; but they certainly make up a remarkable budget for one man. In addition to them, and to a good number of shorter and miscellaneous poems, must be mentioned the *Glass of Government* (a kind of morality or serious comedy, moulded, it would seem, on German originals), and the rather prettily, if fantastically termed *Flowers, Herbs, and Weeds*. Gascoigne has a very fair command of metre : he is not a great sinner in the childish alliteration which, surviving from the older English poetry, helps to convert so much of his contemporaries' work into doggerel. The pretty " Lullaby of a Lover," and "Gascoigne's Good Morrow " may be mentioned, and part of one of them may be quoted, as a fair specimen of his work, which is always tolerable if never first-rate.

> " Sing lullaby, as women do,
>   Wherewith they bring their babes to rest,
> And lullaby can I sing too,
>   As womanly as can the best.
> With lullaby they still the child ;
> And if I be not much beguiled,
> Full many wanton babes have I
> Which must be stilled with lullaby.

> " First lullaby, my youthful years,
>   It is now time to go to bed,
> For crooked age and hoary hairs
>   Have won the hav'n within my head :
> With lullaby then, youth, be still,
> With lullaby content thy will,
> Since courage quails and comes behind,
> Go sleep and so beguile thy mind.

> " Next lullaby, my gazing eyes,
>   Which wanton were to glance apace,
> For every glass may now suffice
>   To show the furrows in my face.
> With lullaby then wink awhile,
> With lullaby your looks beguile ;
> Let no fair face, nor beauty bright,
> Entice you oft with vain delight.

" And lullaby, my wanton will,
      Let reason(s) rule now rein thy thought,
Since all too late I find by skill
      How dear I have thy fancies bought :
With lullaby now take thine ease,
      With lullaby thy doubts appease,
For trust to this, if thou be still
      My body shall obey thy will."

Thomas Churchyard was an inferior sort of Gascoigne, who led a much longer if less eventful life. He was about the Court for the greater part of the century, and had a habit of calling his little books, which were numerous, and written both in verse and prose, by alliterative titles playing on his own name, such as *Churchyard's Chips, Churchyard's Choice,* and so forth. He was a person of no great literary power, and chiefly noteworthy because of his long life after contributing to Tottel's *Miscellany,* which makes him a link between the old literature and the new.

The literary interests and tentative character of the time, together with its absence of original genius, and the constant symptoms of not having "found its way," are also very noteworthy in George Turberville and Barnabe Googe, who were friends and verse writers of not dissimilar character. Turberville, of whom not much is known, was a Dorsetshire man of good family, and was educated at Winchester and Oxford. His birth and death dates are both extremely uncertain. Besides a book on Falconry and numerous translations (to which, like all the men of his school and day, he was much addicted), he wrote a good many occasional poems, trying even blank verse. Barnabe Googe, a Lincolnshire man, and a member of both universities, appears to have been born in 1540, was employed in Ireland, and died in 1594. He was kin to the Cecils, and Mr. Arber has recovered some rather interesting details about his love affairs, in which he was assisted by Lord Burghley. He, too, was an indefatigable translator, and wrote some original poems. Both poets affected the combination of Alexandrine and fourteener (split up or not, as the printer chose, into six, six, eight, six), the popularity of which has been noted, and both succumbed too often to its capacities of doggerel. Turberville's best work is the following song in a pretty metre well kept up :—

> " The green that you did wish me wear
> Aye for your love,
> And on my helm a branch to bear
> Not to remove,
> Was ever you to have in mind
> Whom Cupid hath my feire assigned.
>
> " As I in this have done your will
> And mind to do,
> So I request you to fulfil
> My fancy too ;
> A green and loving heart to have,
> And this is all that I do crave.
>
> " For if your flowering heart should change
> His colour green,
> Or you at length a lady strange
> Of me be seen,
> Then will my branch against his use
> His colour change for your refuse.[1]
>
> " As winter's force cannot deface
> This branch his hue,
> So let no change of love disgrace
> Your friendship true ;
> You were mine own, and so be still,
> So shall we live and love our fill.
>
> " Then I may think myself to be
> Well recompensed,
> For wearing of the tree that is
> So well defensed
> Against all weather that doth fall
> When wayward winter spits his gall.
>
> " And when we meet, to try me true,
> Look on my head,

[1] Refusal.

> And I will crave an oath of you
>   Whe'r[1] Faith be fled ;
> So shall we both answered be,
>   Both I of you, and you of me. "

The most considerable and the most interesting part of Googe's work is a set of eight eclogues which may not have been without influence on *The Shepherd's Calendar*, and a poem of some length entitled *Cupido Conquered*, which Spenser may also have seen.   Googe has more sustained power than Turberville, but is much inferior to him in command of metre and in lyrical swing.   In him, or at least in his printer, the mania for cutting up long verses reaches its height, and his very decasyllables are found arranged in the strange fashion of four and six as thus :—

> " Good aged Bale :
>   That with thy hoary hairs
>   Dost still persist
>   To turn the painful book,
>   O happy man,
>   That hast obtained such years,
>   And leav'st not yet
>   On papers pale to look.
>   Give over now
>   To beat thy wearied brain,
>   And rest thy pen,
>   That long hath laboured sore. "

Thomas Tusser (1524?-1580) has often been regarded as merely a writer of doggerel, which is assuredly not lacking in his *Hundred* (later *Five Hundred*) *Points of Husbandry* (1557-1573). But he has some piquancy of phrase, and is particularly noticeable for the variety, and to a certain extent the accomplishment, of his prosodic experiments—a point of much importance for the time.

To these five, of whom some substantive notice has been given, many shadowy names might be added if the catalogue were of any use : such as those of Kinwelmersh, Whetstone, Phaer,

---

[1] Short for " whether."

Neville, Blundeston, Edwards, Golding, and many others. They seem to have been for the most part personally acquainted with one another ; the literary energies of England being almost confined to the universities and the Inns of Court, so that most of those who devoted themselves to literature came into contact and formed what is sometimes called a clique. They were all studiously and rather indiscriminately given to translation (the body of foreign work, ancient and modern, which was turned into English during this quarter of a century being very large indeed), and all or many of them were contributors of commendatory verses to each other's work and of pieces of different descriptions to the poetical miscellanies of the time. Of these miscellanies and of the chief translations from the classics some little notice may be taken because of the great part which both played in the poetical education of England. It has been said that almost all the original poets were also translators. Thus Googe Englished, among other things, the *Zodiacus Vitæ* of Marcellus Palingenius, the *Regnum Papisticum* of Kirchmayer, the *Four Books of Husbandry* of Conrad Heresbach, and the *Proverbs* of the Marquis of Santillana ; but some of the translators were not distinguished by any original work. Thus Jasper Heywood, followed by Neville above mentioned, by Studley, and others, translated between 1560 and 1580 those tragedies of Seneca which had such a vast influence on foreign literature and, fortunately, so small an influence on English. Arthur Golding gave in 1567 a version, by no means destitute of merit, of the *Metamorphoses* which had a great influence on English poetry. We have already mentioned Surrey's blank-verse translation of Virgil. This was followed up, in 1555-60, by Thomas Phaer, who, like most of the persons mentioned in this paragraph, used the fourteener, broken up or not, as accident or the necessities of the printer brought it about.

It was beyond doubt this abundant translation, and perhaps also the manifest deficiencies of the fourteener thus used, which brought about at the close of the present period and the beginning

of the next the extraordinary attempt to reproduce classical
metres in English verse, which for a time seduced even Spenser,
which was not a little countenanced by most of the critical writer:
of the period, which led Gabriel Harvey and others into such
absurdities, and which was scarcely slain even by Daniel's famou
and capital *Defence of Rhyme*.   The discussion of this absur
attempt (for which rules, not now extant, came from Drant of
Cambridge) in the correspondence of Spenser and Harvey, and the
sensible fashion in which Nash laughed at it, are among the best
known things in the gossiping history of English Letters.   But the
coxcombry of Harvey and the felicitous impertinence of Nash
have sometimes diverted attention from the actual state of the
case.   William Webbe (a very sober-minded person with taste
enough to admire the "new poet," as he calls Spenser) makes
elaborate attempts not merely at hexameters, which, though only a
curiosity, are a possible curiosity in English, but at Sapphics which
could never (except as burlesque) be tolerable.   Sidney, Spenser,
and others gave serious heed to the scheme of substituting classical
metres without rhyme for indigenous metres with rhyme.   And
unless the two causes which brought this about are constantly kept
in mind, the reason of it will not be understood.   It was undoubtedly the weakness of contemporary English verse which
reinforced the general Renaissance admiration for the classics ;
nor must it be forgotten that Wyatt takes, in vernacular metres
and with rhyme, nearly as great liberties with the intonation and
prosody of the language as any of the classicists in their unlucky
hexameters and elegiacs.   The majesty and grace of the learned
tongues, contrasting with the poverty of their own language,
impressed, and to a great extent rightly impressed, the early
Elizabethans, so that they naturally enough cast about for any
means to improve the one, and hesitated at any peculiarity which
was not found in the other.   It was unpardonable in Milton
to sneer at rhyme after the fifty years of magnificent production
which had put English on a level with Greek and above Latin
as a literary instrument.   But for Harvey and Spenser, Sidney

and Webbe, with those fifty years still to come, the state of the
case was very different. The translation mania and the classicising mania together led
to the production of perhaps the most absurd book in all literature
—a book which deserves extended notice here, partly because it
has only recently become accessible to the general reader in its
original form, and partly because it is, though a caricature, yet a
very instructive caricature of the tendencies and literary ideas of
the time.   This is Richard Stanyhurst's translation of the first
four books of the *Æneid*, first printed at Leyden in the summer
of 1582, and reprinted in London a year later.   This wonderful
book (in which the spelling is only less marvellous than the
phraseology and verse) shows more than anything else the active
throes which English literature was undergoing, and though the
result was but a false birth it is none the less interesting.

Stanyhurst was not, as might be hastily imagined, a person of
insufficient culture or insufficient brains.   He was an Irish
Roman Catholic gentleman, brother-in-law to Lord Dunsany, and
uncle to Archbishop Usher, and though he was author of the
Irish part of Holinshed's *History*, he has always been regarded
by the madder sort of Hibernians as a traitor to the nation.   His
father was Recorder of Dublin, and he himself, having been
born about 1547, was educated at University College, Oxford,
and went thence, if not to the Inns of Court, at any rate to
those of Chancery, and became a student of Furnival's Inn.
He died at Brussels in 1618.   Here is an example of his prose,
the latter part of which is profitable for matter as well as for
form :—

" How beyt[1] I haue heere haulf a guesh, that two sorts of carpers wyl seeme
too spurne at this myne enterprise.   Thee one vtterlie ignorant, the oother
meanlye letterd.   Thee ignorant wyl imagin, that thee passage was nothing
craggye, in as much as M. Phaere hath broken thee ice before me : Thee
meaner clarcks wyl suppose my trauail in theese heroical verses too carrye no

---

[1] This and the next extract are given *literatim* to show Stanyhurst's
marvellous spelling.

great difficultie, in that yt lay in my choice too make what word I would short
or long, hauing no English writer beefore mee in this kind of poëtrye with
whose squire I should leauel my syllables.

. . . .

Haue not theese men made a fayre speake?   If they had put in *Mightye Joue*,
and *gods* in thee plural number, and *Venus* with *Cupide thee blynd Boy*, al had
beene in thee nick, thee rythme had been of a right stamp.   For a few such
stiches boch vp oure newe fashion makers.   Prouyded not wythstanding
alwayes that *Artaxerxes*, al be yt hee bee spurgalde, beeing so much gallop,
bee placed in thee dedicatory epistle receauing a cuppe of water of a swayne,
or elles al is not wurth a beane.   Good God what a frye of *wooden rythmours*
dooth swarme in stacioners shops, who neauer enstructed in any grammar
schoole, not atayning too thee paaringes of thee Latin or Greeke tongue, yeet
like blind bayards rush on forward, fostring theyre vayne conceits wyth such
ouerweening silly follyes, as they reck not too bee condemned of thee learned
for ignorant, so they bee commended of thee ignorant for learned.   Thee
reddyest way, therefore, too flap theese droanes from the sweete senting hiues of
Poëtrye, is for thee learned too applye theym selues wholye (yf they be delighted wyth that veyne) too thee true making of verses in such wise as thee
Greekes and *Latins*, thee fathurs of knowledge, haue doone ; and too leaue too
theese doltish coystrels theyre rude rythming and balducktoom ballads."

Given a person capable of this lingo, given the prevalent mania
for English hexameters, and even what follows may not seem too
impossible.

" This sayd, with darcksoom night shade quite clowdye she vannisht.
Grislye faces frouncing, eke against Troy leaged in hatred
Of Saincts soure deities dyd I see.
Then dyd I marck playnely thee castle of Ilion vplayd,
And Troian buyldings quit topsy turvye remooued.
Much lyk on a mountayn thee tree dry wythered oaken
Sliest by the clowne Coridon rusticks with twibbil or hatchet.
Then the tre deepe minced, far chopt dooth terrifye swinckers
With menacing becking thee branches palsye before tyme,
Vntil with sowghing yt grunts, as wounded in hacking.
At length with rounsefal, from stock vntruncked yt harssheth.

. . . .

       Hee rested wylful lyk a wayward obstinat oldgrey.

. . . .

Theese woords owt showting with her howling the house she replennisht."

There is perhaps no greater evidence of the reverence in

which the ancients were held than that such frantic balderdash
as this did not extinguish it.   Yet this was what a man of
undoubted talent, of considerable learning, and of no small
acuteness (for Stanyhurst's Preface to this very translation shows
something more than glimmerings on the subject of classical and
English prosody), could produce.   It must never be forgotten
that the men of this time were at a hopelessly wrong point of
view.   It never occurred to them that English left to itself could
equal Greek or Latin.   They simply endeavoured, with the
utmost pains and skill, to drag English up to the same level
as these unapproachable languages by forcing it into the same
moulds which Greek and Latin had endured.   Properly speaking we ought not to laugh at them.   They were carrying out
in literature what the older books of arithmetic call "The Rule
of False,"—that is to say, they were trying what the English
tongue could *not* bear.   No one was so successful as Stanyhurst in applying this test of the rack : yet it is fair to
say that Harvey and Webbe, nay, Spenser and Sidney, had
practically, though, except in Spenser's case, it would appear
unconsciously, arrived at the same conclusion before.   How
much we owe to such adventurers of the impossible few men
know except those who have tried to study literature as a whole.

A few words have to be said in passing as to the miscellanies
which played such an important part in the poetical literature of
the day.   Tottel and *The Mirror for Magistrates* (which was,
considering its constant accretions, a sort of miscellany) have
been already noticed.   They were followed by not a few others.
The first in date was *The Paradise of Dainty Devices* (1576), edited
by R. Edwards, a dramatist of industry if not of genius, and containing a certain amount of interesting work.   It was very popular,
going through nine or ten editions in thirty years, but with a few
scattered exceptions it does not yield much to the historian of
English poetry.   Its popularity shows what was expected ; its
contents show what, at any rate at the date of its first appearance,
was given.   It is possible that the doleful contents of *The Mirror*

for Magistrates (which was reprinted six times during our present period, and which busied itself wholly with what magistrates should avoid, and with the sorrowful departing out of this life of the subjects) may have had a strong effect on Edwards, though one at least of his contributors, W. Hunnis, was a man of mould. It was followed in 1578 by *A Gorgeous Gallery of Gallant Inventions*, supposed to have been edited by Roydon and Proctor, which is a still drier stick. The next miscellany, six years later, *A Handful of Pleasant Delights*, edited by Clement Robinson, is somewhat better though not much. It is followed by the *Phœnix Nest*, an interesting collection, by no less than three miscellanies in 1600, edited by "A. B." and R. Allot, and named *England's Helicon*, *England's Parnassus*, and *Belvedere* (the two latter being rather anthologies of extracts than miscellanies proper), and by Francis Davison's famous *Poetical Rhapsody*, 1602, all which last belong to a much later date than our present subjects.

To call the general poetical merit of these earlier miscellanies high would be absurd. But what at once strikes the reader, not merely of them but of the collections of individual work which accompany them, as so astonishing, is the level which is occasionally reached. The work is often the work of persons quite unknown or unimportant in literature as persons. But we constantly see in it a flash, a symptom of the presence of the true poetical spirit which it is often impossible to find for years together in other periods of poetry. For instance, if ever there was a "dull dog" in verse it was Richard Edwards. Yet in *The Paradise of Dainty Devices* Edwards's poem with the refrain "The falling out of faithful friends renewing is of love," is one of the most charming things anywhere to be found. So is, after many years, the poem attributed to John Wooton in *England's Helicon* (the best of the whole set), beginning "Her eyes like shining lamps," so is the exquisite "Come, little babe" from *The Arbour of Amorous Devices*, so are dozens and scores more which may be found in their proper places, and many of them in Mr. Arber's admirable *English Garner*. The spirit of poetry, rising slowly, was rising surely in the England of these years : no man knew exactly where it would appear, and the greatest poets were—for their praises of themselves and their fellows are quite unconscious and simple—as ignorant as others. The first thirty years of the reign were occupied with simple education—study of models, efforts in this or that kind, translation, and the rest. But the right models had been provided by Wyatt and Surrey's study of the Italians, and by the study of the classics which all men then pursued ; and the original inspiration, without which the best models are useless, though itself can do little when the best models are not used, was abundantly present. Few things are more curious than to compare, let us say, Googe and Spenser. Yet few things are more certain than that without the study and experiments which Googe represents Spenser could not have existed. Those who decry the historical method in criticism ignore this ; and ignorance like wisdom is justified of all her children.

CHAPTER II

THE history of the earlier Elizabethan prose, if we except the name of Hooker, in whom it culminates, is to a great extent the history of curiosities of literature—of tentative and imperfect efforts, scarcely resulting in any real vernacular style at all. It is, however, emphatically the Period of Origins of modern English prose, and as such cannot but be interesting. We shall therefore rapidly survey its chief developments, noting first what had been done before Elizabeth came to the throne, then taking Ascham (who stands, though part of his work was written earlier, very much as the first Elizabethan prosaist), noticing the schools of historians, translators, controversialists, and especially critics who illustrated the middle period of the reign, and singling out the noteworthy personality of Sidney. We shall also say something of Lyly (as far as *Euphues* is concerned) and his singular attempts in prose style, and shall finish with Hooker, the one really great name of the period. Its curious pamphlet literature, though much of it, especially the Martin Marprelate controversy, might come chronologically within the limit of this chapter, will be better reserved for a notice in Chapter VI. of the whole pamphlet literature of the reigns of Elizabeth and James—an interesting subject, the relation of which to the modern periodical has been somewhat overlooked, and which indeed has, until Dr. Grosart's recent labours, been not very easy to study. Gabriel Harvey alone, as distinctly belonging to the earlier Elizabethans, may be here included with other critics.

It was an inevitable result of the discovery of printing that the cultivation of the vernacular for purposes of all work—that is to say, for prose—should be largely increased. Yet a different influence arising, or at least eked out from the same source, rather checked this increase. The study of the classical writers had at first a tendency to render inveterate the habit of employing Latin for the journey-work of literature, and in the two countries which were to lead Western Europe for the future (the literary date of Italy was already drawing to a close, and Italy had long possessed vernacular prose masterpieces), it was not till the middle of the sixteenth century that the writing of vernacular prose was warmly advocated and systematically undertaken. The most interesting monuments of this crusade, as it may almost be called, in England are connected with a school of Cambridge scholars who flourished a little before our period, though not a few of them, such as Ascham, Wilson, and others, lived into it. A letter of Sir John Cheke's in the very year of the accession of Elizabeth is the most noteworthy document on the subject. It was written to another father of English prose, Sir Thomas Hoby, the translator of Castiglione's *Courtier*. But Ascham had already and some years earlier published his *Toxophilus*, and various not unimportant attempts, detailed notice of which would be an antedating of our proper period, had been made. More's chief work, *Utopia*, had been written in Latin, and was translated into English by another hand, but his *History of Edward V.* was not a mean contribution to English prose. Tyndale's *New Testament* had given a new and powerful impulse to the reading of English ; Elyot's *Governor* had set the example of treating serious subjects in a style not unworthy of them, and Leland's quaint *Itinerary* the example of describing more or less faithfully if somewhat uncouthly. Hall had followed Fabyan as an English historian, and, above all, Latimer's *Sermons* had shown how to transform spoken English of the raciest kind into literature. Lord Berners's translations of

Froissart and of divers *Chansons de Geste* and *Romans d'Aventures* had provided much prose of no mean quality for light reading, and also by their imitation of the florid and fanciful style of the French-Flemish *rhétoriqueurs* (with which Berners was familiar both as a student of French and as governor of Calais) had probably contributed not a little to supply and furnish forth the side of Elizabethan expression which found so memorable an exponent in the author of *Euphues*.

For our purpose, however, Roger Ascham may serve as a starting-point. His *Toxophilus* was written and printed as early as 1545; his *Schoolmaster* did not appear till after his death, and seems to have been chiefly written in the very last days of his life. There is thus nearly a quarter of a century between them, yet they are not very different in style. Ascham was a Yorkshire man born at Kirbywiske, near Northallerton, in 1515; he went to St. John's College at Cambridge, then a notable seat of learning, in 1530; was elected scholar, fellow, and lecturer, became public orator the year after the appearance of *Toxophilus*, acted as tutor to the Princess Elizabeth, went on diplomatic business to Germany, was Latin secretary to Queen Mary, and after her death to his old pupil, and died on the 30th December 1568. A treatise on Cock-fighting (of which sport he was very fond) appears to have been written by him, and was perhaps printed, but is unluckily lost. We have also Epistles from him, and his works, both English and Latin, have been in whole or part frequently edited. The great interest of Ascham is expressed as happily as possible by his own words in the dedication of *Toxophilus* to Henry VIII. "Although," he says, "to have written this book either in Latin or Greek . . . had been more easier and fit for my trade in study, yet . . . I have written this English matter in the English tongue for Englishmen"—a memorable sentence none the worse for its jingle and repetition, which are well in place. Until scholars like Ascham, who with the rarest exceptions were the only persons who were likely to write at all, cared to write "English matters in English tongue for

Englishmen," the formation of English prose style was impossible; and that it required some courage to do so, Cheke's letter, written twelve years later, shows.[1]

"I am of this opinion that our own tongue should be written clean and pure, unmixed and unmingled with borrowing of other tongues, wherein, if we take not heed by time, ever borrowing and never paying, she shall be fain to keep her house as bankrupt.[1] For then doth our tongue naturally and praisably utter her meaning, when she borroweth no counterfeitures of other tongues to attire herself withal, but useth plainly her own with such shift as nature, craft, experience, and following of other excellent doth lead her unto, and if she want at any time (as being imperfect she must) yet let her borrow with such bashfulness that it may appear, that if either the mould of our own tongue could serve us to fashion a word of our own, or if the old denizened words could content and ease this need we would not boldly venture of unknown words."[2]

The *Toxophilus* and the *Schoolmaster* are both in their different ways very pleasant reading; and the English is far more correct than that of much greater men than Ascham in the next century. It is, however, merely as style, less interesting, because it is clear that the author is doing little more than translate in his head, instead of on the paper, good current Latin (such as it would have been "more easier" for him to write) into current English. He does not indulge in any undue classicism; he takes few of the liberties with English grammar which, a little later, it was the habit to take on the strength of classical examples. But, on the other hand, he does not attempt, and it would be rather unreasonable to expect that he should have attempted, experiments in the literary power of English itself. A slight sense of its not being so "easy" to write in English as in Latin, and of the consequent advisableness of keeping to a sober beaten path, to a kind of style which is not much

[1] The letter is given in full by Mr. Arber in his introduction to Ascham's *Schoolmaster*, p. 5.

[2] It will be seen that Cheke writes what he argues for, "clean and pure English." "Other excellent" is perhaps the only doubtful phrase in the extract or in the letter.

more English (except for being composed of good English words in straightforward order) than it is any literary language framed to a great extent on the classics, shows itself in him. One might translate passage after passage of Ascham, keeping almost the whole order of the words, into very good sound Latin prose; and, indeed, his great secret in the *Schoolmaster* (the perpetual translation and retranslation of English into the learned languages, and especially Latin) is exactly what would form such a style. It is, as the following examples from both works will show, clear, not inelegant, invaluable as a kind of go-cart to habituate the infant limbs of prose English to orderly movement ; but it is not original, or striking, or characteristic, or calculated to show the native powers and capacities of the language.

" I can teach you to shoot fair, even as Socrates taught a man once to know God. For when he asked him what was God ? 'Nay,' saith he, ' I can tell you better what God is not, as God is not ill, God is unspeakable, unsearchable, and so forth. Even likewise can I say of fair shooting, it hath not this discommodity with it nor that discommodity, and at last a man may so shift all the discommodities from shooting that there shall be left nothing behind but fair shooting. And to do this the better you must remember how that I told you when I described generally the whole nature of shooting, that fair shooting came of these things of standing, nocking, drawing, holding and loosing ; the which I will go over as shortly as I can, describing the discommodities that men commonly use in all parts of their bodies, that you, if you fault in any such, may know it, and go about to amend it. Faults in archers do exceed the number of archers, which come with use of shooting without teaching. Use and custom separated from knowledge and learning, doth not only hurt shooting, but the most weighty things in the world beside. And, therefore, I marvel much at those people which be the maintainers of uses without knowledge, having no other word in their mouth but this use, use, custom, custom. Such men, more wilful than wise, beside other discommodities, take all place and occasion from all amendment. And this I speak generally of use and custom."

" Time was when Italy and Rome have been, to the great good of us who now live, the best breeders and bringers up of the worthiest men, not only for wise speaking, but also for well-doing in all civil affairs that ever was in the world. But now that time is gone; and though the place remain, yet the old and present manners do differ as far as black and white, as virtue and vice. Virtue once made that country mistress over all the world : vice now maketh that country slave to them that before were glad to serve it.   All man [*i.e.* mankind] seeth it ; they themselves confess it, namely such as be best and wisest amongst them.   For sin, by lust and vanity, hath and doth breed up everywhere common contempt of God's word, private contention in many families, open factions in every city ; and so making themselves bond to vanity and vice at home, they are content to bear the yoke of serving strangers abroad.   Italy now is not that Italy it was wont to be ; and therefore now not so fit a place as some do count it for young men to fetch either wisdom or honesty from thence.   For surely they will make others but bad scholars that be so ill masters to themselves."

This same characteristic, or absence of characteristic, which reaches its climax—a climax endowing it with something like substantive life and merit—in Hooker, displays itself, with more and more admixture of raciness and native peculiarity, in almost all the prose of the early Elizabethan period up to the singular escapade of Lyly, who certainly tried to write not a classical style but a style of his own.   The better men, with Thomas Wilson and Ascham himself at their head, made indeed earnest protests against Latinising the vocabulary (the great fault of the contemporary French *Pléiade*), but they were not quite aware how much they were under the influence of Latin in other matters.   The translators, such as North, whose famous version of Plutarch after Amyot had the immortal honour of suggesting not a little of Shakespere's greatest work, had the chief excuse and temptation in doing this ; but all writers did it more or less : the theologians (to whom it would no doubt have been "more easier" to write in Latin), the historians (though the little known Holinshed has broken off into a much more vernacular but also much more disorderly style), the rare geographers (of whom the chief is Richard Eden, the first English writer on America), and the rest.   Of this rest the most interesting, perhaps, are the small but curious knot of critics who lead up in various ways to Sidney and Harvey, who seem to have excited considerable interest at the time, and who were not succeeded, after the early years of James, by any considerable body of critics of English till John Dryden began to write in the last third of the following century. Of these (putting out of sight Stephen Gosson, the immediate begetter of Sidney's *Apology for Poetry*, Campion, the chief champion of classical metres in English, and by a quaint contrast the author of some of the most charming of English songs in purely romantic style, with his adversary the poet Daniel, Meres, etc.), the chief is the author of the anonymous *Art of English Poesie*, published the year after the Armada, and just before the appearance of *The Faërie Queene*. This *Art* has chiefly to be compared with the *Discourse of English Poetrie*, published three years earlier by William Webbe. Webbe, of whom nothing is known save that he was a private tutor at one or two gentlemen's houses in Essex, exhibits that dislike and disdain of rhyme which was an offshoot of the passion for humanist studies, which was importantly represented all through the sixteenth and early seventeenth century in England, and which had Milton for its last and greatest exponent. The *Art of English Poesie*, which is attributed on no grounds of contemporary evidence to George Puttenham, though the book was generally reputed his in the next generation, is a much more considerable treatise, some four times the length of Webbe's, dealing with a large number of questions subsidiary to *Ars Poetica*, and containing no few selections of illustrative verse, many of the author's own. As far as style goes both Webbe and Puttenham fall into the rather colourless but not incorrect class already described, and are of the tribe of Ascham. Here is a sample of each :—

(Webbe's *Preface to the Noble Poets of England.*)

"Among the innumerable sorts of English books, and infinite fardels of printed pamphlets, wherewith this country is pestered, all shops stuffed, and every study furnished ; the greater part, I think, in any one kind, are such as are either mere poetical, or which tend in some respects (as either in matter or form) to poetry. Of such books, therefore, sith I have been one that have had a desire to read not the fewest, and because it is an argument which men of great learning have no leisure to handle, or at least having to do with more serious matters do least regard. If I write something, concerning what I think of our English poets, or adventure to set down my simple judgment of English poetry, I trust the learned poets will give me leave, and vouchsafe my book passage, as being for the rudeness thereof no prejudice to their noble studies, but even (as my intent is) an *instar cotis* to stir up some other of meet ability to bestow travail in this matter ; whereby, I think, we may not only get the means which we yet want, to discern between good writers and bad, but perhaps also challenge from the rude multitude of rustical rhymers, who will be called poets, the right practice and orderly course of true poetry."

(Puttenham *on Style.*)

" Style is a constant and continual phrase or tenour of speaking and writing, extending to the whole tale or process of the poem or history, and not properly to any piece or member of a tale ; but is of words, speeches, and sentences together ; a certain contrived form and quality, many times natural to the writer, many times his peculiar bye-election and art, and such as either he keepeth by skill or holdeth on by ignorance, and will not or peradventure cannot easily alter into any other. So we say that Cicero's style and Sallust's were not one, nor Cæsar's and Livy's, nor Homer's and Hesiodus',[1] nor Herodotus' and Thucydides', nor Euripides' and Aristophanes', nor Erasmus' and Budeus' styles. And because this continual course and manner of writing or speech sheweth the matter and disposition of the writer's mind more than one or two instances can show, therefore there be that have called style the image of man (*mentis character*). For man is but his mind, and as his mind is tempered and qualified, so are his speeches and language at large ; and his inward conceits be the metal of his mind, and his manner of utterance the very warp and woof of his conceits, more plain or busy and intricate or otherwise affected after the rate.[2]"

Contemporary with these, however, there was growing up a quite different school of English prose which showed itself on one side in the *estilo culto* of Lyly and the university wits of his time ; on the other, in the extremely vernacular and sometimes extremely vulgar manner of the pamphleteers, who were very often the same persons. Lyly himself exhibits both styles in *Euphues ;* and if *Pap with a Hatchet* and *An Almond for a Parrot* are rightly attributed to him, still more in these. So also does Gabriel Harvey, Spenser's friend, a curious coxcomb who endeavoured to dissuade Spenser from continuing *The Faërie Queene*, devoted much time himself and strove to devote other people to the thankless task of composing English hexameters and

[1] The final *s* of such names often at the time appears unaltered.
[2] *I.e.* "in proportion."

trimeters, engaged (very much to his discomfiture) in a furious
pamphlet war with Thomas Nash, and altogether presents one
of the most characteristic though least favourable specimens of
the Elizabethan man of letters. We may speak of him further
when we come to the pamphleteers generally.

John Lyly is a person of much more consequence in English
literature than the conceited and pragmatical pedant who wrote
Pierce's Supererogation. He is familiar, almost literally to every
schoolboy, as the author of the charming piece, "Cupid with my
Campaspe Played," and his dramatic work will come in for notice
in a future chapter; but he is chiefly thought of by posterity,
whether favourably or the reverse, as the author of *Euphues.*
Exceedingly little is known about his life, and it is necessary to
say that the usually accepted dates of his death, his children's
birth, and so forth, depend wholly on the identification of a John
Lilly, who is the subject of such entries in the registers of a
London church, with the euphuist and dramatist—an identification which requires confirmation. A still more wanton attempt
to supplement ignorance with knowledge has been made in the
further identification with Lyly of a certain "witty and bold
atheist," who annoyed Bishop Hall in his first cure at Hawstead,
in Suffolk, and who is called "Mr. Lilly." All supposed facts
about him (or some other John Lyly), his membership of Parliament and so forth, have been diligently set forth by Mr. Bond in
his Oxford edition of the *Works,* with the documents which
are supposed to prove them. He is supposed, on uncertain
but tolerable inferences, to have been born about 1554, and he
certainly entered Magdalen College, Oxford, in 1569, though he
was not matriculated till two years later. He is described as
plebeii filius, was not on the foundation, and took his degree in
1573. He must have had some connection with the Cecils, for
a letter of 1574 is extant from him to Burleigh. He cannot
have been five and twenty when he wrote *Euphues,* which was
licensed at the end of 1578, and was published (the first part)
early next year, while the second part followed with a very short

interval. In 1582 he wrote an unmistakable letter commend-atory to Watson's *Hecatompathia*, and between 1580 and 1590 he must have written his plays. He appears to have continued to reside at Magdalen for a considerable time, and then to have haunted the Court. A melancholy petition is extant to Queen Elizabeth from him, the second of its kind, in which he writes : " Thirteen years your highness' servant, but yet nothing." This was in 1598: he is supposed to have died in 1606. *Euphues* is a very singular book, which was constantly reprinted and eagerly read for fifty years, then forgotten for nearly two hundred, then frequently discussed, but very seldom read, even it may be suspected in Mr. Arber's excellent reprint of it, or in that of Mr. Bond. It gave a word to English, and even yet there is no very distinct idea attaching to the word. It induced one of the most gifted restorers of old times to make a blunder, amusing in itself, but not in the least what its author intended it to be, and of late years especially it has prompted constant discussions as to the origin of the peculiarities which mark it. As usual, we shall try to discuss it with less reference to what has been said about it than to itself.

Euphues (properly divided into two parts, "Euphues, the Anatomy of Wit," and " Euphues and his England," the scene of the first lying in Naples) is a kind of love story; the action, however, being next to nothing, and subordinated to an infinite amount of moral and courtly discourse. Oddly enough, the unfavourable sentence of Hallam, that it is "a very dull story," and the favourable sentence of Kingsley, that it is "a brave, righteous, and pious book," are both quite true, and, indeed, any one can see that there is nothing incompatible in them. At the present day, however, its substance, which chiefly consists of the moral discourses aforesaid, is infinitely inferior in interest to its manner. Of that manner, any one who imagines it to be reproduced by Sir Piercie Shafton's extravagances in *The Monastery* has an entirely false idea. It is much odder than Shaftonese, but also quite different from it. Lyly's two secrets

are in the first place an antithesis, more laboured, more monotonous, and infinitely more pointless than Macaulay's—which
antithesis seems to have met with not a little favour, and was
indeed an obvious expedient for lightening up and giving
character to the correct but featureless prose of Ascham and
other "Latiners." The second was a fancy, which amounts to a
mania, for similes, strung together in endless lists, and derived as
a rule from animals, vegetables, or minerals, especially from the
Fauna and Flora of fancy. It is impossible to open a page of
Euphues without finding an example of this eccentric and tasteless
trick, and in it, as far as in any single thing, must be found the
recipe for euphuism, pure and simple. As used in modern
language for conceited and precious language in general, the
term has only a very partial application to its original, or to that
original's author. Indeed Lyly's vocabulary, except occasionally
in his similes, is decidedly vernacular, and he very commonly
mingles extremely homely words with his highest flights. No
better specimen of him can be given than from the aforesaid
letter commendatory to the *Hecatompathia.*

"My good friend, I have read your new passions, and they have renewed
mine old pleasures, the which brought to me no less delight than they have
done to your self-commendations. And certes had not one of mine eyes about
serious affairs been watchful, both by being too too busy, had been wanton : such
is the nature of persuading pleasure, that it melteth the marrow before it scorch
the skin and burneth before it warmeth. Not unlike unto the oil of jet, which
rotteth the bone and never rankleth the flesh, or the scarab flies which enter
into the root and never touch the fruit.

"And whereas you desire to have my ópinion, you may imagine that my
stomach is rather cloyed than queasy, and therefore mine appetite of less force
than my affection, fearing rather a surfeit of sweetness than desiring a satisfying. The repeating of love wrought in me a semblance of liking ; but
searching the very veins of my heart I could find nothing but a broad scar
where I left a deep wound : and loose strings where I tied hard knots : and a
table of steel where I framed a plot of wax.

"Whereby I noted that young swans are grey, and the old white, young
trees tender and the old tough, young men amorous, and, growing in years,
either wiser or warier. The coral plant in the water is a soft weed, on the
land a hard stone : a sword frieth in the fire like a black eel ; but laid in earth

like white snow : the heart in love is altogether passionate ; but free from desire altogether careless.

" But it is not my intent to inveigh against love, which women account but a bare word and men reverence as the best God. Only this I would add without offence to gentlewomen, that were not men more superstitious in their praises than women are constant in their passions love would either be worn out of use, or men out of love, or women out of lightness. I can condemn none but by conjecture, nor commend any but by lying, yet suspicion is as free as thought, and as far as I can see as necessary as credulity.

"Touching your mistress I must needs think well, seeing you have written so well, but as false glasses shew the fairest faces so fine gloses amend the baddest fancies. Appelles painted the phoenix by hearsay not by sight, and Lysippus engraved Vulcan with a straight leg whom nature framed with a poult foot, which proveth men to be of greater affection their [then?=than] judg-ment. But in that so aptly you have varied upon women I will not vary from you, so confess I must, and if I should not, yet mought I be compelled, that to love would be the sweetest thing in the earth if women were the faithfulest, and that women would be more constant if men were more wise.

"And seeing ycu have used me so friendly as to make me acquainted with your passions, I will shortly make you privy to mine which I would be loth the printer should see, for that my fancies being never so crooked he would put them into straight lines unfit for my humour, necessary for his art, who set-teth down blind in as many letters as seeing.[1]—Farewell."

Many efforts have been made to discover some model for Lyly's oddities. Spanish and Italian influences have been alleged, and there is a special theory that Lord Berners's translations have the credit or discredit of the paternity. The curious similes are certainly found very early in Spanish, and may be due to an Eastern origin. The habit of overloading the sentence with elaborate and far-fetched language, especially with similes, may also have come from the French *rhétori-queurs* already mentioned—a school of pedantic writers (Chastel-lain, Robertet, Crétin, and some others being the chief) who flourished during the last half of the fifteenth century and the first quarter of the sixteenth, while the latest examples of them were hardly dead when Lyly was born. The desire, very laudably

[1] " Blinde " with the *e* according to the old spelling having six letters, the same number as seeing. This curious epistle is both in style and matter an epitome of *Euphues*, which had appeared some three years before.

felt all over Europe, to adorn and exalt the vernacular tongues, so as to make them vehicles of literature worthy of taking rank with Latin and Greek, naturally led to these follies, of which euphuism in its proper sense was only one.

Michael Drayton, in some verse complimentary to Sidney, stigmatises not much too strongly Lyly's prevailing faults, and attributes to the hero of Zutphen the purification of England from euphuism. This is hardly critical. That Sidney—a young man, and a man of fashion at the time when Lyly's oddities were fashionable—should have to a great extent (for his resistance is by no means absolute) resisted the temptation to imitate them, is very creditable. But the influence of *Euphues* was at least as strong for many years as the influence of the *Arcadia* and the *Apology ;* and the chief thing that can be said for Sidney is that he did not wholly follow Lyly to do evil. Nor is his positive excellence in prose to be compared for a moment with his positive excellence in poetry. His life is so universally known that nothing need be said about it beyond reminding the reader that he was born, as Lyly is supposed to have been, in 1554 ; that he was the son of Sir Henry Sidney, afterwards Viceroy of Ireland, and of Lady Mary, eldest daughter of the luckless Dudley, Duke of Northumberland ; that he was educated at Shrewsbury and Christ Church, travelled much, acquiring the repute of one of the most accomplished cavaliers of Europe, loved without success Penelope Devereux ("Stella"), married Frances Walsingham, and died of his wounds at the battle of Zutphen, when he was not yet thirty-two years old. His prose works are the famous pastoral romance of the *Arcadia*, written to please his sister, the Countess of Pembroke, and the short *Apology for Poetry*, a very spirited piece of work, immediately provoked by a rather silly diatribe against the theatre by one Stephen Gosson, once a playwright himself, but turned Puritan clergyman. Both appear to have been written about the same time—that is to say, between 1579 and 1581 ; Sidney being then in London and in the society of Spenser and other men of letters.

The amiability of Sidney's character, his romantic history, the exquisite charm of his verse at its best, and last, not least, the fact of his enthusiastic appreciation and patronage of literature at a time when literary men never failed to give aristocratic patrons somewhat more than *quid pro quo*, have perhaps caused his prose ·work to be traditionally a little overvalued. The *Apology for Poetry* is full of generous ardour, contains many striking and poetical expressions, and explains more than any other single book the secret of the wonderful literary production of the half-century which followed. The *Arcadia*, especially when contrasted with *Euphues*, has the great merit of abundant and stirring incident and interest, of freedom from any single affectation so pestering and continuous as Lyly's similes, and of constant purple patches of poetical description and expression, which are indeed not a little out of place in prose, but which are undeniably beautiful in themselves. But when this is said all is said. Enthusiastic as Sidney's love for poetry and for literature was, it was enthusiasm not at all according to knowledge. In the *Apology*, by his vindication of the unities, and his denunciation of the mixture of tragedy and comedy, he was (of course without knowing it) laying down exactly the two principles, a fortunate abjuration and scouting whereof gave us the greatest possession in mass and variety of merit that any literature possesses—the Elizabethan drama from Shakespere and Marlowe to Ford and Shirley. Follow Sidney, and good-bye to *Faustus*, to *Hamlet*, to *Philaster*, to *The Duchess of Malfi*, to *The Changeling*, to *The Virgin Martyr*, to *The Broken Heart*. We must content ourselves with *Gorboduc* and *Cornelia*, with *Cleopatra* and *Philotas*, at the very best with *Sejanus* and *The Silent Woman*. Again Sidney commits himself in this same piece to the pestilent heresy of prose-poetry, saying that verse is " only an ornament of poetry ;" nor is there any doubt that Milton, whether he meant it or not, fixed a deserved stigma on the *Arcadia* by calling it a " vain and amatorious poem." It is a poem in prose, which is as much as to say, in other words, that it unites the faults of both kinds. Nor is Sidney less an enemy (though a "sweet enemy" in his own or Bruno's words) of the minor and more formal graces of style. If his actual vocabulary is not Latinised, or Italianised, or Lylyfied, he was one of the greatest of sinners in the special Elizabethan sin of convoluting and entangling his phrases (after the fashion best known in the mouths of Shakespere's fine gentlemen), so as to say the simplest thing in the least simple manner. Not Osric nor Iachimo detests the *mot propre* more than Sidney. Yet again, he is one of the arch offenders in the matter of spoiling the syntax of the sentence and the paragraph. As has been observed already, the unpretending writers noticed above, if they have little harmony or balance of phrase, are seldom confused or breathless. Sidney was one of the first writers of great popularity and influence (for the *Arcadia* was very widely read) to introduce what may be called the sentence-and-paragraph-heap, in which clause is linked on to clause till not merely the grammatical but the philosophical integer is hopelessly lost sight of in a tangle of jointings and appendices. It is not that he could not do better ; but that he seems to have taken no trouble not to do worse. His youth, his numerous avocations, and the certainty that he never formally prepared any of his work for the press, would of course be ample excuses, even if the singular and seductive beauty of many scraps throughout this work did not redeem it. But neither of the radical difference in nature and purpose between prose and verse, nor of the due discipline and management of prose itself, does Sidney seem to have had the slightest idea. Although he seldom or never reaches the beauties of the *flamboyant* period of prose, which began soon after his death and filled the middle of the seventeenth century, he contains examples of almost all its defects ; and considering that he is nearly the first writer to do this, and that his writings were (and were deservedly) the favourite study of generous literary youth for more than a generation, it is scarcely uncharitable to hold him directly responsible for much mischief. The faults of *Euphues* were faults which were certain to work their own cure ; those of the *Arcadia* were so engaging in themselves, and linked with so many merits and beauties, that they were sure to set a dangerous example. I believe, indeed, that if Sidney had lived he might have pruned his style not a little without weakening it, and then the richness of his imagination would probably have made him the equal of Bacon and the superior of Raleigh. But as it is, his light in English prose (we shall speak and speak very differently of his verse hereafter) was only too often a will-o'-the-wisp. I am aware that critics whom I respect have thought and spoken in an opposite sense, but the difference comes from a more important and radical difference of opinion as to the nature, functions, and limitations of English prose. Sidney's style may be perhaps best illustrated by part of his Dedication ; the narrative parts of the *Arcadia* not lending themselves well to brief excerpt, while the *Apology* is less remarkable for style than for matter.

To my dear Lady and Sister, the Countess of Pembroke.

"Here have you now, most dear, and most worthy to be most dear, lady, this idle work of mine ; which, I fear, like the spider's web, will be thought fitter to be swept away than wove to any other purpose. For my part, in very truth, as the cruel fathers among the Greeks were wont to do to the babes they would not foster, I could well find in my heart to cast out in some desert of forgetfulness this child which I am loth to father. But you desired me to do it, and your desire to my heart is an absolute commandment. Now it is done only for you, only to you ; if you keep it to yourself, or commend it to such friends who will weigh errors in the balance of good will, I hope, for the father's sake, it will be pardoned, perchance made much of, though in itself it have deformities. For indeed for severer eyes it is not, being but a trifle, and that triflingly handled. Your dear self can best witness the manner, being done in loose sheets of paper, most of it in your presence, the rest by sheets sent unto you as fast as they were done. In sum, a young head, not so well stayed as I would it were, and shall be when God will, having many fancies begotten in it, if it had not been in some way delivered, would have grown a monster, and more sorry might I be that they came in than that they gat out. But his[1] chief safety shall be the walking abroad ; and his chief protection the bearing the livery of your name, which, if much good will do not deceive me, is worthy to be a sanctuary for a greater offender. This say I because I know thy virtue so ; and this say I because it may be for ever so, or, to say better, because it will be for ever so."

---

[1] Apparently = the book's.

The difference referred to above is again well exemplified by the difference of opinions on the style of Hooker as compared with that of Sidney.   Hooker wrote considerably later than the other authors here criticised, but his work is so distinctly the climax of the style started by Ascham, Cheke, and their fellows (the style in which English was carefully adapted to literary purposes for which Latin had been previously employed, under the general idea that Latin syntax should, on the whole, rule the new literary medium), that this chapter would be incomplete without a notice of him.   For the distinguished writers who were contemporary with his later years represent, with rare and only partly distinguished exceptions, not a development of Hooker, but either a development of Sidney or a fresh style, resulting from the blending in different proportions of the academic and classical manner with the romantic and discursive.

The events of Hooker's neither long nor eventful life are well-known from one of the earliest of standard biographies in English—that of Izaak Walton.   He was born at Heavitree, a suburb of Exeter, in 1554 (?).   Though he was fairly connected, his parents were poor, and he was educated as a Bible clerk at Corpus Christi College, Oxford.   He entered here in 1567, and for some fifteen years Oxford was his home, latterly as Fellow and Lecturer of Corpus.   The story of his marriage is slightly pathetic, but more than slightly ludicrous, and he appears to have been greatly henpecked as well as obliged to lead an uncongenial life at a country living.   In 1585 he was made Master of the Temple, and held that post for seven years, distinguishing himself both as a preacher and a controversialist.   But neither was this his vocation ; and the last nine years of his life were spent, it would seem more congenially, in two other country livings, first in Wiltshire, then in Kent.   He died in 1600.   The first four books of the *Ecclesiastical Polity* were published in 1594, the fifth in 1597.   The last three books, published after his death, lie under grave suspicion of having been tampered with.   This, however, as the unquestionably genuine portion is

considerable in bulk, is a matter rather of historical and theological than of purely literary interest. Hooker himself appears
to have been something like the popular ideal of a student :
never so happy as when pen in hand, and by no means
fitted for the rougher kind of converse with his fellow-men,
still less for the life of what is commonly called a man of the
world.

But in the world of literature he is a very great man indeed.
Very few theological books have made themselves a place in
the first rank of the literature of their country, and if the
Ecclesiastical Polity has done so, it has certainly not done so
without cause. If there has been a certain tendency on the part
of strong partisans of the Anglican Church to overestimate the
literary and philosophical merit of this book, which may be called
the first vernacular defence of the position of the English Church,
that has been at least compensated by partisan criticism on the
other side. Nor is there the least fear that the judgment of
impartial critics will ever deprive Hooker of the high rank generally accorded to him. He is, of course, far from being faultless.
In his longer sentences (though long sentences are by no means
the rule with him) he often falls into that abuse of the classical
style which the comparatively jejune writers who had preceded
him avoided, but which constantly manifested itself in the richer
manner of his own contemporaries—the abuse of treating the
uninflected English language as if it were an inflected language,
in which variations and distinctions of case and gender and
number help to connect adjective with substantive, and relative
with antecedent. Sometimes, though less often, he distorts the
natural order of the English in order to secure the Latin desider-
atum of finishing with the most emphatic and important words
of the clause. His subject leads and almost forces him to an
occasional pedantry of vocabulary, and in the region which is not
quite that of form nor quite that of matter, he sometimes fails in
co-ordinating his arguments, his facts, and his citations, and in
directing the whole with crushing force at his enemy. His argu-

ment occasionally degenerates into mere illustration; his logic into mere rhetoric.

But when all these things are admitted, the *Ecclesiastical Polity* remains a book in which matter and manner are wedded as in few other books of the same kind. The one characteristic which has been admitted by Hooker's faintest praisers as well as by his warmest—the golden moderation and judiciousness of his argument — is perhaps rather calculated to extort esteem than to arouse admiration. Moderation, like other kinds of probity, *laudatur et alget:* the adversary is not extremely grateful for not being pushed to extremity, and those on the same side would at least excuse a little more vehemence in driving advantages home. But Hooker has other qualities which are equally estimable and more shining. What especially distinguishes him from the literary point of view is his almost unique faculty of diversifying dry and technical argument with outbursts of rhetoric. These last are not mere purple patches; they do not come in with the somewhat ostentatious usherment and harbingery which, for instance, laid the even more splendid bursts of Jeremy Taylor open to the sharp sarcasm of South. There is nothing theatrical about them; they rise quite naturally out of the level of discussion and sink into it again, with no sudden stumble or drop. Nor are they ever (like some of Sidney's poetical excrescences) tags and hemistichs of unwritten sonnets or songs stuck in anyhow upon the prose. For instance, Sidney writes : "About the time when the candles had begun to inherit the sun's office." Now this in a somewhat quaint and conceited fashion of verse would be excellent. It would also be excellent in burlesque, and in such prose as Browne's it might conquer its place victoriously. But except in such a context (which Sidney cannot weave) it is a *rococo* ornament, a tawdry beautification. Compare with it any of the celebrated passages of Hooker, which may be found in the extract books—the encomium on law, the admirable passage, not so admirable indeed in the context as it might be, but still admirable, about angels, the vindication of music in the church

service.   Here the expression, even at its warmest, is in no sense
poetical, and the flight, as it is called, connects itself with and
continues and drops into the ordinary march of argument in the
most natural and imperceptible manner.   The elevated passages
of Hooker's style resemble more than anything else those convenient exploits common, probably, in most persons' dreams, in
which the dreamer, without any trouble to himself or any apparent
surprise in those about him, lifts himself from the ground and
skims or soars as he pleases, sure that he can return to earth also
when he pleases, and without any shock.   The speculators on the
causes of beauty, admiration, and the like have sometimes sought
them in contrast first of all, and it has been frequently noticed
that the poets who charm us most are those who know how to
alternate pity and terror.   There is something of the same sort in
these variations of the equable procession of Hooker's syllogisms,
these flower-gardens scattered, if not in the wilderness, yet in the
humdrum arable ground of his collections from fathers and philosophers, his marshallings of facts and theories against the counter-
theories of Cartwright and Travers.   Neither before him nor in
his time, nor for generations after him—scarcely, indeed, till
Berkeley—did any one arise who had this profound and unpre-
tentious art of mixing the useful with the agreeable.   Taylor—
already mentioned as inferior to Hooker in one respect, however
superior he may be in the splendour of his rhetoric—is again and
still more inferior to him in the parts that are not ornamental, in
the pedestrian body of his controversy and exposition.   As a mere
controversialist, Hooker, if not exactly a Hobbes or a Bentley, if
not even a Chillingworth, is not likely to be spoken of without
respect by those who understand what evidence means.   If he
sometimes seems to modern readers to assume his premisses, the
conclusions follow much more rigidly than is customary with a
good many of our later philosophers, who protest against the
assumption of premisses ; but having so protested neglect the
ambiguity of terms, and leave their middles undistributed, and
perpetrate illicit process with a gaiety of heart which is extremely

edifying, or who fancy that they are building systems of philosophy when they are in reality constructing dictionaries of
terms.   But his argument is of less concern to us here than the
style in which he clothes it, and the merit of that is indisputable,
as a brief extract will show.

" As therefore man doth consist of different and distinct parts, every part
endued with manifold abilities which all have their several ends and actions
thereunto referred ; so there is in this great variety of duties which belong to
men that dependency and order by means whereof, the lower sustaining always
the more excellent and the higher perfecting the more base, they are in their
times and seasons continued with most exquisite correspondence.   Labours of
bodily and daily toil purchase freedom for actions of religious joy, which
benefit these actions requite with the gift of desired rest—a thing most
natural and fit to accompany the solemn festival duties of honour which are
done to God.   For if those principal works of God, the memory whereof we
use to celebrate at such times, be but certain tastes and says,[1] as it were, of
that final benefit wherein our perfect felicity and bliss lieth folded up, seeing
that the presence of the one doth direct our cogitations, thoughts, and desires
towards the other, it giveth surely a kind of life and addeth inwardly no small
delight to those so comfortable anticipations, especially when the very outward countenance of that we presently do representeth, after a sort, that also
whereunto we tend.   As festival rest doth that celestial estate whereof the
very heathens themselves, which had not the means whereby to apprehend
much, did notwithstanding imagine that it must needs consist in rest, and
have therefore taught that above the highest movable sphere there is no thing
which feeleth alteration, motion, or change ; but all things immutable, unsub-
ject to passion, blest with eternal continuance in a life of the highest perfection, and of that complete abundant sufficiency within itself which no
possibility of want, maim, or defect, can touch."

Hooker's defects have been already admitted, and it has to be
added to them that he was necessarily destitute of much useful
vocabulary which his successors inherited or added, and that he had
absolutely no model of style.   What he lacked was the audacity
to be, not like Sidney more flowery, not like the contemporary
pamphleteers more slangy, but more intelligently vernacular ; to
follow in the mould of his sentences the natural order of English
speech rather than the conventional syntax of Latin, and to
elaborate for himself a clause-architecture or order, so to speak,

[1] " Assays."

of word-building, which should depend upon the inherent qualities of euphony and rhythm possessed by English. It is, however, quite certain that nothing was further from Hooker's thoughts than the composition of English literature merely as English literature. He wanted to bring a certain subject under the notice of readers of the vulgar tongue, and being before all things a scholar he could not help making a scholarly use of that tongue. The wonder is that, in his circumstances and with his purposes, with hardly any teachers, with not a great stock of verbal material, and with little or no tradition of workmanship in the art, he should have turned out such admirable work.

It would be interesting to dwell on the prose of Fulke Greville, Sidney's friend, who long outlived him, and who anticipated not a little of that magnificence of the prose of his later contemporaries, beside which I have ventured to suggest that Sidney's own is sometimes but *rococo*. A place ought to be given to Richard Knolles, who deserves, if not the name of the first historian of England, certainly the credit of making, in his *History of the Turks* (1604), a step from the loose miscellany of the chronicle to the ordered structure of the true historic style. Some would plead for Richard Mulcaster, whose work on education and especially on the teaching of the English tongue in his *Positions* and *First Part of the Elementary* (1582) is most intimately connected with our general subject. But there is no room for more than a mention of these, or for further dwelling on the translators already glanced at and others, the most important and influential of whom was John Florio, the Englisher (1603) of Montaigne.

CHAPTER III

THE FIRST DRAMATIC PERIOD

IT does not belong to the plan of this division of the present book to trace the earliest beginnings of the English theatre, or those intermediate performances by which, in the reigns of the four first Tudors, the Mystery and Morality passed into the Interlude. Even the two famous comedies of *Ralph Roister Doister* and *Gammer Gurton's Needle* stand as it were only at the threshold of our period in this chapter, and everything before them is shut out of it. On the other hand, we can take to be our province the whole rise, flourishing, and decadence of the extraordinary product, known somewhat loosely as the Elizabethan drama. We shall in the present chapter discuss the two comedies or rather farces just mentioned, and notice on the one hand the rather amorphous production which, during the first thirty years of Elizabeth, represented the influence of a growing taste for personal and lively dramatic story on the somewhat arid soil of the Morality and Interlude, and, on the other, the abortive attempt to introduce the regular Senecan tragedy— an attempt which almost immediately broke down and disappeared, whelmed in the abundance of chronicle-play and melodrama. And finally we shall show how the two rival schools of the university wits and the actor playwrights culminated, the first in Marlowe, the second in the earlier and but indistinctly and conjecturally known work of Shakespere. A second chapter will show us the triumph of the untrammelled English play in tragedy and comedy, furnished by Marlowe with the mighty line, but freed to a great extent from the bombast and the unreal scheme which he did not shake off.   Side by side with Shakespere himself we shall have to deal with the learned sock of Jonson, the proud full style of Chapman, the unchastened and ill-directed vigour of Marston, the fresh and charming, if unkempt grace of Dekker, the best known and most remarkable members of a crowd of unknown or half-known playwrights.   A third division will show us a slight gain on the whole in acting qualities, a considerable perfecting of form and scheme, but at the same time a certain decline in the most purely poetical merits, redeemed and illustrated by the abundant genius of Beaumont and Fletcher, of Middleton, of Webster, of Massinger, and of Ford.   And the two latest of these will conduct us into the fourth or period of decadence where, round the voluminous work and still respectable fame of James Shirley, are grouped names like Brome, Glapthorne, Suckling, and others, whose writing, sometimes remarkable and even brilliant, gradually loses not only dramatic but poetical merit, till it drops into the formless plots, the unscannable verse, the coarseness unredeemed by passion, the horrors unlit by any tragic force, which distinguish the last plays before the closing of the theatres, and reappear to some extent at a period beyond ours in the drama (soon to be radically changed in almost every possible characteristic) of the Restoration.   The field of survey is vast, and despite the abundant labour which has been bestowed upon it during the nineteenth century, it is still in a somewhat chaotic condition.   The remarkable collection of old plays which we owe to Mr. A. H. Bullen shows, by sample only and with no pretence of being exhaustive, the amount of absolutely unknown matter which still exists.   The collection and editing of texts has proceeded on the most widely different principles, and with an almost complete absence of that intelligent partition of labour which alone can reduce chaos to order in such a case.   To give but one instance, there is

actually no complete collection, though various attempts have
been made at it, which gives, with or without sufficient editorial
apparatus to supplement the canon, all the dramatic *adespota*
which have been at one time or another attributed to Shakespere.
These at present the painful scholar can only get together in
publications abounding in duplicates, edited on the most
opposite principles, and equally troublesome either for library
arrangement or for literary reference.   The editions of single
authors have exhibited an equal absence of method ; one
editor admitting doubtful plays or plays of part-authorship which
are easily accessible elsewhere, while another excludes those
which are difficult to be got at anywhere.   It is impossible for
any one who reads literature as literature and not as a matter
of idle crotchet, not to reflect that if either of the societies
which, during the nineteenth century, have devoted themselves to the study of Shakespere and his contemporaries, had
chosen to employ their funds on it, a complete Corpus of the
drama between 1560 and 1660, edited with sufficient, but not
superfluous critical apparatus on a uniform plan, and in a decent
if not a luxurious form, might now be obtainable.   Some forty or
fifty volumes at the outside on the scale of the " Globe " series,
or of Messrs. Chatto's useful reprints of Jonson, Chapman, and
other dramatists, would probably contain every play of the
slightest interest, even to a voracious student—who would then
have all his material under his hand.   What time, expense, and
trouble are required to obtain, and that very imperfectly, any
such advantage now, only those who have tried to do it know.
Even Mr. Hazlitt's welcome, if somewhat uncritical, reprint of
Dodsley, long out of print, did not boldly carry out its
principle— though there are plans for improving and supple-
menting it.

Nevertheless, if the difficulties are great so are the rewards.   It
has been the deliberate opinion of many competent judges (neither
unduly prejudiced in favour of English literature nor touched with
that ignorance of other literature which is as fatal to judgment

as actual prejudice) that in no time or country has the literary interest of a short and definite period of production in one well-defined kind approached in value the interest of the Elizabethan drama. Other periods and other countries may produce more remarkable work of different kinds, or more uniformly accomplished, and more technically excellent work in the same kind. But for originality, volume, generic resemblance of character, and individual independence of trait, exuberance of inventive thought, and splendour of execution in detached passages—the Elizabethan drama from Sackville to Shirley stands alone in the history of the world. The absurd overestimate which has sometimes been made of its individual practitioners, the hyperbole of the language which has been used to describe them, the puerile and almost inconceivable folly of some of their scholiasts and parasitic students, find a certain excuse in this truth—a truth which will only be contested by those who have not taken the very considerable trouble necessary to master the facts, or who are precluded by a natural inability from savouring the *goût du terroir* of this abundant and intoxicating wine. There are those who say that nobody but an enthusiast or a self-deceiver can read with real relish any Elizabethan dramatist but Shakespere, and there are those who would have it that the incommunicable and uncommunicated charm of Shakespere is to be found in Nabbes and Davenport, in Glapthorne and Chettle. They are equally wrong, but the second class are at any rate in a more saving way of wrongness. Where Shakespere stands alone is not so much in his actual faculty of poetry as in his command of that faculty. Of the others, some, like Jonson, Fletcher, Massinger, had the art without the power ; others, like Chapman, Dekker, Webster, had flashes of the power without the art. But there is something in the whole crew, jovial or saturnine, which is found nowhere else, and which, whether in full splendour as in Shakespere, or in occasional glimmers as in Tourneur or Rowley, is found in all, save those mere imitators and hangers-on who are peculiar to no period.

This remarkable quality, however, does not show itself in the dramatic work of our present period until quite the close of it. It is true that the period opens (according to the traditional estimate which has not been much altered by recent studies) with three plays of very considerable character, and of no inconsiderable merit — the two comedies already named and the tragedy of *Gorboduc*, otherwise *Ferrex and Porrex*. *Ralph Roister Doister* was licensed and is thought to have been printed in 1566, but it may have been acted at Eton by 1541, and the whole cast of the metre, language, and *scenario*, is of a colour older than Elizabeth's reign. It may be at least attributed to the middle of the century, and is the work of Nicholas Udall, a schoolmaster who has left at two great schools a repute for indulgence in the older methods of instruction not inferior to Busby's or Keate's. *Ralph Roister Doister*, though a fanciful estimate may see a little cruelty of another kind in it, is of no austere or pedagogic character. The author has borrowed not a little from the classical comedy—Plautine or even Aristophanic rather than Terentian—to strengthen and refine the domestic interlude or farce ; and the result is certainly amusing enough. The plot turns on the courtship of Dame Christian Custance [Constance], a widow of repute and wealth as well as beauty, by the gull and coxcomb, *Ralph Roister Doister*, whose suit is at once egged on and privately crossed by the mischievous Matthew Merrygreek, who plays not only parasite but rook to the hero. Although Custance has not the slightest intention of accepting Ralph, and at last resorts to actual violence, assisted by her maids, to get rid of him and his followers, the affair nearly breeds a serious quarrel between herself and her plighted lover, Gawin Goodluck ; but all ends merrily. The metre is the somewhat unformed doggerel couplet of twelve syllables or thereabouts, with a strong cæsura in the middle, and is varied and terminated by songs from Custance's maids and others. Indeed the chief charm of the piece is the genuine and unforced merriment which pervades it. Although Merrygreek's practices on Ralph's silliness sometimes tend a little to tediousness, the action on the whole moves trippingly enough, and despite the strong flavour of the "stock part" in the characters they have considerable individuality. The play is, moreover, as a whole remarkably free from coarseness, and there is no difficulty in finding an illustrative extract.

C. Custance loquitur.

" O Lord ! how necessary it is now o' days,
   That each body live uprightly all manner ways ;
   For let never so little a gap be open,
   And be sure of this, the worst shall be spoken.
   How innocent stand I in this frame o' thought,
   And yet see what mistrust towards me it hath wrought.
   But thou, Lord, knowest all folks' thoughts and eke intents ;
   And thou art the deliverer of all innocents.
   Thou didst keep the advoutress,[1] that she might be amended ;
   Much more then keep, Lord,[2] that never sin intended.
   Thou didst keep Susanna, wrongfully accused,
   And no less dost thou see, how I am now abused.
   Thou didst keep Hester, when she should have died,
   Keep also, good Lord, that my truth may be tried.
   Yet, if Gawin Goodluck with Tristram Trusty speak,
   I trust of ill-report the force shall be but weak ;
   And lo ! yond they come talking sadly together :
   I will abide, and not shrink for their coming hither."

Freedom from coarseness is more than can be predicated of the still more famous *Gammer Gurton's Needle*, attributed to, and all but certainly known to be, by John Still, afterwards bishop. The authorship, indeed, is not quite certain ; and the curious reference in Martin Marprelate's *Epistle* (ed. Arber, p. 11) to "this trifle" as "shewing the author to have had some wit and invention in him" only disputes the claim of Dr. Bridges to those qualities, and does not make any suggestion as to the identity of the more favoured author. Still was the son of a Lincolnshire gentleman, is supposed to have been born about 1543, was educated at Christ's College, Cambridge, and after a course of

    [1] Adulteress.   [2] Understand "me."

preferment through the positions of parish priest in London and at Hadleigh, Dean of Bocking, Canon of Westminster, Master successively of St. John's and Trinity, and Vice-Chancellor of his own University, was at the beginning of 1593 made Bishop of Bath and Wells, an office which he held for fifteen years. His play (taking it as his) was his only work of the kind, and was the first English play acted at either university, though later he himself had to protest officially against the use of the vernacular in a piece performed before the Queen. *Gammer Gurton's Needle*, as has been said, is, despite the subsequent history of its author and the academic character of its appearance, of a much lower order of comedy than *Ralph Roister Doister*, though it is also more spontaneous, less imitative, and, in short, more original. The best thing about it is the magnificent drinking song, " Back and Side go Bare, go Bare," one of the most spirited and genuine of all bacchanalian lyrics ; but the credit of this has sometimes been denied to Still. The metre of the play itself is very similar to that of *Ralph Roister Doister*, though the long swinging couplet has a tendency to lengthen itself still further, to the value of four-teen or even sixteen syllables, the central cæsura being always well marked, as may be seen in the following :—

Diccon. " Here will the sport begin, if these two once may meet,
Their cheer, [I] durst lay money, will prove scarcely sweet.
My gammer sure intends to be upon her bones,
With staves, or with clubs, or else with coble stones.
Dame Chat on the other side, if she be far behind,
I am right far deceived, she is given to it of kind.
He that may tarry by it a while, and that but short,
I warrant him trust to it, he shall see all the sport.
Into the town will I, my friends to visit there,
And hither straight again to see the end of this gear.
In the meantime, fellows, pipe up your fiddles ; I say, take them,
And let your friends hear such mirth as ye can make them."

As for the story, it is of the simplest, turning merely on the losing of her needle by Gammer Gurton as she was mending her man Hodge's breeches, on the search for it by the household, on the tricks by which Diccon the Bedlam (the clown or "vice" of the piece) induces a quarrel between Gammer and her neighbours, and on the final finding of the needle in the exact place on which Gammer Gurton's industry had been employed.   The action is even better sustained and livelier than in Udall's play, and the swinging couplets canter along very cheerfully with great freedom and fluency of language.   Unfortunately this language, whether in order to raise a laugh or to be in strict character with the personages, is anything but choice. There is (barring a possible double meaning or two) nothing of the kind generally known as licentious ; it is the merely foul and dirty language of common folk at all times, introduced, not with humorous extravagance in the Rabelaisian fashion, but with literal realism.   If there had been a little less of this, the piece would have been much improved ; but even as it is, it is a capital example of farce, just as *Ralph Roister Doister* is of a rather rudimentary kind of regular comedy.

The strangeness of the contrast which these two plays offer when compared with the third is peculiar in English literature. Elsewhere it is common enough.   That tragedy should be stately, decorous, and on the whole somewhat uneventful as far as visible action goes,—comedy bustling, crammed with incident, and quite regardless of decorum,—might seem a law of nature to the audience of Æschylus and Aristophanes, of Plautus and Pacuvius, even to the audience of Molière and Racine.   But the vast and final change, the inception of which we have here to record, has made tragedy, tragicomedy, comedy, and farce pass into one another so gradually, and with so little of a break in the English mind, that *Gammer Gurton's Needle* and *Gorboduc*, though they were presented to the same audiences, and in all probability written within ten years of each other at furthest, seem to belong to different worlds of literature and society.   The two comedies just noticed are framed upon no literary model at all as wholes, but simply upon the model of human nature.   *Gorboduc* is framed, though not with absolute fidelity, on the model of the tragedies

of Seneca, which had, during the early years of the sixteenth
century, mastered the attention of the literary playwrights of Italy,
France, and even to some extent Germany, and which determined
for three hundred years, at any rate, the form of the tragedy of
France.   This model—which may be briefly described as the
model of Greek tragedy, still further pruned of action, with the
choruses retained, but estranged from their old close connection
with the dialogue, and reduced to the level of elaborate lyrical
moralisings, and with the tendency to such moralising in dialogue
as well as in chorus largely increased—was introduced in England
with hardly less advantage than abroad.   Sackville, one of the
reputed authors of *Gorboduc*, was far superior to Jodelle, both
as poet and as versifier, and the existence of the two universities in England gave a support, to which nothing in France
corresponded, to the influence of learned writers.   Indeed,
till nearly the close of our present period, the universities had
the practical control of literary production.   But the genius of
the English nation would have none of Seneca.   It refused him
when he was first introduced by Sackville and others ; it refused
him once more when Daniel and the set of the Countess of Pembroke again attempted to introduce him ; it refused him again
and again in the later seventeenth century, when imitation, first
of his earlier French followers, and then of the greater tragedy
of Corneille and Racine (which was only the Senecan model
strengthened and improved) was repeatedly tried by fine gentlemen and by needy hacks, by devotees of the unities, and by
devotees of court fashion.   I hardly know any other instance in
literary history of a similar resistance offered to a similar tide of
literary influence in Europe.   We have little room here for
fanciful comparisons, yet might the dramatic events of 1560-
1590 in England well seem a literary battle of Tours, in which
an English Charles Martel stemmed and turned back for ever
and ever the hitherto resistless march of a literary invader
and spread of a literary heresy.

     To the modern reader *Gorboduc* (part of which is attributed to Thomas Norton, and which was acted on 18th January 1561, published piratically in 1565, and authoritatively under the title of *Ferrex and Porrex* in 1571?) is scarcely inviting, but that is not a criterion of its attractiveness to its own contemporaries. Perhaps the most curious thing about it is the violence done to the Horatian and Senecan theories, or rather the *naïf* outwitting of those theories, by an arrangement of dumb shows between the acts to satisfy the hunger for real action which the model refused to countenance. All the rest is of the most painful regularity : and the scrupulosity with which each of the rival princes is provided with a counsellor and a parasite to himself, and the other parts are allotted with similar fairness, reaches such a point that it is rather surprising that Gorboduc was not provided with two queens—a good and a bad. Such action as there is lies wholly in the mouths of messengers, and the speeches are of excessive length. But even these faults are perhaps less trying to the modern reader than the inchoate and unpolished condition of the metre in the choruses, and indeed in the blank verse dialogue. Here and there, there are signs of the stateliness and poetical imagery of the " Induction " ; but for the most part the decasyllables stop dead at their close and begin afresh at their beginning with a staccato movement and a dull monotony of cadence which is inexpressibly tedious, as will be seen in the following :—

(Videna soliloquises.)

" Why should I live and linger forth my time
In longer life to double my distress?
O me, most woeful wight, whom no mishap
Long ere this day could have bereaved hence.
Might not these hands, by fortune or by fate,
Have pierc'd this breast, and life with iron reft?
Or in this palace here where I so long
Have spent my days, could not that happy hour
Once, once have happ'd in which these hugy frames
With death by fall might have oppressed me?
Or should not this most hard and cruel soil,

So oft where I have press'd my wretched steps,
Some time had ruth of mine accursed life,
To rend in twain and swallow me therein?
So had my bones possessed now in peace
Their happy grave within the closed ground,
And greedy worms had gnawn this pined heart
Without my feeling pain : so should not now
This living breast remain the ruthful tomb
Wherein my heart yielden to death is graved ;
Nor dreary thoughts, with pangs of pining grief,
My doleful mind had not afflicted thus."

There is no blame due to Sackville in that he did not invent
what no single man invented, and what even in England, where
only it has been originally attained, took some thirty years of
the genius of the nation working through innumerable individual
tentatives and failures to bring about. But he did not invent it ;
he did not even make any attempt to invent it ; and had this
first English tragedy been generally followed, we should have
been for an unknown period in the land of bondage, in the
classical dungeon which so long retained the writers of a nation,
certainly not, at the time of the appearance of *Gorboduc*, of less
literary promise than our own.

In describing these tentatives and failures it will be impossible
here to enter into any lengthened criticism of particular works.
We shall have to content ourselves with a description of the
general lines and groups, which may be said to be four in
number : (1) The few unimportant and failing followers of Sackville ; (2) The miscellaneous farce-and-interlude-writers, who,
incult and formless as their work was, at least maintained the
literary tradition ; (3) The important and most interesting group
of "university wits" who, with Marlowe at their head, made the
blank verse line for dramatic purposes, dismissed, cultivated as
they were, the cultivation of classical models, and gave English
tragedy its Magna Charta of freedom and submission to the
restrictions of actual life only, but who failed, from this cause or
that, to achieve perfect life-likeness ; and (4) The actor-play-

wrights who, rising from very humble beginnings, but possessing in their fellow Shakespere a champion unparalleled in ancient and modern times, borrowed the improvements of the University Wits, added their own stage knowledge, and with Shakespere's aid achieved the master drama of the world.

A very few lines will suffice for the first group, who are the merest literary curiosities. Indeed the actual number of Senecan dramas in English is very small indeed, though there may possibly be some undiscovered in MS. The *Tancred and Gismund* of Robert Wilmot (acted 1568, and of some merit), the *Cornelia* of Garnier, translated by Kyd and printed in 1594, the curious play called *The Misfortunes of Arthur*, acted before the Queen in the Armada year, with " triumphs " partly devised by Francis Bacon, the two plays of Samuel Daniel, and a very few others, complete the list; indeed *Cornelia*, *Cleopatra*, and *Philotas* are almost the only three that keep really close to the model. At a time of such unbounded respect for the classics, and when Latin plays of the same stamp were constantly acted at the universities, such a paucity of examples in English can only testify to a strong national distaste—an instinctive feeling that this would never do.

The nondescript followings of morality and farce are infinitely more numerous, and perhaps intrinsically more interesting; but they can hardly be said to be, except in bulk, of much greater importance. Their real interest to the reader as he turns them over in the first seven or eight volumes of Dodsley, or in the rarer single editions where they occur, is again an interest of curiosity—a desire to trace the various shiftings and turnings of the mighty but unorganised genius which was soon to find its way. Next to the difficulty of inventing a conveniently plastic form seems to have been the difficulty of inventing a suitable verse. For some time the swinging or lumbering doggerel in which a tolerably good rhyme is reached by a kind of scramble through four or five feet, which are most like a very shuffling anapæst— the verse which appears in the comedies of Udall and Still—held its ground. We have it in the morality of the *New Custom*,

printed in 1573, but no doubt written earlier, in the Interlude of
The Trial of Treasure, in the farcical comedy of *Like Will to Like*,
a coarse but lively piece, by Ulpian Fulwell (1568).   In the very
curious tragicomedy of *Cambyses* this doggerel appears partly, but
is alternated with the less lawless but scarcely more suitable
"fourteener" (divided or not as usual, according to printer's
exigencies) which, as was shown in the last chapter, for a time
almost monopolised the attention of English poets.   The same
mixture appears to some extent, though the doggerel occupies the
main text, in the *Damon and Pythias* of Richard Edwards, the
editor of *The Paradise of Dainty Devices*.   In *Appius and
Virginia* (a decidedly interesting play) the fourteener on the
contrary is the staple verse, the doggerel being only occasional.   Something the same may be said of a very late morality, *The Conflict of Conscience*.   Both doggerel and fourteeners
appear in the quaint productions called *Three Ladies of London*,
etc. ; but by this time the decasyllable began to appear with them
and to edge them out.   They died hard, however, thoroughly ill-
fitted as they were for dramatic use, and, as readers of *Love's
Labour Lost* know, survived even in the early plays of Shakespere.   Nor were the characters and minor details generally of
this group less disorderly and inadequate than the general
schemes or the versification.   Here we have the abstractions
of the old Morality ; there the farcical gossip of the *Gammer
Gurton's Needle* class ; elsewhere the pale and dignified personages of *Gorboduc:* all three being often jumbled together all in
one play.   In the lighter parts there are sometimes fair touches
of low comedy ; in the graver occasionally, though much more
rarely, a touching or dignified phrase or two.   But the plays as
wholes are like Ovid's first-fruits of the deluge—nondescripts
incapable of life, and good for no useful or ornamental purpose.

It is at this moment that the cleavage takes place.   And
when I say "this moment," I am perfectly conscious that the
exact moment in dates and years cannot be defined.   Not a little
harm has been done to the history of English literature by the

confusion of times in which some of its historians have pleased
themselves.   But even greater harm might be done if one
were to insist on an exact chronology for the efflorescence of
the really poetical era of Elizabethan literature, if the blos-
soming of the aloe were to be tied down to hour and day.
All that we can say is that in certain publications, in certain
passages even of the same publication, we find the old respectable plodding, the old blind tentative experiment in poetry
and drama : and then without warning—without, as it seems, any
possible opportunity of distinguishing chronologically—we find the
unmistakable marks of the new wine, of the unapproachable poetry
proper, which all criticism, all rationalisation can only indicate
and not account for.   We have hardly left (if we take their
counterparts later we have not left) the wooden verse of *Gorboduc*,
the childish rusticity of *Like Will to Like*, when suddenly we
stumble on the bower—

" Seated in hearing of a hundred streams "—

of George Peele, on the myriad graceful fancies of Lyly, on the
exquisite snatches of Greene, on the verses, to this day the high-
water mark of poetry, in which Marlowe speaks of the inexpressible
beauty which is the object and the despair of the poet.   This is
wonderful enough.   But what is more wonderful is, that these
lightning flashes are as evanescent as lightning.   Lyly, Peele,
Greene, Marlowe himself, in probably the very next passages,
certainly in passages not very remote, tell us that this is all matter
of chance, that they are all capable of sinking below the level of
Sackville at his even conceivably worst, close to the level of
Edwards, and the various anonymous or half-anonymous writers
of the dramatic miscellanies just noted.   And then beyond these
unequal wits arises the figure of Shakespere ; and the greatest
work of all literature swims slowly into our ken.   There has been
as yet no history of this unique phenomenon worthy of it ; I have
not the least pretension to supply one that shall be worthy.   But
at least the uniqueness of it shall here have due celebration.   The

age of Pericles, the age of Augustus, the age of Dante, had no
such curious ushering-in unless time has dealt exceptional injustice
to the forerunners of all of them.   We do not, in the period
which comes nearest in time and nature to this, see anything of
the same kind in the middle space between Villon and Ronsard,
between Agrippa d'Aubigné and Corneille.   Here if anywhere is
the concentrated spirit of a nation, the thrice-decocted blood of a
people, forcing itself into literary expression through mediums
more and more worthy of it.   If ever the historical method was
justified (as it always is), now is its greatest justification as
we watch the gradual improvements, the decade-by-decade,
almost year-by-year acquisitions, which lead from Sackville to
Shakespere.

The rising sap showed itself in two very different ways, in
two branches of the national tree.   In the first place, we have
the group of University Wits, the strenuous if not always wise band
of professed men of letters, at the head of whom are Lyly, Marlowe, Greene, Peele, Lodge, Nash, and probably (for his connection with the universities is not certainly known) Kyd.   In the
second, we have the irregular band of outsiders, players and
others, who felt themselves forced into literary and principally
dramatic composition, who boast Shakespere as their chief, and
who can claim as seconds to him not merely the imperfect talents
of Chettle, Munday, and others whom we may mention in this
chapter, but many of the perfected ornaments of a later time.

It may be accident or it may not, but the beginning of this
period is certainly due to the "university wits."   Lyly stands a
good deal apart from them personally, despite his close literary
connection.   We have no kind of evidence which even shows
that he was personally acquainted with any one of the others.
Of Kyd, till Mr. Boas's recent researches, we knew next to
nothing, and we still know very little save that he was at
Merchant Taylors' School and was busy with plays famous
in their day.   But the other five were closely connected in
life, and in their deaths they were hardly divided.   Lodge

only of the five seems to have freed himself, partly in virtue of a
regular profession, and partly in consequence of his adherence to
the Roman faith, from the Bohemianism which has tempted men
of letters at all times, and which was especially dangerous in a
time of such unlimited adventure, such loose public morals, and
such unco-ordinated society as the Elizabethan era. Whatever
details we have of their lives (and they are mostly very meagre
and uncertain) convey the idea of times out of joint or not yet
in joint. The atheism of Marlowe rests on no proof whatever,
though it has got him friends in this later time. I am myself
by no means sure that Greene's supposed debauchery is not, to
a great extent, "copy." The majority of the too celebrated
"jests" attributed to George Peele are directly traceable to
Villon's *Repues Franches* and similar compilations, and have a
suspiciously mythical and traditional air to the student of literary
history. There is something a little more trustworthily autobiographical about Nash. But on the whole, though we need
not doubt that these ancestors of all modern Englishmen who
live by the gray goose quill tasted the inconveniences of the
profession, especially at a time when it was barely constituted
even as a vocation or employment (to quote the Income Tax
Papers), we must carefully avoid taking too gloomy a view of
their life. It was usually short, it was probably merry, but we
know very little else about it. The chief direct documents, the
remarkable pamphlets which some of them have left, will be
dealt with hereafter. Here we are busied only with their dates
and their dramatic work, which was in no case (except perhaps
in that of Kyd) their sole known work, but which in every case
except those of Nash and perhaps Greene was their most
remarkable.

In noticing *Euphues* an account has already been given of
Lyly's life, or rather of the very scanty particulars which are
known of it. His plays date considerably later than *Euphues*.
But they all bear the character of the courtier about them ; and
both in this characteristic and in the absence of any details in

the gossipping literature of the time to connect him with the Bohemian society of the playhouse, the distinction which separates Lyly from the group of "university wits" is noteworthy. He lost as well as gained by the separation.   All his plays were acted "by the children of Paul's before her Majesty," and not by the usual companies before Dick, Tom, and Harry.   The exact date and order of their writing is very uncertain, and in one case at least, that of *The Woman in the Moon*, we know that the order was exactly reversed in publication : this being the last printed in Lyly's lifetime, and expressly described as the first written.   His other dramatic works are *Campaspe, Sappho and Phaon, Endymion, Galathea, Midas, Mother Bombie*, and *Love's Metamorphosis;* another, *The Maid's Metamorphosis*, which has been attributed to him, is in all probability not his.

The peculiar circumstances of the production of Lyly's plays, and the strong or at any rate decided individuality of the author, keep them in a division almost to themselves.   The mythological or pastoral character of their subject in most cases might not of itself have prevented their marking an advance in the dramatic composition of English playwrights.   *A Midsummer Night's Dream* and much other work of Shakespere's show how far from necessary it is that theme, or class of subject, should affect merit of presentment.   But Lyly's work generally has more of the masque than the play.   It sometimes includes charming lyrics, such as the famous *Campaspe* song and others.   But most of it is in prose, and it gave beyond doubt—though Gascoigne had, as we have seen, set the example in drama—no small impetus to the use and perfectioning of that medium.   For Lyly's dramatic prose, though sometimes showing the same faults, is often better than *Euphues*, as here :—

" *End.* O fair Cynthia, why do others term thee unconstant, whom I have ever found immovable?   Injurious time, corrupt manners, unkind men, who finding a constancy not to be matched in my sweet mistress, have christened her with the name of wavering, waxing, and waning.   Is she inconstant that keepeth a settled course, which since her first creation altereth not one minute in her moving? There is nothing thought more admirable, or commendable in the sea, than the ebbing and flowing; and shall the moon, from whom the sea taketh this virtue, be accounted fickle for increasing and decreasing? Flowers in their buds are nothing worth till they be blown; nor blossoms accounted till they be ripe fruit; and shall we then say they be changeable, for that they grow from seeds to leaves, from leaves to buds, from buds to their perfection? then, why be not twigs that become trees, children that become men, and mornings that grow to evenings, termed wavering, for that they continue not at one stay? Ay, but Cynthia being in her fulness decayeth, as not delighting in her greatest beauty, or withering when she should be most honoured. When malice cannot object anything, folly will; making that a vice which is the greatest virtue. What thing (my mistress excepted) being in the pride of her beauty, and latter minute of her age, that waxeth young again? Tell me, Eumenides, what is he that having a mistress of ripe years, and infinite virtues, great honours, and unspeakable beauty, but would wish that she might grow tender again? getting youth by years, and never-decaying beauty by time; whose fair face, neither the summer's blaze can scorch, nor winter's blast chap, nor the numbering of years breed altering of colours. Such is my sweet Cynthia, whom time cannot touch, because she is divine, nor will offend because she is delicate. O Cynthia, if thou shouldest always continue at thy fulness, both gods and men would conspire to ravish thee. But thou, to abate the pride of our affections, dost detract from thy perfections; thinking it sufficient if once in a month we enjoy a glimpse of thy majesty; and then, to increase our griefs, thou dost decrease thy gleams; coming out of thy royal robes, wherewith thou dazzlest our eyes, down into thy swath clouts, beguiling our eyes; and then——"

In these plays there are excellent phrases and even striking scenes. But they are not in the true sense dramatic, and are constantly spoilt by Lyly's strange weakness for conceited style. Everybody speaks in antitheses, and the intolerable fancy similes, drawn from a kind of imaginary natural history, are sometimes as prominent as in *Euphues* itself. Lyly's theatre represents, in short, a mere backwater in the general stream of dramatic progress, though not a few allusions in other men's work show us that it attracted no small attention. With Nash alone, of the University Wits proper, was Lyly connected, and this only problematically. He was an Oxford man, and most of them were of Cambridge; he was a courtier, if a badly-paid one, and they all lived by their wits; and, if we may judge

by the very few documents remaining, he was not inclined to
be hail-fellow-well-met with anybody, while they were all born
Bohemians. Yet none of them had a greater influence on
Shakespere than Lyly, though it was anything but a beneficial
influence, and for this as well as for the originality of his production he deserves notice, even had the intrinsic merit of his
work been less than it is. But, in fact, it is very great, being
almost a typical production of talent helped by knowledge, but
not mastered by positive genius, or directed in its way by the
precedent work of others.

In the work of the University Wits proper—Marlowe, Greene,
Peele, Lodge, Nash, and Kyd, the last of whom, it must again
be said, is not certainly known to have belonged to either university, though the probabilities are all in favour of that hypothesis—a very different kind of work is found. It is always
faulty, as a whole, for even *Dr. Faustus* and *Edward II.*,
despite their magnificent poetry and the vast capabilities of
their form, could only be called good plays or good compositions as any kind of whole by a critic who had entirely lost the
sense of proportion. But in the whole group, and especially in
the dramatic work of Marlowe, Greene, Peele, and Kyd (for that
of Lodge and Nash is small in amount and comparatively unimportant in manner), the presence, the throes of a new dramatic
style are evident. Faults and beauties are more or less common
to the whole quartet. In all we find the many-sided activity of
the Shakesperian drama as it was to be, sprawling and struggling in a kind of swaddling clothes of which it cannot get rid,
and which hamper and cripple its movements. In all there is
present a most extraordinary and unique rant and bombast of
expression which reminds one of the shrieks and yells of a band
of healthy boys just let out to play. The passages which (thanks
chiefly to Pistol's incomparable quotations and parodies of them)
are known to every one, the " Pampered jades of Asia," the
" Have we not Hiren here," the "Feed and grow fat, my fair
Callipolis," the other quips and cranks of mine ancient are

scattered broadcast in their originals, and are evidently meant quite seriously throughout the work of these poets. Side by side with this mania for bombast is another mania, much more clearly traceable to education and associations, but specially odd in connection with what has just been noticed. This is the foible of classical allusion. The heathen gods and goddesses, the localities of Greek and Roman poetry, even the more out-of-the-way commonplaces of classical literature, are put in the mouths of all the characters without the remotest attempt to consider propriety or relevance. Even in still lesser peculiarities the blemishes are uniform and constant—such as the curious and childish habit of making speakers speak of themselves in the third person, and by their names, instead of using "I" and "me." And on the other hand, the merits, though less evenly distributed in degree, are equally constant in kind. In Kyd, in Greene still more, in Peele more still, in Marlowe most of all, phrases and passages of blinding and dazzling poetry flash out of the midst of the bombast and the tedium. Many of these are known, by the hundred books of extract which have followed Lamb's *Specimens*, to all readers. Such, for instance, is the

"See where Christ's blood streams in the firmament"

of Marlowe, and his even more magnificent passage beginning

"If all the pens that ever poets held;"

such Peele's exquisite bower,

"Seated in hearing of an hundred streams,

which is, with all respect to Charles Lamb, to be paralleled by a score of other jewels from the reckless work of "George Pyeboard": such Greene's

"Why thinks King Henry's son that Margaret's love
Hangs in the uncertain balance of proud time?"

such even Kyd's

"There is a path upon your left hand side
That leadeth from a guilty conscience
Unto a forest of distrust and fear."

But the whole point of the thing is that these flashes, which are not to be found at all before the date of this university school, are to be found constantly in its productions, and that, amorphous, inartistic, incomplete as those productions are, they still show *Hamlet* and *A Midsummer Night's Dream* in embryo. Whereas the greatest expert in literary embryology may read *Gorboduc* and *The Misfortunes of Arthur* through without discerning the slightest signs of what was coming.

Nash and Lodge are so little dramatists (the chief, if not only play of the former being the shapeless and rather dull comedy, *Will Summer's Testament*, relieved only by some lyrics of merit which are probably not Nash's, while Lodge's *Marius and Sylla*, while it wants the extravagance, wants also the beauty of its author's companions' work), that what has to be said about them will be better said later in dealing with their other books. Greene's prose pieces and his occasional poems are, no doubt, better than his drama, but the latter is considerable, and was probably his earliest work. Kyd has left nothing, and Peele little, but drama; while beautiful as Marlowe's *Hero and Leander* is, I do not quite understand how any one can prefer it to the faultier but far more original dramas of its author. We shall therefore deal with these four individually here.

The eldest of the four was George Peele, variously described as a Londoner and a Devonshire man, who was probably born about 1558. He was educated at Christ's Hospital (of which his father was " clerk ") and at Broadgates Hall, now Pembroke College, Oxford, and had some credit in the university as an arranger of pageants, etc. He is supposed to have left Oxford for London about 1581, and had the credit of living a Bohemian, not to say disreputable, life for about seventeen years; his death in 1597 (?) being not more creditable than his life. But even the scandals about Peele are much more shadowy than those about Marlowe and Greene. His dramatic work consists of some half-dozen plays, the earliest of which is *The Arraignment of Paris*, 1581 (?), one of the most elaborate and barefaced of the many contemporary flatteries of Elizabeth, but containing some exquisite verse. In the same way Peele has been accused of having in *Edward I.* adopted or perhaps even invented the basest and most groundless scandals against the noble and stainless memory of Eleanor of Castile; while in his *Battle of Alcazar* he certainly gratifies to the utmost the popular ante-Spanish and ante-Popish feeling. So angry have critics been with Peele's outrage on Eleanor, that some of them have declared that none but he could have been guilty of the not dissimilar slur cast on Joan of Arc's character in *Henry VI.*, the three parts of which it has been the good pleasure of Shakesperian commentators to cut and carve between the University Wits *ad libitum.* I cannot myself help thinking that all this has arisen very much from the idea of Peele's vagabondism given by the untrustworthy "Jests." The slander on Queen Eleanor was pretty certainly supplied to him by an older ballad. There is little or nothing else in Peele's undoubted writings which is at all discreditable. His miscellaneous poems show a man by no means given to low company or low thoughts, and one gifted with the truest poetic vein; while his dramas, besides exhibiting a greater command over blank verse than any of his prede- cessors and than any except Marlowe of his contemporaries can claim, are full of charming passages. *Sir Clyomon and Sir Clamydes*, which has been denied to him—an interesting play on the rare basis of the old romance—is written not in blank verse but in the fourteener. The *Old Wives' Tale* pretty certainly furnished Milton with the subject of *Comus*, and this is its chief merit. *Edward I.* and *The Battle of Alcazar*, but especially the latter, contain abundance of the hectoring rant which has been marked as one of the characteristics of the school, and which is half-excused by the sparks of valour that often break from its smoke and clatter. But Peele would undoubtedly stand higher, though he might not be so interesting a literary figure, if we had nothing of his save *The Arraignment of Paris* and *David and Bethsabe*. *The*

Arraignment (written in various metres, but mainly in a musical and varied heroic couplet), is partly a pastoral, partly a masque, and wholly a Court play.   It thus comes nearest to Lyly, but is altogether a more dramatic, livelier, and less conceited perform- ance than anything by the author of *Euphues*.   As for *David and Bethsabe*, it is crammed with beauties, and Lamb's curiously faint praise of it has always been a puzzle to me.   As Marlowe's are the mightiest, so are Peele's the softest, lines in the drama before Shakespere ; while the spirit and humour, which the author also had in plenty, save his work from the merely cloying sweetness of some contemporary writers.   Two of his interposed or occa- sional lyrics will be given later : a blank verse passage may find room here :—

Bethsabe.   " Come, gentle Zephyr, trick'd with those perfumes
            That erst in Eden sweeten'd Adam's love,
            And stroke my bosom with thy silken fan :
            This shade, sun-proof,[1] is yet no proof for thee ;
            Thy body, smoother than this waveless spring,
            And purer than the substance of the same,
            Can creep through that his lances cannot pierce :
            Thou, and thy sister, soft and sacred Air,
            Goddess of life, and governess of health,
            Keep every fountain fresh and arbour sweet ;
            No brazen gate her passage can repulse,
            Nor bushy thicket bar thy subtle breath :
            Then deck thee with thy loose delightsome robes,
            And on thy wings bring delicate perfumes,
            To play the wanton with us through the leaves."

Robert Greene, probably, if not certainly, the next in age of the group to Peele, was born in 1560, the son of apparently well-to-do parents at Norwich, and was educated at Clare Hall, Cambridge, where he took his Master's Degree in 1583.   He was subsequently incorporated at Oxford, and being by no means ill-inclined to make the most of himself, sometimes took the style of a member

---

[1] Cf. Milton's "elms star-proof" in the *Arcades*.   Milton evidently knew Peele well.

" Utriusque Academiæ." After leaving the university he seems
to have made a long tour on the Continent, not (according to his
own account) at all to the advantage of his morals or means.
He is said to have actually taken orders, and held a living for
some short time, while he perhaps also studied if he did not
practice medicine. He married a lady of virtue and some fortune,
but soon despoiled and deserted her, and for the last six years of
his life never saw her. At last in 1592, aged only two and
thirty,—but after about ten years it would seem of reckless living
and hasty literary production,—he died (of a disease caused or
aggravated by a debauch on pickled herrings and Rhenish) so
miserably poor that he had to trust to his injured wife's forgiveness for payment of the money to the extent of which a charitable landlord and landlady had trusted him. The facts of this
lamentable end may have been spitefully distorted by Gabriel
Harvey in his quarrel with Nash; but there is little reason to
doubt that the received story is in the main correct. Of the remarkable prose pamphlets which form the bulk of Greene's work
we speak elsewhere, as also of the pretty songs (considerably exceeding in poetical merit anything to be found in the body of his
plays) with which both pamphlets and plays are diversified. His
actual dramatic production is not inconsiderable : six plays being
his beyond doubt ; while I am myself rather disposed (if the whole
business of crediting these Elizabethan poets with anonymous
plays had not been discredited by the wild dogmatism with which
it has been pursued) to adopt that theory of *Fair Em*, which sets
it down to Greene. His best play without doubt is *The History
of Friar Bacon and Friar Bungay*, in which, after a favourite
fashion of the time, he mingles a certain amount of history, or,
at least, a certain number of historical personages, with a plentiful
dose of the supernatural and of horse play, and with a very
graceful and prettily-handled love story. With a few touches
from the master's hand, Margaret, the fair maid of Fressingfield,
might serve as handmaid to Shakespere's women, and is
certainly by far the most human heroine produced by any of

heroine produced by any of Greene's own group.   There is less
rant in Greene (though there is still plenty of it) than in any of
his friends, and his fancy for soft female characters, loving, and
yet virtuous, appears frequently.   But his power is ill-sustained,
as the following extract will show :—

Margaret.   " Ah, father, when the harmony of heaven
           Soundeth the measures of a lively faith,
           The vain illusions of this flattering world
           Seem odious to the thoughts of Margaret.
           I lovèd once,—Lord Lacy was my love ;
           And now I hate myself for that I loved,
           And doted more on him than on my God,—
           For this I scourge myself with sharp repents.
           But now the touch of such aspiring sins
           Tells me all love is lust but love of heaven ;
           That beauty used for love is vanity :
           The world contains naught but alluring baits,
           Pride, flattery [   ], and inconstant thoughts.
           To shun the pricks of death I leave the world,
           And vow to meditate on heavenly bliss,
           To live in Framlingham a holy nun,
           Holy and pure in conscience and in deed ;
           And for to wish all maids to learn of me
           To seek heaven's joy before earth's vanity."

We do not know anything of Thomas Kyd's, except *The
Spanish Tragedy*, which is a second part of an extremely popular
play (sometimes attributed to Kyd himself, but probably earlier)
called *Jeronimo*, and the translation of *Cornelia*, though others
are doubtfully attributed.   The well-known epithet of Jonson,
" sporting " Kyd, seems to have been either a mere play on the
poet's name, or else a *lucus a non lucendo ;* for both *Jeronimo* and
its sequel are in the ghastliest and bloodiest vein of tragedy, and
Cornelia is a model of stately dullness.   The two " Jeronimo "
or " Hieronimo " plays were, as has been said, extremely popular, and it is positively known that Jonson himself, and probably
others, were employed from time to time to freshen them up ; with
the consequence that the exact authorship of particular passages

is somewhat problematical. Both plays, however, display, nearly in perfection, the rant, not always quite ridiculous, but always extravagant, from which Shakespere rescued the stage ; though, as the following extract will show, this rant is by no means always, or indeed often, smoke without fire :—

> " O ! forbear,
> For other talk for us far fitter were.
> But if you be importunate to know
> The way to him, and where to find him out,
> Then list to me, and I'll resolve your doubt.
> There is a path upon your left hand side,
> That leadeth from a guilty conscience
> Unto a forest of distrust and fear—
> A darksome place and dangerous to pass.
> There shall you meet with melancholy thoughts
> Whose baleful humours if you but uphold,
> It will conduct you to despair and death.
> Whose rocky cliffs when you have once beheld
> Within a hugy dale of lasting night—
> That, kindled with the world's iniquities,
> Doth cast up filthy and detested fumes—
> Not far from thence, where murderers have built
> An habitation for their cursed souls,
> There is a brazon cauldron fixed by Jove
> In his fell wrath upon a sulphur flame.
> Yourselves shall find Lorenzo bathing him
> In boiling lead and blood of innocents."

But nothing, except citation of whole scenes and acts, could show the extraordinary jumble of ghosts, blood, thunder, treachery, and horrors of all sorts which these plays contain.

Now for a very different citation :—

> " If all the pens that ever poets held
> Had fed the feeling of their masters' thoughts,
> And every sweetness that inspir'd their hearts,
> Their minds, and muses, on admirèd themes ;
> If all the heavenly quintessence they 'still
> From their immortal flowers of poesy,
> Wherein as in a mirror we perceive

The highest reaches of a human wit ;
If these had made one poem's period,
And all combined in beauty's worthiness,
Yet should there hover in their restless heads
One thought, one grace, one wonder at the least
Which into words no virtue can digest."

It is no wonder that the whole school has been dwarfed
in the general estimation, since its work was critically considered
and isolated from other work, by the towering excellence of
this author.   Little as is known of all the band, that little
becomes almost least in regard to their chief and leader.   Born
(1564) at Canterbury, the son of a shoemaker, he was educated
at the Grammar School of that city, and at Benet (afterwards
Corpus) College, Cambridge ; he plunged into literary work and
dissipation in London ; and he outlived Greene only to fall a
victim to debauchery in a still more tragical way.   His death (1593)
was the subject of much gossip, but the most probable account
is that he was poniarded in self-defence by a certain Francis
Archer, a serving-man (not by any means necessarily, as Charles
Kingsley has it, a footman), while drinking at Deptford, and that
the cause of the quarrel was a woman of light character.   He
has also been accused of gross vices not to be particularised, and
of atheism.   The accusation is certain ; and Mr. Boas's researches
as to Kyd, who was also concerned in the matter, have thrown
some light on it ; but much is still obscure.   The most offensive
charges were due to one Bame or Baines, who was afterwards
hanged at Tyburn.   That Marlowe was a Bohemian in the fullest
sense is certain ; that he was anything worse there is no evidence
whatever.   He certainly was acquainted with Raleigh and other
distinguished persons, and was highly spoken of by Chapman and
others.

But the interest of Marlowe's name has nothing to do with
these obscure scandals of three hundred years ago, though it
may be difficult to pass them over entirely.   He is the
undoubted author of some of the masterpieces of English verse ;

the hardly to be doubted author of others not much inferior.
Except the very greatest names—Shakespere, Milton, Spenser,
Dryden, Shelley—no author can be named who has produced,
when the proper historical estimate is applied to him, such work
as is to be found in *Tamburlaine, Doctor Faustus, The Jew of
Malta, Edward the Second*, in one department ; *Hero and Leander*
and the *Passionate Shepherd* in another.   I have but very little
doubt that the powerful, if formless, play of *Lust's Dominion* is
Marlowe's, though it may have been rewritten, and the translations
of Lucan and Ovid and the minor work which is more or less
probably attributed to him, swell his tale.   Prose he did not
write, perhaps could not have written.   For the one characteristic
lacking to his genius was measure, and prose without measure, as
numerous examples have shown, is usually rubbish.   Even his
dramas show a singular defect in the architectural quality of
literary genius.   The vast and formless creations of the writer's
boundless fancy completely master him ; his aspirations after the
immense too frequently leave him content with the simply un-
measured.   In his best play as a play, *Edward the Second*, the
limitations of a historical story impose something like a restraining
form on his glowing imagination.   But fine as this play is, it is
noteworthy that no one of his greatest things occurs in it.   *The
Massacre at Paris*, where he also has the confinement of reality
after a fashion, is a chaotic thing as a whole, without any great
beauty in parts.   The *Tragedy of Dido* (to be divided between
him and Nash) is the worst thing he ever did.   But in the
purely romantic subjects of *Tamburlaine, Faustus*, and *The Jew of
Malta*, his genius, untrammelled by any limits of story, showed
itself equally unable to contrive such limits for itself, and able to
develop the most marvellous beauties of detail.   Shakespere
himself has not surpassed, which is equivalent to saying that no
other writer has equalled, the famous and wonderful passages in
Tamburlaine and *Faustus*, which are familiar to every student of
English literature as examples of the *ne plus ultra* of the poetic
powers, not of the language but of language.   The tragic imagina-

tion in its wildest flights has never summoned up images of pity
and terror more imposing, more moving, than those excited by
The Jew of Malta. The riot of passion and of delight in the
beauty of colour and form which characterises his version of
Hero and Leander has never been approached by any writer. But
Marlowe, with the fullest command of the *apeiron*, had not, and,
as far as I can judge, never would have had, any power of introducing into it the law of the *peras*. It is usual to say that had he
lived, and had his lot been happily cast, we should have had two
Shakesperes. This is not wise. In the first place, Marlowe was
totally destitute of humour—the characteristic which, united with
his tragic and imaginative powers, makes Shakespere as, in a less
degree, it makes Homer, and even, though the humour is grim
and intermittent, Dante. In other words, he was absolutely
destitute of the first requisite of self-criticism. In the natural
course of things, as the sap of his youthful imagination ceased
to mount, and as his craving for immensity hardened itself,
he would probably have degenerated from bombast shot through
with genius to bombast pure and simple, from *Faustus* to *Lust's
Dominion,* and from *Lust's Dominion* to *Jeronimo* or *The Distracted Emperor.* Apart from the magnificent passages which he
can show, and which are simply intoxicating to any lover of
poetry, his great title to fame is the discovery of the secret of
that "mighty line" which a seldom-erring critic of his own day,
not too generously given, vouchsafed to him. Up to his time
the blank verse line always, and the semi-couplet in heroics, or
member of the more complicated stanza usually, were either stiff
or nerveless. Compared with his own work and with the
work of his contemporaries and followers who learnt from him,
they are like a dried preparation, like something waiting for the
infusion of blood, for the inflation of living breath. Marlowe
came, and the old wooden versification, the old lay-figure structure
of poetic rhythm, was cast once for all into the lumber-room, where
only poetasters of the lowest rank went to seek it. It is impossible to call Marlowe a great dramatist, and the attempts that

have been made to make him out to be such remind one of the attempts that have been made to call Molière a great poet. Marlowe was one of the greatest poets of the world whose work was cast by accident and caprice into an imperfect mould of drama ; Molière was one of the greatest dramatists of the world who was obliged by fashion to use a previously perfected form of verse. The state of Molière was undoubtedly the more gracious ; but the splendour of Marlowe's uncut diamonds of poetry is the more wonderful.

The characteristics of this strange and interesting school may be summed up briefly, but are of the highest importance in literary history. Unlike their nearest analogues, the French romantics of the 1830 type, they were all of academic education, and had even a decided contempt (despite their Bohemian way of life) for unscholarly innovators. They manifested (except in Marlowe's fortuitous and purely genial discovery of the secret of blank verse) a certain contempt for form, and never, at least in drama, succeeded in mastering it. But being all, more or less, men of genius, and having the keenest sense of poetry, they supplied the dry bones of the precedent dramatic model with blood and breath, with vigour and variety, which not merely informed but transformed it. *David and Bethsabe, Doctor Faustus, Friar Bacon and Friar Bungay,* are chaotic enough, but they are of the chaos that precedes cosmic development. The almost insane bombast that marks the whole school has (as has been noticed) the character of the shrieks and gesticulations of healthy childhood, and the insensibility to the really comic which also marks them is of a similar kind. Every one knows how natural it is to childhood to appreciate bad jokes, how seldom a child sees a good one. Marlowe and his crew, too (the comparison has no doubt often been used before), were of the brood of Otus and Ephialtes, who grew so rapidly and in so disorderly a fashion that it was necessary for the gods to make an end of them. The universe probably lost little, and it certainly gained something.

Side by side with this learned, extravagant, gifted, ill-regulated school, there was slowly growing up a very different one, which was to inherit all the gifts of the University Wits, and to add to them the gifts of measure and proportion.   The early work of the actor school of English dramatists is a difficult subject to treat in any fashion, and a particularly difficult subject to treat shortly. Chronology, an important aid, helps us not very much, though such help as she does give has been as a rule neglected by historians, so that plays before 1590 (which may be taken roughly as the dividing date), and plays after it have been muddled up ruthlessly.   We do not know the exact dates of many of those which are (many of the plays of the earlier time are not) extant ; and of those which are extant, and of which the dates are more or less known, the authors are in not a few most important cases absolutely undiscoverable.   Yet in the plays which belong to this period, and which there is no reason to attribute wholly to any of the Marlowe group, or much reason to attribute to them under the guidance, or perhaps with the collaboration of practical actors (some at least of whom were like Shakespere himself, men of no known regular education), there are characteristics which promise at least as well for the future as the wonderful poetic outbursts of the Marlowe school itself.   Of these outbursts we find few in this other division.   But we find a growing knowledge of what a play is, as distinguished from a series of tableaux acted by not too lifelike characters.   We find a glimmering (which is hardly anywhere to be seen in the more literary work of the other school) of the truth that the characters must be made to work out the play, and not the play be written in a series of disjointed scenes to display, in anything but a suc- cessful fashion, the characters.   With fewer flights we have fewer absurdities ; with less genius we have more talent.   It must be remembered, of course, that the plays of the university school itself were always written for players, and that some of the authors had more or less to do with acting as well as with writing.   But the flame of discord which burns so fiercely on the one side in the famous real or supposed dying utterances of Greene, and which years afterwards breaks out on the other in the equally famous satire of *The Return from Parnassus*,[1] illuminates a real difference—a difference which study of the remains of the lite-rature of the period can only make plainer. The same differ-ence has manifested itself again, and more than once in other departments of literature, but hardly in so interesting a manner, and certainly not with such striking results.

[1] The outburst of Greene about "the only Shakescene," the "upstart crow beautified with our feathers," and so forth, is too well known to need extracting here. *The Return from Parnassus*, a very curious tripartite play, performed 1597-1601 but retrospective in tone, is devoted to the troubles of poor scholars in getting a livelihood, and incidentally gives much matter on the authors of the time from Shakespere downward, and on the jealousy of pro-fessional actors felt by scholars, and *vice versâ*.

CHAPTER IV

"THE FAËRIE QUEENE" AND ITS GROUP

" Velut inter ignes luna minores "

THERE is no instance in English history of a poet receiving such
immediate recognition, and deserving it so thoroughly, as did
Edmund Spenser at the date of *The Shepherd's Calendar.* In
the first chapter of this volume the earlier course of Elizabethan
poetry has been described, and it will have been seen that, with
great intention, no very great accomplishment had been achieved.
It was sufficiently evident that a poetic language and a general
poetic spirit were being formed, such as had not existed in
England since Chaucer's death ; but no one had yet arisen who
could justify the expectation based on such respectable tentatives.
It seems from many minute indications which need not be
detailed here, that at the advent of *The Shepherd's Calendar* all
the best judges recognised the expected poet. Yet they could
hardly have known how just their recognition was, or what
extraordinary advances the poet would make in the twenty
years which passed between its publication and his death.

The life of Spenser is very little known, and here and elsewhere the conditions of this book preclude the reproduction or
even the discussion of the various pious attempts which have
been made to supply the deficiency of documents. The chief
of these in his case is to be found in Dr. Grosart's magnificent

edition, the principal among many good works of its editor. That
he belonged to a branch—a Lancashire branch in all probability—
of the family which produced the Le Despensers of elder, and the
Spencers of modern English history, may be said to be unquestionable. But he appears to have been born about 1552 in
London, and to have been educated at Merchant Taylors', whence
in May 1569 he matriculated at Pembroke Hall, Cambridge, as
a sizar. At or before this time he must have contributed (though
there are puzzles in the matter) certain translations of sonnets
from Petrarch and Du Bellay to a book called *The Theatre of
Voluptuous Worldlings*, published by a Brabanter, John van der
Noodt. These, slightly changed from blank verse to rhyme,
appeared long afterwards with his minor poems of 1590. But
the original pieces had been claimed by the Dutchman ; and
though there are easy ways of explaining this, the thing is
curious. However it may be with these verses, certainly
nothing else of Spenser's appeared in print for ten years. His
Cambridge life, except for some vague allusions (which, as usual
in such cases, have been strained to breaking by commentators
and biographers), is equally obscure ; save that he certainly
fulfilled seven years of residence, taking his Bachelor's Degree in
1573, and his Master's three years later. But he did not gain a
fellowship, and the chief discoverable results of his Cambridge
sojourn were the thorough scholarship which marks his work, and his
friendship with the notorious Gabriel Harvey—his senior by some
years, a Fellow of Pembroke, and a person whose singularly bad
literary taste, as shown in his correspondence with Spenser, may
be perhaps forgiven, first, because it did no harm, and secondly,
because without him we should know even less of Spenser than
we do. It is reasonably supposed from the notes of his friend,
"E. K." (apparently Kirke, a Pembroke man), to *The Shepherd's
Calendar*, that he went to his friends in the north after leaving
Cambridge and spent a year or two there, falling in love with
the heroine, poetically named Rosalind, of *The Calendar*, and no
doubt writing that remarkable book. Then (probably very late in

1578) he went to London, was introduced by Harvey to Sidney and Leicester, and thus mixed at once in the best literary and political society. He was not long in putting forth his titles to its attention, for *The Shepherd's Calendar* was published in the winter of 1579, copiously edited by " E. K.," whom some absurdly suppose to be Spenser himself. The poet seems to have had also numerous works (the titles of which are known) ready or nearly ready for the press. But all were subsequently either changed in title, incorporated with other work, or lost. He had already begun *The Faërie Queene*, much to the pedant Harvey's disgust ; and he dabbled in the fashionable absurdity of classical metres, like his inferiors. But he published nothing more immediately ; and powerful as were his patrons, the only preferment which he obtained was in that Eldorado-Purgatory of Elizabethan ambition—Ireland. Lord Grey took him as private secretary when he was in 1580 appointed deputy, and shortly afterwards he received some civil posts in his new country, and a lease of abbey lands at Enniscorthy, which lease he soon gave up. But he stayed in Ireland, notwithstanding the fact that his immediate patron Grey soon left it. Except a few bare dates and doubtful allusions, little or nothing is heard of him between 1580 and 1590. On the eve of the latter year (the 1st of December 1589) the first three books of *The Faërie Queene* were entered at Stationers' Hall, and were published in the spring of the next year. He had been already established at Kilcolman in the county Cork on a grant of more than three thousand acres of land out of the forfeited Desmond estates. And henceforward his literary activity, at least in publication, became more considerable, and he seems to have been much backwards and forwards between England and Ireland. In 1590 appeared a volume of minor poems (*The Ruins of Time, The Tears of the Muses, Virgil's Gnat, Mother Hubbard's Tale, The Ruins of Rome, Muiopotmos,* and the *Visions*), with an address to the reader in which another list of forthcoming works is promised. These, like the former list of Kirke, seem oddly enough to have also perished. The whole collection was called *Complaints*, and a somewhat similar poem, *Daphnaida*, is thought to have appeared in the same year. On the 11th of June 1594 the poet married (strangely enough it was not known whom, until Dr. Grosart ingeniously identified her with a certain Elizabeth Boyle *alias* Seckerstone), and in 1595 were published the beautiful *Amoretti* or love sonnets, and the still more beautiful *Epithalamion* describing his courtship and marriage, with the interesting poem of *Colin Clout's Come Home Again;* while in the same year (old style; in January 1596, new style) the fourth, fifth, and sixth books of *The Faërie Queene* were entered for publication and soon appeared. The supposed allusions to Mary Stuart greatly offended her son James. The *Hymns* and the *Prothalamion* followed in the same year. Spenser met with difficulties at Court (though he had obtained a small pension of fifty pounds a year), and had had like other Englishmen troubles with his neighbours in Ireland; yet he seemed to be becoming more prosperous, and in 1598 he was named Sheriff of Cork. A few weeks later the Irish Rebellion broke out; his house was sacked and burnt with one of his children; he fled to England and died on the 16th of January 1599 at King Street, Westminster, perhaps not "for lack of bread," as Jonson says, but certainly in no fortunate circumstances. In the year of his misfortune had been registered, though it was never printed till more than thirty years later, his one prose work of substance, the remarkable *View of the Present State of Ireland;* an admirable piece of prose, and a political tract, the wisdom and grasp of which only those who have had to give close attention to Irish politics can fully estimate. It is probably the most valuable document on any given period of Irish history that exists, and is certainly superior in matter, no less than in style, to any political tract in English, published before the days of Halifax eighty years after.

It has been said that *The Shepherd's Calendar* placed Spenser at once at the head of the English poets of his day; and it did so. But had he written nothing more, he would not (as is the case with not a few distinguished poets) have occupied as high

or nearly as high a position in quality, if not in quantity, as he
now does.   He was a young man when he published it ; he was
not indeed an old man when he died ; and it would not appear
that he had had much experience of life beyond college walls.
His choice of models—the artificial pastorals in which the
Renaissance had modelled itself on Virgil and Theocritus, rather
than Virgil and Theocritus themselves—was not altogether happy.
He showed, indeed, already his extraordinary metrical skill,
experimenting with rhyme-royal and other stanzas, fourteeners
or eights and sixes, anapæsts more or less irregular, and an
exceedingly important variety of octosyllable which, whatever
may have been his own idea in practising it, looked back
to early Middle English rhythms and forward to the metre
of *Christabel*, as Coleridge was to start it afresh.   He also
transgressed into religious politics, taking (as indeed he always
took, strange as it may seem in so fanatical a worshipper of
beauty) the Puritan side.   Nor is his work improved as poetry,
though it acquires something in point of quaint attractiveness, by
good Mr. " E. K.'s " elaborate annotations, introductions, explanations, and general gentleman-usherings—the first in English,
but most wofully not the last by hundreds, of such overlayings of
gold with copper.   Yet with all these drawbacks *The Shepherd's
Calendar* is delightful.   Already we can see in it that double
command, at once of the pictorial and the musical elements of
poetry, in which no English poet is Spenser's superior, if any is
his equal.   Already the unmatched power of vigorous allegory,
which he was to display later, shows in such pieces as *The Oak
and the Briar*.   In the less deliberately archaic divisions, such as
"April" and "November," the command of metrical form, in
which also the poet is almost peerless, discovers itself.   Much
the same may be said of the volume of *Complaints*, which, though
published later than *The Faërie Queene*, represents beyond all
question very much earlier work.   Spenser is unquestionably,
when he is not at once spurred and soothed by the play of his
own imagination, as in *The Queene*, a melancholy poet, and the

note of melancholy is as strong in these poems as in their joint
title. It combines with his delight in emblematic allegory
happily enough, in most of these pieces except *Mother Hubbard's
Tale*. This is almost an open satire, and shows that if Spenser's
genius had not found a less mongrel style to disport itself in,
not merely would Donne, and Lodge, and Hall, and Marston
have had to abandon their dispute for the post of first English
satirist, but the attainment of really great satire in English might
have been hastened by a hundred years, and *Absalom and
Achitophel* have been but a second. Even here, however, the
piece still keeps the Chaucerian form and manner, and is only a
kind of exercise. The sonnets from and after Du Bellay and
others are more interesting. As in the subsequent and far finer
Amoretti, Spenser prefers the final couplet form to the so-called
Petrarchian arrangement; and, indeed, though the most recent
fashion in England has inclined to the latter, an impartial judgment must pronounce both forms equally good and equally
entitled to place. The *Amoretti* written in this metre, and
undoubtedly representing some, at least, of Spenser's latest
written work, rank with the best of Sidney's, and hardly below
the best of Shakespere's; while both in them and in the earlier
sonnets the note of regret mingled with delight—the special Renaissance note—sounds as it rarely does in any other English verse.
Of the poems of the later period, however (leaving *The Faërie
Queene* for a moment aside), the *Epithalamion* and the *Four
Hymns* rank undoubtedly highest. For splendour of imagery,
for harmony of verse, for delicate taste and real passion, the
Epithalamion excels all other poems of its class, and the *Four
Hymns* express a rapture of Platonic enthusiasm, which may
indeed be answerable for the unreadable *Psyches* and *Psychozoias*
of the next age, but which is itself married to immortal verse in
the happiest manner.

Still, to the ordinary reader, Spenser is the poet of *The Faërie
Queene*, and for once the ordinary reader is right. Every quality
found in his other poems is found in this greatest of them in

perfection; and much is found there which is not, and indeed could not be, found anywhere else. Its general scheme is so well known (few as may be the readers who really know its details) that very slight notice of it may suffice. Twelve knights, representing twelve virtues, were to have been sent on adventures from the Court of Gloriana, Queen of Fairyland. The six finished books give the legends (each subdivided into twelve cantos, averaging fifty or sixty stanzas each) of Holiness, Temperance, Chastity, Friendship, Justice, and Courtesy; while a fragment of two splendid "Cantos on Mutability" is supposed to have belonged to a seventh book (not necessarily seventh in order) on Constancy. Legend has it that the poem was actually completed; but this seems improbable, as the first three books were certainly ten years in hand, and the second three six more. The existing poem comprehending some four thousand stanzas, or between thirty and forty thousand lines, exhibits so many and such varied excellences that it is difficult to believe that the poet could have done anything new in kind. No part of it is as a whole inferior to any other part, and the fragmentary cantos contain not merely one of the most finished pictorial pieces—the Procession of the Months—to be found in the whole poem, but much of the poet's finest thought and verse. Had fortune been kinder, the volume of delight would have been greater, but its general character would probably not have changed much. As it is, *The Faërie Queene* is the only long poem that a lover of poetry can sincerely wish longer.

It deserves some critical examination here from three points of view, regarding respectively its general scheme, its minor details of form in metre and language, and lastly, its general poetical characteristics. The first is simple enough in its complexity. The poem is a long *Roman d'Aventure* (which it is perhaps as well to say, once for all, is not the same as a "Romance of Chivalry," or a "Romance of Adventure"), redeemed from the aimless prolixity incident to that form by its regular plan, by the intercommunion of the adventures of the several knights (none of whom disappears after having achieved his own quest), and by the constant presence of a not too obtrusive allegory. This last characteristic attaches it on the other side to the poems of the *Roman de la Rose* order, which succeeded the *Romans d'Aventures* as objects of literary interest and practice, not merely in France, but throughout Europe. This allegory has been variously estimated as a merit or defect of the poem. It is sometimes political, oftener religious, very often moral, and sometimes purely personal —the identifications in this latter case being sometimes clear, as that of Gloriana, Britomart, and Belphœbe with Queen Elizabeth, sometimes probable, as that of Duessa with Queen Mary (not one of Spenser's most knightly actions), and of Prince Arthur with Leicester, and sometimes more or less problematical, as that of Artegall with Lord Grey, of Timias the Squire with Raleigh, and so forth. To those who are perplexed by these double meanings the best remark is Hazlitt's blunt one that "the allegory won't bite them." In other words, it is always perfectly possible to enjoy the poem without troubling oneself about the allegory at all, except in its broad ethical features, which are quite unmistakable. On the other hand, I am inclined to think that the presence of these under-meanings, with the interest which they give to a moderately instructed and intelligent person who, without too desperate a determination to see into millstones, understands "words to the wise," is a great addition to the hold of the poem over the attention, and saves it from the charge of mere desultoriness, which some, at least, of the other greatest poems of the kind (notably its immediate exemplar, the *Orlando Furioso*) must undergo. And here it may be noted that the charge made by most foreign critics who have busied themselves with Spenser, and perhaps by some of his countrymen, that he is, if not a mere paraphrast, yet little more than a transplanter into English of the Italian, is glaringly uncritical. Not, perhaps, till Ariosto and Tasso have been carefully read in the original, is Spenser's real greatness understood. He has often, and evidently of purpose, challenged comparison; but in every instance it will be found that his beauties are emphatically his own. He has followed his leaders only as Virgil has followed Homer ; and much less slavishly.

It is strange to find English critics of this great if not greatest English poem even nowadays repeating that Spenser borrowed his wonderful stanza from the Italians. He did nothing of the kind. That the *ottava rima* on the one hand, and the sonnet on the other, may have suggested the idea of it is quite possible. But the Spenserian stanza, as it is justly called, is his own and no one else's, and its merits, especially that primal merit of adaptation to the subject and style of the poem, are unique. Nothing else could adapt itself so perfectly to the endless series of vignettes and dissolving views which the poet delights in giving ; while, at the same time, it has, for so elaborate and apparently integral a form, a singular faculty of hooking itself on to stanzas preceding and following, so as not to interrupt continuous narrative when continuous narrative is needed. Its great com- pass, admitting of an almost infinite variety of cadence and com- position, saves it from the monotony from which even the consum- mate art of Milton could not save blank verse now and then, and from which no writer has ever been able to save the couplet, or the quatrain, or the stanzas ending with a couplet, in narratives of very great length. But the most remarkable instance of harmony between metrical form and other characteristics, both of form and matter, in the metrist has yet to be mentioned. It has been said how well the stanza suits Spenser's pictorial faculty ; it certainly suits his musical faculty as well. The slightly (very slightly, for he can be vigorous enough) languid turn of his grace, the voluptuous cadences of his rhythm, find in it the most perfect exponent possible. The verse of great poets, especially Homer's, has often been compared to the sea. Spenser's is more like a river, wide, and deep, and strong, but moderating its waves and conveying them all in a steady, soft, irresistible sweep forwards. To aid him, besides this extraordinary instrument of metre, he had forged for himself another in his language. A great deal has been written on this—comments, at least of the unfavourable kind, generally echoing Ben Jonson's complaint that Spenser " writ no language "; that his dialect is not the dialect of any actual place or time, that it is an artificial " poetic diction " made up of Chaucer, and of Northern dialect, and of classicisms, and of foreign words, and of miscellaneous archaisms from no matter where. No doubt it is. But if any other excuse than the fact of a beautiful and satisfactory effect is wanted for the formation of a poetic diction different from the actually spoken or the ordinarily written tongue of the day (and I am not sure that any such excuse is required) it is to be found at once. There was no actually spoken or ordinarily written tongue in Spenser's day which could claim to be " Queen's English." Chaucer was obsolete, and since Chaucer there was no single person who could even pretend to authority. Every writer more or less endowed with originality was engaged in beating out for himself, from popular talk, and from classical or foreign analogy, an instrument of speech. Spenser's verse language and Lyly's prose are the most remarkable results of the process; but it was, in fact, not only a common but a necessary one, and in no way to be blamed. As for the other criterion hinted at above, no one is likely to condemn the diction according to that. In its remoteness without grotesqueness, in its lavish colour, in its abundance of matter for every kind of cadence and sound-effect, it is exactly suited to the subject, the writer, and the verse.

It is this singular and complete adjustment of worker and implement which, with other peculiarities noted or to be noted, gives *The Faërie Queene* its unique unicity, if such a conceit may be pardoned. From some points of view it might be called a very artificial poem, yet no poem runs with such an entire absence of effort, with such an easy eloquence, with such an effect, as has been said already, of flowing water. With all his learning, and his archaisms, and his classicisms, and his Platonisms, and his isms without end, hardly any poet smells of the lamp less disagreeably than Spenser. Where Milton forges and smelts, his

gold is native. The endless, various, brightly-coloured, softly
and yet distinctly outlined pictures rise and pass before the eyes
and vanish—the multiform, sweetly-linked, softly-sounding harmonies swell and die and swell again on the ear—without a
break, without a jar, softer than sleep and as continuous, gayer
than the rainbow and as undiscoverably connected with any
obvious cause. And this is the more remarkable because the
very last thing that can be said of Spenser is that he is a poet of
mere words. Milton himself, the severe Milton, extolled his
moral teaching; his philosophical idealism is evidently no mere
poet's plaything or parrot-lesson, but thoroughly thought out and
believed in. He is a determined, almost a savage partisan in
politics and religion, a steady patriot, something of a statesman,
very much indeed of a friend and a lover. And of all this there
is ample evidence in his verse. Yet the alchemy of his poetry
has passed through the potent alembics of verse and phrase all
these rebellious things, and has distilled them into the inimitably
fluent and velvet medium which seems to lull some readers to
inattention by its very smoothness, and deceive others into a
belief in its lack of matter by the very finish and brilliancy of its
form. The show passages of the poem which are most generally known—the House of Pride, the Cave of Despair, the
Entrance of Belphœbe, the Treasury of Mammon, the Gardens
of Acrasia, the Sojourn of Britomart in Busirane's Castle, the
Marriage of the Thames and Medway, the Discovery of the False
Florimel, Artegall and the Giant, Calidore with Melibœus, the
Processions of the Seasons and the Months—all these are not, as
is the case with so many other poets, mere purple patches,
diversifying and relieving dullness, but rather remarkable, and as
it happens easily separable examples of a power which is shown
constantly and almost evenly throughout. Those who admire
them do well; but they hardly know Spenser. He, more than
almost any other poet, must be read continuously and constantly
till the eye and ear and mind have acquired the freedom of his
realm of enchantment, and have learnt the secret (as far as a mere

reader may learn it) of the poetical spells by which he brings together and controls its wonders. The talk of tediousness, the talk of sameness, the talk of coterie-cultivation in Spenser shows bad taste no doubt; but it rather shows ignorance. The critic has in such cases stayed outside his author; he speaks but of what he has *not* seen.

The comparative estimate is always the most difficult in litera-ture, and where it can be avoided it is perhaps best to avoid it. But in Spenser's case this is not possible. He is one of those few who can challenge the title of "greatest English poet," and the reader may almost of right demand the opinion on this point of any one who writes about him. For my part I have no intention of shirking the difficulty. It seems to me that putting Shake-spere aside as *hors concours*, not merely in degree but in kind, only two English poets can challenge Spenser for the primacy. These are Milton and Shelley. The poet of *The Faërie Queene* is generally inferior to Milton in the faculty of concentration, and in the minting of those monumental phrases, impressive of them-selves and quite apart from the context, which often count highest in the estimation of poetry. His vocabulary and general style, if not more remote from the vernacular, have sometimes a touch of deliberate estrangement from that vernacular which is no doubt of itself a fault. His conception of a great work is looser, more excursive, less dramatic. As compared with Shelley he lacks not merely the modern touches which appeal to a par-ticular age, but the lyrical ability in which Shelley has no equal among English poets. But in each case he redeems these defects with, as it seems to me, far more than counterbalancing merits. He is never prosaic as Milton, like his great successor Words-worth, constantly is, and his very faults are the faults of a poet. He never (as Shelley does constantly) dissolves away into a flux of words which simply bids good-bye to sense or meaning, and wanders on at large, unguided, without an end, without an aim. But he has more than these merely negative merits. I have seen long accounts of Spenser in which the fact of his

invention of the Spenserian stanza is passed over almost without
a word of comment.   Yet in the formal history of poetry (and
the history of poetry must always be pre-eminently a history of
form) there is simply no achievement so astonishing as this.
That we do not know the inventors of the great single poetic
vehicles, the hexameter, the iambic Senarius, the English heroic,
the French Alexandrine, is one thing.   It is another that in
Spenser's case alone can the invention of a complicated but
essentially integral form be assigned to a given poet.   It is
impossible to say that Sappho invented the Sapphic, or Alcæus
the Alcaic : each poet may have been a Vespucci to some precedent Columbus.   But we are in a position to say that Spenser
did most unquestionably invent the English Spenserian stanza—
a form only inferior in individual beauty to the sonnet, which is
itself practically *adespoton*, and far superior to the sonnet in its
capacity of being used in multiples as well as singly.   When the
unlikelihood of such a complicated measure succeeding in narrative form, the splendid success of it in *The Faërie Queene*, and
the remarkable effects which have subsequently been got out of
it by men so different as Thomson, Shelley, and Lord Tennyson,
are considered, Spenser's invention must, I think, be counted
the most considerable of its kind in literature.

But it may be very freely admitted that this technical merit,
great as it is, is the least part of the matter.   Whosoever first
invented butterflies and pyramids in poetry is not greatly commendable, and if Spenser had done nothing but arrange a cunning
combination of eight heroics, with interwoven rhymes and an
Alexandrine to finish with, it may be acknowledged at once that
his claims to primacy would have to be dismissed at once.   It is
not so.   Independently of *The Faërie Queene* altogether he has done
work which we must go to Milton and Shelley themselves to equal.
The varied and singularly original strains of *The Calendar*, the
warmth and delicacy combined of the *Epithalamion*, the tone
of mingled regret and wonder (not inferior in its characteristic
Renaissance ring to Du Bellay's own) of *The Ruins of Rome*, the

different notes of the different minor poems, are all things not to
be found in any minor poet.   But as does not always happen,
and as is perhaps not the case with Milton, Spenser's greatest
work is also his best.   In the opinion of some at any rate the
poet of *Lycidas*, of *Comus*, of *Samson Agonistes*, even of the
Allegro and *Penseroso*, ranks as high as, if not above, the poet of
Paradise Lost. But the poet of *The Faërie Queene* could spare all
his minor works and lose only, as has been said, quantity not
quality of greatness.   It is hardly necessary at this time of day
to repeat the demonstration that Macaulay in his famous jibe
only succeeded in showing that he had never read what he jibed
at ; and though other decriers of Spenser's masterpiece may not
have laid themselves open to quite so crushing a retort, they
seldom fail to show a somewhat similar ignorance.   For the
lover of poetry, for the reader who understands and can receive
the poetic charm, the revelation of beauty in metrical language,
no English poem is the superior, or, range and variety being
considered, the equal of *The Faërie Queene*.   Take it up where
you will, and provided only sufficient time (the reading of a
dozen stanzas ought to suffice to any one who has the necessary
gifts of appreciation) be given to allow the soft dreamy versi-
coloured atmosphere to rise round the reader, the languid and yet
never monotonous music to gain his ear, the mood of mixed
imagination and heroism, adventure and morality, to impress
itself on his mind, and the result is certain.   To the influence of
no poet are the famous lines of Spenser's great nineteenth-
century rival so applicable as to Spenser's own.   The enchanted
boat, angel-guided, floating on away, afar, without conscious purpose, but simply obeying the instinct of sweet poetry, is not an
extravagant symbol for the mind of a reader of Spenser.   If
such readers want " Criticisms of Life " first of all, they must go
elsewhere, though they will find them amply given, subject to the
limitations of the poetical method.   If they want story they may
complain of slackness and deviations. If they want glorifications of
science and such like things, they had better shut the book at once,

and read no more on that day nor on any other. But if they want poetry—if they want to be translated from a world which is not one of beauty only into one where the very uglinesses are beautiful, into a world of perfect harmony in colour and sound, of an endless sequence of engaging event and character, of noble passions and actions not lacking their due contrast, then let them go to Spenser with a certainty of satisfaction. He is not, as are some poets, the poet of a certain time of life to the exclusion of others. He may be read in childhood chiefly for his adventure, in later youth for his display of voluptuous beauty, in manhood for his ethical and historical weight, in age for all combined, and for the contrast which his bright universe of invention affords with the work-day jejuneness of this troublesome world. But he never palls upon those who have once learnt to taste him; and no poet is so little of an acquired taste to those who have any liking for poetry at all. He has been called the poet's poet—a phrase honourable but a little misleading, inasmuch as it first suggests that he is not the poet of the great majority of readers who cannot pretend to be poets themselves, and secondly insinuates a kind of intellectual and æsthetic Pharisaism in those who do admire him, which may be justly resented by those who do not. Let us rather say that he is the poet of all others for those who seek in poetry only poetical qualities, and we shall say not only what is more than enough to establish his greatness but what, as I for one believe, can be maintained in the teeth of all gainsayers.[1]

The volume, variety, and vigour of the poetical production of the period in which Spenser is the central figure—the last twenty years of the sixteenth century—is perhaps proportionally the greatest, and may be said to be emphatically the most distinguished in purely poetical characteristics of any period in our

[1] Of Spenser as of two other poets in this volume, Shakespere and Milton, it seemed to be unnecessary and even impertinent to give any extracts. Their works are, or ought to be, in all hands; and even if it were not so, no space at my command could give sample of their infinite varieties.

history.   Every kind of poetical work is represented in it, and
every kind (with the possible exception of the semi-poetical kind
of satire) is well represented.   There is, indeed, no second name
that approaches Spenser's, either in respect of importance or in
respect of uniform excellence of work.   But in the most incomplete
production of this time there is almost always that poetical spark
which is often entirely wanting in the finished and complete
work of other periods.   I shall, therefore, divide the whole mass
into four groups, each with certain distinguished names at its head,
and a crowd of hardly undistinguished names in its rank and file.
These four groups are the sonneteers, the historians, the satirists,
and lastly, the miscellaneous lyrists and poetical miscellanists.

Although it is only recently that its mass and its beauty have
been fully recognised, the extraordinary outburst of sonnet-writing
at a certain period of Elizabeth's reign has always attracted the
attention of literary historians.   For many years after Wyatt and
Surrey's work appeared the form attracted but little imitation or
practice.   About 1580 Spenser himself probably, Sidney and
Thomas Watson certainly, devoted much attention to it ; but it
was some dozen years later that the most striking crop of sonnets
appeared.   Between 1593 and 1596 there were published more
than a dozen collections, chiefly or wholly of sonnets, and almost
all bearing the name of a single person, in whose honour
they were supposed to be composed.   So singular is this
coincidence, showing either an intense *engouement* in literary
society, or a spontaneous determination of energy in individuals,
that the list with dates is worth giving.   It runs thus :—In 1593
came Barnes's *Parthenophil and Parthenophe*, Fletcher's *Licia*,
and Lodge's *Phillis*.   In 1594 followed Constable's *Diana*,
Daniel's *Delia*,[1] the anonymous *Zepheria*, Drayton's *Idea*, Percy's
Cœlia, and Willoughby's *Avisa ;* 1595 added the *Alcilia* of a
certain J. C., and Spenser's perfect *Amoretti ;* 1596 gave
Griffin's *Fidessa*, Lynch's *Diella*, and Smith's *Chloris*, while

[1] *Delia* had appeared earlier in 1592, and partially in 1591 ; but the text
of 1594 is the definitive one.   Several of these dates are doubtful or disputed.

Shakespere's earliest sonnets were probably not much later. Then the fashion changed, or the vein was worked out, or (more fancifully) the impossibility of equalling Spenser and Shakespere choked off competitors. The date of Lord Brooke's singular *Cælica*, not published till long afterwards, is uncertain ; but he may, probably, be classed with Sidney and Watson in period.

Fulke, or, as he himself spelt it, Foulke Greville, in his later years Lord Brooke,[1] was of a noble house in Warwickshire connected with the Beauchamps and the Willoughbys. He was born in 1554, was educated at Shrewsbury with Philip Sidney, whose kinsman, lifelong friend, and first biographer he was—proceeded, not like Sidney to Oxford, but to Cambridge (where he was a member, it would seem, of Jesus College, not as usually said of Trinity)—received early lucrative preferments chiefly in connection with the government of Wales, was a favourite courtier of Elizabeth's during all her later life, and, obtaining a royal gift of Warwick Castle, became the ancestor of the present earls of Warwick. In 1614 he became Chancellor of the Exchequer. Lord Brooke, who lived to a considerable age, was stabbed in a rather mysterious manner in 1628 by a servant named Haywood, who is said to have been enraged by discovering that his master had left him nothing in his will. The story is, as has been said, mysterious, and the affair seems to have been hushed up. Lord Brooke was not universally popular, and a very savage contemporary epitaph on him has been preserved. But he had been the patron of the youthful Davenant, and has left not a little curious literary work, which has only been recently collected, and little of which saw the light in his own lifetime. Of his two singular plays, *Mustapha* and *Alaham* (closet-dramas having something in common with the Senecan model), *Mustapha* was printed in 1609 ; but it would seem

[1] He is a little liable to be confounded with two writers (brothers of a patronymic the same as his title) Samuel and Christopher Brooke, the latter of whom wrote poems of some merit, which Dr. Grosart has edited.

piratically. His chief prose work, the *Life of Sidney*, was not
printed till 1652.   His chief work in verse, the singular *Poems
of Monarchy* (ethical and political treatises), did not appear till
eighteen years later, as well as the allied *Treatise on Religion*.
But poems or tracts on human learning, on wars, and other
things, as singularly inappropriate to verse, had appeared in
1633.   This publication, a folio volume, also contained by far
the most interesting part of his work, the so-called sonnet collection of *Cælica*—a medley, like many of those mentioned in this
chapter, of lyrics and short poems of all lengths and metrical
arrangements, but, unlike almost all of them, dealing with many
subjects, and apparently addressed to more than one person.   It
is here, and almost here only, that the reader who has not a very
great love for Elizabethan literature and some experience of it,
can be recommended to seek confirmation of the estimate in which
Greville was held by Charles Lamb, and of the very excusable
and pious, though perhaps excessive, admiration of his editor Dr.
Grosart.   Even *Cælica* is very unlikely to find readers as a whole,
owing to the strangely repellent character of Brooke's thought,
which is intricate and obscure, and of his style, which is at any
rate sometimes as harsh and eccentric as the theories of poetry
which made him compose verse-treatises on politics.   Nevertheless there is much nobility of thought and expression in him,
and not unfrequent flashes of real poetry, while his very faults
are characteristic.   He may be represented here by a piece from
Cælica, in which he is at his very best, and most poetical because
most simple—

> " I, with whose colours Myra dressed her head,
>   I, that ware posies of her own hand making,
>   I, that mine own name in the chimnies read
>   By Myra finely wrought ere I was waking :
>   Must I look on, in hope time coming may
>   With change bring back my turn again to play ?
>
> " I, that on Sunday at the church-stile found
>   A garland sweet with true love knots in flowers,

Which I to wear about mine arms, was bound
That each of us might know that all was ours :
Must I lead now an idle life in wishes,
And follow Cupid for his loaves and fishes?

" I, that did wear the ring her mother left,
I, for whose love she gloried to be blamed,
I, with whose eyes her eyes committed theft,
I, who did make her blush when I was named :
Must I lose ring, flowers, blush, theft, and go naked,
Watching with sighs till dead love be awaked?

" I, that when drowsy Argus fell asleep,
Like jealousy o'erwatchèd with desire,
Was ever warnèd modesty to keep
While her breath, speaking, kindled Nature's fire :
Must I look on a-cold while others warm them ?
Do Vulcan's brothers in such fine nets arm them?

" Was it for this that I might Myra see
Washing the water with her beauties white ?
Yet would she never write her love to me :
Thinks wit of change when thoughts are in delight?
Mad girls may safely love as they may leave ;
No man can print a kiss : lines may deceive."

Had Brooke always written with this force and directness he
would have been a great poet. As it is, he has but the ore of
poetry, not the smelted metal.

For there is no doubt that Sidney here holds the primacy,
not merely in time but in value, of the whole school, putting
Spenser and Shakespere aside. That thirty or forty years'
diligent study of Italian models had much to do with the extraordinary advance visible in his sonnets over those of Tottel's
Miscellany is, no doubt, undeniable. But many causes besides
the inexplicable residuum of fortunate inspiration, which eludes
the most careful search into literary cause and effect, had to do
with the production of the " lofty, insolent, and passionate vein,"
which becomes noticeable in English poetry for the first time
about 1580, and which dominates it, if we include the late

autumn-summer of Milton's last productions, for a hundred years. Perhaps it is not too much to say that this makes its very first appearance in Sidney's verse, for *The Shepherd's Calendar*, though of an even more perfect, is of a milder strain. The inevitable tendency of criticism to gossip about poets instead of criticising poetry has usually mixed a great deal of personal matter with the accounts of *Astrophel and Stella*, the series of sonnets which is Sidney's greatest literary work, and which was first published some years after his death in an incorrect and probably pirated edition by Thomas Nash. There is no doubt that there was a real affection between Sidney (Astrophel) and Penelope Devereux (Stella), daughter of the Earl of Essex, afterwards Lady Rich, and that marriage proving unhappy, Lady Mountjoy. But the attempts which have been made to identify every hint and allusion in the series with some fact or date, though falling short of the unimaginable folly of scholastic labour-lost which has been expended on the sonnets of Shakespere, still must appear somewhat idle to those who know the usual genesis of love-poetry—how that it is of imagination all compact, and that actual occurrences are much oftener occasions and bases than causes and material of it. It is of the smallest possible importance or interest to a rational man to discover what was the occasion of Sidney's writing these charming poems—the important point is their charm. And in this respect (giving heed to his date and his opportunities of imitation) I should put Sidney third to Shakespere and Spenser. The very first piece of the series, an oddly compounded sonnet of thirteen Alexandrines and a final heroic, strikes the note of intense and fresh poetry which is only heard afar off in Surrey and Wyatt, which is hopelessly to seek in the tentatives of Turberville and Googe, and which is smothered with jejune and merely literary ornament in the less formless work of Sidney's contemporary, Thomas Watson. The second line—

"That she, dear she, might take some pleasure of my pain,"

the couplet—

> " Oft turning others' leaves to see if thence would flow
> Some fresh and fruitful showers upon my sunburnt brain,"

and the sudden and splendid finale—

> " ' Fool ! ' said my muse, ' look in thy heart and write ! ' "

are things that may be looked for in vain earlier.

A little later we meet with that towering soar of verse which is also peculiar to the period :

> " When Nature made her chief work—Stella's eyes,
> In colour black, why wrapt she beams so bright ? "—

lines which those who deprecate insistence on the importance of form in poetry might study with advantage, for the thought is a mere commonplace conceit, and the beauty of the phrase is purely derived from the cunning arrangement and cadence of the verse.   The first perfectly charming sonnet in the English language—a sonnet which holds its own after three centuries of competition—is the famous " With how sad steps, O moon, thou climbst the skies," where Lamb's stricture on the last line as obscure seems to me unreasonable.   The equally famous phrase, " That sweet enemy France," which occurs a little further on is another, and whether borrowed from Giordano Bruno or not is perhaps the best example of the felicity of expression in which Sidney is sur-passed by few Englishmen.   Nor ought the extraordinary variety of the treatment to be missed.   Often as Sidney girds at those who, like Watson, " dug their sonnets out of books," he can write in the learned literary manner with the best.   The pleasant ease of his sonnet to the sparrow, " Good brother Philip," contrasts in the oddest way with his allegorical and mythological sonnets, in each of which veins he indulges hardly less often, though very much more wisely than any of his contemporaries.   Nor do the other " Songs of variable verse," which follow, and in some editions are mixed up with the sonnets, display less extraordinary power.   The first song, with its refrain in the penultimate line of each stanza,

> " To you, to you, all song of praise is due,"

contrasts in its throbbing and burning life with the faint and

misty imagery, the stiff and wooden structure, of most of the verse
of Sidney's predecessors, and deserves to be given in full:—

" Doubt you to whom my Muse these notes intendeth ;
  Which now my breast o'ercharged to music lendeth ?
    To you ! to you ! all song of praise is due :
  Only in you my song begins and endeth.

" Who hath the eyes which marry state with pleasure,
  Who keeps the keys of Nature's chiefest treasure ?
    To you ! to you ! all song of praise is due :
  Only for you the heaven forgat all measure.

" Who hath the lips, where wit in fairness reigneth ?
  Who womankind at once both decks and staineth ?
    To you ! to you ! all song of praise is due :
  Only by you Cupid his crown maintaineth.

" Who hath the feet, whose steps all sweetness planteth ?
  Who else ; for whom Fame worthy trumpets wanteth ?
    To you ! to you ! all song of praise is due :
  Only to you her sceptre Venus granteth.

" Who hath the breast, whose milk doth passions nourish ?
  Whose grace is such, that when it chides doth cherish ?
    To you ! to you ! all song of praise is due :
  Only through you the tree of life doth flourish.

" Who hath the hand, which without stroke subdueth ?
  Who long dead beauty with increase reneweth ?
    To you ! to you ! all song of praise is due :
  Only at you all envy hopeless rueth.

" Who hath the hair, which loosest fastest tieth ?
  Who makes a man live then glad when he dieth ?
    To you ! to you ! all song of praise is due :
  Only of you the flatterer never lieth.

" Who hath the voice, which soul from senses sunders ?
  Whose force but yours the bolts of beauty thunders ?
    To you ! to you ! all song of praise is due :
  Only with you not miracles are wonders.

" Doubt you to whom my Muse these notes intendeth ?
  Which now my breast o'ercharged to music lendeth ?
    To you ! to you ! all song of praise is due :
  Only in you my song begins and endeth. "

Nor is its promise belied by those which follow, and which are among the earliest and the most charming of the rich literature of songs that really are songs—songs to music—which the age was to produce. All the scanty remnants of his other verse are instinct with the same qualities, especially the splendid dirge, "Ring out your bells, let mourning shows be spread," and the pretty lines "to the tune of Wilhelmus van Nassau." I must quote the first :—

> " Ring out your bells ! let mourning shows be spread,
>   For Love is dead.
>   All love is dead, infected
>   With the plague of deep disdain ;
>   Worth as nought worth rejected.
>   And faith, fair scorn doth gain.
>   From so ungrateful fancy,
>   From such a female frenzy,
>   From them that use men thus,
>   Good Lord, deliver us !
>
> ' Weep, neighbours, weep ! Do you not hear it said
>   That Love is dead ?
>   His deathbed, peacock's Folly ;
>   His winding-sheet is Shame ;
>   His will, False Seeming wholly ;
>   His sole executor, Blame.
>   From so ungrateful fancy,
>   From such a female frenzy,
>   From them that use men thus,
>   Good Lord, deliver us !
>
> " Let dirge be sung, and trentals rightly read,
>   For Love is dead.
>   Sir Wrong his tomb ordaineth
>   My mistress' marble heart ;
>   Which epitaph containeth
>   ' Her eyes were once his dart.'
>   From so ungrateful fancy,
>   From such a female frenzy,
>   From them that use men thus,
>   Good Lord, deliver us !

> " Alas, I lie.   Rage hath this error bred,
>> Love is not dead.
>> Love is not dead, but sleepeth
>> In her unmatchèd mind :
>> Where she his counsel keepeth
>> Till due deserts she find.
>> Therefore from so vile fancy
>> To call such wit a frenzy,
>> Who love can temper thus,
>> Good Lord, deliver us ! "

The verse from the *Arcadia* (which contains a great deal of verse) has been perhaps injuriously affected in the general judgment by the fact that it includes experiments in the impossible classical metres.   But both it and the Translations from the Psalms express the same poetical faculty employed with less directness and force.   To sum up, there is no Elizabethan poet, except the two named, who is more unmistakably imbued with poetical quality than Sidney.   And Hazlitt's judgment on him, that he is " jejune " and "frigid" will, as Lamb himself hinted, long remain the chiefest and most astonishing example of a great critic's aberrations when his prejudices are concerned.

Had Hazlitt been criticising Thomas Watson, his judgment, though harsh, would have been not wholly easy to quarrel with. It is probably the excusable but serious error of judgment which induced his rediscoverer, Professor Arber, to rank Watson above Sidney in gifts and genius, that has led other critics to put him unduly low.   Watson himself, moreover, has invited depreciation by his extreme frankness in confessing that his *Passionate Century* is not a record of passion at all, but an elaborate literary *pastiche* after this author and that.   I fear it must be admitted that the average critic is not safely to be trusted with such an avowal of what he is too much disposed to advance as a charge without confession.   Watson, of whom as usual scarcely anything is known personally, was a Londoner by birth, an Oxford man by education, a friend of most of the earlier literary school of the reign, such as Lyly, Peele, and Spenser, and a tolerably industrious writer both in Latin and English during his short life, which can hardly have begun before 1557, and was certainly closed by 1593. He stands in English poetry as the author of the *Hecatompathia* or *Passionate Century* of sonnets (1582), and the *Tears of Fancy*, consisting of sixty similar poems, printed after his death. The *Tears of Fancy* are regular quatorzains, the pieces composing the *Hecatompathia*, though called sonnets, are in a curious form of eighteen lines practically composed of three six-line stanzas rhymed A B, A B, C C, and not connected by any continuance of rhyme from stanza to stanza. The special and peculiar oddity of the book is, that each sonnet has a prose preface as thus : "In this passion the author doth very busily imitate and augment a certain ode of Ronsard, which he writeth unto his mistress. He beginneth as followeth, *Plusieurs*, etc." Here is a complete example of one of Watson's pages :—

" There needeth no annotation at all before this passion, it is of itself so plain and easily conveyed. Yet the unlearned may have this help given them by the way to know what Galaxia is or Pactolus, which perchance they have not read of often in our vulgar rhymes. Galaxia (to omit both the etymology and what the philosophers do write thereof) is a white way or milky circle in the heavens, which Ovid mentioneth in this manner—

> *Est via sublimis cœlo manifesta sereno.*
> *Lactea nomen habet, candore notabilis ipso.*
> —Metamorph. lib. I.

And Cicero thus in Somnio Scipionis : *Erat autem is splendissimo candore inter flammas circulus elucens, quem vos (ut a Graijs accepistis) orbem lacteum nuncupatis.*

Pactolus is a river in Lydia, which hath golden sands under it, as Tibullus witnesseth in this verse :—

> *Nec me regna juvant, nec Lydius aurifer amnis.*—Titul. lib. 3.

> Who can recount the virtues of my dear,
> Or say how far her fame hath taken flight,
> That cannot tell how many stars appear
> In part of heaven, which Galaxia hight,
>   Or number all the moats in Phœbus' rays,
>   Or golden sands whereon Pactolus plays ?

> And yet my hurts enforce me to confess,
> In crystal breast she shrouds a bloody heart,
> Which heart in time will make her merits less,
> Unless betimes she cure my deadly smart :
>   For now my life is double dying still,
>   And she defamed by sufferance of such ill ;
>
> And till the time she helps me as she may,
> Let no man undertake to tell my toil,
> But only such, as can distinctly say,
> What monsters Nilus breeds, or Afric soil :
>   For if he do, his labour is but lost,
>   Whilst I both fry and freeze 'twixt flame and frost."

Now this is undoubtedly, as Watson's contemporaries would have said, " a cooling card " to the reader, who is thus presented with a series of elaborate poetical exercises affecting the acutest personal feeling, and yet confessedly representing no feeling at all. Yet the *Hecatompathia* is remarkable, both historically and intrinsically. It does not seem likely that at its publication the author can have had anything of Sidney's or much of Spenser's before him ; yet his work is only less superior to the work of their common predecessors than the work of these two. By far the finest of his *Century* is the imitation of Ferrabosco—

> " Resolved to dust intombed here lieth love."

The quatorzains of the *Tears of Fancy* are more attractive in form and less artificial in structure and phraseology, but it must be remembered that by their time Sidney's sonnets were known and Spenser had written much. The seed was scattered abroad, and it fell in congenial soil in falling on Watson, but the *Hecatompathia* was self-sown.

This difference shows itself very remarkably in the vast outburst of sonneteering which, as has been remarked, distinguished the middle of the last decade of the sixteenth century. All these writers had Sidney and Spenser before them, and they assume so much of the character of a school that there are certain subjects, for instance, " Care-charming sleep," on which many of them (after Sidney) composed sets of rival poems, almost as definitely competitive as the sonnets of the later "Uranie et Job" and "Belle Matineuse" series in France. Nevertheless, there is in all of them—what as a rule is wanting in this kind of clique verse—the independent spirit, the original force which makes poetry. The Smiths and the Fletchers, the Griffins and the Lynches, are like little geysers round the great ones : the whole soil is instinct with fire and flame. We shall, however, take the production of the four remarkable years 1593-1596 separately, and though in more than one case we shall return upon their writers both in this chapter and in a subsequent one, the unity of the sonnet impulse seems to demand separate mention for them here.

In 1593 the influence of the Sidney poems (published, it must be remembered, in 1591) was new, and the imitators, except Watson (of whom above), display a good deal of the quality of the novice. The chief of them are Barnabe Barnes, with his *Parthenophil and Parthenophe*, Giles Fletcher (father of the Jacobean poets, Giles and Phineas Fletcher), with his *Licia*, and Thomas Lodge, with his *Phillis*. Barnes is a modern discovery, for before Dr. Grosart reprinted him in 1875, from the unique original at Chatsworth, for thirty subscribers only (of whom I had the honour to be one), he was practically unknown. Mr. Arber has since, in his *English Garner*, opened access to a wider circle, to whom I at least do not grudge their entry. As with most of these minor Elizabethan poets, Barnes is a very obscure person. A little later than *Parthenophil* he wrote *A Divine Centurie of Spiritual Sonnets*, having, like many of his contemporaries, an apparent desire poetically to make the best of both worlds. He also wrote a wild play in the most daring Elizabethan style, called *The Devil's Charter*, and a prose political *Treatise of Offices*. Barnes was a friend of Gabriel Harvey's, and as such met with some rough usage from Nash, Marston, and others. His poetical worth, though there are fine passages in *The Devil's Charter* and in the *Divine Centurie*, must rest on *Parthenophil*. This collection consists not merely of sonnets but of madrigals, sestines, canzons, and other attempts after Italian masters.   The style, both verbal and poetical, needs chastising in places, and Barnes's expression in particular is sometimes obscure. He is sometimes comic when he wishes to be passionate, and frequently verbose when he wishes to be expressive.   But the fire, the full-bloodedness, the poetical virility, of the poems is extraordinary.   A kind of intoxication of the eternal-feminine seems to have seized the poet to an extent not otherwise to be paralleled in the group, except in Sidney ; while Sidney's courtly sense of measure and taste did not permit him Barnes's forcible extravagances.   Here is a specimen :—

> " Phœbus, rich father of eternal light,
> And in his hand a wreath of Heliochrise
>   He brought, to beautify those tresses,
> Whose train, whose softness, and whose gloss more bright,
>   Apollo's locks did overprize.
> Thus, with this garland, whiles her brows he blesses,
>   The golden shadow with his tincture
>   Coloured her locks, aye gilded with the cincture."

Giles Fletcher's *Licia* is a much more pale and colourless performance, though not wanting in merit.   The author, who was afterwards a most respectable clergyman, is of the class of *amoureux transis*, and dies for Licia throughout his poems, without apparently suspecting that it was much better to live for her.   His volume contained some miscellaneous poems, with a dullish essay in the historical style (see *post*), called *The Rising of Richard to the Crown.*   Very far superior is Lodge's *Phillis*, the chief poetical work of that interesting person, except some of the madrigals and odd pieces of verse scattered about his prose tracts (for which see Chapter VI.)   *Phillis* is especially remarkable for the grace and refinement with which the author elaborates the Sidneian model.   Lodge, indeed, as it seems to me, was one of the not uncommon persons who can always do best with a model before them.   He euphuised with better taste than Lyly, but in imitation of him ; his tales in prose are more graceful than those

of Greene, whom he copied; it at least seems likely that he out-
Marlowed Marlowe in the rant of the *Looking-Glass for London*,
and the stiffness of the *Wounds of Civil War*, and he chiefly
polished Sidney in his sonnets and madrigals.   It is not to be
denied, however, that in three out of these four departments he
gave us charming work.   His mixed allegiance to Marlowe and
Sidney gave him command of a splendid form of decasyllable,
which appears often in *Phillis*, as for instance—

> " About thy neck do all the graces throng
> And lay such baits as might entangle death,"

where it is worth noting that the whole beauty arises from
the dexterous placing of the dissyllable " graces," and the trisyllable " entangle," exactly where they ought to be among the
monosyllables of the rest.   The madrigals " Love guards the roses
of thy lips," " My Phillis hath the morning sun," and " Love in
my bosom like a bee " are simply unsurpassed for sugared sweetness in English.   Perhaps this is the best of them :—

> " Love in my bosom like a bee,
>   Doth suck his sweet ;
>   Now with his wings he plays with me,
>   Now with his feet.
>   Within mine eyes he makes his nest
>   His bed amidst my tender breast,
>   My kisses are his daily feast ;
>   And yet he robs me of my rest ?
>   ' Ah, wanton ! will ye?'
>
> " And if I sleep, then percheth he,
>   With pretty flight,[1]
>   And makes his pillow of my knee
>   The livelong night.
>   Strike I my lute, he tunes the string
>   He music plays, if so I sing.
>   He lends me every lovely thing
>   Yet cruel ! he, my heart doth sting.
>   ' Whist, wanton ! still ye !'

---

[1] Printed in *England's Helicon* " sleight."

" Else I with roses, every day
          Will whip you hence,
And bind you, when you want to play,
          For your offence.
I'll shut my eyes to keep you in,
I'll make you fast it for your sin,
I'll count your power not worth a pin.
Alas, what hereby shall I win
          If he gainsay me ?

" What if I beat the wanton boy
          With many a rod ?
He will repay me with annoy
          Because a god.
Then sit thou safely on my knee,
And let thy bower my bosom be.
Lurk in mine eyes, I like of thee.
O Cupid ! so thou pity me,
          Spare not, but play thee."

1594 was the most important of all the sonnet years, and here we are chiefly bound to mention authors who will come in for fuller notice later.   The singular book known as Willoughby's *Avisa* which, as having a supposed bearing on Shakespere and as containing much of that personal puzzlement which rejoices critics, has had much attention of late years, is not strictly a collection of sonnets; its poems being longer and of differing stanzas.   But in general character it falls in with the sonnet-collections addressed or devoted to a real or fanciful personage. It is rather satirical than panegyrical in character, and its poetical worth is very far from high.   William Percy, a friend of Barnes (who dedicated the *Parthenophil* to him), son of the eighth Earl of Northumberland, and a retired person who seems to have passed the greater part of a long life in Oxford "drinking nothing but ale," produced a very short collection entitled *Cœlia*, not very noteworthy, though it contains (probably in imitation of Barnes) one of the tricky things called echo-sonnets, which, with dialogue-sonnets and the like, have sometimes amused the leisure of poets. Much more remarkable is the singular anonymous collection

called *Zepheria*.   Its contents are called not sonnets but canzons,
though most of them are orthodox quatorzains somewhat oddly
rhymed and rhythmed.   It is brief, extending only to forty
pieces, and, like much of the poetry of the period, begins and
ends with Italian mottoes or dedication-phrases.   But what is
interesting about it is the evidence it gives of deep familiarity
not only with Italian but with French models.   This appears
both in such words as "jouissance," "thesaurise," "esperance,"
"souvenance," "vatical" (a thoroughly Ronsardising word), with
others too many to mention, and in other characteristics.   Mr.
Sidney Lee, in his most valuable collection of these sonneteers,
endeavours to show that this French influence was less uncommon
than has sometimes been thought.   Putting this aside, the
characteristic of *Zepheria* is unchastened vigour, full of promise,
but decidedly in need of further schooling and discipline, as the
following will show :—

> " O then Desire, father of Jouissance,
>   The Life of Love, the Death of dastard Fear,
>   The kindest nurse to true persèverance,
>   Mine heart inherited, with thy love's revere. [?]
>   Beauty ! peculiar parent of Conceit,
>   Prosperous midwife to a travelling muse,
>   The sweet of life, Nepenthe's eyes receipt,
>   Thee into me distilled, O sweet, infuse !
>   Love then (the spirit of a generous sprite,
>   An infant ever drawing Nature's breast,
>   The Sum of Life, that Chaos did unnight !)
>   Dismissed mine heart from me, with thee to rest.
>   And now incites me cry, ' Double or quit !
>   Give back my heart, or take his body to it ! ' "

This cannot be said of the three remarkable collections yet to
be noticed which appeared in this year, to wit, Constable's *Diana*,
Daniel's *Delia*, and Drayton's *Idea*.   These three head the group
and contain the best work, after Shakespere and Spenser and
Sidney, in the English sonnet of the time.   Constable's sonnets
had appeared partly in 1592, and as they stand in fullest collec-

tion were published in or before 1594. Afterwards he wrote, like others, "divine" sonnets (he was a Roman Catholic) and some miscellaneous poems, including a very pretty "Song of Venus and Adonis." He was a close friend of Sidney, many of whose sonnets were published with his, and his work has much of the Sidneian colour, but with fewer flights of happily expressed fancy. The best of it is probably the following sonnet, which is not only full of gracefully expressed images, but keeps up its flight from first to last—a thing not universal in these Elizabethan sonnets :—

> " My Lady's presence makes the Roses red,
>   Because to see her lips they blush for shame.
>   The Lily's leaves, for envy, pale became ;
>   And her white hands in them this envy bred.
>   The Marigold the leaves abroad doth spread ;
>   Because the sun's and her power is the same.
>   The Violet of purple colour came,
>   Dyed in the blood she made my heart to shed.
>   In brief all flowers from her their virtue take ;
>   From her sweet breath, their sweet smells do proceed ;
>   The living heat which her eyebeams doth make
>   Warmeth the ground, and quickeneth the seed.
>   The rain, wherewith she watereth the flowers,
>   Falls from mine eyes, which she dissolves in showers."

Samuel Daniel had an eminently contemplative genius which might have anticipated the sonnet as it is in Wordsworth, but which the fashion of the day confined to the not wholly suitable subject of Love. In the splendid "Care-charmer Sleep," one of the tournament sonnets above noted, he contrived, as will be seen, to put his subject under the influence of his prevailing faculty.

> " Care-charmer Sleep, son of the sable Night,
>   Brother to Death, in silent darkness born,
>   Relieve my anguish, and restore the light,
>   With dark forgetting of my cares, return ;
>   And let the day be time enough to mourn
>   The shipwreck of my ill-adventured youth ;
>   Let waking eyes suffice to wail their scorn
>   Without the torment of the night's untruth.

> Cease, Dreams, th' imag'ry of our day-desires,
>   To model forth the passions of the morrow,
> Never let rising sun approve you liars,
>   To add more grief to aggravate my sorrow.
> Still let me sleep, embracing clouds in vain ;
> And never wake to feel the day's disdain."

But as a rule he is perhaps too much given to musing, and too little to rapture.   In form he is important, as he undoubtedly did much to establish the arrangement of three alternate rhymed quatrains and a couplet which, in Shakespere's hands, was to give the noblest poetry of the sonnet and of the world.   He has also an abundance of the most exquisite single lines, such as

> " O clear-eyed rector of the holy hill,"

and the wonderful opening of Sonnet xxvii., " The star of my mishap imposed this pain."

The sixty-three sonnets, varied in different editions of Drayton's *Idea*, are among the most puzzling of the whole group.   Their average value is not of the very highest.   Yet there are here and there the strangest suggestions of Drayton's countryman, Shakespere, and there is one sonnet, No. 61, beginning, " Since there's no help, come let us kiss and part," which I have found it most difficult to believe to be Drayton's, and which is Shakespere all over.   That Drayton was the author of *Idea* as a whole is certain, not merely from the local allusions, but from the resemblance to the more successful exercises of his clear, masculine, vigorous, fertile, but occasionally rather unpoetical style.   The sonnet just referred to is itself one of the very finest existing—perhaps one of the ten or twelve best sonnets in the world, and it may be worth while to give it with another in contrast :—

> " Our flood's Queen, Thames, for ships and swans is crowned ;
>   And stately Severn for her shore is praised.
> The crystal Trent for fords and fish renowned ;
>   And Avon's fame to Albion's cliffs is raised ;
> Carlegion Chester vaunts her holy Dee ;
>   York many wonders of her Ouse can tell.

The Peak her Dove, whose banks so fertile be ;
   And Kent will say her Medway doth excel.
Cotswold commends her Isis to the Tame ;
   Our northern borders boast of Tweed's fair flood
Our western parts extol their Wily's fame ;
   And the old Lea brags of the Danish blood.
Arden's sweet Ankor, let thy glory be
That fair Idea only lives by thee ! "

" Since there's no help, come, let us kiss and part !
   Nay, I have done.   You get no more of me.
And I am glad, yea, glad with all my heart
   That thus so cleanly I myself can free.
Shake hands for ever, cancel all our vows,
   And when we meet at any time again
Be it not seen in either of our brows
   That we one jot of former love retain.
Now at the last gasp of Love's latest breath,
   When, his pulse failing, Passion speechless lies ;
When Faith is kneeling by his bed of death,
   And Innocence is closing up his eyes :
Now, if thou would'st, when all have given him over,
From death to life thou might'st him yet recover ! "

1595 chiefly contributed the curious production called *Alcilia*, by J. C., who gives the name of sonnets to a series of six-line stanzas, varied occasionally by other forms, such as that of the following pretty verses.   It may be noted that the citation of proverbs is very characteristic of *Alcilia :*—

" Love is sorrow mixed with gladness,
   Fear with hope, and hope with madness.
Long did I love, but all in vain ;
I loving, was not loved again :
For which my heart sustained much woe.
It fits not maids to use men so,
Just deserts are not regarded,
Never love so ill rewarded.
But ' all is lost that is not sought,'
' Oft wit proves best that's dearest bought.'

" Women were made for men's relief ;
   To comfort, not to cause their grief.

Where most I merit, least I find :
No marvel, since that love is blind.
Had she been kind as she was fair,
My case had been more strange and rare.
But women love not by desert,
Reason in them hath weakest part.
Then henceforth let them love that list,
I will beware of ' had I wist.' "

1596 (putting the *Amoretti*, which is sometimes assigned to this year, aside) was again fruitful with Griffin's *Fidessa*, Lynch's *Diella*, and Smith's *Chloris*. *Fidessa*, though distinctly " young," is one of the most interesting of the clearly imitative class of these sonnets, and contains some very graceful poetry, especially the following, one of the Sleep class, which will serve as a good example of the minor sonneteers :—

" Care-charmer Sleep ! sweet ease in restless misery !
    The captive's liberty, and his freedom's song !
Balm of the bruisèd heart ! man's chief felicity !
    Brother of quiet Death, when Life is too too long !
A Comedy it is, and now an History ;
    What is not sleep unto the feeble mind?
It easeth him that toils, and him that's sorry ;
    It makes the deaf to hear ; to see, the blind ;
Ungentle Sleep ! thou helpest all but me,
    For when I sleep my soul is vexèd most.
It is Fidessa that doth master thee
    If she approach ; alas ! thy power is lost.
But here she is ! See, how he runs amain !
I fear, at night, he will not come again."

Diella, a set of thirty-eight sonnets prefixed to the " Amorous poem of Diego and Genevra," is more elaborate in colouring but somewhat less fresh and genuine ; while *Chloris*, whose author was a friend of Spenser's, approaches to the pastoral in the plan and phrasing of its fifty sonnets.

Such are the most remarkable members of a group of English poetry, which yields to few such groups in interest. It is connected by a strong similarity of feeling—if any one likes, even

by a strong imitation of the same models.   But in following
those models and expressing those feelings, its members, even
the humblest of them, have shown remarkable poetical capacity ;
while of the chiefs we can only say, as has been said more than
once already, that the matter and form together acknowledge,
and indeed admit of, no superior.

In close connection with these groups of sonnets, displaying
very much the same poetical characteristics and in some cases
written by the same authors, there occurs a great body of miscellaneous poetical writing produced during the last twenty years
of the sixteenth century, and ranging from long poems of the
allegorical or amatory kind to the briefest lyrics and madrigals.
Sometimes this work appeared independently ; sometimes it
was inserted in the plays and prose pamphlets of the time.   As
has already been said, some of our authors, notably Lodge and
Greene, did in this way work which far exceeds in merit any
of their more ambitious pieces, and which in a certain unbor-
rowed and incommunicable poetic grace hardly leaves anything
of the time behind it.   Shakespere himself, in *Venus and Adonis*
and *Lucrece*, has in a more elaborate but closely allied kind of
poetry displayed less mature, but scarcely less, genius than in
his dramatic and sonnet work.   It is my own opinion that the
actual poetical worth of Richard Barnfield, to whom an exquisite
poem in *The Passionate Pilgrim*, long ascribed to Shakespere, is
now more·justly assigned, has, owing to this assignment and to
the singular character of his chief other poem, *The Affectionate
Shepherd*, been considerably overrated.   It is unfortunately as
complete if not as common a mistake to suppose that any
one who disdains his country's morality must be a good poet,
as to set down any one who disdains it without further examination for a bad one.   The simple fact, as it strikes a critic,
is that " As it fell upon a day " is miles above anything else
of Barnfield's, and is not like anything else of his, while it is
very like things of Shakespere's.   The best thing to be said for
Barnfield is that he was an avowed and enthusiastic imitator

and follower of Spenser.   His poetical work (we might have
included the short series of sonnets to *Cynthia* in the division
of sonneteers) was all written when he was a very young man,
and he died when he was not a very old one, a bachelor country-
gentleman in Warwickshire.   Putting the exquisite "As it fell
upon a day" out of question (which, if he wrote it, is one of
the not very numerous examples of perfect poetry written by a
very imperfect poet), Barnfield has, in no extraordinary measure,
the common attributes of this wonderful time—poetical enthusiasm, fresh and unhackneyed expression, metrical charm, and
gorgeous colouring, which does not find itself ill-matched with
accurate drawing of nature.   He is above the average Elizabethan, and his very bad taste in *The Affectionate Shepherd* (a following of Virgil's Second Eclogue) may be excused as a humanist
crotchet of the time.   His rarity, his eccentricity, and the curious
mixing up of his work with Shakespere's have done him something more than yeoman's service with recent critics.   But he
may have a specimen :—

> " And thus it happened : Death and Cupid met
>   Upon a time at swilling Bacchus' house,
> Where dainty cates upon the board were set,
>   And goblets full of wine to drink carouse :
>   Where Love and Death did love the liquor so
>   That out they fall, and to the fray they go.
>
> " And having both their quivers at their back
>   Filled full of arrows—the one of fatal steel,
> The other all of gold ; Death's shaft was black,
>   But Love's was yellow—Fortune turned her wheel,
>   And from Death's quiver fell a fatal shaft
>   That under Cupid by the wind was waft.
>
> " And at the same time by ill hap there fell
>   Another arrow out of Cupid's quiver ;
> The which was carried by the wind at will,
>   And under Death the amorous shaft did shiver.[1]
>   They being parted, Love took up Death's dart,
>   And Death took up Love's arrow for his part."

---

[1] Not, of course = " break," but " shudder."

There is perhaps more genuine poetic worth, though there is less accomplishment of form, in the unfortunate Father Robert Southwell, who was executed as a traitor on the 20th of February 1595. Southwell belonged to a distinguished family, and was born (probably) at Horsham St. Faiths, in Norfolk, about the year 1560. He was stolen by a gipsy in his youth, but was recovered; and a much worse misfortune befell him in being sent for education not to Oxford or Cambridge but to Douay, where he got into the hands of the Jesuits, and joined their order. He was sent on a mission to England; and (no doubt conscientiously) violating the law there, was after some years of hiding and suspicion betrayed, arrested, treated with great harshness in prison, and at last, as has been said, executed. No specific acts of treason were even charged against him; and he earnestly denied any designs whatever against the Queen and kingdom, nor can it be doubted that he merely paid the penalty of others' misdeeds. His work both in prose and poetry was not inconsiderable, and the poetry was repeatedly printed in rather confusing and imperfect editions after his death. The longest, but by no means the best, piece is *St. Peter's Complaint.* The best unquestionably is *The Burning Babe,* which, though fairly well known, must be given :—

" As I in hoary winter's night stood shivering in the snow,
  Surpris'd I was with sudden heat, which made my heart to glow ;
  And lifting up a fearful eye to view what fire was near,
  A pretty Babe all burning bright, did in the air appear,
  Who scorchèd with excessive heat, such floods of tears did shed,
  As though His floods should quench His flames which with His tears were fed ;
  ' Alas ! ' quoth He, ' but newly born, in fiery heats I fry,
  Yet none approach to warm their hearts or feel My fire but I !
  My faultless breast the furnace is, the fuel wounding thorns,
  Love is the fire, and sighs the smoke, the ashes shame and scorns ;
  The fuel Justice layeth on, and Mercy blows the coals ;
  The metal in this furnace wrought are men's defilèd souls,
  For which, as now on fire I am, to work them to their good
  So will I melt into a bath to wash them in My blood :'
  With these He vanished out of sight, and swiftly shrunk away,
  And straight I callèd unto mind that it was Christmas Day."

Something of the glow of this appears elsewhere in the poems, which are, without exception, religious. They have not a little of the "hectic" tone, which marks still more strongly the chief English Roman Catholic poet of the next century, Crashaw ; but are never, as Crashaw sometimes is, hysterical. On the whole, as was remarked in a former chapter, they belong rather to the pre-Spenserian class in diction and metre, though with something of the Italian touch. Occasional roughnesses in them may be at least partly attributed to the evident fact that the author thought of nothing less than of merely "cultivating the muses." His religious fervour is of the simplest and most genuine kind, and his poems are a natural and unforced expression of it.

It is difficult in the brief space which can here be allotted to the subject to pass in review the throng of miscellaneous poets and poetry indicated under this group. The reprints of Dr. Grosart and Mr. Arber, supplemented in a few cases by recourse to the older recoveries of Brydges, Haslewood, Park, Collier, and others, bring before the student a mass of brilliant and beautiful matter, often mixed with a good deal of slag and scoriæ, but seldom deficient in the true poetical ore. The mere collections of madrigals and songs, actually intended for casual performance at a time when almost every accomplished and well-bred gentleman or lady was expected to oblige the company, which Mr. Arber's invaluable *English Garner* and Mr. Bullen's *Elizabethan Lyrics* give from the collections edited or produced by Byrd, Yonge, Campion, Dowland, Morley, Alison, Wilbye, and others, represent such a body of verse as probably could not be got together, with the same origin and circumstances, in any quarter-century of any nation's history since the foundation of the world. In Campion especially the lyrical quality is extraordinary. He was long almost inaccessible, but Mr. Bullen's edition of 1889 has made knowledge of him easy. His birth-year is unknown, but he died in 1620. He was a Cambridge man, a member of the Inns of Court, and a physician in good practice. He has left us a masque ; four *Books of Airs*

(1601-17 ?), in which the gems given below, and many others, occur ; and a sometimes rather unfairly characterised critical treatise, *Observations on the Art of English Poesy*, in which he argues against rhyme and for strict quantitative measures, but on quite different lines from those of the craze of Stanyhurst and Harvey. Some of his illustrations of his still rather unnatural fancy (especially " Rose-cheeked Laura," which is now tolerably familiar in anthologies) are charming, though never so charming as his rhymed " Airs." The poetry is, indeed, mostly in flashes, and it is not very often that any song is a complete gem, like the best of the songs from the dramatists, one or two of which will be given presently for comparison. But by far the greater number contain and exemplify those numerous characteristics of poetry, as distinguished from verse, which at one time of literary history seem naturally to occur—seem indeed to be had for the gathering by any one who chooses—while at another time they are but sparingly found in the work of men of real genius, and seem altogether to escape men of talent, accomplishment, and laborious endeavour. Here are a few specimens from Peele and others, especially Campion. As it is, an exceptional amount of the small space possible for such things in this volume has been given to them, but there is a great temptation to give more. Lyly's lyrical work, however, is fairly well known, and more than one collection of " Songs from the Dramatists " has popularised others.

    Æ. " Fair and fair, and twice so fair,
        As fair as any may be ;
        The fairest shepherd on our green,
        A love for any lady.

    Par. Fair and fair, and twice so fair,
        As fair as any may be :
        Thy love is fair for thee alone,
        And for no other lady.

    Æ. My love is fair, my love is gay,
        As fresh as bin the flowers in May,
        And of my love my roundelay

Concludes with Cupid's curse,
They that do change old love for new
Pray gods, they change for worse !

Ambo, simul. They that do change, etc., etc.
Æ. Fair and fair, etc.
Par. Fair and fair, etc.
Æ. My love can pipe, my love can sing,
My love can many a pretty thing,
And of his lovely praises ring
My merry, merry roundelays.
Amen to Cupid's curse,
They that do change, etc."

PEELE.

" His golden locks time hath to silver turned ;
O time too swift, O swiftness never ceasing !
His youth 'gainst time and age hath ever spurned,
But spurned in vain ; youth waneth by increasing :
Beauty, strength, youth, are flowers but fading seen.
Duty, faith, love, are roots, and ever green.

" His helmet now shall make a hive for bees,
And lovers' songs be turned to holy psalms ;
A man-at-arms must now serve on his knees,
And feed on prayers, which are old age's alms :
But though from court to cottage he depart,
His saint is sure of his unspotted heart.

" And when he saddest sits in homely cell,
He'll teach his swains this carol for a song :
' Blessed be the hearts that wish my Sovereign well,
Cursed be the souls that think her any wrong.'
Goddess allow this aged man his right,
To be your beadsman now that was your knight."

PEELE.

" Fain would I change that note
To which fond love hath charm'd me,
Long, long to sing by rote
Fancying that that harm'd me :
Yet when this thought doth come,
' Love is the perfect sum

Of all delight !'
I have no other choice
Either for pen or voice
To sing or write.

" O Love, they wrong thee much
That say thy sweet is bitter,
When thy rich fruit is such
As nothing can be sweeter.
Fair house of joy and bliss
Where truest pleasure is,
I do adore thee ;
I know thee what thou art.
I serve thee with my heart
And fall before thee.

Anon. in BULLEN.

" Turn all thy thoughts to eyes,
Turn all thy hairs to ears,
Change all thy friends to spies,
And all thy joys to fears :
True love will yet be free
In spite of jealousy.

" Turn darkness into day,
Conjectures into truth,
Believe what th' curious say,
Let age interpret youth :
True love will yet be free
In spite of jealousy.

" Wrest every word and look,
Rack every hidden thought ;
Or fish with golden hook,
True love cannot be caught :
For that will still be free
In spite of jealousy."

CAMPION *in* BULLEN.

" Come, O come, my life's delight !
Let me not in langour pine !
Love loves no delay ; thy sight
The more enjoyed, the more divine.
O come, and take from me
The pain of being deprived of thee !

" Thou all sweetness dost enclose
  Like a little world of bliss ;
Beauty guards thy looks, the rose
  In them pure and eternal is :
    Come, then, and make thy flight
    As swift to me as heavenly light ! "
                                CAMPION.

" Follow your saint, follow with accents sweet !
Haste you, sad notes, fall at her flying feet !
There, wrapped in cloud of sorrow, pity move,
And tell the ravisher of my soul I perish for her love.
But if she scorns my never-ceasing pain,
Then burst with sighing in her sight and ne'er return again.

" All that I sang still to her praise did tend,
Still she was first, still she my songs did end ;
Yet she my love and music both doth fly,
The music that her echo is and beauty's sympathy :
Then let my notes pursue her scornful flight !
It shall suffice that they were breathed and died for her delight."
                                CAMPION.

" What if a day, or a month, or a year,
    Crown thy delights with a thousand sweet contentings !
Cannot a chance of a night or an hour
    Cross thy desires with as many sad tormentings ?
Fortune, Honour, Beauty, Youth, are but blossoms dying,
Wanton Pleasure, doating Love, are but shadows flying.
All our joys are but toys ! idle thoughts deceiving :
None have power, of an hour, in their lives bereaving.

" Earth's but a point to the world, and a man
    Is but a point to the world's comparèd centre !
Shall then a point of a point be so vain
    As to triumph in a silly point's adventure ?
All is hazard that we have, there is nothing biding ;
Days of pleasure are like streams through fair meadows gliding.
Weal and woe, time doth go ! time is never turning ;
Secret fates guide our states, both in mirth and mourning."
                                CAMPION.

" 'Twas I that paid for all things,
  'Twas others drank the wine,

I cannot now recall things ;
  Live but a fool, to pine.
'Twas I that beat the bush,
  The bird to others flew ;
For she, alas, hath left me.
  Falero ! lero ! loo !

" If ever that Dame Nature
  (For this false lover's sake)
Another pleasing creature
  Like unto her would make ;
Let her remember this,
  To make the other true !
For this, alas ! hath left me.
  Falero ! lero ! loo !

" No riches now can raise me,
  No want makes me despair,
No misery amaze me,
  Nor yet for want I care :
I have lost a World itself,
  My earthly Heaven, adieu !
Since she, alas ! hath left me.
  Falero ! lero ! loo ! "

Anon. in ARBER.

Beside these collections, which were in their origin and inception chiefly musical, and literary, as it were, only by parergon,
there are successors of the earlier Miscellanies in which, as in
England's Helicon and the celebrated *Passionate Pilgrim*, there
is some of the most exquisite of our verse. And, yet again,
a crowd of individual writers, of few of whom is much known,
contributed, not in all cases their mites by any means, but
often very respectable sums, to the vast treasury of English poetry.
There is Sir Edward Dyer, the friend of Raleigh and Sidney,
who has been immortalised by the famous " My mind to me
a kingdom is," and who wrote other pieces not much inferior.
There is Raleigh, to whom the glorious preparatory sonnet to
The Faërie Queene would sufficiently justify the ascription of
" a vein most lofty, insolent, and passionate," if a very considerable body of verse (independent of the fragmentary *Cynthia*)

did not justify this many times over, as two brief quotations
in addition to the sonnet will show :—

> " Methought I saw the grave where Laura lay,
>   Within that temple where the vestal flame
> Was wont to burn : and, passing by that way
>   To see that buried dust of living fame,
> Whose tomb fair Love and fairer Virtue kept,
>   All suddenly I saw the Fairy Queen,
> At whose approach the soul of Petrarch wept ;
>   And from henceforth those graces were not seen,
> For they this Queen attended ; in whose stead
>   Oblivion laid him down on Laura's hearse.
> Hereat the hardest stones were seen to bleed,
>   And groans of buried ghosts the heavens did pierce :
> Where Homer's spright did tremble all for grief,
> And curse the access of that celestial thief."

> " Three things there be that prosper all apace,
>   And flourish while they are asunder far ;
> But on a day they meet all in a place,
>   And when they meet they one another mar.

> " And they be these—the Wood, the Weed, the Wag :
>   The Wood is that that makes the gallows tree ;
> The Weed is that that strings the hangman's bag ;
>   The Wag, my pretty knave, betokens thee.

> " Now mark, dear boy—while these assemble not,
>   Green springs the tree, hemp grows, the Wag is wild ;
> But when they meet, it makes the timber rot,
>   It frets the halter, and it chokes the child.

> " God Bless the Child ! "

> " Give me my scallop-shell of quiet,
>   My staff of faith to walk upon,
> My scrip of joy, immortal diet,
>   My bottle of salvation,
> My gown of glory, hope's true gage ;
> And thus I'll take my pilgrimage.

> " Blood must be my body's balmer ;
>   No other balm will there be given ;

Whilst my soul, like quiet palmer,
   Travelleth towards the land of heaven ;
Over the silver mountains
Where spring the nectar fountains :
   There will I kiss
   The bowl of bliss ;
And drink mine everlasting fill
Upon every milken hill.
My soul will be a-dry before,
But after it will thirst no more."

There is Lord Oxford, Sidney's enemy (which he might be if
he chose), and apparently a coxcomb (which is less pardonable),
but a charming writer of verse, as in the following :—

" Come hither, shepherd swain !
   Sir, what do you require ?
I pray thee, shew to me thy name !
   My name is Fond Desire.

" When wert thou born, Desire ?
   In pomp and prime of May.
By whom, sweet boy, wert thou begot ?
   By fond Conceit, men say.

" Tell me, who was thy nurse
   Fresh youth, in sugared joy.
What was thy meat and daily food ?
   Sad sighs, with great annoy.

" What hadst thou then to drink ?
   Unfeigned lovers' tears.
What cradle wert thou rocked in ?
   In hope devoid of fears.

" What lulled thee then asleep ?
   Sweet speech which likes me best.
Tell me, where is thy dwelling-place ?
   In gentle hearts I rest.

" What thing doth please thee most ?
   To gaze on beauty still.
Whom dost thou think to be thy foe ?
   Disdain of my good will.

" Doth company displease ?
Yes, surely, many one.
Where doth desire delight to live ?
He loves to live alone.

" Doth either time or age
Bring him unto decay ?
No, no ! Desire both lives and dies
A thousand times a day.

" Then, fond Desire, farewell !
Thou art no mate for me ;
I should be loath, methinks, to dwell
With such a one as thee.

There is, in the less exalted way, the industrious man of all work, Nicholas Breton, whom we shall speak of more at length among the pamphleteers, and John Davies of Hereford, no poet certainly, but a most industrious verse-writer in satiric and other forms. Mass of production, and in some cases personal interest, gives these a certain standing above their fellows. But the crowd of those fellows, about many of whom even the painful industry of the modern commentator has been able to tell us next to nothing, is almost miraculous when we remember that printing was still carried on under a rigid censorship by a select body of monopolists, and that out of London, and in rare cases the university towns, it was impossible for a minor poet to get into print at all unless he trusted to the contraband presses of the Continent. In dealing with this crowd of enthusiastic poetical students it is impossible to mention all, and invidious to single out some only. The very early and interesting *Posy of Gillyflowers* of Humphrey Gifford (1580) exhibits the first stage of our period, and might almost have been referred to the period before it; the same humpty-dumpty measure of eights and sixes, and the same vestiges of rather infantine alliteration being apparent in it, though something of the fire and variety of the new age of poetry appears beside them, notably in this most spirited war-song :—

(*For Soldiers.*)

" Ye buds of Brutus' land, courageous youths now play your parts,[1]
Unto your tackle stand, abide the brunt with valiant hearts,
For news is carried to and fro, that we must forth to warfare go :
Then muster now in every place, and soldiers are pressed forth apace.
Faint not, spend blood to do your Queen and country good :
Fair words, good pay, will make men cast all care away.

" The time of war is come, prepare your corslet, spear, and shield :
Methinks I hear the drum strike doleful marches to the field.
Tantara, tantara the trumpets sound, which makes our hearts with joy
    abound.
The roaring guns are heard afar, and everything announceth war.
Serve God, stand stout ; bold courage brings this gear about ;
Fear not, forth run : faint heart fair lady never won.

" Ye curious carpet-knights that spend the time in sport and play,
Abroad and see new sights, your country's cause calls you away :
Do not, to make your ladies' game, bring blemish to your worthy name.
Away to field and win renown, with courage beat your enemies down ;
Stout hearts gain praise, when dastards sail in slander's seas.
Hap what hap shall, we soon shall die but once for all.

" Alarm ! methinks they cry. Be packing mates, begone with speed,
Our foes are very nigh : shame have that man that shrinks at need.
Unto it boldly let us stand, God will give right the upper hand.
Our cause is good we need not doubt : in sign of courage give a shout ;
March forth, be strong, good hap will come ere it be long.
Shrink not, fight well, for lusty lads must bear the bell.

" All you that will shun evil must dwell in warfare every day.
The world, the flesh, the devil always do seek our souls' decay.
Strive with these foes with all your might, so shall you fight a worthy fight.
That conquest dost deserve most praise, whose vice do[th] yield to virtue's
    ways.
Beat down foul sin, a worthy crown then shall ye win :
If ye live well, in Heaven with Christ our souls shall dwell."

Of the same date, or indeed earlier, are the miscellaneous
poems of Thomas Howell, entitled *The Arbour of Amity*, and

---

[1] I print this as in the original, but perhaps the rhythm, which is an odd
one, would be better marked if lines 1 and 2 were divided into sixes and
eights, lines 3 and 4 into eights, and lines 5 and 6 into fours and eights as the
rhyme ends.

chiefly of an ethical character. Less excusable for the uncouthness of his verse is Matthew Grove, who, writing, or at least publishing, his poems in 1587, should have learnt something, but
apparently had not. It has to be said in excuse of him that
his date and indeed existence are shadowy, even among the
shadowy Elizabethan bards; his editor, in worse doggerel than
his own, frankly confessing that he knew nothing about him,
not so much as whether he was alive or dead. But his work,
Howell's, and even part of Gifford's, is chiefly interesting as
giving us in the very sharpest contrast the differences of the
poetry before and after the melodious bursts of which Spenser,
Sidney, and Watson were the first mouthpieces. Except an
utter dunce (which Grove does not seem to have been by any
means) no one who had before him *The Shepherd's Calendar*,
or the *Hecatompathia*, or a MS. copy of *Astrophel and Stella*,
could have written as Grove wrote. There are echoes of this
earlier and woodener matter to be found later, but, as a whole, the
passionate love of beauty, the sense—if only a groping sense—
of form, and the desire to follow, and if possible improve upon
the models of melodious verse which the Sidneian school had
given, preserved even poetasters from the lowest depths.

To classify the miscellaneous verse of 1590-1600 (for the
second decade is much richer than the first) under subjects
and styles is a laborious and, at best, an uncertain business.
The semi-mythological love-poem, with a more or less tragic
ending, had not a few followers; the collection of poems of
various character in praise of a real or imaginary mistress,
similar in design to the sonnet collections, but either more
miscellaneous in form or less strung together in one long composition, had even more; while the collection pure and simple,
resembling the miscellanies in absence of special character, but
the work of one, not of many writers, was also plentifully represented. Satirical allegory, epigram, and other kinds, had
numerous examples. But there were two classes of verse which
were both sufficiently interesting in themselves and were culti-

vated by persons of sufficient individual repute to deserve separate and detailed mention.   These were the historical poem or
history—a kind of companion production to the chronicle play
or chronicle, and a very popular one—which, besides the names
of Warner, Daniel, and Drayton, counted not a few minor ad-
herents among Elizabethan bards.   Such were the already-mentioned Giles Fletcher ; such Fitz-Geoffrey in a remarkable poem
on Drake, and Gervase Markham in a not less noteworthy
piece on the last fight of *The Revenge;* such numerous others,
some of whom are hardly remembered, and perhaps hardly deserve to be.   The other, and as a class the more interesting,
though nothing actually produced by its practitioners may be
quite equal to the best work of Drayton and Daniel, was the
beginning of English satire.   This beginning is interesting not
merely because of the apparent coincidence of instinct which made
four or five writers of great talent simultaneously hit on the
style, so that it is to this day difficult to award exactly the
palm of priority, but also because the result of their studies, in
some peculiar and at first sight rather inexplicable ways, is some
of the most characteristic, if very far from being some of the
best, work of the whole poetical period with which we are now
busied.   In passing, moreover, from the group of miscellaneous
poets to these two schools, if we lose not a little of the harmony and lyrical sweetness which characterise the best work
of the Elizabethan singer proper, we gain greatly in bulk and
dignity of work and in intrinsic value.   Of at least one of the
poets mentioned in the last paragraph his modern editor—a
most enthusiastic and tolerant godfather of waifs and strays of
literature — confesses that he really does not quite know why
he should be reprinted, except that the original is unique, and
that almost every scrap of literature in this period is of some
value, if only for lexicographic purposes.   No one would dream
of speaking thus of Drayton or of Daniel, of Lodge, Hall,
Donne, or Marston; while even Warner, the weakest of the
names to which we shall proceed to give separate notice, can be

praised without too much allowance. In the latter case, moreover, if not in the first (for the history-poem, until it was taken up
in a very different spirit at the beginning of this century, never
was a success in England), the matter now to be reviewed, after
being in its own kind neglected for a couple of generations,
served as forerunner, if not exactly as model, to the magnificent
satiric work of Dryden, and through his to that of Pope, Young,
Churchill, Cowper, and the rest of the more accomplished English
satirists. The acorn of such an oak cannot be without interest.

The example of *The Mirror for Magistrates* is perhaps
sufficient to account for the determination of a certain number
of Elizabethan poets towards English history; especially if we
add the stimulating effect of Holinshed's *Chronicle*, which was
published in 1580. The first of the so-called historians, William
Warner, belongs in point of poetical style to the pre-Spenserian
period, and like its other exponents employs the fourteener;
while, unlike some of them, he seems quite free from any Italian
influence in phraseology or poetical manner. Nevertheless
Albion's England is, not merely in bulk but in merit, far ahead of
the average work of our first period, and quite incommensurable
with such verse as that of Grove. It appeared by instalments
(1586-1606-1612). Of its author, William Warner, the old phrase
has to be repeated, that next to nothing is known of him. He
was an Oxfordshire man by birth, and an Oxford man by education;
he had something to do with Cary, Lord Hunsdon, became an
Attorney of the Common Pleas, and died at Amwell suddenly in
his bed in 1609, being, as it is guessed rather than known, fifty
years old or thereabouts. *Albion's England* was seized as contraband, by orders of the Archbishop of Canterbury—a proceeding
for which no one has been able to account (the suggestion that
parts of it are indelicate is, considering the manners of the time,
quite ludicrous), and which may perhaps have been due to some
technical informality. It is thought that he is the author of a
translation of Plautus's *Menæchmi*; he certainly produced in 1585?
a prose story, or rather collection of stories, entitled *Syrinx*, which,

however, is scarcely worth reading. *Albion's England* is in no danger of incurring that sentence. In the most easily accessible edition, that of Chalmers's " Poets," it is spoilt by having the fourteeners divided into eights and sixes, and it should if possible be read in the original arrangement. Considering how few persons have written about it, an odd collection of critical slips might be made. Philips, Milton's nephew, in this case it may be hoped, not relying on his uncle, calls Warner a " good plain writer of moral rules and precepts ": the fact being that though he sometimes moralises he is in the main a story-teller, and much more bent on narrative than on teaching. Meres calls him " a refiner of the English tongue," and attributes to him " rare ornaments and resplendent habiliments of the pen ": the truth being that he is (as Philips so far correctly says) a singularly plain, straightforward, and homely writer. Others say that he wrote in " Alexandrines " —a blunder, and a serious one, which has often been repeated up to the present day in reference to other writers of the seven-foot verse. He brings in, according to the taste and knowledge of his time, all the fabulous accounts of the origins of Britain, and diversifies them with many romantic and pastoral histories, classical tales, and sometimes mere *Fabliaux*, down to his own time. The chief of the episodes, the story of Argentile and Curan, has often, and not undeservedly, met with high praise, and sometimes in his declamatory parts Warner achieves a really great success. Probably, however, what commended his poem most to the taste of the day was its promiscuous admixture of things grave and gay—a mixture which was always much to the taste of Elizabeth's men, and the popularity of which produced and fostered many things, from the matchless tragi-comedy of *Hamlet* and *Macbeth* to the singularly formless pamphlets of which we shall speak hereafter. The main interest of Warner is his insensibility to the new influences which Spenser and Sidney directed, and which are found producing their full effect on Daniel and Drayton. There were those in his own day who compared him to Homer : one of the most remarkable instances

of thoroughly unlucky critical extravagance to be found in literary
history, as the following very fair average specimen will show :—

"Henry (as if by miracle preserved by foreigns long,
From hence-meant treasons) did arrive to right his natives' wrong :
And chiefly to Lord Stanley, and some other succours, as
Did wish and work for better days, the rival welcome was.
Now Richard heard that Richmond was assisted and ashore,
And like unkennel'd Cerberus, the crookèd tyrant swore,
And all complexions act at once confusedly in him :
He studieth, striketh, threats, entreats, and looketh mildly grim,
Mistrustfully he trusteth, and he dreadingly did dare,
And forty passions in a trice, in him consort and square.
But when, by his consented force, his foes increasèd more,
He hastened battle, finding his co-rival apt therefore.
When Richmond, orderly in all, had battlèd his aid,
Inringèd by his complices, their cheerful leader said :
' Now is the time and place (sweet friends) and we the persons be
That must give England breath, or else unbreathe for her must we.
No tyranny is fabled, and no tyrant was in deed
Worse than our foe, whose works will act my words, if well he speed :
For ill to ills superlative are easily enticed,
But entertains amendment as the Gergesites did Christ.
Be valiant then, he biddeth so that would not be outbid,
For courage yet shall honour him though base, that better did.
I am right heir Lancastrian, he, in York's destroyèd right
Usurpeth : but through either ours, for neither claim I fight,
But for our country's long-lack'd weal, for England's peace I war :
Wherein He speed us ! unto Whom I all events refer.'
Meanwhile had furious Richard set his armies in array,
And then, with looks even like himself, this or the like did say :
' Why, lads, shall yonder Welshman with his stragglers overmatch ?
Disdain ye not such rivals, and defer ye their dispatch ?
Shall Tudor from Plantagenet, the crown by cracking snatch ?
Know Richard's very thoughts ' (he touch'd the diadem he wore)
' Be metal of this metal : then believe I love it more
Than that for other law than life, to supersede my claim,
And lesser must not be his plea that counterpleads the same.'
The weapons overtook his words, and blows they bravely change,
When, like a lion thirsting blood, did moody Richard range,
And made large slaughters where he went, till Richmond he espied,
Whom singling, after doubtful swords, the valorous tyrant died."

Of the sonnet compositions of Daniel and Drayton something
has been said already. But Daniel's sonnets are a small and
Drayton's an infinitesimal part of the work of the two poets
respectively. Samuel Daniel was a Somersetshire man, born
near Taunton in 1562. He is said to have been the son of a
music master, but was educated at Oxford, made powerful friends,
and died an independent person at Beckington, in the county of
his birth, in the year 1619. He was introduced early to good
society and patronage, became tutor to Lady Anne Clifford, a
great heiress of the North, was favoured by the Earl of Southampton, and became a member of the Pembroke or *Arcadia*
coterie. His friends or his merits obtained for him, it is said,
the Mastership of the Revels, the posts of Gentleman Extraordinary to James I., and Groom of the Privy Chamber to Anne
of Denmark. His literary production besides *Delia* was considerable. With the first authorised edition of that collection
he published *The Complaint of Rosamond*, a historical poem of
great grace and elegance though a little wanting in strength. In
1594 came his interesting Senecan tragedy of *Cleopatra ;* in 1595
the first part of his chief work, *The History of the Civil Wars*,
and in 1601 a collected folio of "Works." Then he rested, at
any rate from publication, till 1605, when he produced *Philotas*,
another Senecan tragedy in verse. In prose he wrote the admirable
Defence of Rhyme, which finally smashed the fancy for classical metres
dear even to such a man as Campion. *Hymen's Triumph*, a
masque of great beauty, was not printed till four years before his
death. He also wrote a History of England as well as minor
works. The poetical value of Daniel may almost be summed up
in two words—sweetness and dignity. He is decidedly wanting
in strength, and, despite *Delia*, can hardly be said to have had a
spark of passion. Even in his own day it was doubted whether
he had not overweighted himself with his choice of historical
subjects, though the epithet of " well-languaged," given to him at
the time, evinces a real comprehension of one of his best claims
to attention. No writer of the period has such a command of pure

English, unadulterated by xenomania and unweakened by purism,
as Daniel. Whatever unfavourable things have been said of him
from time to time have been chiefly based on the fact that his
chaste and correct style lacks the fiery quaintness, the irregular
and audacious attraction of his contemporaries. Nor was he less
a master of versification than of vocabulary. His *Defence of
Rhyme* shows that he possessed the theory : all his poetical works
show that he was a master of the practice. He rarely attempted and
probably would not have excelled in the lighter lyrical measures.
But in the grave music of the various elaborate stanzas in which
the Elizabethan poets delighted, and of which the Spenserian,
though the crown and flower, is only the most perfect, he was a
great proficient, and his couplets and blank verse are not inferior.
Some of his single lines have already been quoted, and many
more might be excerpted from his work of the best Elizabethan
brand in the quieter kind. Quiet, indeed, is the overmastering
characteristic of Daniel. It was this no doubt which made him
prefer the stately style of his Senecan tragedies, and the hardly
more disturbed structure of pastoral comedies and tragi-comedies,
like the *Queen's Arcadia* and *Hymen's Triumph*, to the boisterous
revels of the stage proper in his time. He had something of the
schoolmaster in his nature as well as in his history. Nothing is
more agreeable to him than to moralise ; not indeed in any dull
or crabbed manner, but in a mellifluous and at the same time
weighty fashion, of which very few other poets have the secret.
It is perhaps by his scrupulous propriety, by his anxious decency
(to use the word not in its modern and restricted sense, but in its
proper meaning of the generally becoming), that Daniel brought
upon himself the rather hard saying that he had a manner " better
suiting prose."

The sentence will scarcely be echoed by any one who has
his best things before him, however much a reader of some
of the duller parts of the historical poems proper may feel
inclined to echo it. Of his sonnets one has been given. The
splendid Epistle to the Countess of Cumberland is not surpassed

as ethical poetry by anything of the period, and often as it has
been quoted, it must be given again, for it is not and never can
be too well known:—

> " He that of such a height hath built his mind,
>   And reared the dwelling of his thoughts so strong,
>   As neither fear nor hope can shake the frame
>   Of his resolvèd powers ; nor all the wind
>   Of vanity or malice pierce to wrong
>   His settled peace, or to disturb the same :
>   What a fair seat hath he, from whence he may
>   The boundless wastes and wealds of man survey !
>
> " And with how free an eye doth he look down
>   Upon these lower regions of turmoil !
>   Where all the storms of passion mainly beat
>   On flesh and blood : where honour, power, renown,
>   Are only gay afflictions, golden toil ;
>   Where greatness stands upon as feeble feet
>   As frailty doth ; and only great doth seem
>   To little minds, who do it so esteem.
>
> " He looks upon the mightiest monarch's wars
>   But only as on stately robberies ;
>   Where evermore the fortune that prevails
>   Must be the right : the ill-succeeding mars
>   The fairest and the best fac'd enterprise.
>   Great pirate Pompey lesser pirates quails :
>   Justice, he sees (as if seducèd) still
>   Conspires with power, whose cause must not be ill.
>
> " He sees the face of right t' appear as manifold
>   As are the passions of uncertain man ;
>   Who puts it in all colours, all attires,
>   To serve his ends, and make his courses hold.
>   He sees, that let deceit work what it can,
>   Plot and contrive base ways to high desires,
>   That the all-guiding Providence doth yet
>   All disappoint, and mocks the smoke of wit.
>
> " Nor is he mov'd with all the thunder cracks
>   Of tyrants' threats, or with the surly brow
>   Of Power, that proudly sits on others' crimes ;
>   Charg'd with more crying sins than those he checks.

The storms of sad confusion, that may grow
Up in the present for the coming times
Appal not him ; that hath no side at all,
But of himself, and knows the worst can fall.

" Although his heart (so near allied to Earth)
Cannot but pity the perplexèd state
Of troublous and distress'd Mortality,
That thus make way unto the ugly birth
Of their own sorrows, and do still beget
Affliction upon imbecility :
Yet seeing thus the course of things must run,
He looks thereon not strange, but as fore-done.

" And whilst distraught ambition compasses,
And is encompass'd ; whilst as craft deceives,
And is deceiv'd : whilst man doth ransack man
And builds on blood, and rises by distress ;
And th' inheritance of desolation leaves
To great-expecting hopes : he looks thereon,
As from the shore of peace, with unwet eye,
And bears no venture in impiety."

In sharp contrast with this the passage from *Hymen's Triumph,*

" Ah, I remember well, and how can I,"

shows the sweetness without namby-pambyness which Daniel had
at constant command.   Something of the same contrast may be
found between the whole of *Hymen's Triumph* and the *Queen's
Arcadia* on the one side, and *Cleopatra* and *Philotas* on the
other.   All are written in mixed blank and rhymed verse,
much interlaced and "enjambed."   The best of the historical
poems is, by common consent, *Rosamond,* which is instinct with
a most remarkable pathos, nor are fine passages by any means to
seek in the greater length and less poetical subject of *The Civil
Wars of York and Lancaster.*   The fault of this is that the too
conscientious historian is constantly versifying what must be
called mere expletive matter.   This must always make any one
who speaks with critical impartiality admit that much of Daniel
is hard reading ; but the soft places (to use the adjective in no

ill sense) are frequent enough, and when the reader comes to
them he must have little appreciation of poetry if he does
not rejoice in the foliage and the streams of the poetical oasis
which has rewarded him after his pilgrimage across a rather arid
wilderness.

Michael Drayton was much better fitted for the arduous, and
perhaps not wholly legitimate, business of historical poetry than
Daniel.   If his genius was somewhat less fine, it was infinitely
better thewed and sinewed.   His ability, indeed, to force any
subject which he chose to treat into poetry is amazing, and can
hardly be paralleled elsewhere except in a poet who was born
but just before Drayton's death, John Dryden.   He was pretty
certainly a gentleman by birth, though not of any great possessions, and is said to have been born at Hartshill, in Warwickshire, in the year 1563.   He is also said, but not known, to
have been a member of the University of Oxford, and appears to
have been fairly provided with patrons, in the family of some one
of whom he served as page, though he never received any great
or permanent preferment.[1]   On the other hand, he was not a
successful dramatist (the only literary employment of the time
that brought in much money), and friend as he was of nearly all
the men of letters of the time, it is expressly stated in one of the
few personal notices we have of him, that he could not " swagger
in a tavern or domineer in a hothouse " [house of ill-fame]—that
is to say, that the hail-fellow well-met Bohemianism of the time,
which had led Marlowe and many of his group to evil ends,
and which was continued in a less outrageous form under the
patronage of Ben Jonson till far into the next age, had no charms
for him.   Yet he must have lived somehow and to a good age,
for he did not die till the 23d December 1631.   He was
buried in Westminster Abbey, a fact which drew from Goldsmith,
in *The Citizen of the World*, a gibe showing only the lamentable
ignorance of the best period of English poetry, in which Gold-

---

[1] Drayton has been thoroughly treated by Professor Oliver Elton in *Michael
Drayton* (London, 1905), enlarged from a monograph for the Spenser Society.

smith was not indeed alone, but in which he was perhaps pre-
eminent among contemporaries eminent for it.

Drayton's long life was as industrious as it was long. He
began in 1591 with a volume of sacred verse, the *Harmony of
the Church*, which, for some reason not merely undiscovered but
unguessed, displeased the censors, and was never reprinted with
his other works until recently. Two years later appeared *Idea,
The Shepherd's Garland*—a collection of eclogues not to be
confounded with the more famous collection of sonnets in praise
of the same real or fancied mistress which appeared later. In
the first of these Drayton called himself "Rowland," or "Ro-
land," a fact on which some rather rickety structures of guesswork
have been built as to allusions to him in Spenser. His next
work was *Mortimeriados*, afterwards refashioned and completed
under the title of *The Barons' Wars*, and this was followed in
1597 by one of his best works, *England's Heroical Epistles*.
The Owl, some *Legends*, and other poems succeeded; and in
1605 he began to collect his Works, which were frequently
reprinted. The mighty poem of the *Polyolbion* was the fruit
of his later years, and, in strictness, belongs to the period of a
later chapter; but Drayton's muse is eminently one and indi-
visible, and, notwithstanding the fruits of pretty continual study
which his verses show, they belong, in the order of thought,
to the middle and later Elizabethan period rather than to the
Jacobean.

Few poets of anything like Drayton's volume (of which some
idea may be formed by saying that his works, in the not quite
complete form in which they appear in Chalmers, fill five hundred
of the bulky pages of that work, each page frequently containing
a hundred and twenty-eight lines) show such uniform mixture of
imagination and vigour. In the very highest and rarest graces of
poetry he is, indeed, by common consent wanting, unless one
of these graces in the uncommon kind of the war-song be allowed,
as perhaps it may be, to the famous and inimitable though often
imitated *Ballad of Agincourt*, "To the brave Cambro-Britons

and their Harp," not to be confounded with the narrative
"Battle of Agincourt," which is of a less rare merit.   The Agincourt ballad,

"Fair stood the wind for France,"

is quite at the head of its own class of verse in England—
Campbell's two   masterpieces, and Lord Tennyson's still more
direct imitation in the "Six Hundred," falling, the first somewhat,
and the last considerably, short of it.   The sweep of the metre,
the martial glow of the sentiment, and the skill with which the
names are wrought into the verse, are altogether beyond praise.
Drayton never, unless the enigmatical sonnet to Idea (see *ante*) be
really his, rose to such concentration of matter and such elaborate
yet unforced perfection of manner as here, yet his great qualities
are perceptible all over his work.   The enormous *Polyolbion*,
written in a metre the least suitable to continuous verse of any in
English—the Alexandrine—crammed with matter rebel to poetry,
and obliging the author to find his chief poetical attraction rather
in superadded ornament, in elaborately patched-on passages,
than in the actual and natural evolution of his theme, is still a
very great work in another than the mechanical sense.   Here
is a fairly representative passage :—

"The haughty Cambrian hills enamoured of their praise,
(As they who only sought ambitiously to raise
The blood of God-like Brute) their heads do proudly bear :
And having crown'd themselves sole regents of the air
(Another war with Heaven as though they meant to make)
Did seem in great disdain the bold affront to take,
That any petty hill upon the English side,
Should dare, not (with a crouch) to veil unto their pride.
When Wrekin, as a hill his proper worth that knew,
And understood from whence their insolency grew,
For all that they appear'd so terrible in sight,
Yet would not once forego a jot that was his right,
And when they star'd on him, to them the like he gave,
And answer'd glance for glance, and brave for brave :
That, when some other hills which English dwellers were,
The lusty Wrekin saw himself so well to bear

> Against the Cambrian part, respectless of their power ;
> His eminent disgrace expecting every hour
> Those flatterers that before (with many cheerful look)
> Had grac'd his goodly sight, him utterly forsook,
> And muffled them in clouds, like mourners veiled in black,
> Which of their utmost hope attend the ruinous wrack :
> That those delicious nymphs, fair Team and Rodon clear
> (Two brooks of him belov'd, and two that held him dear ;
> He, having none but them, they having none but he
> Which to their mutual joy might either's object be)
> Within their secret breast conceivèd sundry fears,
> And as they mix'd their streams, for him so mix'd their tears.
> Whom, in their coming down, when plainly he discerns,
> For them his nobler heart in his strong bosom yearns :
> But, constantly resolv'd, that dearer if they were)
> The Britons should not yet all from the English bear ;
> 'Therefore,' quoth he, 'brave flood, tho' forth by Cambria brought,
> Yet as fair England's friend, or mine thou would'st be thought
> (O Severn) let thine ear my just defence partake.' "

Happy phrases abound, and, moreover, every now and then there are set pieces, as they may be called, of fanciful description which are full of beauty ; for Drayton (a not very usual thing in a man of such unflagging industry, and even excellence of work) was full of fancy.   The fairy poem of *Nymphidia* is one of the most graceful trifles in the language, possessing a dancing movement and a felicitous choice of imagery and language which triumphantly avoid the trivial on the one hand, and the obviously burlesque on the other.   The singular satirical or quasi-satirical poems of *The Mooncalf*, *The Owl*, and *The Man in the Moon*, show a faculty of comic treatment less graceful indeed, but scarcely inferior, and the lyrics called *Odes* (of which the *Ballad of Agincourt* is sometimes classed as one) exhibit a command of lyric metre hardly inferior to the command displayed in that masterpiece.   In fact, if ever there was a poet who could write, and write, perhaps beautifully, certainly well, about any conceivable broomstick in almost any conceivable manner, that poet was Drayton.   His historical poems, which are inferior in bulk only to the huge *Polyolbion*, contain a great deal of most admirable work.   They consist of three divisions—*The Barons' Wars* in eight-lined stanzas, the *Heroic Epistles* (suggested, of course, by Ovid, though anything but Ovidian) in heroic couplets, *The Miseries of Queen Margaret* in the same stanza as *The Barons' Wars*, and *Four Legends* in stanzas of various form and range.   That this mass of work should possess, or should, indeed, admit of the charms of poetry which distinguish *The Faërie Queene* would be impossible, even if Drayton had been Spenser, which he was far from being.   But to speak of his "dull creeping narrative," to accuse him of the "coarsest vulgarities," of being "flat and prosaic," and so on, as was done by eighteenth-century critics, is absolutely uncritical, unless it be very much limited.   *The Barons' Wars* is somewhat dull, the author being too careful to give a minute history of a not particularly interesting subject, and neglecting to take the only possible means of making it interesting by bringing out strongly the characters of heroes and heroines, and so infusing a dramatic interest.   But this absence of character is a constant drawback to the historical poems of the time.   And even here we find many passages where the drawback of the stanza for narrative is most skilfully avoided, and where the vigour of the single lines and phrases is unquestionable on any sound estimate.

Still the stanza, though Drayton himself defends it (it should be mentioned that his prose prefaces are excellent, and constitute another link between him and Dryden), is something of a clog; and the same thing is felt in *The Miseries of Queen Margaret* and the *Legends*, where, however, it is again not difficult to pick out beauties.   The *Heroical Epistles* can be praised with less allowance. Their shorter compass, their more manageable metre (for Drayton was a considerable master of the earlier form of couplet), and the fact that a personal interest is infused in each, give them a great advantage; and, as always, passages of great merit are not infrequent.   Finally, Drayton must have the praise (surely not quite irrelevant) of a most ardent and lofty spirit of patriotism.   Never was there a better Englishman, and as his love of his country spirited him up to the brilliant effort of the *Ballad of Agincourt*, so it sustained him through the "strange herculean task" of the *Polyolbion*, and often put light and life into the otherwise lifeless mass of the historic poems.   Yet I have myself no doubt that these historic poems were a mistake, and that their composition, though prompted by a most creditable motive, the burning attachment to England which won the fight with Spain, and laid the foundation of the English empire, was not altogether, perhaps was not by any means, according to knowledge.

The almost invariable, and I fear it must be said, almost invariably idle controversy about priority in literary styles has been stimulated in the case of English satire by a boast of Joseph Hall's made in his own *Virgidemiarum*—

> " Follow me who list,
> And be the *second* English satirist."

It has been pleaded in Hall's favour that although the date of publication of his *Satires* is known, the date of their composition is not known.   It is not even necessary to resort to this kind of special pleading ; for nothing can be more evident than that the bravado is not very serious.   On the serious supposition, however, and if we are to suppose that publication immediately followed composition, Hall was anticipated by more than one or two predecessors, in the production of work not only specifically satirical but actually called satire, and by two at least in the adoption of the heroic couplet form which has ever since been consecrated to the subject.   Satirical poetry, of a kind, is of course nearly if not quite as old as the language, and in the hands of Skelton it had assumed various forms.   But the satire proper—the following of the great Roman examples of Horace, Juvenal, and Persius in general lashing of vice and folly—can hardly trace itself further back in England than George Gascoigne's *Steel Glass*, which preceded Hall's *Virgidemiarum* by twenty years, and is interesting not only for itself but as being ushered in by the earliest known verses of Walter Raleigh.   It is written in blank verse and is a rather rambling commentary on the text *vanitas vanitatum*, but it expressly calls itself a satire and answers sufficiently well to the

description.   More immediate and nearer examples were to be
found in the Satires of Donne and Lodge.   The first named were
indeed, like the other poetical works of their marvellously gifted
writer, not published till many years after; but universal tradition ascribes the whole of Donne's profane poems to his early
youth, and one document exists which distinctly dates "John
Donne, his Satires," as early as 1593.   We shall therefore deal
with them, as with the other closely connected work of their
author, here and in this chapter.   But there has to be mentioned
first the feebler but chronologically more certain work of Thomas
Lodge, *A Fig for Momus*, which fulfils both the requirements of
known date and of composition in couplets.   It appeared in
1595, two years before Hall, and is of the latest and weakest of
Lodge's verse work.   It was written or at least produced when
he was just abandoning his literary and adventurous career and
settling down as a quiet physician with no more wild oats to sow,
except, perhaps, some participation in popish conspiracy.   The
style did not lend itself to the display of any of Lodge's strongest
gifts—romantic fancy, tenderness and sweetness of feeling, or
elaborate embroidery of precious language.   He follows Horace
pretty closely and with no particular vigour.   Nor does the book
appear to have attracted much attention, so that it is just possible
that Hall may not have heard of it.   If, however, he had not, it is
certainly a curious coincidence that he, with Donne and Lodge,
should all have hit on the couplet as their form, obvious as its
advantages are when it is once tried.   For the rhyme points the
satirical hits, while the comparatively brief space of each distich
prevents that air of wandering which naturally accompanies satire
in longer stanzas.   At any rate after the work (in so many ways
remarkable) of Donne, Hall, and Marston, there could hardly
be any more doubt about the matter, though part of the method
which these writers, especially Donne and Marston, took to give
individuality and "bite" to their work was as faulty as it now
seems to us peculiar.

Ben Jonson, the least gushing of critics to his contemporaries,

said of John Donne that he was "the first poet of the world in
some things," and I own that without going through the long
catalogue of singularly contradictory criticisms which have been
passed on Donne, I feel disposed to fall back on and adopt this
earliest, simplest, and highest encomium.   Possibly Ben might
not have meant the same things that I mean, but that does not
matter.   It is sufficient for me that in one special point of the
poetic charm—the faculty of suddenly transfiguring common
things by a flood of light, and opening up strange visions to the
capable imagination—Donne is surpassed by no poet of any
language, and equalled by few.   That he has obvious and great
defects, that he is wholly and in all probability deliberately
careless of formal smoothness, that he adopted the fancy of his
time for quaint and recondite expression with an almost perverse
vigour, and set the example of the topsy-turvified conceits which
came to a climax in Crashaw and Cleveland, that he is almost
impudently licentious in thought and imagery at times, that he
alternates the highest poetry with the lowest doggerel, the noblest
thought with the most trivial crotchet—all this is true, and all
this must be allowed for; but it only chequers, it does not
obliterate, the record of his poetic gifts and graces.   He is, moreover, one of the most historically important of poets, although
by a strange chance there is no known edition of his poems
earlier than 1633, some partial and privately printed issues having
disappeared wholly if they ever existed.   His influence was second
to the influence of no poet of his generation, and completely
overshadowed all others, towards his own latter days and the
decades immediately following his death, except that of Jonson.
Thomas Carew's famous description of him as

> "A king who ruled as he thought fit
> The universal monarchy of wit,"

expresses the general opinion of the time; and even after the
revolt headed by Waller had dethroned him from the position,
Dryden, his successor in the same monarchy, while declining to

allow him the praise of "the best poet" (that is, the most exact
follower of the rules and system of versifying which Dryden himself preferred), allowed him to be "the greatest wit of the nation."

His life concerns us little, and its events are not disputed, or
rather, in the earlier part, are still rather obscure.   Born in 1573,
educated at both universities and at Lincoln's Inn, a traveller, a
man of pleasure, a law-student, a soldier, and probably for a time
a member of the Roman Church, he seems just before reaching
middle life to have experienced some religious change, took
orders, became a famous preacher, was made Dean of St. Paul's,
and died in 1631.

It has been said that tradition and probability point to the
composition of most, and that all but certain documentary
evidence points to the composition of some, of his poems in the
earlier part of his life.   Unless the date of the Harleian MS. is a
forgery, some of his satires were written in or before 1593, when
he was but twenty years old.   The boiling passion, without a
thought of satiety, which marks many of his elegies would also
incline us to assign them to youth, and though some of his
epistles, and many of his miscellaneous poems, are penetrated
with a quieter and more reflective spirit, the richness of fancy
in them, as well as the amatory character of many, perhaps
the majority, favour a similar attribution.   All alike display
Donne's peculiar poetical quality—the fiery imagination shining
in dark places, the magical illumination of obscure and shadowy
thoughts with the lightning of fancy.   In one remarkable respect
Donne has a peculiar cast of thought as well as of manner,
displaying that mixture of voluptuous and melancholy meditation,
that swift transition of thought from the marriage sheet to the
shroud, which is characteristic of French Renaissance poets, but
less fully, until he set the example, of English.   The best known and
most exquisite of his fanciful flights, the idea of the discovery of

"A bracelet of bright hair about the bone"

of his own long interred skeleton : the wish—

> " I long to talk with some old lover's ghost
> Who died before the god of love was born,"

and others, show this peculiarity. And it recurs in the most
unexpected places, as, for the matter of that, does his strong
satirical faculty. In some of his poems, as the *Anatomy of the
World*, occasioned by the death of Mrs. Elizabeth Drury, this
melancholy imagery mixed with touches (only touches here) of the
passion which had distinguished the author earlier (for the
Anatomy is not an early work), and with religious and philosophical meditation, makes the strangest amalgam—shot through,
however, as always, with the golden veins of Donne's incomparable
poetry. Expressions so strong as this last may seem in want of
justification. And the three following pieces, the "Dream," a
fragment of satire, and an extract from the *Anatomy*, may or may
not, according to taste, supply it :—

> " Dear love, for nothing less than thee
> Would I have broke this happy dream.
>   It was a theme
> For reason, much too strong for fantasy :
> Therefore thou wak'dst me wisely ; yet
> My dream thou brok'st not, but continued'st it :
> Thou art so true, that thoughts of thee suffice
> To make dreams true, and fables histories ;
> Enter these arms, for since thou thought'st it best
> Not to dream all my dream, let's act the rest.

> " As lightning or a taper's light
> Thine eyes, and not thy noise, wak'd me ;
>   Yet I thought thee
> (For thou lov'st truth) an angel at first sight,
> But when I saw thou saw'st my heart
> And knew'st my thoughts beyond an angel's art,
> When thou knew'st what I dreamt, then thou knew'st when
> Excess of joy would wake me, and cam'st then ;
> *I must confess, it could not choose but be
> Profane to think thee anything but thee.*

> " Coming and staying show'd thee thee,
> But rising makes me doubt that now
>   Thou art not thou.

That love is weak where fears are strong as he ;
'Tis not all spirit, pure and brave,
If mixture it of fear, shame, honour, have.
Perchance as torches which must ready be
Men light, and put out, so thou deal'st with me.
Thou cam'st to kindle, goest to come : then I
Will dream that hope again, or else would die."

————————

" O age of rusty iron ! some better wit
Call it some worse name, if ought equal it.
Th' iron age was, when justice was sold ; now
Injustice is sold dearer far ; allow
All claim'd fees and duties, gamesters, anon
The money, which you sweat and swear for 's gone
Into other hands ; so controverted lands
'Scape, like Angelica, the striver's hands.
If law be in the judge's heart, and he
Have no heart to resist letter or fee,
Where wilt thou appeal ? power of the courts below
Flows from the first main head, and these can throw
Thee, if they suck thee in, to misery,
To fetters, halters.   But if th' injury
Steel thee to dare complain, alas ! thou go'st
Against the stream upwards when thou art most
Heavy and most faint ; and in these labours they
'Gainst whom thou should'st complain will in thy way
Become great seas, o'er which when thou shalt be
Forc'd to make golden bridges, thou shalt see
That all thy gold was drowned in them before."

————————

" She, whose fair body no such prison was
But that a soul might well be pleased to pass
An age in her ; she, whose rich beauty lent
Mintage to other beauties, for they went
But for so much as they were like to her ;
She, in whose body (if we dare prefer
This low world to so high a mark as she),
The western treasure, eastern spicery,
Europe and Afric, and the unknown rest
Were easily found, or what in them was best ;
And when we've made this large discovery
Of all, in her some one part then will be

> Twenty such parts, whose plenty and riches is
> Enough to make twenty such worlds as this ;
> She, whom had they known, who did first betroth
> The tutelar angels and assigned one both
> To nations, cities, and to companies,
> To functions, offices, and dignities,
> And to each several man, to him and him,
> They would have giv'n her one for every limb ;
> She, of whose soul if we may say 'twas gold,
> Her body was th' electrum and did hold
> Many degrees of that ; we understood
> Her by her sight ; *her pure and eloquent blood*
> *Spoke in her cheeks, and so distinctly wrought*
> *That one might almost say, her body thought ;*
> She, she thus richly and largely hous'd is gone
> And chides us, slow-paced snails who crawl upon
> Our prison's prison earth, nor think us well
> Longer than whilst we bear our brittle shell."

But no short extracts will show Donne, and there is no room for a full anthology. He must be read, and by every catholic student of English literature should be regarded with a respect only " this side idolatry," though the respect need not carry with it blindness to his undoubtedly glaring faults.

Those faults are not least seen in his Satires, though neither the unbridled voluptuousness which makes his Elegies shocking to modern propriety, nor the far-off conceit which appears in his meditative and miscellaneous poems, is very strongly or specially represented here. Nor, naturally enough, is the extreme beauty of thought and allusion distinctly noteworthy in a class of verse which does not easily admit it. On the other hand, the force and originality of Donne's intellect are nowhere better shown. It is a constant fault of modern satirists that in their just admiration for Horace and Juvenal they merely paraphrase them, and, instead of going to the fountainhead and taking their matter from human nature, merely give us fresh studies of *Ibam forte via sacra* or the Tenth of Juvenal, adjusted to the meridians of Paris or London. Although Donne is not quite free from this fault, he is much freer than either of his contemporaries, Regnier or Hall. And the rough vigour of his sketches and single lines is admirable. Yet it is as rough as it is vigorous ; and the breakneck versification and contorted phrase of his satires, softened a little in Hall, roughened again and to a much greater degree in Marston, and reaching, as far as phrase goes, a rare extreme in the *Transformed Metamorphosis* of Cyril Tourneur, have been the subject of a great deal of discussion. It is now agreed by all the best authorities that it would be a mistake to consider this roughness unintentional or merely clumsy, and that it sprung, at any rate in great degree, from an idea that the ancients intended the *Satura* to be written in somewhat un- polished verse, as well as from a following of the style of Persius, the most deliberately obscure of all Latin if not of all classical poets. In language Donne is not (as far as his Satires are con- cerned) a very great sinner ; but his versification, whether by his own intention or not, leaves much to desire. At one moment the ten syllables are only to be made out by a Chaucerian lengthening of the mute *e ;* at another the writer seems to be emulating Wyatt in altering the accent of syllables, and coolly making the final iambus of a line out of such a word as "answer." It is no wonder that poets of the "correct" age thought him in need of rewriting ; though even they could not mistake the force of observation and expression which characterises his Satires, and which very frequently reappears even in his dreamiest metaphysics, his most recondite love fancies, and his warmest and most passionate hymns to Aphrodite Pandemos.

These artificial characteristics are supplemented in the Eliza- bethan satirists, other than Donne, by yet a third, which makes them, I confess, to me rather tedious reading, independently of their shambling metre, and their sometimes almost unconstruable syntax. This is the absurd affectation of extreme moral wrath against the corruptions of their time in which they all indulge. Marston, who is nearly the foulest, if not quite the foulest writer of any English classic, gives himself the airs of the most sensitive

puritan ; Hall, with a little less of this contrast, sins considerably
in the same way, and adds to his delinquencies a most petulant
and idle attempt to satirise from the purely literary point of view
writers who are a whole head and shoulders above himself.   And
these two, followed by their imitator, Guilpin, assail each other
in a fashion which argues either a very absurd sincerity of
literary jealousy, or a very ignoble simulation of it, for the
purpose of getting up interest on the part of the public.   Nevertheless, both Marston and Hall are very interesting figures in
English literature, and their satirical performances cannot be
passed over in any account of it.

Joseph Hall was born near Ashby de la Zouch, of parents in
the lower yeoman rank of life, had his education at the famous
Puritan College of Emanuel at Cambridge, became a Fellow
thereof, proceeded through the living of Hawstead and a canonry
at Wolverhampton to the sees of Exeter and Norwich, of the
latter of which he was violently deprived by the Parliament,
and, not surviving long enough to see the Restoration, died (1656)
in a suburb of his cathedral city.   His later life was important
for religious literature and ecclesiastical politics, in his dealings
with the latter of which he came into conflict, not altogether
fortunately for the younger and greater man of letters, with John
Milton.   His Satires belong to his early Cambridge days, and to
the last decade of the sixteenth century.   They have on the
whole been rather overpraised, though the variety of their matter
and the abundance of reference to interesting social traits of the
time to some extent redeem them.   The worst point about them,
as already noted, is the stale and commonplace impertinence with
which their author, unlike the best breed of young poets and men
of letters, attempts to satirise his literary betters ; while they are
to some extent at any rate tarred with the other two brushes of
corrupt imitation of the ancients, and of sham moral indignation.
Indeed the want of sincerity—the evidence of the literary exercise
—injures Hall's satirical work in different ways throughout.   We
do not, as we read him, in the least believe in his attitude of

Hebrew prophet crossed with Roman satirist, and the occasional presence of a vigorous couplet or a lively metaphor hardly redeems this disbelief.   Nevertheless, Hall is here as always a literary artist—a writer who took some trouble with his writings ; and as some of his satires are short, a whole one may be given:—

> " A gentle squire would gladly entertain
> Into his house some trencher-chaplain ; [1]
> Some willing man that might instruct his sons
> And that would stand to good conditions.
> First, that he lie upon the truckle bed,
> Whiles his young master lieth o'er his head.
> Second, that he do, on no default,[2]
> Ever presume to sit above the salt.
> Third, that he never change his trencher twice.
> Fourth, that he use all common courtesies ;
> Sit bare at meals, and one half rise and wait.
> Last, that he never his young master beat,
> But he must ask his mother to define,
> How many jerks she would his breech should line.
> All these observ'd he could contented be
> To give five marks and winter livery."

John Marston, who out-Halled Hall in all his literary mis-deeds, was, it would appear, a member of a good Shropshire family which had passed into Warwickshire.   He was educated at Coventry School, and at Brasenose College, Oxford, and passed early into London literary society, where he involved himself in the inextricable and not-much-worth-extricating quarrels which have left their mark in Jonson's and Dekker's dramas.   In the first decade of the seventeenth century he wrote several remark-able plays, of much greater literary merit than the work now to be criticised.   Then he took orders, was presented to the living of Christchurch, and, like others of his time, seems to have forsworn literature as an unholy thing.   He died in 1634. Here we are concerned only with two youthful works of his—

---

[1] " Chaplain "—trisyllable like " capellan."
[2] Missing syllable.

Pigmalion's Image and some Satires in 1598, followed in the same year by a sequel, entitled *The Scourge of Villainy.* In these works he called himself " W. Kinsayder," a pen-name for which various explanations have been given.   It is characteristic and rather comical that, while both the earlier Satires and *The Scourge* denounce lewd verse most fullmouthedly, *Pigmalion's Image* is a poem in the *Venus and Adonis* style which is certainly not inferior to its fellows in luscious descriptions.   It was, in fact, with the *Satires* and much similar work, formally condemned and burnt in 1599.   Both in Hall and in Marston industrious commentators have striven hard to identify the personages of the satire with famous living writers, and there may be a chance that some at least of their identifications (as of Marston's Tubrio with Marlowe) are correct.   But the exaggeration and insincerity, the deliberate "society-journalism " (to adopt a detestable phrase for a corresponding thing of our own days), which characterise all this class of writing make the identifications of but little interest. In every age there are writers who delight in representing that age as the very worst of the history of the world, and in ransacking literature and imagination for accusations against their fellows. The sedate philosopher partly brings and partly draws the conviction that one time is very like another.   Marston, however, has fooled himself and his readers to the very top of his and their bent ; and even Churchill, restrained by a more critical atmosphere, has not come quite near his confused and only half-intelligible jumble of indictments for indecent practices and crude philosophy of the moral and metaphysical kind.   A vigorous line or phrase occasionally redeems the chaos of rant, fustian, indecency, ill-nature, and muddled thought.

> " Ambitious Gorgons, wide-mouth'd Lamians,
> Shape-changing Proteans, damn'd Briarians,
> Is Minos dead, is Radamanth asleep,
> That ye thus dare unto Jove's palace creep ?
> What, hath Ramnusia spent her knotted whip,
> That ye dare strive on Hebe's cup to sip ?

> Ye know Apollo's quiver is not spent,
> But can abate your daring hardiment.
> Python is slain, yet his accursed race
> Dare look divine Astrea in the face ;
> Chaos return and with confusion
> Involve the world with strange disunion ;
> For Pluto sits in that adorèd chair
> Which doth belong unto Minerva's heir.
> O hecatombs ! O catastrophe !
> From Midas' pomp to Trus' beggary !
> Prometheus, who celestial fire
> Did steal from heaven, therewith to inspire
> Our earthly bodies with a sense-ful mind,
> Whereby we might the depth of nature find,
> Is ding'd to hell, and vulture eats his heart
> Which did such deep philosophy impart
> To mortal men."

The contrast of this so-called satire, and the really satiric touches of Marston's own plays, when he was not cramped by the affecta-tions of the style, is very curious.

Edward Gilpin or Guilpin, author of the rare book *Skialetheia*, published between the dates of Hall and Marston, is, if not a proved plagiarist from either, at any rate an obvious follower in the same track. There is the same exaggeration, the same petulant ill-nature, the same obscurity of phrase and ungainliness of verse, and the same general insincerity. But the fine flower of the whole school is perhaps to be found in the miraculous *Transformed Metamorphosis*, attributed to the powerful but extra-vagant dramatist, Cyril Tourneur, who wrote this kind of thing:—

> " From out the lake a bridge ascends thereto,
>   Whereon in female shape a serpent stands.
>   Who eyes her eye, or views her blue-vein'd brow,
>   With sense-bereaving glozes she enchants,
>   And when she sees a worldling blind that haunts
>   The pleasure that doth seem there to be found,
>   She soothes with Leucrocutanized sound.

> " Thence leads an entry to a shining hall
>   Bedecked with flowers of the fairest hue ;

> The Thrush, the Lark, and night's-joy Nightingale
>   There minulize their pleasing lays anew.
>   This welcome to the bitter bed of rue ;
>   This little room will scarce two wights contain
>   T' enjoy their joy, and there in pleasure reign.
>
> " But next thereto adjoins a spacious room,
>   More fairly fair adorned than the other :
> (O woe to him at sin-awhaping doom,
>   That to these shadows hath his mind given over)
>   For (O) he never shall his soul recover :
>   If this sweet sin still feeds him with her smack
>   And his repentant hand him hales not back." [1]

We could hardly end with anything farther removed from the clear philosophy and the serene loveliness of *The Faërie Queene*.

---

[1] Mr. Churton Collins is "tolerably confident," and perhaps he might have been quite certain, that Leucrocutanised refers to one of the Fauna of fancy,—a monster that spoke like a man. "Minulise," from μινυρίζω, "I sing."   "To awhape" = "to confound."

CHAPTER V

THE difficulty of writing about Shakespere is twofold ; and though it is a difficulty which, in both its aspects, presents itself when other great writers are concerned, there is no other case in which it besets the critic to quite the same extent. Almost everything that is worth saying has been already said, more or less happily. A vast amount has been said which is not in the least worth saying, which is for the most part demonstrably foolish or wrong. As Shakespere is by far the greatest of all writers, ancient or modern, so he has been the subject of commentatorial folly to an extent which dwarfs the expense of that folly on any other single subject. It is impossible to notice the results of this folly except at great length ; it is doubtful whether they are worth noticing at all ; yet there is always the danger either that some mischievous notions may be left undisturbed by the neglect to notice them, or that the critic himself may be presumed to be ignorant of the foolishness of his predecessors. These inconveniences, however, must here be risked, and it may perhaps be thought that the necessity of risking them is a salutary one. In no other case is it so desirable that an author should be approached by students with the minimum of apparatus.

The scanty facts and the abundant fancies as to Shakespere's life are a commonplace of literature. He was baptized on the 26th of April 1564 at Stratford-on-Avon, and must have been born either on the same day, or on one of those immediately preceding.   His father was John Shakespere, his mother Mary Arden, both belonging to the lower middle class and connected, personally and by their relations, with yeomanry and small landed gentry on the one side, and with well-to-do tradesmen on the other.   Nothing is known of his youth and little of his education ; but it was a constant tradition of men of his own and the immediately succeeding generation that he had little school learning.   Before he was nineteen he was married, at the end of November 1582, to Anne Hathaway, who was seven years his senior.   Their first child, Susannah, was baptized six months later.   He is said to have left Stratford for London in 1585, or thereabouts, and to have connected himself at once with the theatre, first in humble and then in more important positions. But all this is mist and myth.   He is transparently referred to by Robert Greene in the summer or autumn of 1592, and the terms of the reference prove his prosperity.   The same passage brought out a complimentary reference to Shakespere's intellectual and moral character from Chettle, Greene's editor.   He published *Venus and Adonis* in 1593, and *Lucrece* next year.   His plays now began to appear rapidly, and brought him money enough to buy, in 1597, the house of New Place at Stratford, and to establish himself there after, it is supposed, twelve years' almost complete absence from his birthplace and his family.   Documentary references to his business matters now become not infrequent, but, except as showing that he was alive and prosperous, they are quite uninteresting.   The same may be said of the marriages and deaths of his children.   In 1609 appeared the *Sonnets*, some of which had previously been printed in unauthorised and piratical publications.   He died on the 23d of April (supposed generally to be his birthday) 1616, and was buried at Stratford.   His plays had been only surreptitiously printed, the retention of a play in manuscript being of great importance to the actors, and the famous first folio did not appear till seven years after his death.

The canon of Shakespere's plays, like everything else connected with him, has been the subject of endless discussion.
There is no reasonable doubt that in his earlier days (the first
printed play among those ordinarily assigned to him, *Romeo and
Juliet*, dates from 1597) he had taken part in dramatic work
which is now mostly anonymous or assigned to other men, and
there is also no doubt that there may be passages in the accepted
plays which he owed to others. But my own deliberate judgment is that no important and highly probable ascription of
extant work to Shakespere can be made outside the canon as
usually printed, with the doubtful exception of *The Two Noble
Kinsmen;* and I do not believe that in the plays usually accepted,
any very important or characteristic portion is not Shakespere's.
As for Shakespere-Bacon theories, and that kind of folly, they
are scarcely worthy even of mention.   Nor among the numerous
other controversies and errors on the subject shall I meddle with
more than one—the constantly repeated assertion that England
long misunderstood or neglected Shakespere, and that foreign
aid, chiefly German (though some include Voltaire !), was required
to make her discover him.   A very short way is possible with
this absurdity.   It would be difficult to name any men more
representative of cultivated literary opinion and accomplishment
in the six generations (taking a generation at the third of a century) which passed between Shakespere's death and the battle of
Waterloo (since when English admiration of Shakespere will
hardly be denied), than Ben Jonson, John Milton, John Dryden,
Alexander Pope, Samuel Johnson, and Samuel Taylor Coleridge.
Their lives overlapped each other considerably, so that no period
is left uncovered.   They were all typical men of letters, each of
his own time, and four at least of them were literary dictators.
Now, Ben Jonson's estimate of Shakespere in prose and verse is
on record in more places than one, and is as authentic as the silly
stories of his envy are mythical.   If Milton, to his eternal disgrace, flung, for party purposes, the study of Shakespere as a reproach in his dead king's face, he had himself long before put on

record his admiration for him, and his own study is patent to every critical reader of his works.   Dryden, but a year or two after the death of Shakespere's daughter, drew up that famous and memorable eulogy which ought to be familiar to all, and which, long before any German had spoken of Shakespere, and thirty years before Voltaire had come into the world, exactly and precisely based the structure of Shakespere-worship.   Pope edited Shakespere.   Johnson edited him.   Coleridge is acknowledged as, with his contemporaries Lamb and Hazlitt, the founder of modern appreciation.   It must be a curious reckoning which, in face of such a catena as this, stretching its links over the whole period, maintains that England wanted Germans to teach her how to admire the writer whom Germans have done more to mystify and distort than even his own countrymen.

The work of Shakespere falls into three divisions very unequal in bulk.   There is first (speaking both in the order of time and in that of thought, though not in that of literary importance and interest) the small division of poems, excluding the *Sonnets*, but including *Venus and Adonis*, *The Rape of Lucrece*, and the few and uncertain but exquisite scraps, the *Lover's Complaint*, *The Passionate Pilgrim*, and so forth.   All these are likely to have been the work of early youth, and they are much more like the work of other men than any other part of Shakespere's work, differing chiefly in the superior sweetness of those wood-notes wild, which Milton justly, if not altogether adequately, attributed to the poet, and in the occasional appearance of the still more peculiar and unique touches of sympathy with and knowledge of universal nature which supply the main Shakesperian note.   The *Venus* and the *Lucrece* form part of a large collection (see last chapter) of extremely luscious, not to say voluptuous, poetry which the imitation of Italian models introduced into England, which has its most perfect examples in the earlier of these two poems, in numerous passages of Spenser, and in the *Hero and Leander* of Marlowe, but which was written, as will have been seen from what has been already said, with extra-

ordinary sweetness and abundance, by a vast number of Elizabethan
writers. There are extant mere *adespota*, and mere "minor poems"
(such as the pretty " Britain's Ida," which used to be printed as
Spenser's, and which some critics have rather rashly given to
Phineas Fletcher), good enough to have made reputation, if not
fortune, at other times. There is no reason to attribute to
Shakespere on the one hand, any deliberate intention of exe-
cuting a *tour de force* in the composition of these poems or,
in his relinquishment of the style, any deliberate rejection of
the kind as unworthy of his powers on the other. He appears
to have been eminently one of those persons who care neither
to be in nor out of the fashion, but follow it as far as suits
and amuses them. Yet, beautiful as these poems are, they
so manifestly do not present their author at the full of his
powers, or even preluding in the kind wherein the best of those
powers were to be shown, that they require comparatively little
critical notice. As things delightful to read they can hardly be
placed too high, especially the *Venus;* as evidences of the poet's
many-sided nature, they are interesting. But they are in somewhat
other than the usual sense quite "simple, sensuous, and passionate." The misplaced ingenuity which, neglecting the *unum
necessarium*, will busy itself about all sorts of unnecessary things,
has accordingly been rather hard put to it with them, and to find
any pasture at all has had to browse on questions of dialect, and
date, and personal allusion, even more jejune and even more
unsubstantial than usual.

It is quite otherwise with the *Sonnets.* In the first place nowhere in Shakespere's work is it more necessary to brush away
the cobwebs of the commentators. This side of madness, no
vainer fancies have ever entered the mind of man than those
which have been inspired by the immaterial part of the matter.
The very initials of the dedicatee "W. H." have had volumes
written about them ; the *Sonnets* themselves have been twisted
and classified in every conceivable shape ; the persons to whom
they are addressed, or to whom they refer, have been identified

with half the gentlemen and ladies of Elizabeth's court, and half the men of letters of the time ; and every extremity and eccentricity of non-natural interpretation has been applied to them. When they are freed from this torture and studied rationally, there is nothing mysterious about them except the mystery of their poetical beauty.   Some of them are evidently addressed in the rather hyperbolical language of affection, common at the time, and derived from the study of Greek and Italian writers, to a man ; others, in language not hyperbolical at all, to a woman.   Disdain, rivalry, suspense, short-lived joy, long sorrow, all the symptoms and concomitants of the passion of love—which are only commonplaces as death and life are commonplace—form their motives.   For my part I am unable to find the slightest interest or the most rudimentary importance in the questions whether the Mr. W. H. of the dedication was the Earl of Pembroke, and if so, whether he was also the object of the majority of the *Sonnets ;* whether the "dark lady," the "woman coloured ill," was Miss Mary Fitton ; whether the rival poet was Chapman.   Very likely all these things are true : very likely not one of them is true.   They are impossible of settlement, and if they were settled they would not in the slightest degree affect the poetical beauty and the human interest of the *Sonnets,* which, in a strange *reductio ad absurdum* of eighteenth century common-sense criticism, Hallam thought it impossible not to wish that Shakespere had not written, and which some critics, not perhaps of the least qualified, have regarded as the high water-mark of English, if not of all, poetry.

This latter estimate will only be dismissed as exaggerated by those who are debarred from appreciation by want of sympathy with the subject, or distracted by want of comprehension of it.   A harmony of the two chief opposing theories of poetry will teach us that we must demand of the very highest poetry first—the order is not material—a certain quality of expression, and secondly, a certain quality of subject.   What that quality of subject must be has been, as it seems to me, crudely and wrongly stated, but rightly indicated, in Mr. Matthew Arnold's formula of the " Criticism of

Life." That is to say, in less debatable words, the greatest poet
must show most knowledge of human nature. Now both these
conditions are fulfilled in the sonnets of Shakespere with a completeness and intensity impossible to parallel elsewhere. The
merits of the formal and expressive part hardly any one will now
question ; the sonnets may be opened almost at random with the
certainty of finding everywhere the phrases, the verses, the
passages which almost mechanically recur to our minds when we
are asked to illustrate the full poetical capacity and beauty of the
English tongue, such as :

> " The painful warrior, famoused for fight,
> After a thousand victories once foiled,
> Is from the book of honour razed quite
> And all the rest forgot for which he toiled ; "

or

> " When to the sessions of sweet silent thought
> I summon up remembrance of things past ;"

or

> " Was it the proud full sail of his great verse,
> Bound for the prize of all too precious you ? "

or

> " Then hate me if thou wilt,"

with the whole sonnet which it opens ; or

> " When in the chronicle of wasted time
> I see descriptions of the fairest wights,
> And beauty making beautiful old rhyme
> In praise of ladies dead and lovely knights ;"

or that most magnificent quatrain of all,

> " Let me not to the marriage of true minds
> Admit impediments.   Love is not love
> Which alters when it alteration finds,
> Or bends with the remover to remove."

Any competent judge of the formal part of poetry must admit
that its force can no farther go.   Verse and phrase cannot be
better moulded to the melodious suggestion of beauty.   Nor, as

even these scraps show, is the thought below the verse.   Even
if Hallam's postulate of misplaced and ill-regulated passion be
granted (and I am myself very far from granting it), the extraordinary wealth of thought, of knowledge, of nature, of self-
knowledge, of clear vision of others in the very midst of the
circumstances which might make for unclear vision, is still
unmistakable.   And if the poet's object was to catch up the sum
of love and utter it with or even without any special relation to
his own actual feelings for any actual person (a hypothesis which
human nature in general, and the nature of poets in particular,
makes not improbable), then it can only be said that he has
succeeded.   From Sappho and Solomon to Shelley and Mr.
Swinburne, many bards have spoken excellently of love : but
what they have said could be cut out of Shakespere's sonnets
better said than they have said it, and yet enough remain to
furnish forth the greatest of poets.

With the third and in every sense chief division of the work,
the necessities for explanation and allowance cease altogether.
The thirty-seven plays of the ordinary Shakesperian canon
comprise the greatest, the most varied, the most perfect work yet
done by any man in literature ; and what is more, the work of
which they consist is on the whole the most homogeneous and
the least unequal ever so done.   The latter statement is likely
to be more questioned than the former ; but I have no fear of
failing to make it out.   In one sense, no doubt, Shakespere is
unequal—as life is.   He is not always at the tragic heights of
Othello and Hamlet, at the comic raptures of Falstaff and Sir Toby,
at the romantic ecstasies of Romeo and Titania.   Neither is life.
But he is always—and this is the extraordinary and almost
inexplicable difference, not merely between him and all his contemporaries, but between him and all other writers—at the
height of the particular situation.   This unique quality is uniquely
illustrated in his plays.   The exact order of their composition is entirely unknown, and the attempts which have been made to arrange
it into periods, much more to rank play after play in regular

sequence, are obvious failures, and are discredited not merely by the inadequate means—such as counting syllables and attempting to classify the cadence of lines—resorted to in order to effect them, but by the hopeless discrepancy between the results of different investigators and of the same investigator at different times. We know indeed pretty certainly that *Romeo and Juliet* was an early play, and *Cymbeline* a late one, with other general facts of the same kind. We know pretty certainly that the *Henry the Sixth* series was based on a previous series on the same subject in which Shakespere not improbably had a hand ; that *King John* and *The Taming of the Shrew* had in the same way first draughts from the same or other hands, and so forth. But all attempts to arrange and elucidate a chronological development of Shakespere's mind and art have been futile. Practically the Shakesperian gifts are to be found *passim* in the Shakesperian canon—even in the dullest of all the plays, as a whole, *The Two Gentlemen of Verona*, even in work so alien from his general practice, and so probably mixed with other men's work, as *Titus Andronicus* and *Pericles*. There are rarely elsewhere—in *The Maid's Tragedy* of Fletcher, in *The Duchess of Malfy* of Webster, in *The Changeling* of Middleton — passages or even scenes which might conceivably have been Shakespere's. But there is, with the doubtful exception of *The Two Noble Kinsmen*, no play in any other man's work which as a whole or in very great part is Shakesperian, and there is no play usually recognised as Shakespere's which would not seem out of place and startling in the work of any contemporary.

This intense, or rather (for intense is not the right word) this extraordinarily diffused character, is often supposed to be a mere fancy of Shakespere-worshippers. It is not so. There is something, not so much in the individual flashes of poetry, though it is there too, as in the entire scope and management of Shakespere's plays, histories, tragedies, and comedies alike, which distinguishes them, and it is exactly the characteristic noted

above, and well put by Dryden in his famous definition of
Shakespere.   Perhaps the first branch or phase of this distinction
is that Shakespere is never, in the vulgar sense of the word,
unnatural.   He has not the slightest objection to horrors; the
alarmed foreign critics who described his theatre as a " shambles "
need not have gone farther than his greatest plays to justify themselves literally.   But with barely even the exception which has
so often to be made of *Titus Andronicus*, his horrors are never
sought beyond a certain usual and probable round of circumstance,
and are almost always tempered and humanised by touches of
humour or pathos, or both.   The cool sarcastic villany of Aaron
(a mood hit off nowhere out of Shakespere, except in Middleton's
De Flores, and not fully there) is the point on which I should
chiefly put the finger to justify at least a partial Shaksperian
authorship.   Contrast the character with the nightmare ghastlinesses
and extravagances not merely of Tourneur and Webster, but even
of Marlowe in Barabas, and the difference of Shakespere's handling
will be felt at once.   Another point which has been often, yet
perhaps not quite fully, noticed is the distinct and peculiar attitude
of Shakespere towards what is in the common sense called morality.   Nobody can possibly call him squeamish : I do not know
that even any French naturalist of the latest school has charged
the author of *Pericles*, and *Love's Labour Lost*, and *Henry IV.*,
with that *pruderie bête* of which they accuse Scott.   But he
never makes those forms of vice which most trouble and corrupt society triumphant; he never diverges into the morbid
pathology of the amatory passion, and above all, and most
remarkably of all, though I think least remarked, he never makes
his personages show the singular toleration of the most despicable immorality which almost all his dramatic contemporaries
exhibit.   One is constantly astonished at the end of an Elizabethan play, when, after vice has been duly baffled or punished,
and virtue rewarded (for they all more or less follow that rule),
reconciliations and forgivenesses of injuries follow, to observe the
complacency with which husbands who have sold their wives'

favours, wives who have been at the command of the first comer or the highest bidder, mix cheek by jowl, and apparently unrebuked, with the modest maidens, the virtuous matrons, the faithful lovers of the piece. Shakespere never does this. Mrs. Quickly is indeed at one time the confidante of Anne Fenton, and at another the complaisant hostess of Doll Tear-sheet, but not in the same play. We do not find Marina's master and mistress rewarded, as they would very likely have been by Fletcher or Middleton, with comfortable if not prominent posts at the court of Pericles, or the Government-house of Mytilene. The ugly and artistically unmanageable situation of the husband who trades in his wife's honour simply does not occur in all the wide license and variety of Shakespere's forty plays. He is in his own sense liberal as the most easy going can demand, but he never mixes vice and virtue. Yet again, while practising this singular moderation in the main element, in the most fertile motives, of tragedy and comedy respectively, he is equally alone in his use in both of the element of humour. And here we are on dangerous ground. To many excellent persons of all times since his own, as well as in it, Shakespere's humour and his use of it have been stumbling-blocks. Some of them have been less able to away with the use, some with the thing. Shakesperian clowns are believed to be red rags to some experienced playwrights and accomplished wits of our own days : the porter in *Macbeth*, the gravediggers in *Hamlet*, the fool in *Lear*, even the humours in *Love's Labour Lost* and *The Merchant of Venice* have offended. I avow myself an impenitent Shakesperian in this respect also. The constant or almost constant presence of that humour which ranges from the sarcastic quintessence of Iago, and the genial quintessence of Falstaff, through the fantasies of Feste and Edgar, down to the sheer nonsense which not unfrequently occurs, seems to me not only delightful in itself, but, as I have hinted already, one of the chief of those spells by which Shakespere has differentiated his work in the sense of universality from that of all other dramatists. I have used the word nonsense, and I may be thought to have partly given up my case by it. But nonsense, as hardly any critic but Hazlitt has had the courage to avow openly, is no small part of life, and it is a part the relish of which Englishmen, as the same great but unequal critic justly maintains, are almost alone in enjoying and recognising.   It is because Shakespere dares, and dares very frequently, simply *desipere*, simply to be foolish, that he is so pre-eminently wise. The others try to be always wise, and, alas ! it is not necessary to complete the antithesis.

These three things—restraint in the use of sympathy with suffering, restraint in the use of interest in voluptuous excess, and humour—are, as it seems to me, the three chief distinguishing points in Shakespere's handling which are not found in any of his contemporaries, for though there is humour in not a few of these, none of them is a perfect humorist in the same sense. Here, as well as in that general range or width of subject and thought which attracted Dryden's eulogium, he stands alone.   In other respects he shares the qualities which are perceptible almost throughout this wonderfully fertile department of literature ; but he shares them as infinitely the largest shareholder.   It is difficult to think of any other poet (for with Homer we are de- prived of the opportunity of comparison) who was so completely able to meet any one of his contemporaries on that contemporary's own terms in natural gift.   I say natural gift because, though it is quite evident that Shakespere was a man of no small reading, his deficiencies in general education are too constantly recorded by tradition, and rendered too probable by internal evidence, to be ignored or denied by any impartial critic.   But it is difficult to mention a quality possessed by any of the school (as it is loosely called), from Marlowe to Shirley, which he had not in greater measure ; while the infinite qualities which he had, and the others each in one way or another lacked, are evident.   On only one subject—religion—is his mouth almost closed ; certainly, as the few utterances that touch it show, from no incapacity of dealing with it, and apparently from no other dislike than a dislike to meddle with anything outside of the purely human province of which he felt that he was universal master—in short from an infinite reverence.

It will not be expected that in a book like the present—the whole space of which might very well be occupied, without any of the undue dilation which has been more than once rebuked, in dealing with Shakespere alone—any attempt should be made to criticise single plays, passages, and characters.   It is the less of a loss that in reality, as the wisest commentators have always either begun or ended by acknowledging, Shakespere is your only commentator on Shakespere.   Even the passages which corrupt printing, or the involved fashion of speaking peculiar to the time, make somewhat obscure at first, will in almost every case yield to the unassisted cogitation of any ordinarily intelligent person ; and the results so reached are far more likely to be the true results than the elaborate emendations which delight a certain class of editors.   A certain amount of mere glossary is of course necessary, but otherwise the fewer corks and bladders the swimmer takes with him when he ventures into " the ocean which is Shakespere," the better.   There are, however, certain common errors, some of which have survived even the last century of Shakespere-study and Shakespere-worship, which must perhaps be discussed.   For in the case of the greatest writers, the business of the critic is much more to shovel away the rubbish of his predecessors than to attempt any accumulation of his own.   The chief of these errors—or rather that error which practically swallows up all the others and can produce them again at any time—is that Shakespere was, if not exactly an inspired idiot, at any rate a mainly tentative if not purely unconscious artist, much of whose work is only not bad as art, while most, if not all of it, was originally produced with a minimum of artistic consciousness and design.   This enormous error, which is protean in form, has naturally induced the counter error of a too great insistence on the consciousness and elaboration of Shakespere's art.   The most elaborate theories of this art have been framed—theories involving the construction of perhaps as much baseless fabric as anything else connected with the subject,

which is saying a great deal. It appears to me in the highest
degree improbable that Shakespere had before him consciously
more than three purposes; but these three I think that he constantly had, and that he was completely successful in achieving
them. The first was to tell in every play a dramatically complete
story; the second was to work that story out by the means of
purely human and probable characters; and the third was to
give such form and ornaments to the working out as might please
the playgoers of his day. In pursuing the first two he was the
poet or dramatist of all time. In pursuing the third he was the
intelligent playwright. But (and here is the source of the
common error) it by no means follows that his attention, and his
successful attention, to his third purpose in any way interferes with,
or degrades, his excellence as a pursuer of the first two. In the
first place, it can escape no careful student that the merely playwright part of Shakespere's work is (as is the case with no other
dramatic author whatever) singularly separable. No generation
since his death has had the slightest difficulty in adapting by far
the greater part of his plays to use and popularity in its own day,
though the adaptation may have varied in liberty and in good
taste with the standards of the time. At the present day, while
almost all other old dramatists have ceased to be acted at all,
or are acted merely as curiosities, the adaptation of Shakespere
has become more and more a process of simple omission (without
the addition or alteration of anything) of parts which are either
unsuited to modern manners or too long for modern patience.
With the two usual exceptions, *Pericles* and *Titus Andronicus*
(which, despite the great beauty of parts, are evidently less Shakesperian as wholes than any others), there is not a single play of
the whole number that could not be—there are not many that
have not been—acted with success in our time. It would be
difficult to find a stronger differentia from the work of the mere
playwright, who invariably thinks first of the temporary conditions
of success, and accordingly loses the success which is not
temporary. But the second great difference of Shakespere is,

that even what may be in comparison called the ephemeral
and perishable parts of him have an extraordinary vitality, if
not theatrical yet literary, of their own.   The coarser scenes
of *Measure for Measure* and *The Comedy of Errors*, the satire on
fleeting follies in *Love's Labour Lost*, the uncomelier parts of *All's
Well that Ends Well*, the Doll Tear-sheet business of *Henry IV.*,
the comic by-play of *Troilus and Cressida*, may seem mere wood,
hay, and stubble in comparison with the nobler portions.   Yet
the fire of time has not consumed them : they are as delightful as
ever in the library if not on the stage.

Little or nothing need be said in defence of Shakespere as an
artist from the attacks of the older or Unity criticism.   That
maleficent giant can now hardly grin at the pilgrims whom he
once harassed.   But there are many persons who, not dreaming
of the Unities, still object in language less extravagant than
Voltaire's or George the Third's, but with hardly less decision,
to the "sad stuff," the *fumier* of Shakespere's admixture of
comedy with tragedy, of his digressions and episodes, of his
multifarious underplots and minor groups, and ramifications of
interest or intrigue.   The reply to this is not (as it might be, if
any reply were not superfluous, in the case of the Unity objection)
a reply of demonstration.   If any person experienced in literature,
and with an interest in it, experienced in life and with an interest
in that, asserts that Caliban and Trinculo interfere with his enjoyment of Ferdinand and Miranda ;   that the almost tragedy
of Hero is marred for him by the comedy of Beatrice and the
farce of Dogberry ; that he would have preferred *A Midsummer
Night's Dream* without the tedious brief effort of Quince and his
companions ; that the solemnity and passion of *Hamlet* and
Macbeth cause in him a revulsion against the porter and the
gravedigger ; that the Fool and Edgar are out of place in *Lear*,—
it is impossible to prove to him by the methods of any Euclid
or of any Aldrich that he is wrong.   The thing is essentially, if
not wholly, a matter of taste.   It is possible, indeed, to point
out, as in the case of the Unities, that the objectors, if they will

maintain their objection, must deny the position that the dramatic art holds up the mirror to Nature, and that if they deny it, the burden—a burden never yet successfully taken up by any one—of framing a new definition rests upon them.   But this is only a partial and somewhat inconclusive argument, and the person who genuinely dislikes these peculiarities of Shakespere is like a man who genuinely dislikes wine or pictures or human faces, that seem delightful and beautiful to others.   I am not aware of any method whereby I can prove that the most perfect claret is better than zoedone in flavour, or that the most exquisite creation of Botticelli or Lionardo is more beautiful than the cuts on the sides of railway novels.   Again, it is matter of taste.

It will be seen that I am not for my part afraid to avow myself a thoroughgoing Shakesperian, who accepts the weak points of his master as well as the strong.   It is often forgotten (indeed I do not know where I have seen it urged) that there is in Shakespere's case an excuse for the thousand lines that good Ben Jonson would have liked him to blot,—an excuse which avails for no one else.   No one else has his excuse of universality ; no one else has attempted to paint, much less has painted, the whole of life. It is because Shakespere has attempted this, and, in the judgment of at least some, has succeeded in it, that the spots in his sun are so different from the spots in all other suns.   I do not know an unnatural character or an unnatural scene in Shakespere, even among those which have most evidently been written to the gallery.   Everything in him passes, in some mysterious way, under and into that "species of eternity" which transforms all the great works of art, which at once prevents them from being mere copies of Nature, and excuses whatever there is of Nature in them that is not beautiful or noble.   If this touch is wanting anywhere (and it is wanting very seldom), that, I take it, is the best, indeed the only, sign that that passage is not Shakespere's,—that he had either made use of some other man's work, or that some other man had made use of his.   If such passages were of more frequent occurrence, this argument might be called a circular one.

But the proportion of such passages as I at least should exclude is so small, and the difference between them and the rest is so marked, that no improper begging of the question can be justly charged.   The plays in the *Globe* edition contain just a thousand closely-printed pages.   I do not think that there are fifty in all, perhaps not twenty—putting scraps and patches together—in which the Shakesperian touch is wanting, and I do not think that that touch appears outside the covers of the volume once in a thousand pages of all the rest of English literature.   The finest things of other men,—of Marlowe, of Fletcher, of Webster (who no doubt comes nearest to the Shake-sperian touch, infinitely as he falls short of the Shakesperian range),—might conceivably be the work of others.   But the famous passages of Shakespere, too numerous and too well known to quote, could be no one else's.   It is to this point that æsthetic criticism of Shakespere is constantly coming round with an almost monotonous repetition.   As great as all others in their own points of greatness ; holding points of greatness which no others even approach ; such is Shakespere.

There is a certain difficulty—most easily to be appreciated by those who have most carefully studied the literature of the period in question, and have most fully perceived the mistakes which confusion of exact date has induced in the consideration of the very complex subject before us—in selecting dramatists to group with Shakespere.   The obvious resource of taking him by himself would frustrate the main purpose of this volume, which is to show the general movement at the same time as the individual developments of the literature of 1560–1660.   In one sense Shakespere might be included in any one of three out of the four chapters which we have here devoted to the Elizabethan dramatists.   His earliest known, and probably much of his un-known work coincides with the period of tentative ; and his latest work overlaps very much of that period of ripe and somewhat over-ripe performance, at the head of which it has here been thought good to set Beaumont and Fletcher.   But there is a group of four notable persons who appear to have especial rights to be classed with him, if not in greatness, yet in character of work, and in the influences which played on that work.   They all, like him, took an independent part in the marvellous wit-combat of the last decade of Elizabeth, and they all like him survived, though for different lengths of time, to set an example to the third generation.   They are all, even the meanest of them, distinctly great men, and free alike from the immaturity, visible even in Lyly and Marlowe, which marked some of their older contemporaries, and from the decadence, visible even in Fletcher and Massinger, which marred their younger followers.   Furthermore, they were mixed up, as regards one another, in an inextricable but not uninteresting series of broils and friendships, to some part of which Shakespere himself may have been by no means a stranger.   These reasons have seemed sufficient for separating them from the rest, and grouping them round the captain.   They are Benjamin Jonson, George Chapman, John Marston, and Thomas Dekker.

The history of Ben Jonson (the literary history that is to for the known facts of his life are simple enough) is curious and perhaps unique.   Nothing is really known of his family; but as, at a time when Scotchmen were not loved in England, he maintained his Annandale origin, there should be, especially after Mr. Symonds's investigations as to his career, no doubt that he at least believed himself to be of Border extraction, as was also, it may be remembered, his great disciple, panegyrist, slanderer, and (with the substitution of an easy for a rugged temper), analogue, John Dryden.   The fact of these two typical Englishmen being of half or whole Scotch descent will not surprise any one who does not still ignore the proper limits of England. Nobody doubts that his father (or rather stepfather, for he was a posthumous child, born 1573, and his mother married again) was a bricklayer, or that he went to Westminster School; it seems much more dubious whether he had any claim to anything but an honorary degree from either university, though he received

that from both.   Probably he worked at bricklaying, though the
taunts of his rivals would, in face of the undoubted fact of his
stepfather's profession, by no means suffice to prove it.   Certainly he went through the chequered existence of so many
Elizabethan men of letters ; was a soldier in Flanders, an actor, a
duellist (killing his man, and escaping consequences only by
benefit of clergy), a convert to Romanism, a "revert" to the
Anglican Church, a married man, a dramatist.   The great play
of *Every Man in his Humour*, though afterwards much altered, was
perhaps acted first at the Rose Theatre in 1596, and it established
Jonson's reputation, though there is no reasonable doubt that he
had written other things.   His complicated associations and
quarrels with Dekker, Marston, Chapman, and others, have
occupied the time of a considerable number of persons ; they
lie quite beyond our subject, and it may be observed without
presumption that their direct connection, even with the literary
work (*The Poetaster*, *Satiro-mastix*, and the rest) which is usually
linked to them, will be better established when critics have left
off being uncertain whether *A* was *B*, or *B*, *C*.   Even the most
famous story of all (the disgrace of Jonson with others for
Eastward Ho! as a libel against the Scots, for which he was
imprisoned, and, being threatened with mutilation, was by his
Roman mother supplied with poison), though told by himself, does not rest on any external evidence.   What is certain
is that Jonson was in great and greater request, both as a writer
of masks and other *divertissements* for the Court, and as a head
and chief of literary conviviality at the "Mermaid," and other
famous taverns.   Here, as he grew older, there grew up round
him that "Tribe of Ben," or admiring clique of young literary
men, which included almost all the most remarkable poets, except
Milton, of the late Jacobean and early Caroline period, and
which helped to spread his fame for at least two generations, and
(by Waller's influence on St. Evremond) to make him the first
English man of letters who was introduced by a great critic of
the Continent to continental attention as a worker in the English

vernacular.   At last he was made Poet Laureate, and in 1618
he took a journey to Scotland, and stayed there for some time
with Drummond of Hawthornden.   The celebrated conversations
noted by the host have been the very centre battle-ground of all
fights about Ben Jonson's character.   It is sufficient here to say that
though Ben's chief defender, Gifford, may have been too hard on
Drummond, it is difficult, if not impossible, to think that the
"Notes of Conversations" were made in a friendly spirit.   They
contain for their bulk an extraordinary amount of interesting
matter, and much sound criticism ; but which of us in modern
days would care to have such "notes" taken ?   A man thinks
that there are faults in a friend's work, and in the usual exaggeration of conversation he says that it is "rubbish."   The Drum-
monds of this world note it down and it passes as a deliberate
judgment.   He must be a fortunate man, or an exceptional recluse,
who has not found some good-natured friend anticipate Drummond, and convey the crude expression (probably heightened in
conveyance) direct to the person concerned.   After this visit
(which must have been at the end of 1618) Jonson suffered the
calamity of having his study destroyed by fire, and lost much
MS. work.   He lived many years longer and retained his literary
primacy, but was unfortunate in money matters, and even in
reception of his work by the public, though the literary men of
his day made no mistake about him.   He died in 1637, and the
last of the many stories clustering round his name is the famous
one of the inscription, "O rare Ben Jonson !"   A year later, a
tombeau, or collection of funeral poems, entitled *Jonsonus Virbius*,
showed the estimate entertained of him by the best and brightest
wits of the time.

His life was thus a life of struggle, for he was never rich, and
lived for the most part on the most unsatisfactory of all sources
of income—casual bounties from the king and others.   It is not
improbable that his favour with the Court and with Templar society
(which was then very unpopular with the middle classes), had
something to do with the ill-reception of his later plays.   But his

literary influence was very great, and with Donne he determined
much of the course of English poetry for many years, and retained
a great name even in the comparative eclipse of the "Giant
Race" after the Restoration.   It was only when the study of
Shakespere became a favourite subject with persons of more
industry than intelligence in the early eighteenth century, that a
singular fabric of myth grew up round Ben Jonson.   He was
pictured as an incarnation of envy, hatred, malice, and all un-
charitableness, directed in the first place towards Shakespere, and
then towards all other literary craftsmen.   William Gifford, his
first competent editor, set himself to work to destroy this, and
undoubtedly succeeded.   But the acrimony with which Gifford
tinctured all his literary polemic perhaps rather injured his treatment of the case; even yet it may be doubted whether Ben
Jonson has attained anything like his proper place in English
literary history.

Putting aside the abiding influence of a good long-continued
course of misrepresentation, it is still not difficult to discover the
source of this under-estimate, without admitting the worst view or
even any very bad view of Ben Jonson's character, literary and
personal.   It may be granted that he was rough and arrogant, a
scholar who pushed scholarship to the verge of pedantry, a critic
who sometimes forgot that though a schoolmaster may be a critic,
a critic should not be merely a schoolmaster.   His work is
saturated with that contempt of the *profanum vulgus* which the
profanum vulgus (humanly enough) seldom fails to return.
Moreover, it is extremely voluminous, and it is by no means equal.
Of his eighteen plays, three only—*Every Man in his Humour,
The Alchemist*, and the charming fragment of *The Sad Shepherd*—
can be praised as wholes.   His lovely *Masques* are probably unread by all but a few scores, if so many, in each generation.
His noble sinewy prose is, for the most part, unattractive in
subject.   His minor poems, though not a few of them are known
even to smatterers in literature, are as a whole (or at least it
would seem so) unknown.   Yet his merits are extraordinary.

"Never" in his plays (save *The Sad Shepherd*) "tender," and still more rarely "sublime," he yet, in words much better applied to him than to his pupil Dryden, "wrestles with and conquers time." Even his enemies admit his learning, his vigour, his astonishing power of work. What is less generally admitted, despite in one case at least the celebrity of the facts that prove it, is his observation, his invention, and at times his anomalous and seemingly contradictory power of grace and sweetness. There is no more singular example of the proverb, "Out of the eater came forth meat, and out of the strong sweetness," which has been happily applied to Victor Hugo, than the composition, by the rugged author of *Sejanus* and *Catiline*, of *The Devil is an Ass* and *Bartholomew Fair*, of such things as

> "Here lies to each her parents ruth;"

or the magnificent song,

> "Drink to me only with thine eyes;"

or the crown and flower of all epitaphs,

> "Underneath this sable herse." [1]

But these three universally-known poems only express in quintessence a quality of Jonson's which is spread all about his minor pieces, which appears again perfectly in *The Sad Shepherd*, and which he seems to have kept out of his plays proper rather from bravado than for any other reason. His prose will be noticed separately in the next chapter, but it may be observed here that it is saturated with the same literary flavour which pervades all his work. None of his dramatic fellows wrote anything that can compare to it, just as none of them wrote anything that surpasses the songs and snatches in his plays, and the best things in his miscellaneous works. The one title which no competent criticism has ever grudged him is that of best epitaph-writer in the English language, and only those who have failed to consider the difficulties and the charm of that class of composition will

---

[1] Ben is sometimes deprived of this, *me judice*, most irreligiously.

consider this faint praise.   Nevertheless, it was no doubt upon
drama that Jonson concentrated his powers, and the unfavourable
judgments which have been delivered on him chiefly refer to
this.

A good deal of controversy has arisen out of the attribution
to him, which is at least as old as *The Return from Parnassus*, of
being minded to classicise the English drama.   It is certain that
he set a value on the Unities which no other English dramatist
has set, and that in *The Alchemist* at least he has given something like a perfect example of them, which is at the same time
an admirable play.   Whether this attention is at all responsible
for the defects which are certainly found in his work is a very
large question.   It cannot be denied that in that work, with perhaps
the single exception just mentioned, the reader (it is, except in the
case of *Every Man in his Humour*, generations since the playgoer
had any opportunity of judging) finds a certain absence of sympathetic attraction, as well as, for all the formal unity of the pieces,
a lack of that fusing poetic force which makes detail into a whole.
The amazing strength of Jonson's genius, the power with which
he has compelled all manner of unlikely elements into his service,
is evident enough, but the result usually wants charm.   The
drawbacks are (always excepting *The Alchemist*) least perceptible
in *Every Man in his Humour*, the first sprightly runnings (unless
The Case is Altered is older) of Jonson's fancy, the freshest
example of his sharp observation of "humours."   Later he sometimes overdid this observation, or rather he failed to bring its results
sufficiently into poetic or dramatic form, and, therefore, is too
much for an age and too little for all time.   But *Every Man in
his Humour* is really charming.   Bobadil, Master Stephen, and
Kitely attain to the first rank of dramatic characters, and others
are not far behind them in this respect.   The next play, *Every
Man out of his Humour*, is a great contrast, being, as even the
doughty Gifford admits, distinctly uninteresting as a whole, despite
numerous fine passages.   Perhaps a little of its want of attraction
must be set down to a pestilent habit of Jonson's, which he had

at one time thought of applying to *Every Man in his Humour*, the habit of giving foreign, chiefly Italian, appellations to his characters, describing, and as it were labelling them—Deliro, Macilente, and the like.   This gives an air of unreality, a figurehead and type character.   *Cynthia's Revels* has the same defects, but is to some extent saved by its sharp raillery of euphuism.   With *The Poetaster* Jonson began to rise again.   I think myself that the personages and machinery of the Augustan Court would be much better away, and that the implied satire on contemporaries would be tedious if it could not, as it fortunately can, be altogether neglected.   But in spite of these drawbacks, the piece is good.   Of *Sejanus* and Jonson's later Roman play *Catiline* I think, I confess, better than the majority of critics appear to think.   That they have any very intense tragic interest will, indeed, hardly be pretended, and the unfortunate but inevitable comparison with *Coriolanus* and *Julius Cæsar* has done them great and very unjust harm.   Less human than Shakespere's "godlike Romans" (who are as human as they are godlike), Jonson's are undoubtedly more Roman, and this, if it is not entirely an attraction, is in its way a merit.   But it was not till after *Sejanus* that the full power of Jonson appeared.   His three next plays, *Volpone*, *Epicene*, and *The Alchemist*, could not have been written by any one but himself, and, had they not been written, would have left a gap in English which nothing from any other literature could supply.   If his attitude had been a little less virtuous and a little more sarcastic, Jonson would in these three plays have anticipated Swift.   Of the three, I prefer the first and the last—the last being the best of all.   *Epicene* or the *Silent Woman* was specially liked by the next generation because of its regularity, and of the skill with which the various humours are all wrought into the main plot.   Both these things are undeniable, and many of the humours are in themselves amusing enough.   But still there is something wanting, which is supplied in *Volpone* and *The Alchemist*.   It has been asked whether that disregard of probability, which is one of Jonson's greatest faults, does not appear in the recklessness with which "The Fox" exposes himself to utter ruin, not so much to gratify any sensual desire or obtain any material advantage, as simply to indulge his combined hypocrisy and cynicism to the very utmost. The answer to this question will very much depend on each reader's taste and experience. It is undeniable that there have been examples of perverse indulgence in wickedness for wickedness' sake, which, rare as they are, go far to justify the creation of Volpone. But the unredeemed villany of the hero, with whom it is impossible in any way to sympathise, and the sheer brutality of the fortune-hunting dupes who surround him, make it easier to admire than to like the play. I have little doubt that Jonson was to some extent sensible of this, for the comic episode or underplot of Sir Politick and Lady Would-be is very much more loosely connected with the centre interest (it is only by courtesy that it can be said to be connected at all), than is usual with him, and this is an argument in favour of its having been introduced as a makeweight.

From the drawbacks of both these pieces *The Alchemist* is wholly free. Jonson here escaped his usual pitfall of the unsympathetic, for the vices and follies he satirises are not loathsome, only contemptible at worst, and not always that. He found an opportunity of exercising his extraordinary faculty of concentration as he nowhere else did, and has given us in Sir Epicure Mammon a really magnificent picture of concupiscence, of sensual appetite generally, sublimed by heat of imagination into something really poetic. The triumvirate of adventurers, Subtle, Dol and Face (for Dol has virile qualities), are not respectable, but one does not hate them ; and the gulls are perfection. If any character could be spared it is the "Angry Boy," a young person whose humours, as Jonson himself admits of another character elsewhere, are "more tedious than diverting." *The Alchemist* was followed by *Catiline*, and *Catiline* by *Bartholomew Fair*, a play in which singularly vivid and minute pictures of manners, very amusing sketches of character,

and some capital satire on the Puritans, do not entirely redeem a
profusion of the coarsest possible language and incident. *The Devil
is an Ass* comes next in time, and though no single character is
the equal of Zeal-of-the-land Busy in *Bartholomew Fair*, the
play is even more amusing.   The four last plays, *The Staple
of News, The Magnetic Lady, The New Inn*, and *The Tale of a
Tub*, which Jonson produced after long absence from the stage,
were not successful, and were both unkindly and unjustly called
by Dryden "Ben's dotages."   As for the charming *Sad Shepherd*,
it was never acted, and is now unfinished, though it is believed that
the poet completed it.   It stands midway as a pastoral *Féerie*
between his regular plays and the great collection of ingenious
and graceful masques and entertainments, which are at the top
of all such things in England (unless *Comus* be called a masque),
and which are worth comparing with the ballets and spectacle
pieces of Molière.   Perhaps a complete survey of Jonson's work
indicates, as his greatest defect, the want of passion.   He could
be vigorous, he could be dignified, he could be broadly humorous,
and, as has been said, he could combine with these the apparently
incompatible, or, at least, not closely-connected faculty of grace.
Of passion, of rapture, there is no trace in him, except in the
single instance—in fire mingled with earth—of Sir Epicure
Mammon.   But the two following passages—one from *Sejanus*,
one from *The Sad Shepherd*—will show his dignity and his
pathos.   No extract in brief could show his humour :—

> *Arr.* " I would begin to study 'em,[1] if I thought
>   They would secure me.   May I pray to Jove
>   In secret and be safe ? ay, or aloud,
>   With open wishes, so I do not mention
>   Tiberius or Sejanus ? Yes I must,
>   If I speak out.   'Tis hard that.   May I think
>   And not be racked ?   What danger is't to dream,
>   Talk in one's sleep or cough ?   Who knows the laws ?
>   May I shake my head without a comment ?   Say

---

[1] To wit the "arts" of suffering and being silent, by which his interlocutor
Lepidus has explained his own safety from delation.

It rains, or it holds up, and not be thrown
Upon the Gemonies? These now are things,
Whereon men's fortune, yea, their fate depends.
Nothing hath privilege 'gainst the violent ear.
No place, no day, no hour, we see, is free,
Not our religious and most sacred times
From some one kind of cruelty : all matter,
Nay, all occasion pleaseth. Madmen's rage,
The idleness of drunkards, women's nothing,
Jester's simplicity, all, all is good
That can be catcht at. Nor is now the event
Of any person, or for any crime
To be expected ; for 'tis always one :
Death, with some little difference of place
Or time. What's this? Prince Nero, guarded !"

_Æg._ "A spring, now she is dead ! of what? of thorns,
Briars and brambles? thistles, burs and docks?
Cold hemlock, yews? the mandrake, or the box?
These may grow still ; but what can spring beside?
Did not the whole earth sicken when she died
As if there since did fall one drop of dew,
But what was wept for her ! or any stalk
Did bear a flower, or any branch a bloom,
After her wreath was made ! In faith, in faith,
You do not fair to put these things upon me,
Which can in no sort be : Earine
Who had her very being and her name
With the first knots or buddings of the spring,
Born with the primrose and the violet
Or earliest roses blown : when Cupid smiled
And Venus led the Graces out to dance,
And all the flowers and sweets in nature's lap
Leaped out and made their solemn conjuration
To last but while she lived ! Do not I know
How the vale withered the same day? how Dove,
Dean, Eye, and Erwash, Idel, Snite and Soare
Each broke his urn, and twenty waters more
That swelled proud Trent, shrunk themselves dry, that since
No sun or moon, or other cheerful star,
Looked out of heaven, but all the cope was dark
As it were hung so for her exequies !
And not a voice or sound to ring her knell

But of that dismal pair, the screeching owl
And buzzing hornet ! Hark ! hark ! hark ! the foul
Bird ! how she flutters with her wicker wings !
Peace ! you shall hear her screech.

Cla. Good Karolin, sing,
Help to divert this phant'sy.

Kar. All I can :

Sings while Æg. reads the song.

‘ Though I am young and cannot tell
Either what Death or Love is well,
Yet I have heard they both bear darts
And both do aim at human hearts :
And then again, I have been told,
Love wounds with heat, as Death with cold ;
So that I fear they do but bring
Extremes to touch and mean one thing.

‘ As in a ruin we it call
One thing to be blown up, or fall ;
Or to our end, like way may have,
By a flash of lightning or a wave :
So Love's inflamèd shaft or brand
May kill as soon as Death's cold hand,
Except Love's fires the virtue have
To fright the frost out of the grave.' ”

Of no two contemporary men of letters in England can it be
said that they were, intellectually speaking, so near akin as Ben
Jonson and George Chapman. The translator of Homer was a
good deal older than Jonson, and exceedingly little is known of
his life. He was pretty certainly born near Hitchin in Hertford-
shire, the striking situation of which points his reference to it
even in these railroad days. The date is uncertain—it may have
been 1557, and was certainly not later than 1559—so that he
was the oldest of the later Elizabethan school who survived into
the Caroline period. He perhaps entered the University of Oxford
in 1574. His first known work, *The Shadow of Night*, dates from
1594 ; and a reference of Meres's shows that he was known for
tragedy four years later. In 1613 he, Jonson (a constant friend of his

whose mutual fidelity refutes of itself the silly calumnies as to
Jonson's enviousness, for of Chapman only, among his colleagues,
was he likely to be jealous), and Marston were partners in the
venture of *Eastward Ho!* which, for some real or fancied slight
on Scotland, exposed the authors to danger of the law. He was
certainly a *protégé* of Prince Henry, the English Marcellus, and he
seems to have received patronage from a much less blameless
patron, Carr, Earl of Somerset. His literary activity was continuous and equal, but it was in his later days that he attempted
and won the crown of the greatest of English translators.
"Georgius Chapmannus, Homeri metaphrastes" the posy of his
portrait runs, and he himself seems to have quite sunk any expectation of fame from his original work in the expectation of
remembrance as a translator of the Prince of Poets. Many
other interesting traits suggest, rather than ascertain, themselves in
reference to him, such as his possible connection with the early
despatch of English troupes of players to Germany, and his
adoption of contemporary French subjects for English tragedy.
But of certain knowledge of him we have very little. What is
certain is that, like Drayton (also a friend of his), he seems to
have lived remote and afar from the miserable quarrels and
jealousies of his time ; that, as has been already shown by dates,
he was a kind of English Fontenelle in his overlapping of both
ends of the great school of English poets ; and that absolutely
no base personal gossip tarnishes his poetical fame. The splendid
sonnet of Keats testifies to the influence which his work long had
on those Englishmen who were unable to read Homer in the
original. A fine essay of Mr. Swinburne's has done, for the first
time, justice to his general literary powers, and a very ingenious
and, among such hazardous things, unusually probable conjecture
of Mr. Minto's identifies him with the "rival poet" of Shakespere's
Sonnets. But these are adventitious claims to fame. What is
not subject to such deduction is the assertion that Chapman
was a great Englishman who, while exemplifying the traditional
claim of great Englishmen to originality, independence, and

versatility of work, escaped at once the English tendency to lack of scholarship, and to ignorance of contemporary continental achievements, was entirely free from the fatal Philistinism in taste and in politics, and in other matters, which has been the curse of our race, was a Royalist, a lover, a scholar, and has left us at once one of the most voluminous and peculiar collections of work that stand to the credit of any literary man of his country.   It may be that his memory has gained by escaping the danger of such revelations or scandals as the Jonson confessions to Drummond, and that the lack of attraction to the ordinary reader in his work has saved him from that comparison which (it has perhaps been urged *ad nauseam*) is the bane of just literary judgment.   To those who always strive to waive all such considerations, these things will make but little difference.

The only complete edition of Chapman's works dates from our own days, and its three volumes correspond to a real division of subject.   Although, in common with all these writers, Chapman has had much uncertain and some improbable work fathered on him, his certain dramas supply one of the most interesting studies in our period.   As usual with every one except Shakespere and (it is a fair reason for the relatively disproportionate estimate of these so long held) Beaumont and Fletcher, they are extremely unequal.   Not a certain work of Chapman is void of interest.   The famous *Eastward Ho!* (one of the liveliest comedies of the period dealing with London life) was the work of three great writers, and it is not easy to distribute its collaboration.   That it is not swamped with "humours" may prove that Jonson's learned sock was put on by others.   That it is neither grossly indecent nor extravagantly sanguinary, shows that Marston had not the chief hand in it, and so we are left to Chapman.   What he could do is not shown in the list of his own certain plays till *All Fools*. *The Blind Beggar of Alexandria* (1596 ?) and *An Humorous Day's Mirth* show that singular promiscuousness—that heaping together of scenes without order or connection—which we have noticed in the first dramatic period, not to mention that the way in which the characters speak of themselves, not as "I" but by their names in the third person, is also unmistakable. But *All Fools* is a much more noteworthy piece, and though Mr. Swinburne may have praised it rather highly, it would certainly take place in a collection of the score best comedies of the time not written by Shakespere. *The Gentleman Usher* and *Monsieur d'Olive* belong to the same school of humorous, not too pedantic comedy, and then we come to the strange series of Chapman's French trage-dies, *Bussy d'Ambois*, *The Revenge of Bussy d'Ambois*, *Byron's Conspiracy*, *The Tragedy of Charles*, *Duke of Byron*, and *The Tragedy of Philip Chabot*, *Admiral of France*. These singular plays stand by themselves. Whether the strong influence which Marlowe exercised on Chapman led the later poet (who it must be remembered was not the younger) to continue *The Massacre of Paris*, or what other cause begat them, cannot now be asserted or even guessed without lost labour. A famous criticism of Dryden's attests his attention to them, but does not, perhaps, to those who have studied Dryden deeply, quite express the influence which Chapman had on the leader of post-Restoration tragedy. As plays, the whole five are models of what plays should not be ; in parts, they are models of what plays should be. Then Chapman re-turned to the humour-comedy and produced two capital specimens of it in *May-Day* and *The Widow's Tears*. *Alphonsus*, *Emperor of Germany*, which contains long passages of German, and *Revenge for Honour*, two tragedies which were not published till long after Chap-man's death, are to my mind very dubiously his. Mr. Swinburne, in dealing with them, availed himself of the hypothesis of a mellowing, but at the same time weakening of power by age. It may be so, and I have not the slightest intention of pronouncing decidedly on the subject. They bear to my mind much more mark of the decadent period of Charles I., when the secret of blank verse was for a time lost, and when even men who had lived in personal friendship with their great predecessors lapsed into the slipshod stuff that we find in Davenant, in his followers, and among them even in the earlier plays of Dryden. It is, of

course, true that this loosening and slackening of the standard
betrays itself even before the death of Chapman, which happened
in 1634. But I cannot believe that the author of *Bussy d'Ambois*
(where the verse is rude enough but never lax) and the contemporary or elder of Shakespere, Marlowe, and all the great race,
could ever have been guilty of the slovenliness which, throughout,
marks *Revenge for Honour*.

The second part of Chapman's work, his original verse, is
much inferior in bulk and in interest of matter to the first and
third. Yet, is it not perhaps inferior to either in giving evidence
of the author's peculiarities; while the very best thing he ever
wrote (a magnificent passage in *The Tears of Peace*) is contained
in it. Its component parts are, however, sufficiently odd. It
opens with a strange poem called *The Shadow of Night*, which
Mr. Swinburne is not wrong in classing among the obscurest
works in English. The mischievous fashion of enigmatic writing,
already glanced at in the section on satire, was perhaps an
offshoot of euphuism; and certainly Chapman, who never exhibits
much taint of euphuism proper, here out-Herods Herod and out-
Tourneurs Tourneur. It was followed by an equally singular
attempt at the luscious school of which *Venus and Adonis* is the
most famous. *Ovid's Banquet of Sense* has received high praise
from critics whom I esteem. For my own part I should say that
it is the most curious instance of a radically unpassionate nature,
trying to lash itself into passion, that our language contains. Then
Chapman tried an even bolder flight in the same dialect—the
continuation of Marlowe's unfinished *Hero and Leander*. In this
attempt, either by sheer force of his sinewy athletics, or by
some inspiration derived from the " Dead Shepherd," his pre-
decessor, he did not fail, curious as is the contrast of the two
parts. *The Tears of Peace*, which contains his finest work, is in
honour of Prince Henry—a worthy work on a worthy subject,
which was followed up later by an epicedium on the prince's
lamented death. Besides some epigrams and sonnets, the chief
other piece of this division is the disastrous *Andromeda Liberata,*

which unluckily celebrates the nuptials—stained with murder,
adultery, and crime of all sorts — of Frances Howard and
Robert Carr. It is in Chapman's most allusive and thorniest
style, but is less interesting intrinsically than as having given
occasion to an indignant prose vindication by the poet, which,
considering his self-evident honesty, is the most valuable document
in existence for explaining the apparently grovelling panegyric of
the sixteenth and seventeenth century. It makes clear (what
indeed an intelligent reader might gather for himself) that the
traditional respect for rank and station, uniting with the tendency
to look for patterns and precedents in the classics for almost
everything, made of these panegyrics a kind of school exercise, in
which the excellence of the subject was taken for granted, and
the utmost hyperbole of praise was only a "common form" of
composition, to which the poet imparted or added what grace of
style or fancy he could, with hardly a notion of his ascriptions
being taken literally.

But if Chapman's dramas have been greatly undervalued, and
if his original poems are an invaluable help to the study of the
time, there is no doubt that it is as a translator that he made and
kept the strongest hold on the English mind. He himself spoke
of his Homeric translations (which he began as early as 1598,
doing also Hesiod, some Juvenal, and some minor fragments,
Pseudo-Virgilian, Petrarchian and others) as "the work that he
was born to do." His version, with all its faults, outlived the
popularity even of Pope, was for more than two centuries the
resort of all who, unable to read Greek, wished to know what the
Greek was, and, despite the finical scholarship of the present day,
is likely to survive all the attempts made with us. I speak with
all humility, but as having learnt Homer from Homer himself, and
not from any translation, prose or verse. I am perfectly aware of
Chapman's outrageous liberties, of his occasional unfaithfulness
(for a libertine need not necessarily be unfaithful in translation),
and of the condescension to his own fancies and the fancies of
his age, which obscures not more perhaps than some condescen-

sions which nearness and contemporary influences prevent some of us from seeing the character of the original. But at the same time, either I have no skill in criticism, and have been reading Greek for fifty years to none effect, or Chapman is far nearer Homer than any modern translator in any modern language. He is nearer in the Iliad than in the Odyssey—an advantage resulting from his choice of vehicle. In the Odyssey he chose the heroic couplet, which never can give the rise and fall of the hexameter. In the Iliad, after some hesitation between the two (he began as early as 1598), he preferred the fourteener, which, at its best, is the hexameter's nearest substitute. With Chapman it is not always at its best—very far from it. If he never quite relapses into the sheer doggerel of the First Period, he sometimes comes perilously near to it. But he constantly lifts his wings and soars in a quite different measure which, when he keeps it up for a little, gives a narrative vehicle unsurpassed, and hardly equalled, in English poetry for variation of movement and steady forward flow combined. The one point in which the Homeric hexameter is unmatched among metres is its combination of steady advance with innumerable ripples and eddies in its course, and it is here that Chapman (though of course not fully) can partly match it. It is, however, one of the testimonies to the supreme merit of the Homeric poems that every age seems to try to imitate them in its own special mannerisms, and that, consequently, no age is satisfied with the attempts of another. It is a second, that those who know the original demur at all.

The characteristics of Chapman, then, are very much those of Jonson with a difference. Both had the same incapacity of unlaboured and forceless art, the same insensibility to passion, the same inability to rise above mere humours and contemporary oddities into the region of universal poetry. Both had the same extensive learning, the same immense energy, the same (if it must be said) arrogance and contempt of the vulgar. In casual strokes, though not in sustained grasp, Chapman was Jonson's superior;

but unlike Jonson he had no lyric gift, and unlike Jonson he let his learning and his ambitious thought clog and obscure the flow of his English. Nor does he show in any of his original work the creative force of his younger friend. With the highest opinion reasonably possible of Chapman's dramas, we cannot imagine him for a moment composing a *Volpone* or an *Alchemist*—even a *Bartholomew Fair;* while he was equally, or still more, incapable of Jonson's triumphs in epigram and epitaph, in song and ode. A certain shapelessness is characteristic of everything that Chapman did—an inability, as Mr. Swinburne (to whom every one who now writes on Chapman must acknowledge indebtedness), has said, "to clear his mouth of pebbles, and his brow of fog." His long literary life, which must have exceeded half a century, and his great learning, forbid our setting this down as it may be set in the case of many of his contemporaries, and especially in the case of those two to whom we are now coming, as due to youth, to the imperfect state of surrounding culture, to want of time for perfecting his work, and so forth. He is the "Bègue de Vilaines," the heroic Stammerer of English literature—a man who evidently had some congenital defect which all his fire and force, all his care and curiosity, could not overcome. Yet are his doings great, and it is at least probable that if he had felt less difficulty in original work, he would not have been prompted to set about and finish the noble work of translation which is among the best products of an unsatisfactory kind, and which will outlive the cavils of generations of etymologists and aorist-grinders. He has been so little read that four specimens of his different manners—the early "tenebrous" style of *The Shadow of Night*, the famous passage from *Bussy d'Ambois* which excited Lamb's enthusiasm, and a sample from both *Iliad* and *Odyssey*—may be given :

> " In this vast thicket (whose description's task
> The pens of fairies and of fiends would ask :
> So more than human-thoughted horrible)
> The souls of such as lived implausible,

In happy empire of this goddess' glories,
And scorned to crown her fanes with sacrifice, [1]
Did ceaseless walk ; exspiring fearful groans,
Curses and threats for their confusions.
Her darts, and arrows, some of them had slain :
Others her dogs eat, painting her disdain,
After she had transformed them into beasts :
Others her monsters carried to their nests,
Rent them in pieces, and their spirits sent
To this blind shade, to wail their banishment.
The huntsmen hearing (since they could not hear)
Their hounds at fault, in eager chase drew near,
Mounted on lions, unicorns, and boars,
And saw their hounds lie licking of their sores
Some yearning at the shroud, as if they chid
Her stinging tongues, that did their chase forbid :
By which they knew the game was that way gone.
Then each man forced the beast he rode upon,
T' assault the thicket ; whose repulsive thorns
So gall'd the lions, boars, and unicorns,
Dragons and wolves, that half their courages
Were spent in roars, and sounds of heaviness :
Yet being the princeliest, and hardiest beasts,
That gave chief fame to those Ortygian forests,
And all their riders furious of their sport,
A fresh assault they gave, in desperate sort :
And with their falchions made their way in wounds,
The thicket open'd, and let in the hounds."

Bu. "What dismal change is here ; the good old Friar
Is murther'd, being made known to serve my love ;
And now his restless spirit would forewarn me
Of some plot dangerous and imminent.
Note what he wants ?   He wants his upper weed,
He wants his life and body ; which of these
Should be the want he means, and may supply me
With any fit forewarning ?   This strange vision
(Together with the dark prediction
Used by the Prince of Darkness that was raised
By this embodied shadow) stir my thoughts
With reminiscion of the spirit's promise,

---

[1] The rhyme, bad as it is, is not unprecedented.

Who told me, that by any invocation
I should have power to raise him, though it wanted
The powerful words and decent rites of art ;
Never had my set brain such need of spirit
T' instruct and cheer it ; now, then, I will claim
Performance of his free and gentle vow
T' appear in greater light and make more plain
His rugged oracle.   I long to know
How my dear mistress fares, and be inform'd
What hand she now holds on the troubled blood
Of her incensèd lord.   Methought the spirit
(When he had utter'd his perplex'd presage)
Threw his changed countenance headlong into clouds,
His forehead bent, as it would hide his face,
He knock'd his chin against his darken'd breast,
And struck a churlish silence through his powers.
Terror of darkness ! O, thou king of flames !
That with thy music-footed horse dost strike
The clear light out of crystal on dark earth,
And hurl'st instructive fire about the world,
Wake, wake, the drowsy and enchanted night
That sleeps with dead eyes in this heavy riddle ;
Or thou great prince of shades where never sun
Sticks his far darted beams, whose eyes are made
To shine in darkness, and see ever best
Where sense is blindest : open now the heart
Of thy abashed oracle, that for fear
Of some ill it includes, would fain lie hid,
And rise thou with it in thy greater light."

"For Hector's glory still he stood, and ever went about
To make him cast the fleet such fire, as never should go out ;
Heard Thetis' foul petition, and wished in any wise
The splendour of the burning ships might satiate his eyes.[1]
From him yet the repulse was then to be on Troy conferred,
The honour of it given the Greeks ; which thinking on, he stirr'd
With such addition of his spirit, the spirit Hector bore
To burn the fleet, that of itself was hot enough before.
But now he fared like Mars himself, so brandishing his lance
As, through the deep shades of a wood, a raging fire should glance,

---

[1] This line alone would suffice to exhibit Chapman's own splendour at his best.

Held up to all eyes by a hill ; about his lips a foam
Stood as when th' ocean is enraged ; his eyes were overcome
With fervour and resembled flames, set off by his dark brows,
And from his temples his bright helm abhorrèd lightnings throws ;
For Jove, from forth the sphere of stars, to his state put his own
And all the blaze of both the hosts confined in him alone.
And all this was, since after this he had not long to live,
This lightning flew before his death, which Pallas was to give
(A small time thence, and now prepared) beneath the violence
Of great Pelides.   In meantime, his present eminence
Thought all things under it ; and he, still where he saw the stands
Of greatest strength and bravest arm'd, there he would prove his hands,
Or no where ; offering to break through, but that passed all his power
Although his will were past all theirs, they stood him like a tower
Conjoined so firm, that as a rock, exceeding high and great,
And standing near the hoary sea, bears many a boisterous threat
Of high-voiced winds and billows huge, belched on it by the storms ;
So stood the Greeks great Hector's charge, nor stirred their battellous forms."

                    " This the Goddess told,
        And then the morning in her throne of gold
        Surveyed the vast world ; by whose orient light
        The nymph adorn'd me with attires as bright,
        Her own hands putting on both shirt and weed
        Robes fine, and curious, and upon my head
        An ornament that glittered like a flame ;
        Girt me in gold ; and forth betimes I came
        Amongst my soldiers, roused them all from sleep,
        And bade them now no more observance keep
        Of ease, and feast, but straight a shipboard fall,
        For now the Goddess had inform'd me all.
        Their noble spirits agreed ; nor yet so clear
        Could I bring all off, but Elpenor there
        His heedless life left.   He was youngest man
        Of all my company, and one that wan
        Least fame for arms, as little for his brain ;
        Who (too much steep'd in wine and so made fain
        To get refreshing by the cool of sleep,
        Apart his fellows plung'd in vapours deep,
        And they as high in tumult of their way)
        Suddenly waked and (quite out of the stay
        A sober mind had given him) would descend
        A huge long ladder, forward, and an end

> Fell from the very roof, full pitching on
> The dearest joint his head was placed upon,
> Which quite dissolved, let loose his soul to hell."

With regard to Marston (of whose little-known personality something has been said in connection with his satires) I find myself somewhat unable to agree with the generality of critics, who seem to me to have been rather taken in by his blood-and-thunder work, his transpontine declamation against tyrants, and his affectation of a gloomy or furious scorn against mankind. The uncouthness, as well as the suspicion of insincerity, which we noted in his satirical work, extend, as it seems to me, also to his dramas ; and if we class him as a worker in horrors with Marlowe earlier, and with Webster and Ford later, the chief result will be to show his extreme inferiority to them. He is even below Tourneur in this respect, while, like Tourneur, he is exposed to the charge of utterly neglecting congruity and proportion. With him we relapse not merely from the luminous perfection of Shakespere, from the sane order of work which was continued through Fletcher, and the best of Fletcher's followers, but from the more artificial unity of Jonson, back into the chaotic extravagances of the First Period. Marston, like the rest, is fond of laughing at *Jeronimo*, but his own tragic construction and some of his own tragic scenes are hardly less bombastic, and scarcely at all less promiscuous than the tangled horrors of that famous melodrama. Marston, it is true, has lucid intervals— even many of them. Hazlitt has succeeded in quoting many beautiful passages, one of which was curiously echoed in the next age by Nat. Lee, in whom, indeed, there was a strong vein of Elizabethan melodrama. The sarcasm on philosophical study in *What You Will* is one of the very best things of its own kind in the range of English drama,—light, sustained, not too long nor too short, in fact, thoroughly "hit off."

> "*Delight* my spaniel slept, whilst I baused[1] leaves,
> Tossed o'er the dunces, pored on the old print

---

[1] Kissed.

Of titled words, and still my spaniel slept.
Whilst I wasted lamp oil, bated my flesh,
Shrunk up my veins, and still my spaniel slept,
And still I held converse with Zabarell,
Aquinas, Scotus, and the musty saws
Of antique Donate : still my spaniel slept.
Still on went I : first *an sit anima*,
Then, an' 'twere mortal.   O hold, hold !
At that they are at brain buffets, fell by the ears,
Amain [pell-mell] together—still my spaniel slept.
Then whether 'twere corporeal, local, fixed,
Ex traduce ; but whether 't had free will
Or no, hot philosophers
Stood banding factions all so strongly propped,
I staggered, knew not which was firmer part ;
But thought, quoted, read, observed and pried,
Stuffed noting-books, and still my spaniel slept.
At length he waked and yawned, and by yon sky
For aught I know, he knew as much as I."

There is real pathos in *Antonio and Mellida*, and real satire in *Parasitaster* and *The Malcontent*.   Hazlitt (who had a very high opinion of Marston) admits that the remarkable inequalities of this last piece "seem to show want of interest in the subject."   This is an odd explanation, but I suspect it is really only an anticipation in more favourable words of my own theory, that Marston's tragic and satiric moods were not really sincere ; that he was a clever man who found a fashion of satire and a fashion of blood-and-thunder tragedy prevailing, and threw himself into both without much or any heart in the matter.   This is supported by the curious fact that almost all his plays (at least those extant) were produced within a very few years, 1602—1605, though he lived thirty years after the latter date, and more than twenty af.er his last dated appearances in literature, *The Insatiate Countess*, and *Eastward Ho !*   That he was an ill-tempered person with considerable talents, who succeeded, at any rate for a time, in mistaking his ill-temper for *sæva indignatio*, and his talents for genius, is not, I think, too harsh a description of Marston.   In the hotbed of the literary influences of the time, these conditions of his produced some remarkable fruit. But when my friend Professor Minto attributes to him "amazing and almost Titanic energy," mentions "life" several times over as one of the chief characteristics of his personages (I should say that they had as much life as violently-moved marionettes), and discovers "amiable and admirable characters" among them, I am compelled not, of course, to be positive that my own very different estimate is right, but to wonder at the singularly different way in which the same things strike different persons, who are not as a rule likely to look at them from very different points of view.

Marston's plays, however, are both powerful enough and famous enough to call for a somewhat more detailed notice. *Antonio and Mellida*, the earliest and if not the best as a whole, that which contains the finest scenes and fragments, is in two parts —the second being more properly called *The Revenge of Antonio*. The revenge itself is of the exaggerated character which was so popular with the Elizabethan dramatists, but in which (except in the famous Cornwall and Gloucester scene in *Lear*) Shakespere never indulged after his earliest days. The wicked tyrant's tongue is torn out, his murdered son's body is thrown down before him, and then the conspirators, standing round, gibe, curse, and rant at him for a couple of pages before they plunge their swords into his body. This goodly conclusion is led up to by a sufficient quantity of antecedent and casual crimes, together with much not very excellent fooling by a court gull, Balurdo, who might be compared with Shakespere's fools of the same kind, with very great advantage, by those who do not appreciate the latter. The beautiful descriptive and reflective passages which, in Lamb's *Extracts*, gave the play its reputation, chiefly occur towards the beginning, and this is the best of them :—

> *And.* "Why man, I never was a Prince till now.
> 'Tis not the bared pate, the bended knees,
> Gilt tipstaves, Tyrian purple, chairs of state,
> Troops of pied butterflies, that flutter still
> In greatness summer, that confirm a prince :

> 'Tis not the unsavoury breath of multitudes,
> Shouting and clapping, with confusèd din ;
> That makes a prince.   No, Lucio, he's a king,
> A true right king, that dares do aught save wrong,
> Fears nothing mortal, but to be unjust,
> Who is not blown up with the flattering puffs
> Of spungy sycophants : who stands unmov'd
> Despite the jostling of opinion :
> Who can enjoy himself, maugre the throng
> That strive to press his quiet out of him :
> Who sits upon Jove's footstool as I do
> Adoring, not affecting majesty :
> Whose brow is wreathèd with the silver crown
> Of clear content : this, Lucio, is a king,
> And of this empire, every man's possessed
> That's worth his soul."

Sophonisba, which followed, is much less rambling, but as bloody and extravagant.   The scene where the witch Erichtho plays Succubus to Syphax, instead of the heroine, and in her form, has touches which partly, but not wholly, redeem its extravagance, and the end is dignified and good.   *What You Will*, a comedy of intrigue, is necessarily free from Marston's worst faults, and here the admirable passage quoted above occurs.   But the main plot—which turns not only on the courtship, by a mere fribble, of a lady whose husband is supposed to be dead, and who has very complacently forgotten all about him, but on a ridiculous plot to foist a pretender off as the dead husband itself—is simply absurd.   The lack of probability, which is the curse of the minor Elizabethan drama, hardly anywhere appears more glaringly.   *Parasitaster*, or *The Fawn*, a satirical comedy, is much better, but the jealous hatred of *The Dutch Courtesan* is again not made probable.   Then came Marston's completest work in drama, *The Malcontent*, an anticipation, after Elizabethan fashion, of *Le Misanthrope* and *The Plain Dealer*.   Though not free from Marston's two chief vices of coarseness and exaggerated cynicism, it is a play of great merit, and much the best thing he has done, though the reconciliation,

at the end, of such a husband and such a wife as Piero and
Aurelia, between whom there is a chasm of adultery and murder,
again lacks verisimilitude.   It is to be observed that both in *The
Fawn* and *The Malcontent* there are disguised dukes—a fact not
testifying any very great originality, even in borrowing.   Of
Eastward Ho! we have already spoken, and it is by no means
certain that *The Insatiate Countess* is Marston's.   His reputation
would not lose much were it not.   A *fabliau*-like underplot of
the machinations of two light-o'-love citizens' wives against their
husbands is not unamusing, but the main story of the Countess
Isabella, a modern Messalina (except that she adds cruelty to the
vices of Messalina) who alternately courts lovers and induces their
successors to assassinate them, is in the worst style of the whole
time—the tragedy of lust that is not dignified by the slightest
passion, and of murder that is not excused by the slightest poetry
of motive or treatment.   Though the writing is not of the lowest
order, it might have been composed by any one of some thirty or
forty writers.   It was actually attributed at the time to William
Barksted, a minor poet of some power, and I am inclined to
think it not Marston's, though my own estimate of him is, as will
have been seen, not so high as some other estimates.   It is
because those estimates appear to me unduly high that I have
rather accentuated the expression of my own lower one.   For the
last century, and perhaps longer, the language of hyperbole has
been but too common about our dramatists, and I have known
more than one case in which the extravagant praise bestowed
upon them has, when students have come to the works themselves, had a very disastrous effect of disappointment.   It is,
therefore, all the more necessary to be candid in criticism where
criticism seems to be required.

As to the last of our good company, there is fortunately very
little risk of difference of opinion.   A hundred years ago Thomas
Dekker was probably little more than a name to all but professed
students of Elizabethan literature, and he waited longer than any
of his fellows for due recognition by presentation of his work in

a complete form.   It is not fifteen years since his plays were
collected ; it is scarcely as many months since his prose works
had the same honour.   Yet, since attention was directed to
Dekker in any way, the best authorities have been unanimous in
his praise.   Lamb's famous outburst of enthusiasm, that he had
" poetry enough for anything," has been soberly endorsed by two
full generations of the best judges, and whatever differences of
detail there may be as to his work, it is becoming more and more
the received, and correctly-received opinion, that, as his collaborator Webster came nearest to Shakespere in universalising
certain types in the severer tragedy, so Dekker has the same
honour on the gently pathetic side.   Yet this great honour is
done to one of the most shadowy personalities in literature.   We
have four goodly volumes of his plays and five of his other works ;
yet of Thomas Dekker, the man, we know absolutely less
than of any one of his shadowy fellows.   We do not know when
he was born, when he died, what he did other than writing in
the certainly long space between the two unknown dates.   In
1637 he was by his own words a man of threescore, which, as
it has been justly remarked, may mean anything between fifty-five
and seventy.   He was in circumstances a complete contrast to
his fellow-victim in Jonson's satire, Marston.   Marston was apparently a gentleman born and bred, well connected, well educated,
possessed of some property, able to make testamentary disposi-
tions, and probably in the latter part of his life, when Dekker
was still toiling at journalism of various kinds, a beneficed clergyman in country retirement.   Dekker was, it is to be feared, what
the arrogance of certain members of the literary profession has
called, and calls, a gutter-journalist—a man who had no regular
preparation for the literary career, and who never produced
anything but hand-to-mouth work.   Jonson went so far as to
say that he was a "rogue ;" but Ben, though certainly not a
rogue, was himself not to be trusted when he spoke of people
that he did not like ; and if there was any but innocent roguery
in Dekker he has contrived to leave exactly the opposite im-

pression stamped on every piece of his work. And it is particularly interesting to note, that constantly as he wrote in collaboration, one invariable tone, and that the same as is to be found in his undoubtedly independent work, appears alike in plays signed with him by persons so different as Middleton and Webster, as Chettle and Ford. When this is the case, the inference is certain, according to the strictest rules of logic. We can define Dekker's idiosyncrasy almost more certainly than if he had never written a line except under his own name. That idiosyncrasy consists, first, of an exquisite lyrical faculty, which, in the songs given in all collections of extracts, equals, or almost equals, that of Shakespere; secondly, of a faculty for poetical comedy, for the comedy which transcends and plays with, rather than grasps and exposes, the vices and follies of men; thirdly, for a touch of pathos again to be evened only to Shakespere's; and lastly, for a knack of representing women's nature, for which, except in the master of all, we may look in vain throughout the plentiful dramatic literature of the period, though touches of it appear in Greene's Margaret of Fressingfield, in Heywood, in Middleton, and in some of the anonymous plays which have been fathered indifferently, and with indifferent hopelessness of identification, on some of the greatest of names of the period, on some of the meanest, and on an equal number of those that are neither great nor mean.

Dekker's very interesting prose works we shall treat in the next chapter, together with the other tracts into whose class they fall, and some of his plays may either go unnoticed, or, with those of the dramatists who collaborated with him, and whose (notably in the case of *The Roaring Girl*) they pretty evidently were more than his. His own characteristic pieces, or those in which his touch shows most clearly, though they may not be his entirely, are *The Shoemaker's Holiday*, *Old Fortunatus*, *Satiromastix*, *Patient Grissil*, *The Honest Whore*, *The Whore of Babylon*, *If it be not Good the Devil is in it*, *The Virgin Martyr*, *Match me in London*, *The Son's Darling*, and *The Witch of Edmonton*. In every one of these the same characteristics appear, but the strangely composite fashion of writing of the time makes them appear in differing measures. *The Shoemaker's Holiday* is one of those innumerable and yet singular pieces in which the taste of the time seems to have so much delighted, and which seem so odd to modern taste,—pieces in which a plot or underplot, as the case may be, of the purest comedy of manners, a mere picture of the life, generally the lower middle-class life of the time, is united with hardly a thought of real dramatic conjunction to another plot of a romantic kind, in which noble and royal personages, with, it may be, a dash of history, play their parts. The crowning instance of this is Middleton's *Mayor of Queenborough ;* but there are scores and hundreds of others, and Dekker specially affects it. *The Shoemaker's Holiday* is principally distinguished by the directness and raciness of its citizen sketches. *Satiromastix* (the second title of which is " The Untrussing of the Humorous Poet ") is Dekker's reply to *The Poetaster*, in which he endeavours to retort Jonson's own machinery upon him. With his customary disregard of congruity, however, he has mixed up the personages of Horace, Crispinus, Demetrius, and Tucca, not with a Roman setting, but with a purely romantic story of William Rufus and Sir Walter Tyrrel, and the king's attempt upon the fidelity of Tyrrel's bride. This incongruous mixture gives one of the most charming scenes of his pen, the apparent poisoning of Celestina by her father to save her honour. But as Lamb himself candidly confessed, the effect of this in the original is marred, if not ruined, by the farcical surroundings, and the more farcical upshot of the scene itself,—the poisoning being, like Juliet's, a mere trick, though very differently fortuned. In *Patient Grissil* the two exquisite songs, " Art thou poor " and " Golden slumbers kiss thine eyes," and the sympathetic handling of Griselda's character (the one of all others to appeal to Dekker) mark his work. In all the other plays the same notes appear, and there is no doubt that Mr. Swinburne is wholly right in singling out from *The Witch of Edmonton* the feminine characters of Susan, Winifred, and the witch herself, as showing Dekker's unmatched command of the colours in which to paint womanhood. In the great debate as to the authorship of *The Virgin Martyr*, everything is so much conjecture that it is hard to pronounce authoritatively. Gifford's cool assumption that everything bad in the play is Dekker's, and everything good Massinger's, will not hold for a moment ; but, on the other side, it must be remembered that since Lamb there has been a distinct tendency to depreciate Massinger. All that can be said is, that the grace and tenderness of the Virgin's part are much more in accordance with what is certainly Dekker's than with what is certainly Massinger's, and that either was quite capable of the Hircius and Spungius passages which have excited so much disgust and indignation—disgust and indignation which perhaps overlook the fact that they were no doubt inserted with the express purpose of heightening, by however clumsily designed a contrast, the virgin purity of Dorothea the saint.

It will be seen that I have reserved *Old Fortunatus* and *The Honest Whore* for separate notice. They illustrate, respectively, the power which Dekker has in romantic poetry, and his command of vivid, tender, and subtle portraiture in the characters, especially, of women. Both, and especially the earlier play, exhibit also his rapid careless writing, and his ignorance of, or indifference to, the construction of a clear and distinctly outlined plot. *Old Fortunatus* tells the well-known story of the wishing cap and purse, with a kind of addition showing how these fare in the hands of *Fortunatus's* sons, and with a wild intermixture (according to the luckless habit above noted) of kings and lords, and pseudo-historical incidents. No example of the kind is more chaotic in movement and action. But the interlude of Fortune with which it is ushered in is conceived in the highest romantic spirit, and told in verse of wonderful effectiveness, not to mention two beautiful songs ; and throughout the play the allegorical or supernatural passages show the same character. Nor are the more prosaic parts inferior, as, for instance, the pretty dialogue of Orleans and Galloway, cited by Lamb, and the fine passage where Andelocia says what he will do " to-morrow."

Fort. "No more : curse on : your cries to me are music,
    And fill the sacred roundure of mine ears
    With tunes more sweet than moving of the spheres.
    Curse on : on our celestial brows do sit
    Unnumbered smiles, which then leap from their throne
    When they see peasants dance and monarchs groan.
    Behold you not this Globe, this golden bowl,
    This toy call'd world at our Imperial feet?
    This world is Fortune's ball wherewith she sports.
    Sometimes I strike it up into the air,
    And then create I Emperors and Kings.
    Sometimes I spurn it : at which spurn crawls out
    That wild beast multitude : curse on, you fools.
    'Tis I that tumble Princes from their thrones,
    And gild false brows with glittering diadems.
    'Tis I that tread on necks of conquerors,
    And when like semi-gods they have been drawn,
    In ivory chariots to the capitol,
    Circled about with wonder of all eyes
    The shouts of every tongue, love of all hearts
    Being swoll'n with their own greatness, I have prick'd
    The bladder of their pride, and made them die,
    As water bubbles, without memory.
    I thrust base cowards into honour's chair,
    Whilst the true spirited soldier stands by
    Bare headed, and all bare, whilst at his scars
    They scoff, that ne'er durst view the face of wars.
    I set an Idiot's cap on virtue's head,
    Turn learning out of doors, clothe wit in rags
    And paint ten thousand images of loam
    In gaudy silken colours : on the backs
    Of mules and asses I make asses ride
    Only for sport, to see the apish world
    Worship such beasts with sound idolatry.
    This Fortune does, and when this is done,
    She sits and smiles to hear some curse her name,
    And some with adoration crown her fame.

And. "To-morrow? ay to-morrow thou shalt buy them.
    To-morrow tell the Princess I will love her,
    To-morrow tell the King I'll banquet him,
    To-morrow, Shadow, will I give thee gold,
    To-morrow pride goes bare, and lust a-cold.

> To-morrow will the rich man feed the poor,
> And vice to-morrow virtue will adore.
> To-morrow beggars shall be crownèd kings.
> This no-time, morrow's time, no sweetness sings.
> I pray thee hence : bear that to Agripyne."

The whole is, as a whole, to the last degree crude and un-digested, but the ill-matured power of the writer is almost the more apparent.

The Honest Whore, in two parts, is, as far as general character goes, a mixed comedy of intrigue and manners combining, or rather uniting (for there is little combination of them), four themes —first, the love of Hippolito for the Princess Infelice, and his vir-tuous motions followed by relapse; secondly, the conversion by him of the courtesan Bellafront, a damsel of good family, from her evil ways, and her marriage to her first gallant, a hairbrained courtier named Matheo ; thirdly, Matheo's ill-treatment of Bellafront, her constancy and her rejection of the temptations of Hippolito, who from apostle has turned seducer, with the humours of Orlando Friscobaldo, Bellafront's father, who, feigning never to forgive her, watches over her in disguise, and acts as guardian angel to her reckless and sometimes brutal husband ; and lastly, the other humours of a certain marvellously patient citizen who allows his wife to hector him, his customers to bully and cheat him, and who pushes his eccentric and unmanly patience to the point of enduring both madhouse and jail. Lamb, while ranking a single speech of Bellafront's very high, speaks with rather oblique approval of the play, and Hazlitt, though enthusiastic for it, admires chiefly old Friscobaldo and the ne'er-do-weel Matheo. My own reason for preferring it to almost all the non-tragical work of the time out of Shakespere, is the wonderful character of Bellafront, both in her unreclaimed and her reclaimed condition. In both she is a very woman—not as conventional satirists and conven-tional encomiasts praise or rail at women, but as women are. If her language in her unregenerate days is sometimes coarser than is altogether pleasant, it does not disguise her nature,—the very nature of such a woman misled by giddiness, by curiosity, by love of pleasure, by love of admiration, but in no thorough sense depraved.   Her selection of Matheo not as the instrument of her being "made an honest woman," not apparently because she had any love for him left, or had ever had much, but because he was her first seducer, is exactly what, after a sudden convincing of sin, such a woman would have done; and if her patience under the long trial of her husband's thoughtlessness and occasional brutality seem excessive, it will only seem so to one who has been unlucky in his experience.   Matheo indeed is a thorough good-for-nothing, and the natural man longs that Bellafront might have been better parted; but Dekker was a very moral person in his own way, and apparently he would not entirely let her—Imogen gone astray as she is—off her penance.

CHAPTER VI

LATER ELIZABETHAN AND JACOBEAN PROSE

ONE name so far dominates the prose literature of the last years of Elizabeth, and that of the whole reign of James, that it has probably alone secured attention in the general memory, except such as may be given to the purple patches (of the true Tyrian dye, but not extremely numerous) which decorate here and there the somewhat featureless expanse of Sir Walter Raleigh's *History of the World*. That name, it is scarcely necessary to say, is the name of Francis Bacon. Bacon's eventful life, his much debated character, his philosophical and scientific position, are all matters beyond our subject. But as it is of the first importance in study-ing that subject to keep dates and circumstances generally, if not minutely, in view, it may be well to give a brief summary of his career. He was born in 1561, the son of Sir Nicholas Bacon, Lord Keeper ; he went very young to Cambridge, and though early put to the study of the law, discovered an equally early bent in another direction. He was unfortunate in not obtaining the patronage then necessary to all men not of independent fortune. Though Elizabeth was personally familiar with him, she gave him nothing of importance—whether owing to the jealousy of his uncle and cousin, Burleigh and Robert Cecil, is a point not quite certain. The patronage of Essex did him very little good, and drew him into the worst action of his life. But after Elizabeth's death, and when a man of middle age, he at last began to mount the ladder, and came with some rapidity to the summit of his profession, being made Lord Chancellor, and created Baron Verulam and Viscount St. Alban.   The title Lord Bacon he never bore in strictness, but it has been consecrated by the use of many generations, and it is perhaps pedantry to object to it.   Entangled as a courtier in the rising hatred of the Court felt by the popular party, exposed by his own carelessness, if not by actual venality in office, to the attacks of his enemies, and weakly supported, if supported at all, by the favourite Buckingham (who seems to have thought that Bacon took too much upon himself in state affairs), he lost, in 1621, all his places and emoluments, and was heavily fined.   The retirement of his last few years produced much literary fruit, and he died (his death being caused or hastened by an injudicious experiment) in 1626.

Great as is the place that Bacon occupies in English literature, he occupies it, as it were, *malgré lui*.   Unlike almost all the greatest men of his own and even of the preceding generation, he seems to have thought little of the capacities, and less of the chances of the English language.   He held (and, unluckily for him, expressed his opinion in writing) that "these modern languages will at one time or the other play the bankrupt with books," and even when he wrote in the despised vernacular he took care to translate his work, or have it translated, into Latin in order to forestall the oblivion he dreaded.   Nor is this his only phrase of contempt towards his mother-tongue—the tongue which in his own lifetime served as a vehicle to a literature compared with which the whole literary achievement of Latin antiquity is but a neat school exercise, and which in every point but accomplished precision of form may challenge comparison with Greek itself.   This insensibility of Bacon's is characteristic enough, and might, if this were the place for any such subtlety, be connected with the other defects of his strangely blended character —his pusillanimity, his lack of passion (let any one read the Essay on Love, and remember that some persons, not always inmates of lunatic asylums, have held that Bacon wrote the plays of

Shakespere), his love of empty pomp and display, and so
forth.

But the English language which he thus despised had a noble
and worthy revenge on Bacon. Of his Latin works hardly anything but the *Novum Organum* is now read even for scholastic
purposes, and it is not certain that, but for the saving influences
of academical study and prescription, even that might not slip
out of anything like common knowledge. But with the wider
and wider spread and study of English the *Essays* and *The
Advancement of Learning* are read ever more and more, and the
only reason that *The History of Henry VII.*, *The New Atlantis*, and
the *Sylva Sylvarum* do not receive equal attention, lies in the
comparative obsoleteness of their matter, combined with the fact
that the matter is the chief thing on which attention is bestowed
in them. Even in the two works noted, the *Essays* and *The
Advancement*, which can go both together in a small volume,
Bacon shows himself at his very greatest in all respects, and
(ignorant or careless as he was of the fact) as one of the greatest
writers of English prose before the accession of Charles I.

The characteristics of style in these two works are by no
means the same ; but between them they represent fairly enough
the characteristics of all Bacon's English prose, though it might
be desirable in studying it to add to them the *Henry the Seventh*,
which is a model of clear historical narration, not exactly
picturesque, but never dull ; and though not exactly erudite, yet
by no means wanting in erudition, and exhibiting conclusions
which, after two centuries and a half of record-grubbing, have not
been seriously impugned or greatly altered by any modern historian. In this book, which was written late, Bacon had, of
course, the advantage of his long previous training in the actual
politics of a school not very greatly altered since the time he was
describing, but this does not diminish the credit due to him for
formal excellence.

The *Essays*—which Bacon issued for the first time, to the
number of twelve, in 1597, when he was, comparatively speaking,

a young man, which he reissued largely augmented in 1612, and
yet again just before his death, and in their final and fullest condition—are not so much in the modern sense essays as collections of thoughts more or less connected.   We have, indeed, the
genesis of them in the very interesting commonplace book called
the *Promus* [butler or storekeeper] *of Elegancies*, the publication
of which, as a whole, was for some reason or other not undertaken by Mr. Spedding, and is due to Mrs. Henry Pott.   Here
we have the quaint, but never merely quaint, analogies, the apt
quotations, the singular flashes of reflection and illustration, which
characterise Bacon, in their most unformed and new-born condition.   In the *Essays* they are worked together, but still sententiously, and evidently with no attempt at sustained and fluent
connection of style.   That Montaigne must have had some influence on Bacon is, of course, certain ; though few things can be
more unlike than the curt severity of the scheme of the English
essays and the interminable diffuseness of the French.   Yet here
and there are passages in Montaigne which might almost be the
work of a French Bacon, and in Bacon passages which might
easily be the work of an English Montaigne.   In both there is
the same odd mixture of dignity and familiarity—the familiarity
predominating in Montaigne, the dignity in Bacon—and in both
there is the union of a rich fancy and a profound interest in
ethical questions, with a curious absence of passion and enthusiasm
—a touch, as it may almost be called, of Philistinism, which in
Bacon's case contrasts most strangely with his frequently gorgeous
language, and the evident richness of his imagination, or at least
his fancy.

The scheme and manner of these essays naturally induced a
sententious and almost undeveloped manner of writing.   An
extraordinary number of separate phrases and sentences, which
have become the common property of all who use the language,
and are probably most often used without any clear idea of their
author, may be disinterred from them, as well as many striking
images and pregnant thoughts, which have had less general cur-

rency.   But the compression of them (which is often so great that
they might be printed sentence by sentence like verses of the
Bible) prevents the author from displaying his command of a
consecutive, elaborated, and harmonised style.   What command
he had of that style may be found, without looking far, in the
Henry the Seventh, in the *Atlantis*, and in various minor works,
some originally written in Latin and translated, such as the
magnificent passage which Dean Church has selected as describing the purpose and crown of the Baconian system.   In such
passages the purely oratorical faculty which he undoubtedly had
(though like all the earlier oratory of England, with rare exceptions,
its examples remain a mere tradition, and hardly even that) displays itself; and one cannot help regretting that, instead of going
into the law, where he never attained to much technical excellence, and where his mere promotion was at first slow, and was
no sooner quickened than it brought him into difficulties and
dangers, he had not sought the safer and calmer haven of the
Church, where he would have been more at leisure to "take all
knowledge to be his province;" would have been less tempted
to engage in the treacherous, and to him always but half-con-
genial, business of politics, and would have forestalled, and perhaps excelled, Jeremy Taylor as a sacred orator.   If Bacon be
Jeremy's inferior in exuberant gorgeousness, he is very much his
superior in order and proportion, and quite his equal in sudden
flashes of a quaint but illuminative rhetoric.   For after all that
has been said of Bacon and his philosophy, he was a rhetorician
rather than a philosopher.   Half the puzzlement which has arisen
in the efforts to get something exact out of the stately periods
and splendid promises of the *Novum Organum* and its companions
has arisen from oversight of this eminently rhetorical character;
and this character is the chief property of his style.   It may
seem presumptuous to extend the charges of want of depth which
were formulated by good authorities in law and physics against
Bacon in his own day, yet he is everywhere "not deep."   He is
stimulating beyond the recorded power of any other man except

Socrates; he is inexhaustible in analogy and illustration, full of wise saws, and of instances as well ancient as modern. But he is by no means an accurate expositor, still less a powerful reasoner, and his style is exactly suited to his mental gifts ; now luminously fluent, now pregnantly brief; here just obscure enough to kindle the reader's ambition to penetrate the obscurity, there flashing with ornament which perhaps serves to conceal a flaw in the reasoning, but which certainly serves to allure and retain the attention of the student.   All these characteristics are the characteristics rather of the great orator than of the great philosopher.   His constant practice in every kind of literary composition, and in the meditative thought which constant literary composition perhaps sometimes tempts its practitioners to dispense with, enabled him to write on a vast variety of subjects, and in many different styles. But of these it will always be found that two were most familiar to him, the short sententious apothegm, parallel, or image, which suggests and stimulates even when it does not instruct, and the half-hortatory half-descriptive *discours d'ouverture*, where the writer is the unwearied panegyrist of promised lands not perhaps to be identified with great ease on any chart.[1]

A parallel in the Plutarchian manner between Bacon and Raleigh would in many ways be pleasant, but only one point of it concerns us here,—that both had been happier and perhaps had done greater things had they been simple men of letters.   Unlike Bacon, who, though he wrote fair verse, shows no poetical bent, Raleigh was *homo utriusque linguæ*, and his works in verse, unequal as they are, occasionally touch the loftiest summits of poetry.   It is very much the same in his prose.   His minor books, mostly written hurriedly, and for a purpose, have hardly any share of the graces of style; and his masterpiece, the famous *History of the World*, is made up of short passages of the most extraordinary beauty, and long stretches of monotonous narration and digression, showing not much grace of style, and absolutely no sense of proportion or skill in arrange-

[1] Of Bacon in prose, as of Spenser, Shakespere, and Milton in verse, it does not seem necessary to give extracts, and for the same reason.

ment.   The contrast is so strange that some have sought to see
in the undoubted facts that Raleigh, in his tedious prison labours,
had assistants and helpers (Ben Jonson among others), a reason
for the superior excellence of such set pieces as the Preface, the
Epilogue, and others, which are scattered about the course of the
work.   But independently of the other fact that excellence of the
most varied kind meets us at every turn, though it also deserts us
at every turn, in Raleigh's varied literary work, and that it would
be absurd to attribute all these passages to some "affable familiar
ghost," there is the additional difficulty that in none of his
reported helpers' own work do the peculiar graces of the purple
passages of the *History* occur.   The immortal descant on
mortality with which the book closes, and which is one of the
highest achievements of English prose, is not in the least like
Jonson, not in the least like Selden, not in the least like any
one of whose connection with Raleigh there is record.   Donne
might have written it; but there is not the smallest reason for
supposing that he did, and many for being certain that he did
not.   Therefore, it is only fair to give Raleigh himself the credit
for this and all other passages of the kind.   Their character and,
at the same time, their comparative rarity are both easily explic-
able.   They are all obviously struck off in moments of excitement
—moments when the writer's variable and fanciful temperament
was heated to flashing-point and gave off almost spontaneously
these lightnings of prose as it did on other occasions, such
lightnings of poetry as *The Faërie Queene* sonnet, as "the Lie,"
and as the other strange jewels (cats' eyes and opals, rather than
pearls or diamonds), which are strung along with very many
common pebbles on Raleigh's poetical necklace.   In style they
anticipate Browne (who probably learnt not a little from them)
more than any other writer; and they cannot fairly be said to
have been anticipated by any Englishman.   The low and stately
music of their cadences is a thing, except in Browne, almost
unique, and it is not easy to trace it to any peculiar mannerism
of vocabulary or of the arrangement of words.   But Raleigh's

usual style differs very little from that of other men of his day, who kept clear at once of euphuism and burlesque. Being chiefly narrative, it is rather plainer than Hooker, who has some few points of resemblance with Raleigh, but considerably freer from the vices of desultoriness and awkward syntax, than most writers of the day except Hooker. But its most interesting characteristic to the student of literature must always be the way in which it leads up to, without in the least foretelling, the bursts of eloquence already referred to. Even Milton's alternations of splendid imagery with dull and scurrilous invective, are hardly so strange as Raleigh's changes from jog-trot commonplace to almost inspired declamation, if only for the reason that they are much more intelligible. It must also be mentioned that Raleigh, like Milton, seems to have had little or no humour.

The opening and closing passages of the *History* are almost universally known ; a quainter, less splendid, but equally characteristic one may be given here though Mr. Arber has already extracted it :—

" The four complexions resemble the four elements ; and the seven ages of man, the seven planets. Whereof our infancy is compared to the moon ; in which we seem only to live and grow, as plants.

" The second age, to Mercury ; wherein we are taught and instructed.

" Our third age, to Venus ; the days of Love, Desire and Vanity.

" The fourth, to the Sun ; the strong, flourishing and beautiful age of man's life.

" The fifth, to Mars ; in which we seek honour and victory ; and in which our thoughts travel to ambitious ends.

" The sixth age is ascribed to Jupiter; in which we begin to take account of our times, judge of ourselves, and grow to the perfection of our understanding.

" The last and seventh, to Saturn ; wherein our days are sad and overcast ; and in which we find by dear and lamentable experience, and by the loss which can never be repaired, that, of all our vain passions and affections past, the sorrow only abideth. Our attendants are sicknesses and variable infirmities : and by how much the more we are accompanied with plenty, by so much the more greedily is our end desired. Whom, when Time hath made unsociable to others, we become a burden to ourselves : being of no other use than to hold the riches we have from our successors. In this time it is, when we, for the most part (and never before) prepare for our Eternal Habitation, which we pass on unto with many sighs, groans and sad thoughts : and in the end (by the workmanship of Death) finish the sorrowful business of a wretched life. Towards which we always travel, both sleeping and waking. Neither have those beloved companions of honour and riches any power at all to hold us any one day by the glorious promise of entertainments : but by what crooked path soever we walk, the same leadeth on directly to the House of Death, whose doors lie open at all hours, and to all persons."

But great as are Bacon and Raleigh, they cannot approach, as writers of prose, the company of scholarly divines who produced —what is probably the greatest prose work in any language—the Authorised Version of the Bible in English. Now that there is at any rate some fear of this masterpiece ceasing to be what it has been for three centuries—the school and training ground of every man and woman of English speech in the noblest uses of English tongue—every one who values that mother tongue is more especially bound to put on record his own allegiance to it. The work of the Company appears to have been loyally performed in common ; and it is curious that such an unmatched result should have been the result of labours thus combined, and not, as far as is known, controlled by any one guiding spirit. Among the trans- lators were many excellent writers,—an advantage which they possessed in a much higher degree than their revisers in the nineteenth century, of whom few would be mentioned among the best living writers of English by any competent authority. But, at the same time, no known translator under James has left any- thing which at all equals in strictly literary merit the Authorised Version, as it still is and as long may it be. The fact is, however, less mysterious after a little examination than it may seem at first sight. Putting aside all questions as to the intrinsic value of the subject-matter as out of our province, it will be generally admitted that the translators had in the greater part of the Old Testament, in a large part of the Apocrypha, and in no small part of the New Testament, matter as distinguished from form, of very high literary value to begin with in their originals. In the second place, they had, in the Septuagint and in the Vulgate, versions also of no small literary merit to help them.   In the third place, they had in the earlier English versions excellent quarries of suitable English terms, if not very accomplished models of style. These, however, were not in any way advantages peculiar to themselves.   The advantages which, in a manner at least, were peculiar to themselves may be divided into two classes.   They were in the very centre of the great literary ferment of which in this volume I am striving to give a history as little inadequate as possible.   They had in the air around them an English purged of archaisms and uncouthnesses, fully adapted to every literary purpose, and yet still racy of the soil, and free from that burden of hackneyed and outworn literary platitudes and commonplaces with which centuries of voluminous literary production have vitiated and loaded the English of our own day.   They were not afraid of Latinising, but they had an ample stock of the pure vernacular to draw on.   These things may be classed together.   On the other side, but equally healthful, may be put the fact that the style and structure of the originals and earlier versions, and especially that verse division which has been now so unwisely abandoned, served as safeguards against the besetting sin of all prose writers of their time, the habit of indulging in long wandering sentences, in paragraphs destitute of proportion and of grace, destitute even of ordinary manageableness and shape.   The verses saved them from that once for all ; while on the other hand their own taste, and the help given by the structure of the original in some cases, prevented them from losing sight of the wood for the trees, and omitting to consider the relation of verse to verse, as well as the antiphony of the clauses within the verse. Men without literary faculty might no doubt have gone wrong ; but these were men of great literary faculty, whose chief liabilities to error were guarded against precisely by the very conditions in which they found their work.   The hour had come exactly, and so for once had the men.

The result of their labours is so universally known that it is not necessary to say very much about it ; but the mere fact of

the universal knowledge carries with it a possibility of under-
valuation.   In another place, dealing with the general subject of
English prose style, I have selected the sixth and seventh verses of
the eighth chapter of Solomon's Song as the best example known to
me of absolutely perfect English prose—harmonious, modulated,
yet in no sense trespassing the limits of prose and becoming
poetry.   I have in the same place selected, as a companion
passage from a very different original, the Charity passage of the
First Epistle to the Corinthians, which has been so miserably
and wantonly mangled and spoilt by the bad taste and ignorance
of the late revisers.   I am tempted to dwell on this because it is
very germane to our subject.   One of the blunders which spoils
this passage in the Revised Version is the pedantic substitution
of "mirror" for "glass," it having apparently occurred to some
wiseacre that glass was not known to the ancients, or at least used
for mirrors.   Had this wiseacre had the slightest knowledge of
English literature, a single title of Gascoigne's, "The Steel Glass,"
would have dispensed him at once from any attempt at emen-
dation; but this is ever and always the way of the sciolist.
Fortunately such a national possession as the original Authorised
Version, when once multiplied and dispersed by the press, is out
of reach of vandalism.   The improved version, constructed on
very much the same principle as Davenant's or Ravenscroft's
improvements on Shakespere, may be ordered to be read in
churches, and substituted for purposes of taking oaths.   But the
original (as it may be called in no burlesque sense such as that
of a famous story) will always be the text resorted to by scholars
and men of letters for purposes of reading, and will remain the
authentic lexicon, the recognised source of English words and
constructions of the best period.   The days of creation; the
narratives of Joseph and his brethren, of Ruth, of the final
defeat of Ahab, of the discomfiture of the Assyrian host of Sen-
nacherib; the moral discourses of Ecclesiastes and Ecclesiasticus
and the Book of Wisdom; the poems of the Psalms and the
prophets; the visions of the Revelation,—a hundred other pas-

sages which it is unnecessary to catalogue,—will always be the *ne plus ultra* of English composition in their several kinds, and the storehouse from which generation after generation of writers, sometimes actually hostile to religion and often indifferent to it, will draw the materials, and not unfrequently the actual form of their most impassioned and elaborate passages. Revision after revision, constructed in corrupt following of the transient and embarrassed phantoms of ephemeral fashion in scholarship, may sink into the Great Mother of Dead Dogs after setting right a tense here, and there transferring a rendering from text to margin or from margin to text. But the work of the unrevised version will remain unaffected by each of these futile exercitations. All the elements, all the circumstances of a translation as perfect as can be accomplished in any circumstances and with any elements, were then present, and the workers were worthy of the work. The plays of Shakespere and the English Bible are, and will ever be, the twin monuments not merely of their own period, but of the perfection of English, the complete expressions of the literary capacities of the language, at the time when it had lost none of its pristine vigour, and had put on enough but not too much of the adornments and the limitations of what may be called literary civilisation.

The boundary between the prose of this period and that which we shall treat later as "Caroline" is not very clearly fixed. Some men, such as Hall and Donne, whose poetical work runs parallel to that in prose which we are now noticing, come as prose writers rather under the later date ; others who continued to write till long after Elizabeth's death, and even after that of James, seem, by their general complexion, to belong chiefly to the earlier day. The first of these is Ben Jonson, whose high reputation in other ways has somewhat unduly damaged, or at least obscured, his merits as a prose writer. His two chief works in this kind are his *English Grammar*, in which a sound knowledge of the rules of English writing is discovered, and the quaintly named *Explorata* or *Discoveries* and *Timber*—a collection of notes varying from a mere

aphorism to a respectable essay.   In these latter a singular power of
writing prose appears.   The book was not published till after
Ben's death, and is thought to have been in part at least written
during the last years of his life.   But there can be no greater
contrast than exists between the prose style usual at that time—a
style tourmenté, choked with quotation, twisted in every direction
by allusion and conceit, and marred by perpetual confusions of
English with classical grammar—and the straightforward, vigorous
English of these *Discoveries.*   They come, in character as in time,
midway between Hooker and Dryden, and they incline rather to
the more than to the less modern form.   Here is found the prose
character of Shakespere which, if less magniloquent than that in
verse, has a greater touch of sheer sincerity.   Here, too, is an
admirable short tractate on Style which exemplifies what it
preaches ; and a large number of other excellent things.   Some,
it is true, are set down in a short-hand fashion as if (which
doubtless they were) they were commonplace-book notes for
working up in due season.   But others and perhaps the majority
(they all Baconian-wise have Latin titles, though only one or two
have the text in Latin) are written with complete attention to
literary presentment; seldom though sometimes relapsing into
loose construction of sentences and paragraphs, the besetting sin
of the day, and often presenting, as in the following, a model of
sententious but not dry form :—

" We should not protect our sloth with the patronage of difficulty.   It is
a false quarrel against nature that she helps understanding but in a few, when
the most part of mankind are inclined by her thither, if they would take the
pains ; no less than birds to fly, horses to run, etc., which if they lose it is
through their own sluggishness, and by that means become her prodigies, not
her children.   I confess nature in children is more patient of labour in study
than in age ; for the sense of the pain, the judgment of the labour is absent,
they do not measure what they have done.   And it is the thought and consideration that affects us more than the weariness itself.   Plato was not content with the learning that Athens could give him, but sailed into Italy, for
Pythagoras' knowledge : and yet not thinking himself sufficiently informed,
went into Egypt, to the priests, and learned their mysteries.   He laboured, so
must we.   Many things may be learned together and performed in one point

of time ; as musicians exercise their memory, their voice, their fingers, and sometimes their head and feet at once. And so a preacher, in the invention of matter, election of words, composition of gesture, look, pronunciation, motion, useth all these faculties at once : and if we can express this variety together, why should not divers studies, at divers hours, delight, when the variety is able alone to refresh and repair us ? As when a man is weary of writing, to read ; and then again of reading, to write. Wherein, howsoever we do many things, yet are we (in a sort) still fresh to what we begin ; we are recreated with change as the stomach is with meats. But some will say, this variety breeds confusion, and makes that either we lose all or hold no more than the last. Why do we not then persuade husbandmen that they should not till land, help it with marle, lime, and compost ? plant hop gardens, prune trees, look to beehives, rear sheep, and all other cattle at once ? It is easier to do many things and continue, than to do one thing long."

No other single writer until we come to the pamphleteers deserves separate or substantive mention ; but in many divisions of literature there were practitioners who, if they have not kept much notoriety as masters of style, were well thought of even in that respect in their day, and were long authorities in point of matter. The regular theological treatises of the time present nothing equal to Hooker, who in part overlapped it, though the Jesuit Parsons has some name for vigorous writing. In history, Knolles, the historian of the Turks, and Sandys, the Eastern traveller and sacred poet, bear the bell for style among their fellows, such as Hayward, Camden, Spelman, Speed, and Stow. Daniel the poet, a very good prose writer in his way, was also a historian of England, but his chief prose work was his *Defence of Rhyme.* He had companions in the critical task ; but it is curious and by no means uninstructive to notice, that the immense creative production of the time seems to have to a great extent smothered the theoretic and critical tendency which, as yet not resulting in actual performance, betrayed itself at the beginning of the period in Webbe and Puttenham, in Harvey and Sidney. The example of Eden in collecting and Englishing travels and voyages was followed by several writers, of whom two, successively working and residing, the elder at Oxford, and the younger at Cambridge, made the two greatest collections of the kind in the language for interest of matter, if not for perfection of style. These were Richard Hakluyt and Samuel Purchas, a venerable pair. The perhaps overpraised, but still excellent Characters of the unfortunate Sir Thomas Overbury and the prose works, such as the *Counterblast* and *Demonology*, of James I., are books whose authors have made them more famous than their intrinsic merits warrant, and in the various collections of " works " of the day, older and newer, we shall find examples nearly as miscellaneous as those of the class of writers now to be noticed. Of all this miscellaneous work it is impossible to give examples, but one critical passage from Daniel, and one descriptive from Hakluyt may serve :—

" Methinks we should not so soon yield up our consents captive to the authority of antiquity, unless we saw more reason ; all our understandings are not to be built by the square of Greece and Italy. We are the children of nature as well as they, we are not so placed out of the way of judgment but that the same sun of discretion shineth upon us ; we have our portion of the same virtues, as well as of the same vices, et Catilinam quocunque in populo videas, quocunque sub axe. Time and the turn of things bring about these faculties according to the present estimation ; and, res temporibus, non tempore rebus servire opportet. So that we must never rebel against use ; quem penes arbitrium est, et vis et norma loquendi. It is not the observing of trochaics nor their iambics, that will make our writings aught the wiser : all their poesy and all their philosophy is nothing, unless we bring the discerning light of conceit with us to apply it to use. It is not books, but only that great book of the world, and the all-overspreading grace of Heaven that makes men truly judicial. Nor can it but touch of arrogant ignorance to hold this or that nation barbarous, these or those times gross, considering how this manifold creature man, wheresoever he stand in the world, hath always some disposition of worth, entertains the order of society, affects that which is most in use, and is eminent in some one thing or other that fits his humour or the times. The Grecians held all other nations barbarous but themselves ; yet Pyrrhus, when he saw the well ordered marching of the Romans, which made them see their pre- sumptuous error, could say it was no barbarous manner of proceeding. The Goths, Vandals, and Longobards, whose coming down like an inundation overwhelmed, as they say, all the glory of learning in Europe, have yet left us still their laws and customs, as the originals of most of the provincial con- stitutions of Christendom ; which, well considered with their other courses of government, may serve to clear them from this imputation of ignorance. And though the vanquished never speak well of the conqueror, yet even through the unsound coverings of malediction appear these monuments of truth, as argue well their worth, and proves them not without judgment, though without Greek and Latin."

"To speak somewhat of these islands, being called, in old time, *Insulæ fortunæ*, by the means of the flourishing thereof. The fruitfulness of them doth surely exceed far all other that I have heard of. For they make wine better than any in Spain : and they have grapes of such bigness that they may be compared to damsons, and in taste inferior to wine. For sugar, suckets, raisons of the sun, and many other fruits, abundance : for rosin, and raw silk, there is great store. They want neither corn, pullets, cattle, nor yet wild fowl.

"They have many camels also : which, being young, are eaten of the people for victuals ; and being old, they are used for carriage of necessities. Whose property is, as he is taught, to kneel at the taking of his load, and the unlading again ; of understanding very good, but of shape very deformed ; with a little belly ; long misshapen legs ; and feet very broad of flesh, without a hoof, all whole saving the great toe ; a back bearing up like a molehill, a large and thin neck, with a little head, with a bunch of hard flesh which Nature hath given him in his breast to lean upon. This beast liveth hardly, and is contented with straw and stubble ; but of strong force, being well able to carry five hundredweight.

"In one of these islands called Ferro, there is, by the reports of the inhabitants, a certain tree which raineth continually ; by the dropping whereof the inhabitants and cattle are satisfied with water : for other water have they none in all the island. And it raineth in such abundance that it were in-credible unto a man to believe such a virtue to be in a tree ; but it is known to be a Divine matter, and a thing ordained by God : at Whose power therein, we ought not to marvel, seeing He did, by His Providence (as we read in the Scriptures) when the Children of Israel were going into the Land of Promise, feed them with manna from heaven, for the space of forty years. Of these trees aforesaid, we saw in Guinea many ; being of great height, dropping con-tinually ; but not so abundantly as the other, because the leaves are narrower and are like the leaves of a pear tree. About these islands are certain flitting islands, which have been oftentimes seen ; and when men approach near them, they vanished : as the like hath been of these now known (by the report of the inhabitants) which were not found but of a long time, one after the other ; and, therefore, it should seem he is not yet born, to whom God hath appointed the finding of them.

"In this island of Teneriff, there is a hill called the Pike, because it is piked ; which is, in height, by their report, twenty leagues : having, both winter and summer, abundance of snow on the top of it. This Pike may be seen, in a clear day, fifty leagues off ; but it sheweth as though it were a black cloud a great height in the element. I have heard of none to be compared with this in height ; but in the Indies I have seen many, and, in my judgment, not inferior to the Pike : and so the Spaniards write."

One of the most remarkable developments of English prose at the time, and one which has until very recently been almost inaccessible, except in a few examples, to the student who has not the command of large libraries, while even by such students it has seldom been thoroughly examined, is the abundant and very miscellaneous collection of what are called, for want of a better name, Pamphlets. The term is not too happy, but there is no other (except the still less happy Miscellany) which describes the thing. It consists of a vast mass of purely popular literature, seldom written with any other aim than that of the modern journalist. That is to say, it was written to meet a current demand, to deal with subjects for one reason or other interesting at the moment, and, as a matter of course, to bring in some profit to the writer. These pamphlets are thus as destitute of any logical community of subject as the articles which compose a modern newspaper—a production the absence of which they no doubt supplied, and of which they were in a way the forerunners. Attempts to classify their subjects could only end in a hopeless cross division. They are religious very often ; political very seldom (for the fate of the luckless Stubbes in his dealings with the French marriage was not suited to attract) ; politico religious in at least the instance of one famous group, the so-called Martin Marprelate Controversy ; moral constantly ; in very many, especially the earlier instances, narrative, and following to a large extent in the steps of Lyly and Sidney ; besides a large class of curious tracts dealing with the manners, and usually the bad side of the manners, of the town. Of the vast miscellaneous mass of these works by single unimportant or unknown authors it is almost impossible to give any account here, though valuable instances will be found of them in Mr. Arber's *English Garner.* But the works of the six most important individual writers of them—Greene, Nash, Harvey, Dekker, Lodge, Breton (to whom might be added the verse-pamphleteer, but in no sense poet, Rowlands)—are luckily now accessible as wholes, Lodge and Rowlands having been published, or at least privately printed for subscribers, by the Hunterian Club of Glasgow, and the other five by the prolific industry of Dr. Grosart. The reprints of Petheram and of Mr. Arber, with new editions of Lyly and others, have made most of the Marprelate tracts accessible. Some notice of these collections will not only give a fair idea of the entire miscellaneous prose of the Elizabethan period, but will also fill a distinct gap in most histories of it. It will not be necessary to enter into much personal detail about their authors, for most of them have been noticed already in other capacities, and of Breton and Rowlands very little indeed is known. Greene and Lodge stand apart from their fellows in this respect, that their work is, in some respects at any rate, much more like literature and less like journalism, though by an odd and apparently perverse chance, this difference has rather hurt than saved it in the estimation of posterity. For the kind of literature which both wrote in this way has gone out of fashion, and its purely literary graces are barely sufficient to save it from the point of view of form ; while the bitter personalities of Nash, and the quaint adaptations of bygone satire to contemporary London life in which Dekker excelled, have a certain lasting interest of matter. On the other hand, the two companions of Marlowe have the advantage (which they little anticipated, and would perhaps less have relished) of surviving as illustrations of Shakespere, of the Shakescene who, decking himself out in their feathers, has by that act rescued *Pandosto* and *Euphues' Golden Legacy* from oblivion by associating them with the immortality of *As You Like It* and *The Winter's Tale*.

Owing to the different forms in which this fleeting and unequal work has been reprinted, it is not very easy to decide off-hand on the relative bulk of the authors' works. But the palm in this respect must be divided between Robert Greene and Nicholas Breton, the former of whom fills eleven volumes of loosely-printed crown octavo, and the latter (in prose only) a thick quarto of very small and closely-printed double columns.   Greene, who began his work early under the immediate inspiration first of his travels and then of Lyly's *Euphues*, started, as early as 1583, with *Mamillia, a Looking-Glass for the Ladies of England*, which, both in general character and in peculiarities of style, is an obvious copy of *Euphues*.   *The Mirror of Modesty* is more of a lay sermon, based on the story of Susanna.   *The Tritameron of Love* is a dialogue without action, but *Arbasto, or the Anatomie of Fortune* returns to the novel form, as does *The Card of Fancy*.   *Planeto-machia* is a collection of stories, illustrating the popular astrological notions, with an introduction on astrology generally.   *Penelope's Web* is another collection of stories, but *The Spanish Masquerado* is one of the most interesting of the series.   Written just at the time of the Armada, it is pure journalism—a *livre de circonstance* composed to catch the popular temper with aid of a certain actual knowledge, and a fair amount of reading.   Then Greene returned to euphuism in *Menaphon*, and in *Euphues, his Censure to Philautus;* nor are *Perimedes the Blacksmith* and *Tully's Love* much out of the same line.   *The Royal Exchange* again deviates, being a very quaint collection, quaintly arranged, of moral maxims, apophthegms, short stories, etc., for the use of the citizens.   Next, the author began the curious series, at first perhaps not very sincere, but certainly becoming so at last, of half-personal reminiscences and regrets, less pointed and well arranged than Villon's, but remarkably similar.   The first and longest of these was *Greene's Never too Late*, with its second part *Francesco's Fortunes*.   *Greene's Metamorphosis* is Euphuist once more, and *Greene's Mourning Garment* and *Greene's Farewell to Folly* are the same, with a touch of personality.   Then he diverged into the still more curious series on "conny-catching"—rooking, gulling, cheating, as we should call it.   There are five or six of these tracts, and though there is not a little bookmaking in them, they are unquestionably full of instruction as to the ways of the time.   *Philomela* returns once more to euphuism, but Greene is soon back again with *A Quip for an Upstart Courtier*, a piece of social satire, flying rather higher than his previous attempts. The zigzag is kept up in *Orpharion*, the last printed (at least in the only edition now known) of the author's works during his lifetime. Not till after his death did the best known and most personal of all his works appear, the famous *Groat's Worth of Wit Bought with a Million of Repentance*, in which the "Shakescene" passage and the exhortation to his friends to repentance occur. Two more tracts in something the same style—*Greene's Repentance* and *Greene's Vision*—followed. Their genuineness has been questioned, but seems to be fairly certain.

This full list—to which must be added the already mentioned *Pandosto, the Triumph of Time*, or *Dorastus and Fawnia*, and the translated *Debate between Folly and Love*—of a certainly not scanty life-work (Greene died when he was quite a young man, and wrote plays besides) has been given, because it is not only the earliest, but perhaps the most characteristic of the whole. Despite the apparently unsuitable forms, it is evident that the writer is striving, without knowing it, at what we call journalism. But fashion and the absence of models cramp and distort his work. Its main features are to be found in the personal and satirical pieces, in the vivid and direct humanity of some touches in the euphuist tract-romances, in the delightful snatches of verse which intersperse and relieve the heterogeneous erudition, the clumsy dialogue, and the rococo style. The two following extracts give, the first a specimen of Greene's ornate and Euphuist style from *Orpharion*, the second a passage from his autobiographical or semi-autobiographical confesssions in the *Groat's Worth :*—

" I am Lydia that renowned Princess, whose never matched beauty seemed like the gorgeous pomp of Phœbus, too bright for the day : rung so strongly out of the trump of Fame as it filled every ear with wonder : Daughter to Astolpho, the King of Lydia : who thought himself not so fortunate for his diadem, sith other kings could boast of crowns, nor for his great possessions, although endued with large territories, as happy that he had a daughter whose excellency in favour stained Venus, whose austere chastity set Diana to silence with a blush. Know whatsoever thou art that standest attentive to my tale, that the ruddiest rose in all Damasco, the whitest lilies in the creeks of Danuby, might not if they had united their native colours, but have bashed at the vermilion stain, flourish'd upon the pure crystal of my face : the Marguerites of the western Indies, counted more bright and rich than that which Cleopatra quaffed to Anthony, the coral highest in his pride upon the Afric shores, might well be graced to resemble my teeth and lips, but never honoured to over-reach my pureness. Remaining thus the mirror of the world, and nature's strangest miracle, there arrived in our Court a Thracian knight, of personage tall, proportioned in most exquisite form, his face but too fair for his qualities, for he was a brave and a resolute soldier. This cavalier coming amongst divers others to see the royalty of the state of Lydia, no sooner had a glance of my beauty, but he set down his staff, resolving either to perish in so sweet a labyrinth, or in time happily to stumble out with Theseus. He had not stayed long in my father's court, but he shewed such knightly deeds of chivalry amongst the nobility, lightened with the extraordinary sparks of a courageous mind, that not only he was liked and loved of all the chief peers of the realms, but the report of his valour coming to my father's ears, he was highly honoured of him, and placed in short time as General of his warlike forces by land. Resting in this estimation with the king, preferment was no means to quiet his mind, for love had wounded so deep, as honour by no means might remedy, that as the elephants can hardly be haled from the sight of the waste, or the roe buck from gazing at red cloth, so there was no object that could so much allure the wavering eyes of this Thracian called Acestes, as the surpassing beauty of the Princess Lydia, yea, so deeply he doted, that as the Chameleon gorgeth herself with gazing into the air, so he fed his fancy with staring on the heavenly face of his Goddess, so long dallying in the flame, that he scorched his wings and in time consumed his whole body. Being thus passionate, having none so familiar as he durst make his confidant he fell thus to debate with himself."

" On the other side of the hedge sat one that heard his sorrow, who getting over, came towards him, and brake off his passion. When he approached, he saluted Roberto in this sort : Gentleman, quoth he (for so you seem) I have by chance heard you discourse some part of your grief ; which appeareth to be more than you will discover, or I can conceit. But if you vouchsafe such simple comfort as my ability will yield, assure yourself, that I will endeavour to do the best, that either may procure your profit, or bring you pleasure : the rather, for that I suppose you are a scholar, and pity it is men of learning should live in lack.

" Roberto wondering to hear such good words, for that this iron age affords few that esteem of virtue ; returned him thankful gratulations and (urged by necessity) uttered his present grief, beseeching his advice how he might be employed. 'Why, easily,' quoth he, 'and greatly to your benefit : for men of my profession get by scholars their whole living.' 'What is your profession?' said Roberto. 'Truly, sir,' said he, 'I am a player.' 'A player!' quoth Roberto. 'I took you rather for a gentleman of great living, for if by outward habit men should be censured, I tell you, you would be taken for a substantial man.' 'So am I, where I dwell' (quoth the player) 'reputed able, at my proper cost, to build a windmill. What though the world once went hard with me, when I was fain to carry my playing fardel a foot-back; *Tempora mutantur*, I know you know the meaning of it better than I, but I thus construe it; it is otherwise now; for my very share in playing apparel will not be sold for two hundred pounds.' 'Truly' (said Roberto) 'it is strange that you should so prosper in that vain practise, for that it seems to me your voice is nothing gracious.' 'Nay, then,' said the player, 'I mislike your judgment: why, I am as famous for Delphrigas, and the King of Fairies, as ever was any of my time. The twelve labours of Hercules have I terribly thundered on the stage, and placed three scenes of the devil on the highway to heaven.' 'Have ye so?' (said Roberto) 'then I pray you, pardon me.' 'Nay more' (quoth the player) 'I can serve to make a pretty speech, for I was a country author, passing at a moral, for it was I that penn'd the moral of man's wit, the Dialogue of Dives, and for seven years' space was absolute interpreter of the puppets. But now my Almanach is out of date.

> The people make no estimation
> Of morals teaching education.

Was not this pretty for a plain rhyme extempore? if ye will ye shall have more.' 'Nay, it is enough,' said Roberto, 'but how mean you to use me?' 'Why, sir, in making plays,' said the other, 'for which you shall be well paid, if you will take the pains."

These same characteristics, though without the prevailing and in part obviously sincere melancholy which marks Greene's regrets, also distinguish Lodge's prose work to such an extent that remarks on the two might sometimes be made simply interchangeable. But fortune was kinder to Lodge than to his friend and collaborator. Nor does he seem to have had any occasion to "tread the burning marl" in company with conny-catchers and their associates. Lodge began with critical and polemical work —an academic if not very urbane reply to Stephen Gosson's *School of Abuse;* but in the *Alarum against Usurers*, which resembles and even preceded Greene's similar work, he took to the satirical-story-form. Indeed, the connection between Lodge and Greene was so close, and the difficulty of ascertaining the exact dates of their compositions is so great, that it is impossible to be sure which was the precise forerunner.   Certainly if Lodge set Greene an example in the *Alarum against Usurers*, he followed Greene's lead in *Forbonius and Prisceria* some years afterwards, having written it on shipboard in a venture against the Spaniards.   Lodge produced much the most famous book of the euphuist school, next to *Euphues* itself, as well as the best known of this pamphlet series, in *Rosalynde* or *Euphues' Golden Legacy*, from which Shakespere took the story of *As You Like It*, and of which an example follows :—

" ' Ah Phœbe,' quoth he, 'whereof art thou made, that thou regardest not thy malady?   Am I so hateful an object, that thine eyes condemn me for an abject? or so base, that thy desires cannot stoop so low as to lend me a gracious look?   My passions are many, my loves more, my thoughts loyalty, and my fancy faith : all devoted in humble devoir to the service of Phœbe ; and shall I reap no reward for such fealties ?   The swain's daily labours is quit with the evening's hire, the ploughman's toil is eased with the hope of corn, what the ox sweats out at the plough he fatteneth at the crib : but unfortunate Montanus[1] hath no salve for his sorrows, nor any hope of recompense for the hazard of his perplexed passions.   If Phœbe, time may plead the proof of my truth, twice seven winters have I loved fair Phœbe : if constancy be a cause to further my suit, Montanus' thoughts have been sealed in the sweet of Phœbe's excellence, as far from change as she from love : if outward passions may discover inward affections, the furrows in my face may discover the sorrows of my heart, and the map of my looks the grief of my mind.   Thou seest (Phœbe) the tears· of despair have made my cheeks full of wrinkles, and my scalding sighs have made the air echo her pity conceived in my plaints ; Philomel hearing my passions, hath left her mournful tunes to listen to the discourse of miseries.   I have portrayed in every tree the beauty of my mistress, and the despair of my loves.   What is it in the woods cannot witness my woes? and who is it would not pity my plaints? only Phœbe.   And why?   Because I am Montanus, and she Phœbe : I a worthless swain, and she the most excellent of all fairies.   Beautiful Phœbe ! oh might I say pitiful, then happy were I though I tasted but one minute of that good hap.   Measure Montanus, not by his fortunes, but by his loves, and balance not his wealth but his desires, and lend but one gracious look to cure a heap of disquieted cares : if not, ah if Phœbe cannot love, let a storm of frowns end the discontent of my thoughts, and so

---

[1] The Silvius, it may be just necessary to observe, of *As You Like It*.

let me perish in my desires, because they are above my deserts : only at my death this favour cannot be denied me, that all shall say Montanus died for love of hard hearted Phœbe.' At these words she filled her face full of frowns and made him this short and sharp reply.

" ' Importunate shepherd, whose loves are lawless because restless : are thy passions so extreme, that thou canst not conceal them with patience? or art thou so folly-sick, that thou must needs be fancy-sick, and in thy affection tied to such an exigent as none serves but Phœbe? Well, sir, if your market can be made nowhere else, home again, for your mart is at the fairest. Phœbe is no lettuce for your lips, and her grapes hang so high, that gaze at them you may, but touch them you cannot. Yet Montanus I speak not this in pride, but in disdain : not that I scorn thee, but that I hate love : for I count it as great honour to triumph over fancy as over fortune. Rest thee content therefore Montanus, cease from thy loves, and bridle thy looks, quench the sparkles before they grow to a farther flame ; for in loving me, thou shalt but live by loss, and what thou utterest in words are all written in the wind. Wert thou (Montanus) as fair as Paris, as hardy as Hector, as constant as Troilus, as loving as Leander, Phœbe could not love, because she cannot love at all : and therefore if thou pursue me with Phœbus, I must flie with Daphne.' "

This book seems to have been very successful, and Lodge began to write pamphlets vigorously, sometimes taking up the social satire, sometimes the moral treatise, sometimes (and then most happily) the euphuist romance, salted with charming poems. His last prose work in this kind (he wrote other things later) was the pretty and prettily-named *Margarite of America*, in 1596.

The names of Nash and Harvey are intertwined even more closely than those of Greene and Lodge ; but the conjunction is not a grasp of friendship but a grip of hatred—a wrestle, not an embrace. The fact of the quarrel has attracted rather disproportionate attention from the days of Isaac Disraeli onwards ; and its original cause is still extremely obscure and very unimportant. By some it is connected, causally as well as accidentally, with the Martin Marprelate business ; by some with the fact that Harvey belonged to the inner Sidneian clique, Nash to the outer ring of professional journalists and Bohemians. It at any rate produced some remarkable varieties of the pamphlet, and demonstrated the keen interest which the world takes in the proceedings of any couple of literary men who choose to abuse and befoul

one another.   Harvey, though no mean scholar, was in mere
writing no match for Nash ; and his chief answer to the latter,
Pierce's Supererogation, is about as rambling, incoherent, and
ineffective a combination of pedantry and insolence as need be
wished for.   It has some not uninteresting, though usually very
obscure, hints on literary matters.   Besides this, Harvey wrote
letters to Spenser with their well-known criticism and recommendation of classical forms, and *Foure Letters Touching Robert
Greene and Others : with the Trimming of Thomas Nash, Gentleman.*   A sample of him, not in his abusive-dull, but in his
scholarly dull manner, may be given :—

" Mine own rules and precepts of art, I believe will fall out not greatly
repugnant, though peradventure somewhat different : and yet I am not so
resolute, but I can be content to reserve the copying out and publishing
thereof, until I have a little better consulted with my pillow, and taken some
further advice of Madame Sperienza.   In the mean time, take this for a general
caveat, and say I have revealed one great mystery unto you : I am of opinion,
there is no one more regular and justifiable direction, either for the assured
and infallible certainty of our English artificial prosody particularly, or generally
to bring our language into art, and to frame a grammar or rhetoric thereof ;
than first of all universally to agree upon one and the same orthography in
all points conformable and proportionate to our common natural prosody :
whether Sir Thomas Smithies in that respect be the most perfit, as surely
it must needs be very good ; or else some other of profounder learning and
longer experience, than Sir Thomas was, shewing by necessary demonstration, wherein he is defective, will undertake shortly to supply his wants and
make him more absolute.   Myself dare not hope to hop after him, till I see
something or other, to or fro, publicly and authentically established, as it
were by a general council, or Act of Parliament : and then peradventure,
standing upon firmer ground, for company sake, I may adventure to do as
others do.   *Interim,* credit me, I dare give no precepts, nor set down any
certain general art : and yet see my boldness, I am not greatly squeamish of
my *Particular Examples,* whereas he that can but reasonably skill of the one,
will give easily a shrewd guess at the other : considering that the one fetcheth
his original and offspring from the other.   In which respect, to say troth, we
beginners have the start, and advantage of our followers, who are to frame
and conform both their examples and precepts, according to precedent which
they have of us : as no doubt Homer or some other in Greek, and Ennius, or
I know not who else in Latin, did prejudice, and overrule those that followed

them, as well for the quantities of syllables, as number of feet, and the like :
their only examples going for current payment, and standing instead of laws,
and rules with the posterity."

In Harvey, more perhaps than anywhere else in prose, appears the abusive exaggeration, not humorous or Rabelaisian,
but simply rancorous and dull, which mars so much Elizabethan
work.   In order not to fall into the same error ourselves, we
must abstain from repeating the very strong language which has
sometimes been applied to his treatment of dead men, and such
dead men as Greene and Marlowe, for apparently no other fault
than their being friends of his enemy Nash.   It is sufficient to
say that Harvey had all the worst traits of " donnishness," without having apparently any notion of that dignity which sometimes
half excuses the don.   He was emphatically of Mr. Carlyle's
" acrid-quack" genus.

Thomas Nash will himself hardly escape the charge of acrid-
ity, but only injustice or want of discernment will call him a
quack.   Unlike Harvey, but like Greene and Lodge, he was a
verse as well as a prose writer.   But his verse is in comparison
unimportant.   Nor was he tempted to intersperse specimens of
it in his prose work.   The absolutely best part of that work—the
Anti-Martinist pamphlets to be noticed presently—is only attributed
to him conjecturally, though the grounds of attribution are very
strong.   But his characteristics are fully evident in his undoubted
productions.   The first of these in pamphlet form is the very
odd thing called *Pierce Penniless* [the name by which Nash
became known], *his Supplication to the Devil.*   It is a kind of
rambling condemnation of luxury, for the most part delivered in the
form of burlesque exhortation, which the mediæval *sermons joyeux*
had made familiar in all European countries.   Probably some allusions in this refer to Harvey, whose pragmatical pedantry may have
in many ways annoyed Nash, a Cambridge man like himself.   At
any rate the two soon plunged into a regular battle, the documents
of which on Nash's side are, first a prognostication, something
in the style of Rabelais, then a formal confutation of the *Four*

Letters, and then the famous lampoon entitled *Have with you to Saffron Walden* [Harvey's birthplace], of which here is a specimen :—

"His father he undid to furnish him to the Court once more, where presenting himself in all the colours of the rainbow, and a pair of moustaches like a black horse tail tied up in a knot, with two tufts sticking out on each side, he was asked by no mean personage, *Unde hæc insania ?* whence proceedeth this folly or madness ? and he replied with that weather-beaten piece of a verse out of the Grammar, *Semel insanivimus omnes*, once in our days there is none of us but have played the idiots ; and so was he counted and bade stand by for a Nodgscomb. He that most patronized him, prying more searchingly into him, and finding that he was more meet to make sport with than any way deeply to be employed, with fair words shook him off, and told him he was fitter for the University, than for the Court or his turn, and so bade God prosper his studies, and sent for another Secretary to Oxford.

"Readers, be merry; for in me there shall want nothing I can do to make you merry. You see I have brought the Doctor out of request at Court, and it shall cost me a fall, but I will get him hooted out of the University too, ere I give him over. What will you give me when I bring him upon the Stage in one of the principalest Colleges in Cambridge ? Lay any wager with me, and I will ; or if you lay no wager at all, I'll fetch him aloft in Pedantius, that exquisite Comedy in Trinity College ; where under the chief part, from which it took his name, as namely the concise and firking finicaldo fine School master, he was full drawn and delineated from the sole of his foot to the crown of his head. The just manner of his phrase in his Orations and Disputations they stuffed his mouth with, and no Buffianism throughout his whole books, but they bolstered out his part with ; as those ragged remnants in his four familiar epistles 'twixt him and *Senior Immerito*, *raptim scripta*, *noste manum et stylum*, with innumerable other of his rabble-routs: and scoffing his *Musarum Lachrymæ* with *Flebo amorem meum etiam musarum lachrymis ;* which, to give it his due, was a more collachrymate wretched Treatise than my *Piers Penniless*, being the pitifulest pangs that ever any man's Muse breathed forth. I leave out half ; not the carrying up of his gown, his nice gait on his pantoffles, or the affected accent of his speech, but they personated. And if I should reveal all, I think they borrowed his gown to play the part in, the more to flout him. Let him deny this (and not damn himself) for his life if he can. Let him deny that there was a Shew made at Clare Hall of him and his two brothers, called,

> " *Tarra, rantantara turba tumultuosa Trigonum*
> *Tri-Harveyorum Tri-harmonia*

Let him deny that there was another Shew made of the little Minnow his brother, *Dodrans Dick*, at Peter-house called,

"*Duns furens.* Dick Harvey in a frensy.

Whereupon Dick came and broke the College glass windows; and Doctor Perne (being then either for himself or deputy Vice-Chancellor) caused him to be fetched in, and set in the Stocks till the Shew was ended, and a great part of the night after."

The Terrors of the Night, a discourse of apparitions, for once, among these oddly-named pieces, tells a plain story. Its successor, *Christ's Tears over Jerusalem*, Nash's longest book, is one of those rather enigmatical expressions of repentance for loose life which were so common at the time, and which, according to the charity of the reader, may be attributed to real feeling, to a temporary access of *Katzen-jammer*, or to downright hypocrisy, bent only on manufacturing profitable "copy," and varying its style to catch different tastes. The most unfavourable hypothesis is probably unjust, and a certain tone of sincerity also runs through the next book, *The Unfortunate Traveller*, in which Nash, like many others, inveighs against the practice of sending young Englishmen to be corrupted abroad. It is noteworthy that this (the place of which in the history of the novel has been rather exaggerated) is the oldest authority for the romance of Surrey and Geraldine; but it is uncertain whether this was pure invention on Nash's part or not. Nash's *Lenten Stuff* is very interesting, being a panegyric on Great Yarmouth and its famous staple commodity (though Nash was actually born at Lowestoft).

In Nash's work we find a style both of treatment and language entirely different from anything of Greene's or Lodge's. He has no euphuism, his forte being either extravagant burlesque (in which the influence of Rabelais is pretty directly perceptible, while he himself acknowledges indebtedness to some other sources, such as Bullen or Bullein, a dialogue writer of the preceding generation), or else personal attack, boisterous and unscrupulous, but often most vigorous and effective. Diffuseness and want of keeping to the point too frequently mar Nash's work; but when he shakes himself free from them, and goes straight for his enemy or his subject, he is a singularly forcible writer. In his case more than in any of the others, the journalist born out of due time is perceptible. He had perhaps not much original message for the world. But he had eminently the trick both of damaging controversial argument made light to catch the popular taste, and of easy discussion or narrative. The chief defects of his work would probably have disappeared of themselves if he had had to write not pamphlets, but articles. He did, however, what he could; and he is worthy of a place in the history of literature if only for the sake of *Have with you to Saffron Walden*—the best example of its own kind to be found before the end of the seventeenth century, if not the beginning of the eighteenth.

Thomas Dekker was much less of a born prose writer than his half-namesake, Nash. His best work, unlike Nash's, was done in verse, and, while he was far Nash's superior, not merely in poetical expression but in creative grasp of character, he was entirely destitute of Nash's incisive and direct faculty of invective. Nevertheless his work, too, is memorable among the prose work of the time, and for special reasons. His first pamphlet (according to the peculiarity already noted in Rowlands's case) is not prose at all, but verse—yet not the verse of which Dekker had real mastery, being a very lamentable ballad of the destruction of Jerusalem, entitled *Canaan's Calamity* (1598). The next, *The Wonderful Year*, is the account of London in plague time, and has at least the interest of being comparable with, and perhaps that of having to some extent inspired, Defoe's famous performance. Then, and of the same date, follows a very curious piece, the foreign origin of which has not been so generally noticed as that of Dekker's most famous prose production. *The Bachelor's Banquet* is in effect only a free rendering of the immortal fifteenth century satire, assigned on no very solid evidence to Antoine de la Salle, the *Quinze Joyes de Mariage*, the resemblance being kept down to the recurrence at the end of each section of the same phrase, "in Lob's pound," which reproduces the less grotesque "dans la nasse" of the original. But here, as later, the skill with which Dekker adapts and brings in telling circumstances appropriate to his own day deserves every acknowledgment. *Dekker's Dreame* is chiefly verse and chiefly pious; and then at a date somewhat later than that of our present period, but connected with it by the fact of authorship, begins a very interesting series of pieces, more vivid if somewhat less well written than Greene's, and connected with his "conny-catching" course. *The Bellman of London, Lanthorn and Candlelight, A Strange Horse-Race, The Seven Deadly Sins of London, News from Hell, The Double P.P.*, and *The Gull's Hornbook*, are all pamphlets of this class; the chief interest resting in *News from Hell* (which, according to the author's scheme, connects itself with Nash's *Pierce Penniless*, and is the devil's answer thereto) and *The Gull's Hornbook* (1609). This last, the best known of Dekker's work, is an Englishing of the no less famous *Grobianus* of Frederick Dedekind, and the same skill of adaptation which was noticed in *The Bachelor's Banquet* is observable here. The spirit of these works seems to have been so popular that Dekker kept it up in *The Dead Term* [long vacation], *Work for Armourers* (which, however, is less particular and connects itself with Nash's sententious work), *The Raven's Almanack*, and *A Rod for Runaways* (1625). *The Four Birds of Noah's Ark*, which Dr. Grosart prints last, is of a totally different character, being purely a book of piety. It is thus inferior in interest to the series dealing with the low life of London, which contains most curious studies of the ancient order of ragamuffins (as a modern satirist has pleasantly called them), and bears altogether marks of greater sincerity than the parallel studies of other writers. For about Dekker, hack and penny-a-liner as he undoubtedly was, there was a simplicity, a truth to nature, and at the same time a faculty of dramatic presentation in which Greene, Lodge, and Nash were wholly wanting; and his prose pamphlets smack of these good gifts in their measure as much as *The Honest Whore*. Indeed, on the whole, he seems to be the most trustworthy of these chroniclers of the English picaroons; and one feels disposed to believe that if the things which he tells did not actually happen, something very like them was probably happening every day in London during the time of "Eliza and our James." For the time of Eliza and our James was by no means a wholly heroic period, and it only loses, not gains, by the fiction that every man of letters was a Spenser and every man of affairs a Sidney or even a Raleigh. Extracts from *The Seven Deadly Sins* and *The Gull's Hornbook* may be given :—

"O Candle-light! and art thou one of the cursed crew? hast thou been set at the table of Princes and Noblemen? have all sorts of people done reverence unto thee, and stood bare so soon as ever they have seen thee? have thieves, traitors, and murderers been afraid to come in thy presence, because they knew thee just, and that thou wouldest discover them? And art thou now a harbourer of all kinds of vices? nay, dost thou play the capital Vice thyself? Hast thou had so many learned Lectures read before thee, and is the light of thy understanding now clean put out, and have so many profound scholars profited by thee? hast thou done such good to Universities, been such a guide to the lame, and seen the doing of so many good works, yet dost thou now look dimly, and with a dull eye, upon all goodness? What comfort have sick men taken (in weary and irksome nights) but only in thee? thou hast been their physician and apothecary, and when the relish of nothing could please them, the very shadow of thee hath been to them a restorative consolation. The nurse hath stilled her wayward infant, shewing it but to thee: What gladness hast thou put into mariners' bosoms when thou hast met them on the sea! What joy into the faint and benighted traveller when he has met thee on the land! How many poor handicraftsmen by thee have earned the best part of their living! And art thou now become a companion for drunkards, for leachers, and for prodigals? Art thou turned reprobate? thou wilt burn for it in hell. And so odious is this thy apostasy, and hiding thyself from the light of the truth, that at thy death and going out of the world, even they that love thee best will tread thee under their feet: yea, I that have thus played the herald, and proclaimed thy good parts, will now play the crier and call thee into open court, to arraign thee for thy misdemeanours."

"For do but consider what an excellent thing sleep is: it is so inestimable a jewel that, if a tyrant would give his crown for an hour's slumber, it cannot be bought: of so beautiful a shape is it, that though a man lie with an Empress, his heart cannot be at quiet till he leaves her embracements to be at rest with the other: yea, so greatly indebted are we to this kinsman of death, that we owe the better tributary, half of our life to him: and there is good cause why we should do so: for sleep is that golden chain that ties health and our bodies together. Who complains of want? of wounds? of cares? of great men's oppressions? of captivity? whilst he sleepeth? Beggars in their beds take as much pleasure as kings: can we therefore surfeit on this delicate Ambrosia? can we drink too much of that whereof to taste too little tumbles us into a churchyard, and to use it but indifferently throws us into Bedlam? No, no, look upon Endymion, the moon's minion, who slept three score and fifteen years, and was not a hair the worse for it. Can lying abed till noon (being not the three score and fifteenth thousand part of his nap) be hurtful?

" Besides, by the opinion of all philosophers and physicians, it is not good to trust the air with our bodies till the sun with his flame-coloured wings hath fanned away the misty smoke of the morning, and refined that thick tobacco-breath which the rheumatic night throws abroad of purpose to put out the eye of the element: which work questionless cannot be perfectly finished till the sun's car-horses stand prancing on the very top of highest noon: so that then (and not till then) is the most healthful hour to be stirring. Do you require examples to persuade you? At what time do Lords and Ladies use to rise but then? Your simpering merchants' wives are the fairest lyers in the world: and is not eleven o'clock their common hour? they find (no doubt) unspeakable sweetness in such lying, else they would not day by day put it so in practice. In a word, mid-day slumbers are golden; they make the body fat, the skin fair, the flesh plump, delicate and tender; they set a russet colour on the cheeks of young women, and make lusty courage to rise up in men; they make us thrifty, both in sparing victuals (for breakfasts thereby are saved from the hell-mouth of the belly) and in preserving apparel; for while we warm us in our beds our clothes are not worn.

" The casements of thine eyes being then at this commendable time of the day newly set open, choose rather to have thy wind-pipe cut in pieces than to salute any man. Bid not good-morrow so much as to thy father, though he be an emperor. An idle ceremony it is and can do him little good; to thyself it may bring much harm: for if he be a wise man that knows how to hold his peace, of necessity must he be counted a fool that cannot keep his tongue."

The voluminous work in pamphlet kind of Nicholas Breton, still more the verse efforts closely akin to it of Samuel Rowlands, John Davies of Hereford and some others, must be passed over with very brief notice. Dr. Grosart's elaborate edition of the first-named has given a vast mass of matter very interesting to the student of literature, but which cannot be honestly recommended

to the general reader.   Breton, whose long life and perpetual
literary activity fill up great part of our whole period, was an
Essex gentleman of a good family (a fact which he never forgot),
and apparently for some time a dependent of the well-known
Countess of Pembroke, Sidney's sister.   A much older man than
most of the great wits of Elizabeth's reign, he also survived most
of them, and his publications, if not his composition, cover a full
half century, though he was *nel mezzo del cammin* at the date of
the earliest.   He was probably born some years before the middle
of the sixteenth century, and certainly did not die before the first
year of Charles I.   If we could take as his the charming lullaby of
The Arbour of Amorous Devices he would stand (if only as a kind
of " single-speech") high as a poet.   But I fear that Dr. Grosart's
attribution of it to him is based on little external and refuted by
all internal evidence.   His best certain thing is the pretty
"Phillida and Corydon" idyll, which may be found in *England's
Helicon* or in Mr. Ward's *Poets*.   But I own that I can never
read this latter without thinking of two lines of Fulke Greville's
in the same metre and on no very different theme—

> " O'er enamelled meads they went,
> Quiet she, he passion-rent,"

which are simply worth all the works of Breton, prose and verse,
unless we count the *Lullaby*, put together.   In the *mots rayon-
nants*, the *mots de lumière*, he is sadly deficient.   But his work
(which is nearly as plentiful in verse as in prose) is, as has been
said, very interesting to the literary student, because it shows better
perhaps than anything else the style of literature which a man, disdaining to condescend to burlesque or bawdry, not gifted with any
extraordinary talent, either at prose or verse, but possessed of a
certain literary faculty, could then produce with a fair chance of
being published and bought.   It cannot be said that the result
shows great daintiness in Breton's public.   The verse, with an
improvement in sweetness and fluency, is very much of the
doggerel style which was prevalent before Spenser ; and the prose,

though showing considerable faculty, if not of invention, yet of adroit imitation of previously invented styles, is devoid of distinction and point.   There are, however, exercises after Breton's own fashion in almost every popular style of the time—euphuist romances, moral treatises, packets of letters, collections of jests and short tales, purely religious tractates, characters (after the style later illustrated by Overbury and Earle), dialogues, maxims, pictures of manners, collections of notes about foreign countries, —in fact, the whole farrago of the modern periodical.   The pervading characteristics are Breton's invariable modesty, his pious and, if I may be permitted to use the word, gentlemanly spirit, and a fashion of writing which, if not very pointed, picturesque, or epigrammatic, is clear, easy, and on the whole rather superior, in observance of the laws of grammar and arrangement, to the work of men of much greater note in his day.

The verse pamphlets of Rowlands (whom I have not studied as thoroughly as most others), Davies, and many less voluminous men, are placed here with all due apology for the liberty.   They are seldom or never of much formal merit, but they are interesting, first, because they testify to the hold which the mediæval conception of verse, as a general literary medium as suitable as prose and more attractive, had upon men even at this late time ; and secondly, because, like the purely prose pamphlets, they are full of information as to the manners of the time.   For Rowlands I may refer to Mr. Gosse's essay.   John Davies of Hereford, the writing-master, though he has been carefully edited for students, and is by no means unworthy of study, has had less benefit of exposition to the general reader. He was not a genius, but he is a good example of the rather dull man who, despite the disfavour of circumstance, contrives by much assiduity and ingenious following of models to attain a certain position in literature.   There are John Davieses of Hereford in every age, but since the invention and filing of newspapers their individuality has been not a little merged.   The anonymous journalist of our days is simply to the historian such

and such a paper, volume so-and-so, page so much, column this
or that.   The good John Davies, living in another age, still
stands as *nominis umbra*, but with a not inconsiderable body of
work to throw the shadow.

One of the most remarkable, and certainly one of not the
least interesting developments of the Elizabethan pamphlet
remains to be noticed.   This is the celebrated series of " Martin
Marprelate " tracts, with the replies which they called forth.
Indeed the popularity of this series may be said to have given a
great impulse to the whole pamphleteering system.   It is somewhat unfortunate that this interesting subject has never been
taken up in full by a dispassionate historian of literature,
sufficiently versed in politics and in theology.   In mid-nineteenth
century most, but by no means all of the more notable tracts
were reprinted by John Petheram, a London bookseller, whose
productions have since been issued under the well-known imprint of John Russell Smith, the publisher of the *Library of
Old Authors*.   This gave occasion to a review in *The Christian
Remembrancer*, afterwards enlarged and printed as a book by
Mr. Maskell, a High Churchman who subsequently seceded to the
Church of Rome.   This latter accident has rather unfavourably
and unfairly affected later judgments of his work, which, however,
is certainly not free from party bias.   It has scarcely been less
unlucky that the chief recent dealers with the matter, Professor
Arber (who projected a valuable reprint of the whole series in
his *English Scholars' Library*, and who prefaced it with a quite
invaluable introductory sketch), and Dr. Grosart, who also included
divers Anti-Martinist tracts in his privately printed *Works of
Nashe*, are very strongly prejudiced on the Puritan side.[1]   Between
these authorities the dispassionate inquirer who attacks the texts
for himself is likely to feel somewhat in the position of a man who
exposes himself to a cross fire.   The Martin Marprelate controversy, looked at without prejudice but with sufficient information,

[1] This prejudice is naturally still stronger in some American writers,
notably Dr. Dexter.

shows itself as a very early example of the reckless violence of private crotcheteers on the one hand, and of the rather considerable unwisdom of the official defenders of order on the other. "Martin's" method was to a certain extent an anticipation of the famous move by which Pascal, fifty years later, "took theology out of the schools into drawing-rooms," except that Martin and his adversaries transferred the venue rather to the tap-room than to the drawing-room. The controversy between the framers of the Church of England in its present state, and the hot gospellers who, with Thomas Cartwright at their head, denied the proposition (not deniable or denied now by any sane and scholarly disputant) that church discipline and government are points left to a great extent undefined in the Scriptures, had gone on for years before Martin appeared. Cartwright and Whitgift had fought, with a certain advantage of warmth and eloquence on Cartwright's side, and with an immense preponderance of logical cogency on Whitgift's. Many minor persons had joined in the struggle, and at last a divine, more worthy than wise, John Bridges, Dean of Salisbury, had produced on the orthodox side one of those enormous treatises (it had some fifteen hundred quarto pages) which are usually left unread by the side they favour, and which exasperate the side they oppose. The ordinary law of the time, moreover, which placed large powers in the hands of the bishops, and especially entrusted them with a rigid and complete censorship of the press, had begun to be put in force severely against the more outspoken partisans. Any one who will take the trouble to read the examination of Henry Barrow, which Mr. Arber has reprinted,[1] or even the "moderate" tracts of Nicholas Udall, which in a manner ushered in the Marprelate controversy, will probably be more surprised at the long-suffering of the judges than at the sufferings of their prisoners. Barrow, in a long and patient

---

[1] Arber, *Introductory Sketch*, p. 40 *sqq.* All the quotations and references which follow will be found in Arber's and Petheram's reprints or in Grosart's *Nash*, vol. I. If the works cited are not given as wholes in them, the fact will be noted. (See also Mr. Bond's *Lyly*.)

examination before the council, of which the Bishop of London and the Archbishop of Canterbury were members, called them to their faces the one a "wolf," a "bloody persecutor," and an "apostate," the other "a monster" and "the second beast that is spoken of in the Revelations." The "moderate" Udall, after publishing a dialogue (in which an Anglican bishop called Diotrephes is represented, among other things, as planning measures against the Puritans in consort with a papist and an usurer), further composed a' *Demonstration of Discipline* in which, writing, according to Mr. Arber, "without any satire or invective," he calls the bishops merely *qua* bishops, "the wretched fathers of a filthy mother," with abundant epithets to match, and rains down on every practice of the existing church government such terms as "blasphemous," "damnable," "hellish," and the like. To the modern reader who looks at these things with the eyes of the present day, it may of course seem that it would have been wiser to let the dogs bark. But that was not the principle of the time : and as Mr. Arber most frankly admits, it was certainly not the principle of the dogs themselves. The Puritans claimed for themselves a not less absolute right to call in the secular arm if they could, and a much more absolute certainty and righteousness for their tenets than the very hottest of their adversaries.

Udall was directly, as well as indirectly, the begetter of the Martin Marprelate controversy : though after he got into trouble in connection with it, he made a sufficiently distinct expression of disapproval of the Martinist methods, and it seems to have been due more to accident and his own obstinacy than anything else that he died in prison instead of being obliged with the honourable banishment of a Guinea chaplaincy. His printer, Waldegrave, had had his press seized and his license withdrawn for *Diotrephes*, and resentment at this threw what, in the existing arrangements of censorship and the Stationers' monopoly, was a very difficult thing to obtain—command of a practical printer—into the hands of the malcontents. Chief among these malcontents was a certain Reverend John Penry, a Welshman by birth, a member, as was then not uncommon, of both universities, and the author, among other more dubious publications, of a plea, intemperately stated in parts, but very sober and sensible at bottom, for a change in the system of allotting and administering the benefices of the church in Wales.   Which plea, be it observed in passing, had it been attended to, it would have been better for both the church and state of England at this day.   The pamphlet [1] contained, however, a distinct insinuation against the Queen, of designedly keeping Wales in ignorance and subjection —an insinuation which, in those days, was equivalent to high treason.   The book was seized, and the author imprisoned (1587).   Now when, about a year after, and in the very height of the danger from the Armada, Waldegrave's livelihood was threatened by the proceedings above referred to, it would appear that he obtained from the Continent, or had previously secreted from his confiscated stock, printing tools, and that he and Penry, at the house of Mistress Crane, at East Molesey, in Surrey, printed a certain tract, called, for shortness, " The Epistle." [2]   This tract, of the authorship and character of which more presently, created a great sensation.   It was immediately followed, the press being

[1] Large extracts from it are given by Arber.

[2] As the titles of these productions are highly characteristic of the style of the controversy, and, indeed, are sometimes considerably more poignant than the text, it may be well to give some of them in full as follows :—

The Epistle.—Oh read over D. John Bridges, for it is a worthy work : Or an Epitome of the first book of that right worshipful volume, written against the Puritans, in the defence of the noble Clergy, by as worshipful a Priest, John Bridges, Presbyter, Priest or Elder, Doctor of Divillity (*sic*), and Dean of Sarum, Wherein the arguments of the Puritans are wisely presented, that when they come to answer M. Doctor, they must needs say something that hath been spoken.   Compiled for the behoof and overthrow of the Parsons Fyckers and Currats [*sic*] that have learnt their catechisms, and are past grace : by the reverend and worthy Martin Marprelate, gentleman, and dedicated to the Confocation [*sic*] house.   The Epitome is not yet published, but it shall be when the Bishops are at convenient leisure to view the same.   In the mean time let them be content with this learned Epistle.   Printed, oversea, in Europe, within two furlongs of a Bouncing Priest, at the cost and charges of M. Marprelate, gentleman.

shifted for safety to the houses of divers Puritan country gentlemen, by the promised *Epitome*.   So great was the stir, that a
formal answer of great length was put forth by " T. C." (well
known to be Thomas Cooper, Bishop of Winchester), entitled,
An Admonition to the People of England.   The Martinists, from
their invisible and shifting citadel, replied with perhaps the
cleverest tract of the whole controversy, named, with deliberate
quaintness, *Hay any Work for Cooper ?*[1] (" Have You any Work
for the Cooper ?" said to be an actual trade London cry).   Thence-
forward the *mêlée* of pamphlets, answers, " replies, duplies, quadru-
plies," became in small space indescribable.   Petheram's prospectus
of reprints (only partially carried out) enumerates twenty-six, almost
all printed in the three years 1588-1590 ; Mr. Arber, including
preliminary works, counts some thirty.   The perambulating press
was once seized (at Newton Lane, near Manchester), but Martin
was not silenced.   It is certain (though there are no remnants
extant of the matter concerned) that Martin was brought on the
stage in some form or other, and though the duration of the
controversy was as short as its character was hot, it was rather
suppressed than extinguished by the death of Udall in prison,
and the execution of Penry and Barrow in 1593.

The actual authorship of the Martinist Tracts is still purely a
matter of hypothesis.   Penry has been the general favourite, and
perhaps the argument from the difference of style in his known
works is not quite convincing.   The American writer Dr. Dexter,

[1] Hay any work for Cooper, or a brief pistle directed by way of an hublica-
tion [*sic*] to the reverend bishops, counselling them if they will needs be barrelled
up for fear of smelling in the nostrils of her Majesty and the State, that they
would use the advice of Reverend Martin for the providing of their Cooper ;
because the Reverend T. C. (by which mystical letters is understood either the
bouncing parson of East Meon or Tom Cokes his chaplain), hath shewed himself in his late admonition to the people of England to be an unskilful and
beceitful [*sic*] tub-trimmer.   Wherein worthy Martin quits him like a man, I
warrant you in the modest defence of his self and his learned pistles, and
makes the Cooper's hoops to fly off, and the bishops' tubs to leak out of all cry.
Penned and compiled by Martin the metropolitan.   Printed in Europe, not
far from some of the bouncing priests.

a fervent admirer, as stated above, of the Puritans, is for
Barrow. Mr. Arber thinks that a gentleman of good birth named
Job Throckmorton, who was certainly concerned in the affair, was
probably the author of the more characteristic passages. Fantastic
suggestions of Jesuit attempts to distract the Anglican Church have
also been made,—attempts sufficiently refuted by the improbability of the persons known to be concerned lending themselves
to such an intrigue, for, hotheads as Penry and the rest were,
they were transparently honest. On the side of the defence,
authorship is a little better ascertained. Of Cooper's work there
is no doubt, and some purely secular men of letters were oddly
mixed up in the affair. It is all but certain that John Lyly wrote
the so-called *Pap with a Hatchet*,[1] which in deliberate oddity of
phrase, scurrility of language, and desultoriness of method out-
vies the wildest Martinist outbursts. The later tract, *An Almond
for a Parrot*,[2] which deserves a very similar description, may not
improbably be the same author's ; and Dr. Grosart has reasonably
attributed four anti-Martinist tracts (*A Countercuff to Martin Junior*
[*Martin Junior* was one of the Marprelate treatises], *Pasquil's
Return, Martin's Month's Mind*, and *Pasquil's Apology*), to Nash.
But the discussion of such questions comes but ill within the
limits of such a book as the present.

The discussion of the characteristics of the actual tracts, as

[1] Pap with a Hatchet, alias A fig for my godson ! or Crack me this nut, or
A country cuff that is a sound box of the ear for the idiot Martin for to hold his
peace, seeing the patch will take no warning. Written by one that dares call
a dog a dog, and made to prevent Martin's dog-days. Imprinted by John-a-
noke and John-a-stile for the baylive [*sic*] of Withernam, *cum privilegio
perennitatis ;* and are to be sold at the sign of the crab-tree-cudgel in Thwack-
coat Lane. A sentence. Martin hangs fit for my mowing.

[2] An Almond for a Parrot, or Cuthbert Curryknaves alms. Fit for the
knave Martin, and the rest of those impudent beggars that cannot be content to
stay their stomachs with a benefice, but they will needs break their fasts with
our bishops. *Rimarum sum plenus.* Therefore beware, gentle reader, you
catch not the hicket with laughing. Imprinted at a place, not far from a place,
by the assigns of Signior Somebody, and are to be sold at his shop in Trouble-
knave Street at the sign of the Standish.

they present themselves and whosoever wrote them, is, on the
other hand, entirely within our competence.   On the whole the
literary merit of the treatises has, I think, been overrated.   The
admirers of Martin have even gone so far as to traverse Penry's
perfectly true statement that in using light, not to say ribald,
treatment of a serious subject, he was only following [Marnix de
Sainte Aldegonde and] other Protestant writers, and have attributed
to him an almost entire originality of method, owing at most
something to the popular "gags" of the actor Richard Tarleton,
then recently dead.   This is quite uncritical.   An exceedingly
free treatment of sacred and serious affairs had been characteristic
of the Reformers from Luther downward, and the new Martin
only introduced the variety of style which any writer of considerable talents is sure to show.   His method, at any rate for a time,
is no doubt sufficiently amusing, though it is hardly effective.
Serious arguments are mixed up with the wildest buffoonery, and
unconscious absurdities (such as a solemn charge against the
unlucky Bishop Aylmer because he used the phrase " by my faith,"
and enjoyed a game at bowls) with the most venomous assertion
or insinuation of really odious offences.   The official answer to
the *Epistle* and the *Epitome* has been praised by no less a person
than Bacon[1] for its gravity of tone.   Unluckily Dr. Cooper was
entirely destitute of the faculty of relieving argument with humour.
He attacks the theology of the Martinists with learning and logic
that leave nothing to desire ; but unluckily he proceeds in precisely the same style to deal laboriously with the quips assigned
by Martin to Mistress Margaret Lawson (a noted Puritan shrew
of the day), and with mere idle things like the assertion that Whitgift "carried Dr. Perne's cloakbag."   The result is that, as has
been said, the rejoinder *Hay any Work for Cooper* shows Martin,
at least at the beginning, at his very best.   The artificial simplicity
of his distortions of Cooper's really simple statements is not unworthy of Swift, or of the best of the more recent practitioners of

---

[1] In his *Advertisement Touching the Controversies of the Church of England*
(Works.   Folio, 1753, ii. p. 375).

the grave and polite kind of political irony. But this is ˌat the beginning, and soon afterwards Martin relapses for the most part into the alternation between serious argument which will not hold water and grotesque buffoonery which has little to do with the matter. A passage from the *Epistle* lampooning Aylmer, Bishop of London, and a sample each of *Pap with a Hatchet* and the *Almond*, will show the general style. But the most characteristic pieces of all are generally too coarse and too irreverent to be quotable :—

"Well now to mine eloquence, for I can do it I tell you. Who made the porter of his gate a dumb minister? Dumb John of London. Who abuseth her Majesty's subjects, in urging them to subscribe contrary to law? John of London. Who abuseth the high commission, as much as any? John London (and D. Stanhope too). Who bound an Essex minister, in 200*l.* to wear the surplice on Easter Day last? John London. Who hath cut down the elms at Fulham? John London. Who is a carnal *I'll make you* defender of the breach of the Sabbath in all the places of his *weary of it dumb* abode? John London. Who forbiddeth men to humble *John, except you* themselves in fasting and prayer before the Lord, and then can *leave perse-* say unto the preachers, now you were best to tell the people *cuting.* that we forbid fasts? John London. Who goeth to bowls upon the Sabbath? Dumb Dunstical John of good London hath done all this. I will for this time leave this figure, and tell your venerable masterdoms a tale worth the hearing : I had it at the second hand : if he that told it me added anything, I do not commend him, but I forgive him : The matter is this. A man dying in Fulham, made one of the Bishop of London's men his executor. The man had bequeathed certain legacies unto a poor shepherd in the town. The shepherd could get nothing of the Bishop's man, and therefore made his moan unto a gentleman of Fulham, that belongeth to the court of requests. The gentleman's name is M. Madox. The poor man's case came to be tried in the Court of Requests. The B. man desired his master's help : Dumb John wrote to the masters of requests to this effect, and I think these were his words :

"'My masters of the requests, the bearer hereof being my man, hath a cause before you : inasmuch as I understand how the matter standeth, I pray you let my man be discharged the court, and I will see an agreement made. Fare you well.' The letter came to M. D. Dale, he answered it in this sort :

"'My Lord of London, this man delivered your letter, I pray you give him his dinner on Christmas Day for his labour, and fare you well.'

"Dumb John not speeding this way, sent for the said M. Madox : he came, some rough words passed on both sides, Presbyter John said, Master Madox was very saucy, especially seeing he knew before whom he spake : namely, the Lord of Fulham. Whereunto the gentleman answered that he had been a poor free-holder in Fulham, before Don John came to be L. there, hoping also to be so, when he and all his brood (my Lady his daughter and all) should be gone. At the hearing of this speech, the wasp got my brother by the nose, which made him in his rage to affirm, that he would be L. of Fulham as long as he lived in despite of all England. Nay, soft there, quoth M. Madox, except her Majesty. I pray you, that is my meaning, call dumb John, and I tell thee Madox that thou art but a Jack to use me so : Master Madox replying, said that indeed his name was John, and if every John were a Jack, he was content to be a Jack (there he hit my L. over the thumbs). The B. growing in choler, said that Master Madox his name did shew what he was, for saith he, thy name is mad ox, which declareth thee to be an unruly and mad beast. M. Madox answered again, that the B. name, if it were descanted upon, did most significantly shew his qualities. For said he, you are called Elmar, but you may be better called marelm, for you have marred all the elms in Fulham : having cut them all down. This far is my worthy story, as worthy to be printed, as any part of Dean John's book, I am sure."

" To the Father and the two Sons,
" HUFF, RUFF, and SNUFF,[1]
"the three tame ruffians of the Church, which take pepper
"in the nose, because they cannot
" mar Prelates :
"greeting.

" Room for a royster ; so that's well said. Ach, a little farther for a good fellow. Now have at you all my gaffers of the railing religion, 'tis I that must take you a peg lower. I am sure you look for more work, you shall have wood enough to cleave, make your tongue the wedge, and your head the beetle. I'll make such a splinter run into your wits, as shall make them ramkle till you become fools. Nay, if you shoot books like fools' bolts, I'll be so bold as to make your judgments quiver with my thunderbolts. If you mean to gather clouds in the Commonwealth, to threaten tempests, for your flakes of snow, we'll pay you with stones of hail ; if with an easterly wind you bring caterpillers into the Church, with a northern wind we'll drive barrens into your wits.

" We care not for a Scottish mist, though it wet us to the skin, you shall be sure your cockscombs shall not be missed, but pierced to the skulls. I profess railing, and think it as good a cudgel for a martin, as a stone for a dog, or a whip for an ape, or poison for a rat.

---

[1] Well-known stage characters in Preston's *Cambyses.*

"Yet find fault with no broad terms, for I have measured yours with mine, and I find yours broader just by the list. Say not my speeches are light, for I have weighed yours and mine, and I find yours lighter by twenty grains than the allowance. For number you exceed, for you have thirty ribald words for my one, and yet you bear a good spirit. I was loth so to write as I have done, but that I learned, that he that drinks with cutters, must not be without his ale daggers; nor he that buckles with Martin, without his lavish terms.

"Who would curry an ass with an ivory comb? Give the beast thistles for provender. I do but yet angle with a silken fly, to see whether martins will nibble; and if I see that, why then I have worms for the nonce, and will give them line enough like a trout, till they swallow both hook and line, and then, Martin, beware your gills, for I'll make you dance at the pole's end.

"I know Martin will with a trice bestride my shoulders. Well, if he ride me, let the fool sit fast, for my wit is very hickish; which if he spur with his copper reply, when it bleeds, it will all to besmear their consciences.

"If a martin can play at chess, as well as his nephew the ape, he shall know what it is for a scaddle pawn to cross a Bishop in his own walk. Such diedappers must be taken up, else they'll not stick to check the king. Rip up my life, discipher my name, fill thy answer as full of lies as of lines, swell like a toad, hiss like an adder, bite like a dog, and chatter like a monkey, my pen is prepared and my mind; and if ye chance to find any worse words than you brought, let them be put in your dad's dictionary. And so farewell, and be hanged, and I pray God ye fare no worse.

"Yours at an hour's warning,

"DOUBLE V."

"By this time I think, good-man Puritan, that thou art persuaded, that I know as well as thy own conscience thee, namely Martin Makebate of England, to be a most scurvy and beggarly benefactor to obedience, and *per consequens*, to fear neither men, nor that God Who can cast both body and soul into unquenchable fire. In which respect I neither account you of the Church, nor esteem of your blood, otherwise than the blood of Infidels. Talk as long as you will of the joys of heaven, or pains of hell, and turn from yourselves the terror of that judgment how you will, which shall bereave blushing iniquity of the fig-leaves of hypocrisy, yet will the eye of immortality discern of your painted pollutions, as the ever-living food of perdition. The humours of my eyes are the habitations of fountains, and the circumference of my heart the enclosure of fearful contrition, when I think how many souls at that moment shall carry the name of Martin on their foreheads to the vale of confusion, in whose innocent blood thou swimming to hell, shalt have the torments of ten thousand thousand sinners at once, inflicted upon thee. There will envy, malice, and dissimulation be ever-calling for vengeance against thee, and incite whole legions of devils to thy deathless lamentation. Mercy will say unto thee, I know thee not, and Repentance, what have I to do with thee? All hopes shall shake the head at thee, and say : there goes the poison of purity, the perfection of impiety, the serpentine seducer of simplicity. Zeal herself will cry out upon thee, and curse the time that ever she was mashed by thy malice, who like a blind leader of the blind, sufferedst her to stumble at every step in Religion, and madest her seek in the dimness of her sight, to murder her mother the Church, from whose paps thou like an envious dog but yester-day pluckedst her. However, proud scorner, thy whorish impudency may happen hereafter to insist in the derision of these fearful denunciations, and sport thy jester's pen at the speech of my soul, yet take heed least despair be predominant in the day of thy death, and thou instead of calling for mercy to thy Jesus, repeat more oftener to thyself, *Sic morior damnatus ut Judas!* And thus much, Martin, in the way of compassion, have I spoke for thy edification, moved thereto by a brotherly commiseration, which if thou be not too desperate in thy devilish attempts, may reform thy heart to remorse, and thy pamphlets to some more profitable theme of repentance."

If Martin Marprelate is compared with the *Epistolæ Obscurorum Virorum* earlier, or the *Satire Menippée* very little later, the want of polish and directness about contemporary English satire will be strikingly apparent. At the same time he does not compare badly with his own antagonists. The divines like Cooper are, as has been said, too serious. The men of letters like Lyly and Nash are not nearly serious enough, though some exception may be made for Nash, especially if *Pasquil's Apology* be his. They out-Martin Martin himself in mere abusiveness, in deliberate quaintness of phrase, in fantastic vapourings and promises of the dreadful things that are going to be done to the enemy. They deal some shrewd hits at the glaring faults of their subject, his outrageous abuse of authorities, his profanity, his ribaldry, his irrelevance ; but in point of the three last qualities there is not much to choose between him and them. One line of counter attack they did indeed hit upon, which was followed up for generations with no small success against the Nonconformists, and that is the charge of hypocritical abuse of the influence which the Noncon-formist teachers early acquired over women. The germs of the unmatched passages to this effect in *The Tale of a Tub* may be found in the rough horseplay of *Pap with a Hatchet* and *An*

Almond for a Parrot.   But the spirit of the whole controversy is in fact a spirit of horseplay.   Abuse takes the place of sarcasm, Rabelaisian luxuriance of words the place of the plain hard hitting, with no flourishes or capers, but with every blow given straight from the shoulder, which Dryden and Halifax, Swift and Bentley, were to introduce into English controversy a hundred years later.   The peculiar exuberance of Elizabethan literature, evident in all its departments, is nowhere more evident than in this department of the prose pamphlet, and in no section of that department is it more evident than in the Tracts of the Martin Marprelate Controversy.   Never perhaps were more wild and whirling words used about any exceedingly serious and highly technical matter of discussion; and probably most readers who have ventured into the midst of the tussle will sympathise with the adjuration of *Plain Percivall the Peacemaker of England* (supposed to be Richard Harvey, brother of Gabriel, who was himself not entirely free from suspicion of concernment in the matter), "My masters, that strive for this supernatural art of wrangling, let all be husht and quiet a-God's name."   It is needless to say that the disputants did not comply with Plain Percivall's request.   Indeed they bestowed some of their choicest abuse on him in return for his advice.   Not even by the casting of the most peacemaking of all dust, that of years and the grave, can it be said that these jars at last *compacta quiescunt.*   For it is difficult to find any account of the transaction which does not break out sooner or later into strong language.

CHAPTER VII

THE THIRD DRAMATIC PERIOD

I HAVE chosen, to fill the third division of our dramatic chapters, seven chief writers of distinguished individuality, reserving a certain fringe of anonymous plays and of less famous personalities for the fourth and last. The seven exceptional persons are Beaumont and Fletcher, Webster, Middleton, Heywood, Tourneur, and Day. It would be perhaps lost labour to attempt to make out a severe definition, shutting these off on the one hand from their predecessors, on the other from those that followed them. We must be satisfied in such cases with an approach to exactness, and it is certain that while most of the men just named had made some appearance in the latest years of Elizabeth, and while one or two of them lasted into the earliest years of Charles, they all represent, in their period of flourishing and in the character of their work, the Jacobean age. In some of them, as in Middleton and Day, the Elizabethan type prevails; in others, as in Fletcher, a distinctly new flavour—a flavour not perceptible in Shakespere, much less in Marlowe—appears. But in none of them is that other flavour of pronounced decadence, which appears in the work of men so great as Massinger and Ford, at all perceptible. We are still in the creative period, and in some of the work to be now noticed we are in a comparatively unformed stage of it. It has been said, and not unjustly said, that the work of Beaumont and Fletcher belongs, when looked at

on one side, not to the days of Elizabeth at all, but to the later
seventeenth century ; and this is true to the extent that the post-
Restoration dramatists copied Fletcher and followed Fletcher
very much more than Shakespere.   But not only dates but other
characteristics refer the work of Beaumont and Fletcher to a distinctly earlier period than the work of their, in some sense, successors Massinger and Ford.

It will have been observed that I cleave to the old-fashioned
nomenclature, and speak of " Beaumont and Fletcher."   Until
very recently, when two new editions have made their appearance,
there was for a time a certain tendency to bring Fletcher into
greater prominence than his partner, but at the same time and on
the whole to depreciate both.   I am in all things but ill-disposed
to admit innovation without the clearest and most cogent proofs ;
and although the comparatively short life of Beaumont makes it
impossible that he should have taken part in some of the fifty-two
plays traditionally assigned to the partnership (we may perhaps
add Mr. Bullen's remarkable discovery of *Sir John Barneveldt*,
in which Massinger probably took Beaumont's place), I see no
reason to dispute the well-established theory that Beaumont contributed at least criticism, and probably original work, to a large
number of these plays ; and that his influence probably survived
himself in conditioning his partner's work.   And I am also
disposed to think that the plays attributed to the pair have
scarcely had fair measure in comparison with the work of their
contemporaries, which was so long neglected.   Beaumont and
Fletcher kept the stage—kept it constantly and triumphantly—
till almost, if not quite, within living memory ; while since the
seventeenth century, and since its earlier part, I believe that very
few plays of Dekker's or Middleton's, of Webster's or of Ford's, have
been presented to an English audience.   This of itself constituted
at the great revival of interest in Elizabethan literature something
of a prejudice in favour of *les oubliés et les dédaignés*, and this
prejudice has naturally grown stronger since all alike have been
banished from the stage.   The Copper Captain and the Humorous

Lieutenant, Bessus and Monsieur Thomas, are no longer on the boards to plead for their authors.   The comparative depreciation of Lamb and others is still on the shelves to support their rivals.

Although we still know but little about either Beaumont or Fletcher personally, they differ from most of their great contemporaries by having come of "kenned folk," and by having to all appearance, industrious as they were, had no inducement to write for money.   Francis Beaumont was born at Gracedieu, in Leicestershire in 1584.   He was the son of a chief-justice ; his family had for generations been eminent, chiefly in the law ; his brother, Sir John Beaumont, was not only a poet of some merit, but a man of position, and Francis himself, two years before his death in 1616, married a Kentish heiress.   He was educated at Broadgates Hall (now Pembroke College), Oxford, and seems to have made acquaintance with John Fletcher soon after quitting the University. Fletcher was five years older than his friend, and of a clerical family, his father being Bishop of London, and his uncle, Giles Fletcher (the author of *Licia*), a dignitary of the Church.   The younger Giles Fletcher and his brother Phineas were thus cousins of the dramatist.   Fletcher was a Cambridge man, having been educated at Benet College (at present and indeed originally known as Corpus Christi).   Little else is known of him except that he died of the plague in 1625, nine years after Beaumont's death, as he had been born five years before him.   These two men, however, one of whom was but thirty and the other not fifty when he died, have left by far the largest collection of printed plays attributed to any English author.   A good deal of dispute has been indulged in as to their probable shares,—the most likely opinion being that Fletcher was the creator and Beaumont (whose abilities in criticism were recognised by such a judge as Ben Jonson) the critical and revising spirit.   About a third of the whole number have been supposed to represent Beaumont's influence more or less directly.   These include the two finest, *The Maid's Tragedy* and *Philaster ;* while as to the third play, which may be put on the same level, *The Two Noble Kinsmen,* early assertion, confirmed by a constant catena of the best critical authority, maintains that Beaumont's place was taken by no less a collaborator than Shakespere.   Fletcher, as has been said, wrote in conjunction with Massinger (we know this for certain from Sir Aston Cokaine), and with Rowley and others, while Shirley seems to have finished some of his plays.   Some modern criticism has manifested a desire to apply the always uncertain and usually unprofitable tests of separation to the great mass of his work. With this we need not busy ourselves.   The received collection has quite sufficient idiosyncrasy of its own as a whole to make it superfluous for any one, except as a matter of amusement, to try to split it up.

Its characteristics are, as has been said, sufficiently marked, both in defects and in merits.   The comparative depreciation which has come upon Beaumont and Fletcher naturally fixes on the defects.   There is in the work of the pair, and especially in Fletcher's work when he wrought alone, a certain loose fluency, an ungirt and relaxed air, which contrasts very strongly with the strenuous ways of the elder playwrights.   This exhibits itself not in plotting or playwork proper, but in style and in versification (the redundant syllable predominating, and every now and then the verse slipping away altogether into the strange medley between verse and prose, which we shall find so frequent in the next and last period), and also in the characters.   We quit indeed the monstrous types of cruelty, of lust, of revenge, in which many of the Elizabethans proper and of Fletcher's own contemporaries delighted.   But at the same time we find a decidedly lowered standard of general morality—a distinct approach towards the *fay ce que voudras* of the Restoration.   We are also nearer to the region of the commonplace.   Nowhere appears that attempt to grapple with the impossible, that wrestle with the hardest problems, which Marlowe began, and which he taught to some at least of his followers.   And lastly—despite innumerable touches of tender and not a few of heroic poetry—the actual poetical value of the dramas at their best is below that of the best

work of the preceding time, and of such contemporaries as
Webster and Dekker.   Beaumont and Fletcher constantly delight,
but they do not very often transport, and even when they do, it
is with a less strange rapture than that which communicates itself
to the reader of Shakespere *passim*, and to the readers of many
of Shakespere's fellows here and there.

This, I think, is a fair allowance.   But, when it is made, a
goodly capital whereon to draw still remains to our poets.   In
the first place, no sound criticism can possibly overlook the
astonishing volume and variety of their work.   No doubt they
did not often (if they ever did) invent their fables.   But they
have never failed to treat them in such a way as to make them
original, and this of itself shows a wonderful faculty of invention
and constitutes an inexhaustible source of pleasure.   This pleasure
is all the more pleasurable because the matter is always presented
in a thoroughly workmanlike form.   The shapelessness, the incoherence, the necessity for endless annotation and patching together,
which mar so many even of the finest Elizabethan plays, have no
place in Beaumont and Fletcher.   Their dramatic construction
is almost narrative in its clear and easy flow, in its absence of
puzzles and piecings.   Again, their stories are always interesting,
and their characters (especially the lighter ones) always more or
less attractive.   It used to be fashionable to praise their "young
men," probably because of the agreeable contrast which they present with the brutality of the Restoration hero ; but their girls are
more to my fancy.   They were not straightlaced, and have left some
sufficiently ugly and (let it be added) not too natural types of
sheer impudence, such as the Megra of *Philaster*.   Nor could
they ever attain to the romantic perfection of Imogen in one
kind, of Rosalind in another, of Juliet in a third.   But for portraits
of pleasant English girls not too squeamish, not at all afraid of
love-making, quite convinced of the hackneyed assertion of the
mythologists that jests and jokes go in the train of Venus, but
true-hearted, affectionate, and of a sound, if not a very nice
morality, commend me to Fletcher's Dorotheas, and Marys, and

Celias. Add to this the excellence of their comedy (there is little better comedy of its kind anywhere than that of *A King and no King*, of the *Humorous Lieutenant*, of *Rule a Wife and have a Wife*), their generally high standard of dialogue verse, their charming songs, and it will be seen that if they have not the daemonic virtue of a few great dramatic poets, they have at any rate very good, solid, pleasant, and plentiful substitutes for it.

It is no light matter to criticise more than fifty plays in not many times fifty lines; yet something must be said about some of them at any rate. The play which usually opens the series, *The Maid's Tragedy*, is perhaps the finest of all on the purely tragic side, though its plot is a little improbable, and to modern notions not very agreeable. Hazlitt disliked it much ; and though this is chiefly to be accounted for by the monarchical tone of it, it is certainly faulty in parts. It shows, in the first place, the authors' greatest dramatic weakness—a weakness common indeed to all their tribe except Shakespere—the representation of sudden and quite insufficiently motived moral revolutions ; and, secondly, another fault of theirs in the representation of helpless and rather nerveless virtue punished without fault of its own indeed, but also without any effort. The Aspatia of *The Maid's Tragedy* and the Bellario of *Philaster*, pathetic as they are, are also slightly irritating. Still the pathos is great, and the quarrel or threatened quarrel of the friends Amintor and Melantius, the horrible trial put upon Amintor by his sovereign and the abandoned Evadne, as well as the whole part of Evadne herself when she has once been (rather improbably) converted, are excellent. A passage of some length from the latter part of the play may supply as well as another the sufficient requirement of an illustrative extract :—

> *Evad.* " O my lord !
> *Amin.* How now ?
> *Evad.* My much abused lord ! (*Kneels.*)
> *Amin.* This cannot be.
> *Evad.* I do not kneel to live, I dare not hope it ;
>   The wrongs I did are greater ; look upon me
>   Though I appear with all my faults. *Amin.* Stand up.

This is a new way to beget more sorrow.
Heav'n knows, I have too many ; do not mock me ;
Though I am tame and bred up with my wrongs
Which are my foster-brothers, I may leap
Like a hand-wolf into my natural wildness
And do an outrage : pray thee, do not mock me.

Evad. My whole life is so leprous, it infects
All my repentance : I would buy your pardon
Though at the highest set, even with my life :
That slight contrition, that's no sacrifice
For what I have committed.   *Amin.* Sure I dazzle.
There cannot be a Faith in that foul woman
That knows no God more mighty than her mischiefs :
Thou dost still worse, still number on thy faults
To press my poor heart thus.   Can I believe
There's any seed of virtue in that woman
Left to shoot up, that dares go on in sin
Known, and so known as thine is ?   O Evadne !
'Would, there were any safety in thy sex,
That I might put a thousand sorrows off,
And credit thy repentance !   But I must not ;
Thou'st brought me to that dull calamity,
To that strange misbelief of all the world
And all things that are in it ; that, I fear
I shall fall like a tree, and find my grave,
Only remembering that I grieve.

Evad. My lord,
Give me your griefs : you are an innocent,
A soul as white as Heav'n.   Let not my sins
Perish your noble youth : I do not fall here
To shadows by dissembling with my tears
(As, all say, women can) or to make less
What my hot will hath done, which Heav'n and you
Knows to be tougher than the hand of time
Can cut from man's remembrance ; no, I do not ;
I do appear the same, the same Evadne
Drest in the shames I liv'd in ; the same monster :
But these are names of honour, to what I am ;
I do present myself the foulest creature
Most pois'nous, dang'rous, and despis'd of men,
Lerna e'er bred, or Nilus : I am hell,
Till you, my dear lord, shoot your light into me

The beams of your forgiveness : I am soul-sick ;
And wither with the fear of one condemn'd,
Till I have got your pardon. *Amin.* Rise, Evadne.
Those heavenly Powers, that put this good into thee,
Grant a continuance of it : I forgive thee ;
Make thyself worthy of it, and take heed,
Take heed, Evadne, this be serious ;
Mock not the Pow'rs above, that can and dare
Give thee a great example of their justice
To all ensuing eyes, if that thou playest
With thy repentance, the best sacrifice.

Evad. I have done nothing good to win belief,
My life hath been so faithless ; all the creatures
Made for Heav'n's honours, have their ends, and good ones,
All but the cozening crocodiles, false women ;
They reign here like those plagues, those killing sores,
Men pray against ; and when they die, like tales
Ill told, and unbeliev'd they pass away
And go to dust forgotten : But, my lord,
Those short days I shall number to my rest,
(As many must not see me) shall, though late
(Though in my evening, yet perceive a will,)
Since I can do no good, because a woman,
Reach constantly at something that is near it ;
I will redeem one minute of my age,
Or, like another Niobe, I'll weep
Till I am water.

Amin. I am now dissolv'd.
My frozen soul melts : may each sin thou hast
Find a new mercy ! rise, I am at peace :
Hadst thou been thus, thus excellently good,
Before that devil king tempted thy frailty,
Sure, thou hadst made a star.   Give me thy hand ;
From this time I will know thee, and as far
As honour gives me leave, be thy Amintor.
When we meet next, I will salute thee fairly
And pray the gods to give thee happy days.
My charity shall go along with thee
Though my embraces must be far from thee.
I should ha' kill'd thee, but this sweet repentance
Locks up my vengeance, for which thus I kiss thee,
The last kiss we must take."

The beautiful play of *Philaster* has already been glanced at ; it is sufficient to add that its detached passages are deservedly the most famous of all. The insufficiency of the reasons of Philaster's jealousy may be considered by different persons as affecting to a different extent the merit of the piece. In these two pieces tragedy, or at least tragi-comedy, has the upper hand ; it is in the next pair as usually arranged (for the chronological order of these plays is hitherto unsolved) that Fletcher's singular *vis comica* appears. *A King and no King* has a very serious plot ; and the loves of Arbaces and Panthea are most lofty, insolent, and passionate. But the comedy of Bessus and his two swordsmen, which is fresh and vivid even after Bobadil and Parolles (I do not say Falstaff, because I hold it a vulgar error to consider Falstaff as really a coward at all), is perhaps more generally interesting. As for *The Scornful Lady* it is comedy pure and simple, and very excellent comedy too. The callousness of the younger Loveless—an ugly forerunner of Restoration manners—injures it a little, and the instantaneous and quite unreasonable conversion of the usurer Morecraft a little more. But the humours of the Lady herself (a most Moliéresque personage), and those of Roger and Abigail, with many minor touches, more than redeem it. The plays which follow[1] are all comical and mostly farcical. The situations, rather than the expressions of *The Custom of the Country*, bring it under the ban of a rather unfair condemnation of Dryden's, pronounced when he was quite unsuccessfully trying to free the drama of himself and his contemporaries from Collier's damning charges. But there are many lively traits in it. *The Elder Brother* is one of those many variations on *cedant arma togæ* which men of letters have always been somewhat prone to overvalue ; but the excellent comedy of *The Spanish Curate* is not impaired by the fact that Dryden chose to adapt it after his own fashion in *The Spanish Friar*. In *Wit Without Money*, though it is as usual amusing, the stage preference for a " roaring boy," a senseless

---

[1] It may perhaps be well to mention that the references to "volumes" are to the ten-volume edition of 1750, by Theobald, Seward, and others.

crack-brained spendthrift, appears perhaps a little too strongly.
The Beggar's Bush is interesting because of its early indications
of cant language, connecting it with Brome's *Jovial Crew*, and
with Dekker's thieves' Latin pamphlets.   But the faults and the
merits of Fletcher have scarcely found better expression anywhere
than in *The Humorous Lieutenant.*   Celia is his masterpiece in
the delineation of the type of girl outlined above, and awkward as
her double courtship by Demetrius and his father Antigonus is,
one somehow forgives it, despite the nauseous crew of go-betweens
of both sexes whom Fletcher here as elsewhere seems to take a
pleasure in introducing.   As for the Lieutenant he is quite charming ; and even the ultra-farcical episode of his falling in love with
the king owing to a philtre is well carried off.   Then follows the
delightful pastoral of *The Faithful Shepherdess*, which ranks with
Jonson's *Sad Shepherd* and with *Comus*, as the three chiefs of its
style in English.   *The Loyal Subject* falls a little behind, as also
does *The Mad Lover;* but *Rule a Wife and have a Wife* again
rises to the first class.   Inferior to Shakespere in the power of
transcending without travestying human affairs, to Jonson in
sharply presented humours, to Congreve and Sheridan in rattling
fire of dialogue, our authors have no superior in half-farcical, half-
pathetic comedy of a certain kind, and they have perhaps nowhere
shown their power better than in the picture of the Copper
Captain and his Wife.   The flagrant absurdity of *The Laws of
Candy* (which put the penalty of death on ingratitude, and apparently fix no criterion of what ingratitude is, except the decision of
the person who thinks himself ungratefully treated), spoils a play
which is not worse written than the rest.   But in *The False One*,
based on Egyptian history just after Pompey's death, and *Valentinian*, which follows with a little poetical license the crimes and
punishment of that Emperor, a return is made to pure tragedy—
in both cases with great success.   The magnificent passage which
Hazlitt singled out from *The False One* is perhaps the author's or
authors' highest attempt in tragic declamation, and may be considered to have stopped not far short of the highest tragic poetry.

" ' Oh thou conqueror,
         Thou glory of the world once, now the pity :
         Thou awe of nations, wherefore didst thou fall thus?
         What poor fate followed thee, and plucked thee on
         To trust thy sacred life to an Egyptian?
         The life and light of Rome to a blind stranger,
         That honourable war ne'er taught a nobleness
         Nor worthy circumstance show'd what a man was?
         That never heard thy name sung but in banquets
         And loose lascivious pleasures? to a boy
         That had no faith to comprehend thy greatness
         No study of thy life to know thy goodness? . . . .
         Egyptians, dare you think your high pyramides
         Built to out-dure the sun, as you suppose,
         Where your unworthy kings lie rak'd in ashes,
         Are monuments fit for him !   No, brood of Nilus,
         Nothing can cover his high fame but heaven ;
         No pyramid set off his memories,
         But the eternal substance of his greatness,
         To which I leave him.' "

The chief fault of *Valentinian* is that the character of Maxi-
mus is very indistinctly drawn, and that of Eudoxia nearly unintelligible.   These two pure tragedies are contrasted with two
comedies, *The Little French Lawyer* and *Monsieur Thomas*, which
deserve high praise.   The fabliau-motive of the first is happily
contrasted with the character of Lamira and the friendship of
Clerimont and Dinant ; while no play has so many of Fletcher's
agreeable young women as *Monsieur Thomas*.   *The Bloody
Brother*, which its title speaks as sufficiently tragical, comes
between two excellent comedies, *The Chances* and *The Wild Goose
Chase*, which might serve as well as any others for samples of the
whole work on its comic side.   In *The Chances* the portrait of the
hare-brained Don John is the chief thing ; in *The Wild Goose
Chase*, as in *Monsieur Thomas*, a whole bevy of lively characters,
male and female, dispute the reader's attention and divide his preference.   *A Wife for a Month* sounds comic, but is not a little
alloyed with tragedy ; and despite the pathos of its central situation,
is marred by some of Fletcher's ugliest characters—the characters

which Shakespere in Pandarus and the nurse in *Romeo and Juliet*
took care to touch with his lightest finger. *The Lover's Progress*,
a doubtful tragedy, and *The Pilgrim*, a good comedy (revived at
the end of the century, as was *The Prophetess* with certain help
from Dryden), do not require any special notice. Between these
two last comes *The Captain*, a comedy neither of the best nor yet
of the worst. The tragi-comic *Queen of Corinth* is a little heavy;
but in *Bonduca* we have one of the very best of the author's
tragedies, the scenes with Caratach and his nephew, the boy
Hengo, being full of touches not wholly unworthy of Shakespere.
The Knight of the Burning Pestle (where Fletcher, forsaking his
usual fantastic grounds of a France that is scarcely French, and
an Italy that is extremely un-Italian, comes to simple pictures of
London middle-class life, such as those of Jonson or Middleton)
is a very happy piece of work indeed, despite the difficulty of
working out its double presentment of burlesque knight-errantry
and straightforward comedy of manners. In *Love's Pilgrimage*,
with a Spanish subject and something of a Spanish style, there is
not enough central interest, and the fortunes by land and sea of
The Double Marriage do not make it one of Fletcher's most interesting plays. But *The Maid in the Mill* and *The Martial Maid*
are good farce, which almost deserves the name of comedy ; and
The Knight of Malta is a romantic drama of merit. In *Women
Pleased* the humours of avarice and hungry servility are ingeniously treated, and one of the starveling Penurio's speeches is
among the best-known passages of all the plays, while the anti-
Puritan satire of Hope-on-High Bomby is also noteworthy. The
next four plays are less noticeable, and indeed for two volumes, of
the edition referred to, we come to fewer plays that are specially
good. *The Night Walker ; or, The Little Thief*, though not very
probable in its incidents, has a great deal of lively business, and
is particularly noteworthy as supplying proof of the singular popularity of bell-ringing with all classes of the population in the
seventeenth century,—a popularity which probably protected many
old bells in the mania for church desecration. Not much can

be said for *The Woman's Prize*, or, *The Tamer Tamed*, an
avowed sequel, and so to speak, antidote to *The Taming of the
Shrew*, which chiefly proves that it is wise to let Shakespere
alone.   The authors have drawn to some extent on the *Lysistrata*
to aid them, but have fallen as far short of the fun as of the
indecency of that memorable play.   With *The Island Princess* we
return to a fair, though not more than a fair level of romantic tragi-
comedy, but *The Noble Gentleman* is the worst play ever attributed
(even falsely) to authors of genius.   The subject is perfectly
uninteresting, the characters are all fools or knaves, and the
means adopted to gull the hero through successive promotions to
rank, and successive deprivations of them (the genuineness of
neither of which he takes the least trouble to ascertain), are preposterous.   *The Coronation* is much better, and *The Sea Voyage*,
with a kind of Amazon story grafted upon a hint of *The Tempest*,
is a capital play of its kind.   Better still, despite a certain looseness both of plot and moral, is *The Coxcomb*, where the heroine
Viola is a very touching figure.   The extravagant absurdity of
the traveller Antonio is made more probable than is sometimes
the case with our authors, and the situations of the whole join
neatly, and pass trippingly.   *Wit at Several Weapons* deserves a
somewhat similar description, and so does *The Fair Maid of the
Inn ;* while *Cupid's Revenge*, though it shocked the editors of 1750
as a pagan kind of play, has a fine tragical zest, and is quite true
to classical belief in its delineation of the ruthlessness of the
offended Deity.   Undoubtedly, however, the last volume of this
edition supplies the most interesting material of any except the
first.   Here is *The Two Noble Kinsmen*, a play founded on the
story of Palamon and Arcite, and containing what I think irrefrag-
able proofs of Shakespere's writing and versification, though I am
unable to discern anything very Shakesperian either in plot or character.   Then comes the fine, though horrible tragedy of *Thierry
and Theodoret*, in which the misdeeds of Queen Brunehault find
chroniclers who are neither squeamish nor feeble.   The beautiful
part of Ordella in this play, though somewhat sentimental and

improbable (as is always the case with Fletcher's very virtuous characters) ranks at the head of its kind, and is much superior to that of Aspasia in *The Maid's Tragedy*.   *The Woman Hater*, said to be Fletcher's earliest play, has a character of rare comic, or at least farcical virtue in the smell-feast Lazarillo with his Odyssey in chase of the Umbrana's head (a delicacy which is perpetually escaping him) ; and *The Nice Valour* contains, in Chamont and his brother, the most successful attempts of the English stage at the delineation of the point of honour gone mad.   Not so much, perhaps, can be said for *An Honest Man's Fortune*, which, with a mask and a clumsy, though in part beautiful, piece entitled *Four Plays in One*, makes up the tale.   But whosoever has gone through that tale will, if he has any taste for the subject, admit that such a total of work, so varied in character, and so full of excellences in all its variety, has not been set to the credit of any name or names in English literature, if we except only Shakespere.   Of the highest and most terrible graces, as of the sweetest and most poetical, Beaumont and Fletcher may have little to set beside the masterpieces of some other men ; for accomplished, varied, and fertile production, they need not fear any competition.

It has not been usual to put Thomas Middleton in the front rank among the dramatists immediately second to Shakespere ; but I have myself no hesitation in doing so.   If he is not such a poet as Webster, he is even a better, and certainly a more versatile, dramatist ; and if his plays are inferior as plays to those of Fletcher and Massinger, he has a mastery of the very highest tragedy, which neither of them could attain.   Except the best scenes of *The White Devil*, and *The Duchess of Malfi*, there is nothing out of Shakespere that can match the best scenes of *The Changeling;* while Middleton had a comic faculty, in which, to all appearance, Webster was entirely lacking.   A little more is known about Middleton than about most of his fellows.   He was the son of a gentleman, and was pretty certainly born in London about 1570.   It does not appear that he was a university man, but he seems to have been at Gray's Inn. His earliest known work was not dramatic, and was exceedingly bad. In 1597 he published a verse paraphrase of the *Wisdom of Solomon,* which makes even that admirable book unreadable; and if, as seems pretty certain, the *Microcynicon* of two years later is his, he is responsible for one of the worst and feeblest exercises in the school—never a very strong one—of Hall and Marston. Some prose tracts of the usual kind are not better; but either at the extreme end of the sixteenth century, or in the very earliest years of the next, Middleton turned his attention to the then all absorbing drama, and for many years was (chiefly in collaboration) a busy playwright. We have some score of plays which are either his alone, or in greatest part his. The order of their composition is very uncertain, and as with most of the dramatists of the period, not a few of them never appeared in print till long after the author's death. He was frequently employed in composing pageants for the City of London, and in 1620 was appointed city chronologer. In 1624 Middleton got into trouble. His play, *The Game of Chess,* which was a direct attack on Spain and Rome, and a personal satire on Gondomar, was immensely popular, but its nine days' run was abruptly stopped on the complaint of the Spanish ambassador; the poet's son, it would seem, had to appear before the Council, and Middleton himself was (according to tradition) imprisoned for some time. In this same year he was living at Newington Butts. He died there in the summer of 1627, and was succeeded as chronologer by Ben Jonson. His widow, Magdalen, received a gratuity from the Common Council, but seems to have followed her husband in a little over a year.

Middleton's acknowledged, or at least accepted, habit of collaboration in most of the work usually attributed to him, and the strong suspicion, if not more than suspicion, that he collaborated in other plays, afford endless opportunity for the exercise of a certain kind of criticism. By employing another kind we can discern quite sufficiently a strong individuality in the work that is certainly, in part or in whole, his ; and we need not go farther. He seems to have had three different kinds of dramatic aptitude, in all of which he excelled. The larger number of his plays consist of examples of the rattling comedy of intrigue and manners, often openly representing London life as it was, sometimes transplanting what is an evident picture of home manners to some foreign scene apparently for no other object than to make it more attractive to the spectators. To any one at all acquainted with the Elizabethan drama their very titles speak them. These titles are *Blurt Master Constable, Michaelmas Term, A Trick to Catch the Old One, The Family of Love* [a sharp satire on the Puritans], *A Mad World, my Masters, No Wit no Help Like a Woman's, A Chaste Maid in Cheapside, Anything for a Quiet Life, More Dissemblers besides Women.* As with all the humour-comedies of the time, the incidents are not unfrequently very improbable, and the action is conducted with such intricacy and want of clearly indicated lines, that it is sometimes very difficult to follow. At the same time, Middleton has a faculty almost peculiar to himself of carrying, it might almost be said of hustling, the reader or spectator along, so that he has no time to stop and consider defects. His characters are extremely human and lively, his dialogue seldom lags, his catastrophes, if not his plots, are often ingenious, and he is never heavy. The moral atmosphere of his plays is not very refined,—by which I do not at all mean merely that he indulges in loose situations and loose language. All the dramatists from Shakespere downwards do that; and Middleton is neither better nor worse than the average. But in striking contrast to Shakespere and to others, Middleton has no kind of poetical morality in the sense in which the term poetical justice is better known. He is not too careful that the rogues shall not have the best of it ; he makes his most virtuous and his vilest characters hobnob together very contentedly ; and he is, in short, though never brutal, like the post-Restoration school, never very delicate. The style, however, of these works of his did not easily admit of such delicacy, except in the infusion of a strong romantic element such as that which Shakespere almost always infuses. Middleton has hardly done it more than once—in the charming comedy of *The Spanish Gipsy*,—and the result there is so agreeable that the reader only wishes he had done it oftener.

Usually, however, when his thoughts took a turn of less levity than in these careless humorous studies of contemporary life, he devoted himself not to the higher comedy, but to tragedy of a very serious class, and when he did this an odd phenomenon generally manifested itself. In Middleton's idea of tragedy, as in that of most of the playwrights, and probably all the playgoers of his day, a comic underplot was a necessity ; and, as we have seen, he was himself undoubtedly able enough to furnish such a plot. But either because he disliked mixing his tragic and comic veins, or for some unknown reason, he seems usually to have called in on such occasions the aid of Rowley, a vigorous writer of farce, who had sometimes been joined with him even in his comic work. Now, not only was Rowley little more than a farce writer, but he seems to have been either unable to make, or quite careless of making, his farce connect itself in any tolerable fashion with the tragedy of which it formed a nominal part. The result is seen in its most perfect imperfection in the two plays of *The Mayor of Queenborough* and *The Changeling*, both named from their comic features, and yet containing tragic scenes, the first of a very high order, the second of an order only overtopped by Shakespere at his best. The humours of the cobbler Mayor of Queenborough in the one case, of the lunatic asylum and the courting of its keeper's wife in the other, are such very mean things that they can scarcely be criticised. But the desperate love of Vortiger for Rowena in *The Mayor*, and the villainous plots against his chaste wife, Castiza, are real tragedy. Even these, however, fall far below the terrible loves, if loves they are to be called, of Beatrice-Joanna, the heroine of *The Changeling*, and her servant, instrument, and murderer. De Flores. The plot of the tragic part of this play is intricate and not wholly savoury. It is sufficient to say that

Beatrice having enticed De Flores to murder a lover whom she does not love, that so she may marry a lover whom she does love, is suddenly met by the murderer's demand of her honour as the price of his services.   She submits, and afterwards has to purchase fresh aid of murder from him by a continuance of her favours that she may escape detection by her husband.   Thus, roughly described, the theme may look like the undigested horrors of *Lust's Dominion*, of *The Insatiate Countess*, and of *The Revenger's Tragedy*.   It is, however, poles asunder from them.   The girl, with her southern recklessness of anything but her immediate desires, and her southern indifference to deceiving the very man she loves, is sufficiently remarkable, as she stands out of the canvas.   But De Flores,— the broken gentleman, reduced to the position of a mere dependant, the libertine whose want of personal comeliness increases his mistress's contempt for him, the murderer double and treble dyed, as audacious as he is treacherous, and as cool and ready as he is fiery in passion,—is a study worthy to be classed at once with Iago, and inferior only to Iago in their class.   The several touches with which these two characters and their situations are brought out are as Shakesperian as their conception, and the whole of that part of the play in which they figure is one of the most wonderful triumphs of English or of any drama.   Even the change of manners and a bold word or two here and there, may not prevent me from giving the latter part of the central scene :—

> *Beat.* " Why, 'tis impossible thou canst be so wicked,
>   Or shelter such a cunning cruelty,
>   To make his death the murderer of my honour !
>   Thy language is so bold and vicious,
>   I cannot see which way I can forgive it
>   With any modesty.
> *De F.* Pish !¹ you forget yourself :
>   A woman dipped in blood, and talk of modesty !
> *Beat.* O misery of sin ! would I'd been bound

---

¹ In orig. " Push," cf. " Tush."

    Perpetually unto my living hate
    In that Pisacquo, than to hear [1] these words.
    Think but upon the distance that creation
    Set 'twixt thy blood and mine, and keep thee there.
De F. Look but unto your conscience, read me *there ;*
    'Tis a true book, you'll find me there your equal :
    Pish ! fly not to your birth, but settle you
    In what the act has made you ; you're no more now.
    You must forget your parentage to me ;
    You are the deed's creature ; [2] by that name
    You lost your first condition, and I shall urge [3] you
    As peace and innocency has turn'd you out,
    And made you one with me.
Beat. With thee, foul villain !
De F. Yes, my fair murderess : do *you* urge *me ?*
    Though thou writ'st maid, thou whore in thine affection !
    'Twas changed from thy first love, and that's a kind
    Of whoredom in thy heart : and he's changed now
    To bring thy second on, thy Alsemero,
    Whom by all sweets that ever darkness tasted
    If I enjoy thee not, thou ne'er enjoyest !
    I'll blast the hopes and joys of marriage,
    I'll confess all ; my life I rate at nothing.
Beat. De Flores !
De F. I shall rest from all (lover's) [4] plagues then,
    I live in pain now ; that [love] shooting eye
    Will burn my heart to cinders.
Beat. O sir, hear me !
De F. She that in life and love refuses me,
    In death and shame my partner she shall be.
Beat. (kneeling). Stay, hear me once for all : I make thee master
    Of all the wealth I have in gold and jewels ;
    Let me go poor unto my bed with honour
    And I am rich in all things.
De F. Let this silence thee ;
    The wealth of all Valencia shall not buy
    My pleasure from me.

---

[1] Rather than hear.   [2] A trisyllable, as in strictness it ought to be.
[3] = " claim."

[4] This omission and the substitution in the next line are due to Dyce, and may be called *certissima emendatio.*

> Can you weep Fate from its determined purpose?
> So soon may you weep me.
> *Beat.* Vengeance begins ;
>   Murder, I see, is followed by more sins :
>   Was my creation in the womb so curst
>   It must engender with a viper first ?
> *De F.* (*raising her*). Come, rise and shroud your blushes in my bosom,
>   Silence is one of pleasure's best receipts.
>   Thy peace is wrought for ever in this yielding.
>   'Las, how the turtle pants ! thou'lt love anon
>   What thou so fear'st and faint'st to venture on."

Two other remarkable plays of Middleton's fall with some differences under the same second division of his works. These are *The Witch* and *Women Beware Women.* Except for the inevitable and rather attractive comparison with *Macbeth*, *The Witch* is hardly interesting. It consists of three different sets of scenes most inartistically blended,—an awkward and ineffective variation on the story of Alboin, Rosmunda and the skull for a serious main plot, some clumsy and rather unsavoury comic or tragi-comic interludes, and the witch scenes. The two first are very nearly worthless ; the third is intrinsically, though far below *Macbeth*, interesting enough and indirectly more interesting because of the questions which have been started, as to the indebtedness of the two poets to each other. The best opinion seems to be that Shakespere most certainly did not copy Middleton, nor (a strange fancy of some) did he collaborate with Middleton, and that the most probable thing is that both borrowed their names, and some details from Reginald Scot's *Discovery of Witchcraft.* *Women Beware Women* on the other hand is one of Middleton's finest works, inferior only to *The Changeling* in parts, and far superior to it as a whole. The temptation of Bianca, the newly-married wife, by the duke's instrument, a cunning and shameless woman, is the title-theme, and in this part again Middleton's Shakesperian verisimilitude and certainty of touch appear. The end of the play is something marred by a slaughter more wholesale even than that of *Hamlet*, and by no means so well justified. Lastly, *A Fair Quarrel* must be mentioned, because of the very high praise which it has received from Lamb and others. This praise has been directed chiefly to the situation of the quarrel between Captain Ager and his friend, turning on a question (the point of family honour), finely but perhaps a little tediously argued. The comic scenes, however, which are probably Rowley's, are in his best vein of bustling swagger.

I have said that Middleton, as it seems to me, has not been fully estimated. It is fortunately impossible to say the same of Webster, and the reasons of the difference are instructive. Middleton's great fault is that he never took trouble enough about his work. A little trouble would have made *The Change-ling* or *Women Beware Women*, or even *The Spanish Gipsy*, worthy to rank with all but Shakespere's very masterpieces. Webster also was a collaborator, apparently an industrious one ; but he never seems to have taken his work lightly. He had, moreover, that incommunicable gift of the highest poetry in scattered phrases which, as far as we can see, Middleton had not. Next to nothing is known of him. He may have been parish clerk of St. Andrew's, Holborn ; but the authority is very late, and the commentators seemed to have jumped at it to explain Webster's fancy for details of death and burial—a cause and effect not sufficiently pro-portioned. Mr. Dyce has spent much trouble in proving that he could not have been the author of some Puritan tracts published a full generation after the date of his masterpieces. Heywood tells us that he was generally called " Jack," a not uncommon thing when men are christened John. He himself has left us a few very sententiously worded prefaces which do not argue great critical taste. We know from the usual sources (Henslowe's Diaries) that he was a working furnisher of plays, and from many rather dubious title-pages we suppose or know some of the plays he worked at. *Northward Ho ! Westward Ho !* and *Sir John Wyatt* are pieces of dramatic journalism in which he seems to have helped Dekker. He adapted, with additions, Marston's *Mal-content*, which is, in a crude way, very much in his own vein ; he contributed (according to rather late authority) some charming scenes (elegantly extracted, on a hint of Mr. Gosse's, by a recent editor) to *A Cure for a Cuckold*, one of Rowley's characteristic and not ungenial botches of humour-comedy ; he wrote a bad pageant or two, and some miscellaneous verses. But we know nothing of his life or death, and his fame rests on four plays, in which no other writer is either known or even hinted to have had a hand, and which are in different ways of the first order of interest, if not invariably of the first order of merit. These are *The Duchess of Malfi, The White Devil, The Devil's Law Case*, and *Appius and Virginia*.

Of *Appius and Virginia* the best thing to be said is to borrow Sainte-Beuve's happy description of Molière's *Don Garcie de Navarre*, and to call it an *essai pale et noble*. Webster is sometimes very close to Shakespere ; but to read *Appius and Virginia*, and then to read *Julius Cæsar* or *Coriolanus*, is to appreciate, in perhaps the most striking way possible, the universality which all good judges from Dryden downwards have recognised in the prince of literature. Webster, though he was evidently a good scholar, and even makes some parade of scholarship, was a Romantic to the core, and was all abroad in these classical measures. *The Devil's Law Case* sins in the opposite way, being hopelessly undigested, destitute of any central interest, and, despite fine passages, a mere " salmagundi." There remain the two famous plays of *The White Devil* or *Vittoria Corombona* and *The Duchess of Malfi*—plays which were rarely, if ever, acted after their author's days, and of which the earlier and, to my judgment, better was not a success even then, but which the judgment of three generations has placed at the very head of all their class, and which contain magnificent poetry.

I have said that in my judgment *The White Devil* is the better of the two ; I shall add that it seems to me very far the better. Webster's plays are comparatively well known, and there is no space here to tell their rather intricate arguments. It need only be said that the contrast of the two is striking and unmistakable ;

and that Webster evidently meant in the one to indicate the
punishment of female vice, in the other to draw pity and terror by
the exhibition of the unprevented but not unavenged sufferings
of female virtue.   Certainly both are excellent subjects, and if
the latter seem the harder, we have Imogen and Bellafront to
show, in the most diverse material, and with the most diverse
setting possible, how genius can manage it.   With regard to *The
White Devil*, it has been suggested with some plausibility that
it wants expansion.   Certainly the action is rather crowded, and
the recourse to dumb show (which, however, Webster again
permitted himself in *The Duchess*) looks like a kind of shorthand
indication of scenes that might have been worked out.   Even
as it is, however, the sequence of events is intelligible, and
the presentation of character is complete.   Indeed, if there is
any fault to find with it, it seems to me that Webster has sinned
rather by too much detail than by too little.   We could spare
several of the minor characters, though none are perhaps quite
so otiose as Delio, Julio, and others in *The Duchess of Malfi*.
We feel (or at least I feel) that Vittoria's villainous brother
Flamineo is not as Iago and Aaron and De Flores are each in
his way, a thoroughly live creature.   We ask ourselves (or I ask
myself) what is the good of the repulsive and not in the least
effective presentment of the Moor Zanche.   Cardinal Monticelso
is incontinent of tongue and singularly feeble in deed,—for no
rational man would, after describing Vittoria as a kind of pest to
mankind, have condemned her to a punishment which was
apparently little more than residence in a rather disreputable
but by no means constrained boarding-house, and no omnipotent
pope would have let Ludivico loose with a clear inkling of his
murderous designs.   But when these criticisms and others are
made, *The White Devil* remains one of the most glorious works
of the period.   Vittoria is perfect throughout ; and in the justly-
lauded trial scene she has no superior on any stage.   Brachiano
is a thoroughly life-like portrait of the man who is completely
besotted with an evil woman.   Flamineo I have spoken of, and

not favourably ; yet in literature, if not in life, he is a triumph ;
and above all the absorbing tragic interest of the play, which it
is impossible to take up without finishing, has to be counted in.
But the real charm of *The White Devil* is the wholly miraculous
poetry in phrases and short passages which it contains.   Vittoria's
dream of the yew-tree, almost all the speeches of the unfortunate
Isabella, and most of her rival's, have this merit.   But the most
wonderful flashes of poetry are put in the mouth of the scoundrel
Flamineo, where they have a singular effect.   The famous dirge
which Cornelia sings can hardly be spoken of now, except in
Lamb's artfully simple phrase " I never saw anything like it," and
the final speeches of Flamineo and his sister deserve the same
endorsement.   Nor is even the proud farewell of the Moor
Zanche unworthy.   It is impossible to describe the "whirl of
spirits " (as the good old-fashioned phrase has it) into which the
reading of this play sets the reader, except by saying that the
cause of that whirl is the secret of the best Elizabethan writers,
and that it is nowhere, out of Shakespere, better exemplified than
in the scene partly extracted from Middleton, and in such passages
of *Vittoria Corombona* as the following :—

> *Cor.*   " Will you make me such a fool ? here's a white hand :
>   Can blood so soon be wash'd out ? let me see ;
>   When screech-owls croak upon the chimney-tops
>   And the strange cricket i' the oven sings and hops,
>   When yellow spots do on your hands appear,
>   Be certain then you of a corse shall hear.
>   Out upon 't, how 'tis speckled ! 'h'as handled a toad, sure.
>   Cowslip-water is good for the memory :
>   Pray, buy me three ounces of 't.
> *Flam.* I would I were from hence.
>   *Cor.* Do you hear, sir ?
>   I'll give you a saying which my grand-mother
>   Was wont, when she heard the bell toll, to sing o'er
>   Unto her lute.
> *Flam.* Do, an' you will, do.
>   *Cor.* ' Call for the robin-red-breast and the wren,
>   [*Cornelia doth this in several forms of distraction.*

Since o'er shady groves they hover,
And with leaves and flowers do cover
The friendless bodies of unburied men.
Call unto his funeral dole
The ant, the field mouse, and the mole,
To rear him hillocks that shall keep him warm
And (when gay tombs are robb'd) sustain no harm,
But keep the wolf far thence, that's foe to men,
For with his nails he'll dig them up again.'
They would not bury him 'cause he died in a quarrel ;
But I have an answer for them :
' Let holy Church receive him duly
Since he paid the church-tithes truly.'
His wealth is summ'd, and this is all his store.
This poor men get, and great men get no more.
Now the wares are gone, we may shut up shop.
Bless you, all good people.

                        [*Exeunt* CORNELIA, ZANCHE, *and* LADIES.

Flam. I have a strange thing in me, to the which
I cannot give a name, without it be
Compassion. I pray, leave me.

                          [*Exit* FRANCISCO DE MEDICIS.

This night I'll know the utmost of my fate ;
I'll be resolved what my rich sister means
To assign me for my service. I have liv'd
Riotously ill, like some that live in court,
And sometimes when my face was full of smiles
Have felt the maze of conscience in my breast,
Oft gay and honoured robes those tortures try :
We think cag'd birds sing when indeed they cry.

*Enter Brachiano's ghost, in his leather cassock and breeches, and boots ; with
a cowl ; in his hand a pot of lily flowers, with a skull in't.*

Ha ! I can stand thee : nearer, nearer it.
What a mockery hath death made thee ! thou look'st sad.
In what place art thou ? in yon starry gallery ?
Or in the cursèd dungeon ?—No ? not speak ?
Pray, sir, resolve me, what religion's best
For a man to die in ? or is it in your knowledge
To answer me how long I have to live ?
That's the most necessary question.
Not answer ? are you still like some great men

That only walk like shadows up and down,
And to no purpose ? Say :—
    [The Ghost throws earth upon him and shows him the skull.
What's that ? O, fatal ! he throws earth upon me !
A dead man's skull beneath the roots of flowers !—
I pray [you], speak, sir : our Italian Church-men
Make us believe dead men hold conference
With their familiars, and many times
Will come to bed to them, and eat with them.

                                [Exit GHOST.

He's gone ; and see, the skull and earth are vanished.
This is beyond melancholy.   I do dare my fate
To do its worst.   Now to my sister's lodging
And sum up all these horrors : the disgrace
The prince threw on me ; next the piteous sight
Of my dead brother ; and my mother's dotage ;
And last this terrible vision : all these
Shall with Vittoria's bounty turn to good,
Or I will drown this weapon in her blood."

                                       [Exit.

The Duchess of Malfi is to my thinking very inferior—full of beauties as it is.   In the first place, we cannot sympathise with the duchess, despite her misfortunes, as we do with the " White Devil."   She is neither quite a virtuous woman (for in that case she would not have resorted to so much concealment) nor a frank professor of " All for Love."   Antonio, her so-called husband, is an unromantic and even questionable figure.   Many of the minor characters, as already hinted, would be much better away.   Of the two brothers the Cardinal is a cold-blooded and uninteresting debauchee and murderer, who sacrifices sisters and mistresses without any reasonable excuse.   Ferdinand, the other, is no doubt mad enough, but not interestingly mad, and no attempt is made to account in any way satisfactorily for the delay of his vengeance. By common consent, even of the greatest admirers of the play, the fifth act is a kind of gratuitous appendix of horrors stuck on without art or reason.   But the extraordinary force and beauty of the scene where the duchess is murdered ; the touches of poetry, pure and simple, which, as in the *The White Devil*, are scattered all over the play; the fantastic accumulation of terrors before the climax; and the remarkable character of Bosola,—justify the high place generally assigned to the work. True, Bosola wants the last touches, the touches which Shakespere would have given. He is not wholly conceivable as he is. But as a " Plain Dealer " gone wrong, a " Malcontent " (Webster's work on that play very likely suggested him), turned villain, a man whom ill-luck and fruitless following of courts have changed from a cynic to a scoundrel, he is a strangely original and successful study. The dramatic flashes in the play would of themselves save it. " I am Duchess of Malfi still," and the other famous one " Cover her face; mine eyes dazzle; she died young," often as they have been quoted, can only be quoted again. They are of the first order of their kind, and, except the " already *my* De Flores ! " of *The Changeling*, there is nothing in the Elizabethan drama out of Shakespere to match them.

There is no doubt that some harm has been done to Thomas Heywood by the enthusiastic phrase in which Lamb described him as " a prose Shakespere." The phrase itself is in the original quite carefully and sufficiently explained and qualified. But unluckily a telling description of the kind is sure to go far, while its qualifications remain behind; and (especially since a reprint by Pearson in the year 1874 made the plays of Heywood, to which one or two have since been added more or less conjecturally by the industry of Mr. Bullen, accessible as a whole) a certain revolt has been manifested against the encomium. This revolt is the effect of haste. " A prose Shakespere " suggests to incautious readers something like Swift, like Taylor, like Carlyle, —something approaching in prose the supremacy of Shakespere in verse. But obviously that is not what Lamb meant. Indeed when one remembers that if Shakespere is anything, he is a poet, the phrase may run the risk of receiving an under—not an over— valuation. It is evident, however, to any one who reads Lamb's remarks in full and carefully—it is still more evident to any one who without much caring what Lamb or any one else has said, reads Heywood for himself—what he did mean. He was looking only at one or two sides of the myriad-sided one, and he justly saw that Heywood touched Shakespere on these sides, if only in an incomplete and unpoetic manner. What Heywood has in common with Shakespere, though his prosaic rather than poetic treatment brings it out in a much less brilliant way, is his sympathy with ordinary and domestic character, his aversion from the fantastic vices which many of his fellows were prone to attribute to their characters, his humanity, his kindness. The reckless tragedy of blood and massacre, the reckless comedy of revelry and intrigue, were always repulsive to him, as far as we can judge from the comparatively scanty remnant of the hundreds of plays in which he boasted that he had had a hand, if not a chief hand. Besides these plays (he confesses to authorship or collaboration in two hundred and twenty) he was a voluminous writer in prose and verse, though I do not myself pretend to much knowledge of his non-dramatic work. Its most interesting part would have been a *Lives of the Poets*, which we know that he intended, and which could hardly have failed to give much information about his famous contemporaries. As it is, his most remarkable and best-known work, not contained in one of his dramas, is the curious and constantly quoted passage half complaining that all the chief dramatists of his day were known by abbreviations of their names, but characteristically and good-humouredly ending with the license—

" I hold he loves me best who calls me Tom."

We have unfortunately no knowledge which enables us to call him many names except such as are derived from critical examination of his works. Little, except that he is said to have been a Lincolnshire man and a Fellow of Peterhouse, is known of his history. His masterpiece, *The Woman killed with Kindness* (in which a deceived husband, coming to the knowledge of his shame, drives his rival to repentance, and his wife to repentance and death, by his charity), is not wholly admirable.

Shakespere would have felt, more fully than Heywood, the
danger of presenting his hero as something of a wittol without
sufficient passion of religion or affection to justify his tolerance.
But the pathos is so great, the sense of "the pity of it" is so
simply and unaffectedly rendered, that it is impossible not to
rank Heywood very high.   The most famous "beauties" are in
the following passage :—

> *Anne.* " O with what face of brass, what brow of steel,
>   Can you unblushing speak this to the face
>   Of the espoused wife of so dear a friend ?
>   It is my husband that maintains your state,
>   Will you dishonour him that in your power
>   Hath left his whole affairs ?   I am his wife,
>   Is it to *me* you speak ?

> *Wendoll.*   " O speak no more :
>   For more than this I know and have recorded
>   Within the red-leaved table of my heart.
>   Fair and of all beloved, I was not fearful
>   Bluntly to give my life unto your hand,
>   And at one hazard all my worldly means.
>   Go, tell your husband ; he will turn me off
>   And I am then undone : I care not, I,
>   'Twas for your sake.   Perchance in rage he'll kill me ;
>   I care not, 'twas for you.   Say I incur
>   The general name of villain through the world,
>   Of traitor to my friend.   I care not, I.
>   Beggary, shame, death, scandal and reproach
>   For you I'll hazard all—why, what care I ?
>   For you I'll live and in your love I'll die."

Anne capitulates with a suddenness which has been generally
and rightly pronounced a blot on the play ; but her husband is
informed by a servant and resolves to discover the pair.   The
action is prolonged somewhat too much, and the somewhat
unmanly strain of weakness in Frankford is too perceptible ; but
these scenes are full of fine passages, as this :—

> *Fr.* " A general silence hath surprised the house,
>   And this is the last door.   Astonishment,

> Fear and amazement beat [1] upon my heart
> Even as a madman beats upon a drum.
> O keep my eyes, you heavens, before I enter,
> From any sight that may transfix my soul :
> Or if there be so black a spectacle,
> O strike mine eyes stark blind ! Or if not so,
> Lend me such patience to digest my grief
> That I may keep this white and virgin hand
> From any violent outrage, or red murder,
> And with that prayer I enter."

A subsequent speech of his—

> " O God, O God that it were possible
> To undo things done,"

only just comes short of the touch which would have given us instead of a prose Shakespere a Shakespere indeed ; and all the rest of the play, as far as the main plot is concerned, is full of pathos.

In the great number of other pieces attributed to him, written in all the popular styles, except the two above referred to, merits and defects are mixed up in a very curious fashion. Never sinking to the lowest depth of the Elizabethan playwright, including some great ones, Heywood never rises to anything like the highest height. His chronicle plays are very weak, showing no grasp of heroic character, and a most lamentable slovenliness of rhythm. Few things are more curious than to contrast with *Henry VI.* (to which some critics will allow little of Shakespere's work) and *Richard III.* the two parts of *Edward IV.*, in which Heywood, after a manner, fills the gap. There are good lines here and there, and touching traits ; but the whole, as a whole, is quite ludicrously bad, and "written to the gallery," the City gallery, in the most innocent fashion. *If You Know Not Me You Know Nobody*, or *The Troubles of Queen Elizabeth*, also in two parts, has the same curious innocence, the same prosaic character, but hardly as many redeeming flashes. Its

---

[1] First ed. " Play," which I am half inclined to prefer.

first part deals with Elizabeth's real "troubles," in her sister's days; its second with the Armada period and the founding of the Royal Exchange. For Heywood, unlike most of the dramatists, was always true to the City, even to the eccentric extent of making, in *The Four Prentices of London*, Godfrey of Bouillon and his brethren members of the prentice-brotherhood. His classical and allegorical pieces, such as *The Golden Age* and its fellows, are most tedious and not at all brief. The four of them (*The Iron Age* has two parts) occupy a whole volume of the reprint, or more than four hundred closely printed pages; and their clumsy dramatisation of Ovid's *Metamorphoses*, with any other classical learning that Heywood could think of thrust in, presents (together with various minor pieces of a somewhat similar kind) as striking a contrast with *Troilus and Cressida*, as *Edward IV.* does with *Henry VI.* His spectacles and pageants, chiefly in honour of London (*London's Jus Honorarium*, with other metaphorical Latin titles of the same description) are heavy, the weakness of his versification being especially felt in such pieces. His strength lies in the domestic and contemporary drama, where his pathos had free play, unrestrained by the necessity of trying to make it rise to chivalrous or heroic height, and where his keen observation of his fellow-men made him true to mankind in general, at the same time that he gave a vivid picture of contemporary manners. Of this class of his plays *A Woman killed with Kindness* is undoubtedly the chief, but it has not a few companions, and those in a sufficiently wide and varied class of subject. *The Fair Maid of the Exchange* is, perhaps, not now found to be so very delectable and full of mirth as it is asserted to be on its title-page, because it is full of that improbability and neglect of verisimilitude which has been noted as the curse of the minor Elizabethan drama. The "Cripple of Fenchurch," the real hero of the piece, is a very unlikely cripple; the heroines chop and change their affections in the most surprising manner; and the characters generally indulge in that curious self-description and soliloquising in dialogue which is never found in Shakespere, and is found everywhere else. But it is still a lively picture of contemporary manners. We should be sorry to lose *The Fair Maid of the West* with its picture of Devonshire sailors, foreign merchants, kings of Fez, Bashaws of various parts, Italian dukes, and what not. The two parts make anything but a good play, but they are decidedly interesting, and their tone supports Mr. Bullen's conjecture that we owe to Heywood the, in parts, admirable play of *Dick of Devonshire*, a dramatisation of the quarter-staff feats in Spain of Richard Peake of Tavistock. *The English Traveller* may rank with *A Woman killed with Kindness* as Heywood's best plays (there is, indeed, a certain community of subject between them), but *A Maidenhead well Lost*, and *The Witches of Lancashire*, are not far behind it; nor is *A Challenge for Beauty*. We can hardly say so much for *Love's Mistress*, which dramatises the story of *Cupid and Psyche*, or for *The Wise Woman of Hogsdon* (Hoxton), a play rather of Middleton's type. But in *The Royal King and Loyal Subject*, and in *Fortune by Land and Sea*, the author shows again the sympathy with chivalrous character and adventure which (if he never can be said to be fully up to its level in the matter of poetic expression) was evidently a favourite and constant motive with him. In short, Heywood, even at his worst, is a writer whom it is impossible not to like. His very considerable talent, though it stopped short of genius, was united with a pleasant and genial temper, and little as we know of his life, his dedications and prefaces make us better acquainted with his personality than we are with that of much more famous men.

No greater contrast is possible than that between our last two names—Day and Tourneur. As is the case with so many of our authors, very little is known of the personality of either; next to nothing of that of Tourneur. Both, it is pretty certain, were young men at the end of Elizabeth's reign, and were influenced strongly by the literary fashions set by greater men than themselves. But whereas Day took to the graceful fantasticalities of Lyly and to the not very savage social satire of Greene, Tourneur (or Turner)

addressed himself to the most ferocious school of sub-Marlovian
tragedy, and to the rugged and almost unintelligible satire of
Marston.   Something has been said of his effort in the latter vein,
the *Transformed Metamorphosis*. His two tragedies, *The Atheist's
Tragedy* and *The Revenger's Tragedy*, have been rather variously
judged.   The concentration of gloomy and almost insane vigour
in *The Revenger's Tragedy*, the splendid poetry of a few passages
which have long ago found a home in the extract books, and the
less separable but equally distinct poetic value of scattered lines
and phrases, cannot escape any competent reader.   But, at
the same time, I find it almost impossible to say anything
for either play as a whole, and here only I come a long way
behind Mr. Swinburne in his admiration of our dramatists.
The *Atheist's Tragedy* is an inextricable imbroglio of tragic
and comic scenes and characters, in which it is hardly possible
to see or follow any clue ; while the low extravagance of all
the comedy and the frantic rant of not a little of the tragedy
combine to stifle the real pathos of some of the characters.   *The
Revenger's Tragedy* is on a distinctly higher level ; the determination of Vindice to revenge his wrongs, and the noble and hap-
less figure of Castiza, could not have been presented as they are
presented except by a man with a distinct strain of genius, both
in conception and execution.   But the effect, as a whole, is
marred by a profusion of almost all the worst faults of the drama
of the whole period from Peele to Davenant.   The incoherence
and improbability of the action, the reckless, inartistic, butcherly
prodigality of blood and horrors, and the absence of any kind of
redeeming interest of contrasting light to all the shade, though
very characteristic of a class, and that no small one, of Elizabethan drama, cannot be said to be otherwise than characteristic
of its faults.   As the best example (others are *The Insatiate
Countess*, Chettle's *Hoffmann*, *Lust's Dominion*, and the singular
production which Mr. Bullen has printed as *The Distracted
Emperor*) it is very well worth reading, and contrasting with
the really great plays of the same class, such as *The Jew of*

Malta and *Titus Andronicus*, where, though the horrors are still overdone, yet genius has given them a kind of passport. But intrinsically it is mere nightmare.

Of a very different temper and complexion is the work of John Day, who may have been a Cambridge graduate, and was certainly a student of Gonville and Caius, as he describes himself on the title-page of some of his plays and of a prose tract printed by Mr. Bullen. He appears to have been dead in 1640, and the chief thing positively known about him is that between the beginning of 1598 and 1608 he collaborated in the surprising number of twenty-one plays (all but *The Blind Beggar of Bethnal Green* unprinted) with Haughton, Chettle, Dekker, and others. *The Parliament of Bees*, his most famous and last printed work, is of a very uncommon kind in English —being a sort of dramatic allegory, touched with a singularly graceful and fanciful spirit. It is indeed rather a masque than a play, and consists, after the opening Parliament held by the Master, or Viceroy Bee (quaintly appearing in the original, which may have been printed in 1607, though no copy seems now discoverable earlier than 1641, as " Mr. Bee "), of a series of characters or sketches of Bee-vices and virtues, which are very human. The termination, which contains much the best poetry in the piece, and much the best that Day ever wrote, introduces King Oberon giving judgment on the Bees from " Mr. Bee " downwards and banishing offenders. Here occurs the often-quoted passage, beginning —

> " And whither must these flies be sent ? "

and including the fine speech of Oberon—

> " You should have cried so in your youth."

It should be observed that both in this play and elsewhere passages occur in Day which seem to have been borrowed or stolen from or by other writers, such as Dekker and Samuel Rowley ; but a charitable and not improbable explanation of this has been found in the known fact of his extensive and intricate collaboration. *The Isle of Gulls*, suggested in a way by the *Arcadia*, though in general plan also fantastic and, to use a much abused but decidedly convenient word, pastoral, has a certain flavour of the comedy of manners and of contemporary satire. Then we have the quaint piece of *Humour out of Breath*, a kind of study in the for once conjoined schools of Shakespere and Jonson—an attempt at a combination of humorous and romantic comedy with some pathetic writing, as here :—

> "[O] Early sorrow art got up so soon ?
> What, ere the sun ascendeth in the east ?
> O what an early waker art thou grown !
> But cease discourse and close unto thy work.
> Under this drooping myrtle will I sit,
> And work awhile upon my corded net ;
> And as I work, record my sorrows past,
> Asking old Time how long my woes shall last.
> And first—but stay ! alas ! what do I see ?
> Moist gum-like tears drop from this mournful tree ;
> And see, it sticks like birdlime ; 'twill not part,
> Sorrow is even such birdlime at my heart.
> Alas ! poor tree, dost thou want company ?
> Thou dost, I see't, and I will weep with thee;
> Thy sorrows make me dumb, and so shall mine,
> It shall be tongueless, and so seem like thine.
> Thus will I rest my head unto thy bark,
> Whilst my sighs ease my sorrows."

Something the same may be said of *Law Tricks*, or *Who would have Thought it ?* which has, however, in the character of the Count Horatio, a touch of tragedy. Another piece of Day's is in quite a different vein, being an account in dramatised form of the adventures of the three brothers Shirley—a kind of play which, from *Sir Thomas Stukeley* downwards, appears to have been a very favourite one with Elizabethan audiences, though (as might indeed be expected) it was seldom executed in a very successful manner. Lastly, or first, if chronological order is taken, comes *The Blind Beggar of Bethnal Green*, written by Day in conjunction with Chettle, and ranging itself with the half

historical, half romantic plays which were, as has been pointed
out above, favourites with the first school of dramatists.   It
seems to have been very popular, and had a second and third
part, not now extant, but is by no means as much to modern
taste as some of the others.   Indeed both Day and Tourneur,
despite the dates of their pieces, which, as far as known, are
later, belong in more ways than one to the early school, and
show how its traditions survived alongside of the more perfect
work of the greater masters.   Day himself is certainly not a
great master—indeed masterpieces would have been impossible,
if they would not have been superfluous, in the brisk purveying
of theatrical matter which, from Henslowe's accounts, we see
that he kept up.   He had fancy, a good deal of wit, considerable
versatility, and something of the same sunshiny temper, with less
of the pathos, that has been noticed in Heywood.   If he wrote
The Maid's Metamorphosis (also ascribed conjecturally to Lyly),
he did something less dramatically good, but perhaps poetically
better, than his other work ; and if, as has sometimes been
thought,[1] *The Return from Parnassus* is his, he is richer still.
But even without these, his existing poetical baggage (the least
part of the work which we know he accomplished) is more than
respectable, and shows more perhaps than that of any other
distinctly minor writer the vast amount of loose talent—of miscellaneous inspiration—which was afloat in the air of his time.

[1] I agree with Professor Hales in thinking it very improbable.

CHAPTER VIII

THE reign of James I. is not, in mere poetry, quite such a brilliant period as it is in drama. The full influence of Donne and of Jonson, which combined to produce the exquisite if not extraordinarily strong school of Caroline poets, did not work in it. Of its own bards the best, such as Jonson himself and Drayton, were survivals of the Elizabethan school, and have accordingly been anticipated here. Nevertheless, there were not a few verse-writers of mark who may be most conveniently assigned to this time, though, as was the case with so many of their contemporaries, they had sometimes produced work of note before the accession of the British Solomon, and sometimes continued to produce it until far into the reign of his son. Especially there are some of much mark who fall to be noticed here, because their work is not, strictly speaking, of the schools that flourished under Elizabeth, or of the schools that flourished under Charles. We shall not find anything of the first interest in them; yet in one way or in another there were few of them who were unworthy to be contemporaries of Shakespere.

Joshua Sylvester is one of those men of letters whom accident rather than property seems to have made absurd. He has existed in English literature chiefly as an Englisher of the Frenchman Du Bartas, whom an even greater ignorance has chosen to regard as something grotesque. Du Bartas is one of the grandest, if also one of the most unequal, poets of Europe, and Joshua Sylvester, his translator, succeeded in keeping some of his grandeur if he even added to his inequality. His original work is insignificant compared with his translation; but it is penetrated with the same qualities. He seems to have been a little deficient in humour, and his portrait —crowned with a singularly stiff laurel, throated with a stiffer ruff, and clothed, as to the bust, with a doublet so stiff that it looks like textile armour—is not calculated to diminish the popular ridicule. Yet is Sylvester not at all ridiculous. He was certainly a Kentish man, and probably the son of a London clothier. His birth is guessed, on good grounds, at 1563; and he was educated at Southampton under the famous refugee, Saravia, to whom he owed that proficiency in French which made or helped his fame. He did not, despite his wishes, go to either university, and was put to trade. In this he does not seem to have been prosperous; perhaps he gave too much time to translation. He was probably patronised by James, and by Prince Henry certainly. In the last years of his life he was resident secretary to the English company of Merchant Venturers at Middleburgh, where he died on the 28th September 1618. He was not a fortunate man, but his descendants seem to have flourished both in England, the West Indies and America. As for his literary work, it requires no doubt a certain amount of good will to read it. It is voluminous, even in the original part not very original, and constantly marred by that loquacity which, especially in times of great inspiration, comes upon the uninspired or not very strongly inspired. The point about Sylvester, as about so many others of his time, is that, unlike the minor poets of our day and of some others, he has constant flashes—constant hardly separable, but quite perceivable, scraps, which show how genially heated the brain of the nation was. Nor should it be forgotten that his Du Bartas had a great effect for generations. The man of pure science may regret that generations should have busied themselves about anything so thoroughly unscientific; but with that point of view we are unconcerned. The important thing is that the generations in question learnt from Sylvester to take a poetical interest in the natural world.

John Davies of Hereford, who must have been born at about the same time as Sylvester, and who certainly died in the same year, is another curiosity of literature. He was only a writing-master,—a professor of the curious, elaborate penmanship which is now quite dead,—and he seems at no time to have been a man of wealth. But he was, in his vocation or otherwise, familiar with very interesting people, both of the fashionable and the literary class. He succeeded, poor as he was, in getting thrice married to ladies born; and, though he seems to have been something of a coxcomb, he was apparently as little of a fool as coxcombry will consist with. His work (of the most miscellaneous character and wholly in verse, though in subject as well as treatment often better suiting prose) is voluminous, and he might have been wholly treated (as he has already been referred to) with the verse pamphleteers, especially Rowlands, of an earlier chapter. But fluent and unequal as his verse is—obviously the production of a man who had little better to offer than journalism, but for whom the times did not provide the opening of a journalist— there is a certain salt of wit in it which puts him above the mere pamphleteers. His epigrams (most of which are contained in *The Scourge of Folly*, undated, like others of his books) are by no means despicable; the Welsh ancestors, whom he did not fail to commemorate, seem to have endowed him with some of that faculty for lampooning and "flyting" which distin- guished the Celtic race. That they are frequently lacking in point ought hardly to be objected to him; for the age had construed the miscellaneous examples of Martial indulgently, and Jonson in his own generation, and Herrick after him (two men with whom Davies cannot compare for a moment in general power), are in their epigrams frequently as pointless and a good deal coarser. His variations on English proverbs are also remark- able. He had a respectable vein of religious moralising, as the following sonnet from *Wit's Pilgrimage* will show :—

" When Will doth long to effect her own desires,
She makes the Wit, as vassal to the will,
To do what she, howe'er unright, requires,
Which wit doth, though repiningly, fulfil.
Yet, as well pleased (O languishing wit !)
He seems to effect her pleasure willingly,
And all his reasons to her reach doth fit ;
So like the world, gets love by flattery.
That this is true a thousand witnesses,
Impartial conscience, will directly prove;
Then if we would not willingly transgress,
Our will should swayed be by rules of love,
Which holds the multitude of sins because
Her sin morally to him his servants draws. "

The defect of Davies, as of not a few of his contemporaries, is
that, having the power of saying things rememberable enough, he
set himself to wrap them up and merge them in vast heaps of
things altogether unrememberable.   His successors have too
often resembled him only in the latter part of his gift.
His longer works (*Mirum in Modum*, *Summa Totalis*, *Microcosmus*, *The Holy Rood*, *Humours Heaven on Earth*, are some
of their eccentric titles) might move simple wonder if a
century which has welcomed *The Course of Time*, and *Yesterday*,
To-day, and For Ever, not to mention examples even more recent
than these, had any great reason to throw stones at its forerunners.   But to deal with writers like Davies is a little difficult in
a book which aims both at being nothing if not critical, and at
doing justice to the minor as well as to the major luminaries of
the time : while the difficulty is complicated by the necessity of
not saying ditto to the invaluable labourers who have reintroduced
him and others like him to readers.   I am myself full of the
most unfeigned gratitude to my friend Dr. Grosart, to Professor
Arber, and to others, for sparing students, whose time is the least
disposable thing they have, visits to public libraries or begging at
rich men's doors for the sight of books.   I should be very sorry
both as a student and as a lover of literature not to possess

Davies, Breton, Sylvester, Quarles, and the rest, and not to read
them from time to time.   But I cannot help warning those who
are not professed students of the subject that in such writers they
have little good to seek ; I cannot help noting the difference
between them and other writers of a very different order, and
above all I cannot help raising a mild protest against the en-
comiums which are sometimes passed on them.   Southey, in that
nearly best of modern books unclassified, *The Doctor*, has a story
of a glover who kept no gloves that were not " Best."   But when
the facts came to be narrowly inquired into, it was found that
the ingenious tradesman had no less than five qualities—" Best,"
" Better than Best," " Better than better than Best," " Best of
All," and the " Real Best."   Such language is a little delusive,
and when I read the epithets of praise which are sometimes
lavished, not by the same persons, on Breton and Watson, I ask
myself what we are to say of Spenser and Shakespere.

   Davies has no doubt also suffered from the fact that he had a
contemporary of the same name and surname, who was not only
of higher rank, but of considerably greater powers.   Sir John
Davies was a Wiltshire man of good family : his mother, Mary
Bennet of Pyt-house, being still represented by the Benett-Stan-
fords of Dorsetshire and Brighton.   Born about 1560, he was a
member of the University of Oxford, and a Templar ; but appears
to have been anything but a docile youth, so that both at
Oxford and the Temple he came to blows with the authorities.
He seems, however, to have gone back to Oxford, and to have
resided there till close of middle life ; some if not most of his
poems dating thence.   He entered Parliament in 1601, and after
figuring in the Opposition during Elizabeth's last years, was taken
into favour, like others in similar circumstances, by James.   Immediately after the latter's accession Davies became a law officer
for Ireland, and did good and not unperilous service there.   He
was mainly resident in Ireland for some thirteen years, producing
during the time a valuable " Discovery of the Causes of the Irish
Discontent."   For the last ten years of his life he seems to have

practised as serjeant-at-law in England, frequently serving as judge or commissioner of assize, and he died in 1626.   His poetical work consists chiefly of three poems or collections of poems.   These are *Nosce Teipsum*, or the immortality of the soul, in quatrains, and as light as the unsuitableness of the subject to verse will allow ; a singularly clever collection of acrostics called *Astraea*, all making the name of Elizabetha Regina ; and the *Orchestra*, or poem on dancing, which has made his fame. Founded as it is on a mere conceit—the reduction of all natural phenomena to a grave and regulated motion which the author calls dancing—it is one of the very best poems of the school of Spenser, and in harmony of metre (the seven-lined stanza) and grace of illustration is sometimes not too far behind Spenser himself.   An extract from it may be fitly followed by one of the acrostics of *Astraea :*—

    " As the victorious twins of Leda and Jove,
      (That taught the Spartans dancing on the sands
      Of swift Eurotas) dance in heaven above,
      Knit and united with eternal bands ;
      Among the stars, their double image stands,
      Where both are carried with an equal pace,
      Together jumping in their turning race.

    " This is the net, wherein the sun's bright eye,
      Venus and Mars entangled did behold ;
      For in this dance, their arms they so imply,
      As each doth seem the other to enfold.
      What if lewd wits another tale have told
      Of jealous Vulcan, and of iron chains !
      Yet this true sense that forgèd lie contains.

    " These various forms of dancing Love did frame,
      And besides these, a hundred millions more ;
      And as he did invent, he taught the same :
      With goodly gesture, and with comely show,
      Now keeping state, now humbly honouring low.
      And ever for the persons and the place
      He taught most fit, and best according grace."

> " Each day of thine, sweet month of May,
> Love makes a solemn Holy Day.
> I will perform like duty ;
> Since thou resemblest every way
> Astraea, Queen of Beauty.
> Both you, fresh beauties do partake,
> Either's aspect, doth summer make,
> Thoughts of young Love awaking,
> Hearts you both do cause to ache ;
> And yet be pleased with aching.
> Right dear art thou, and so is She,
> Even like attractive sympathy
> Gains unto both, like dearness.
> I ween this made antiquity
> Name thee, sweet May of majesty,
> As being both like in clearness."

The chief direct followers of Spenser were, however, Giles and Phineas Fletcher, and William Browne. The two first were, as has been said, the cousins of John Fletcher the dramatist, and the sons of Dr. Giles Fletcher, the author of *Licia*. The exact dates and circumstances of their lives are little known. Both were probably born between 1580 and 1590. Giles, who was the eldest, died vicar of Alderton in Suffolk in 1623 : Phineas, the younger, who was educated at Eton and King's College, Cambridge (Giles was a member of Trinity College in the same university), also took orders, and was for nearly thirty years incumbent of Hilgay-in-the-Fens.

Giles's extant work is a poem in four cantos or parts, generally entitled *Christ's Victory and Triumph*. It is written in a very curious and by no means successful stanza (rhymed A, B, A, B, B, C, C, C, the last line being an Alexandrine), with a lyrical interlude here and there. The whole treatment is highly allegorical, and the lusciousness of Spenser is imitated and overdone. Nevertheless the versification and imagery are often very beautiful, as samples of the two kinds will show :—

> " The garden like a lady fair was cut
> That lay as if she slumber'd in delight,

And to the open skies her eyes did shut ;
The azure fields of Heav'n were 'sembled right
In a large round, set with the flow'rs of light :
The flow'rs-de-luce, and the round sparks of dew,
That hung upon their azure leaves did shew
Like twinkling stars, that sparkle in the evening blue.

" Upon a hilly bank her head she cast,
On which the bower of Vain-delight was built,
White and red roses for her face were placed,
And for her tresses marigolds were spilt :
Them broadly she displayed like flaming gilt,
Till in the ocean the glad day were drowned :
Then up again her yellow locks she wound,
And with green fillets in their pretty cauls them bound.

" What should I here depaint her lily hand,
Her veins of violets, her ermine breast,
Which there in orient colours living stand :
Or how her gown with living leaves is drest,
Or how her watchman, armed with boughy crest,
A wall of prim hid in his bushes bears
Shaking at every wind their leafy spears
While she supinely sleeps, nor to be wakèd fears."

" See, see the flowers that below,
Now as fresh as morning blow,
And of all the virgin rose,
That as bright Aurora shows :
How they all unleavèd die,
Losing their virginity ;
Like unto a summer shade,
But now born and now they fade.
Everything doth pass away,
There is danger in delay.
Come, come gather then the rose,
Gather it, or it you lose.
All the sand of Tagus' shore
Into my bosom casts his ore :
All the valleys' swimming corn
To my house is yearly borne :
Every grape of every vine
Is gladly bruis'd to make me wine,

While ten thousand kings, as proud,
To carry up my train have bow'd,
And a world of ladies send me
In my chambers to attend me.
All the stars in Heaven that shine,
And ten thousand more, are mine :
Only bend thy knee to me,
Thy wooing shall thy winning be."

The Purple Island, Phineas Fletcher's chief work, is an allegorical poem of the human body, written in a stanza different only from that of *Christ's Victory* in being of seven lines only, the quintett of Giles being cut down to a regular elegiac quatrain. This is still far below the Spenserian stanza, and the colour is inferior to that of Giles. Phineas follows Spenser's manner, or rather his mannerisms, very closely indeed, and in detached passages not unsuccessfully, as here, where the transition from Spenser to Milton is marked :—

" The early morn lets out the peeping day,
  And strew'd his path with golden marigolds :
  The Moon grows wan, and stars fly all away.
  Whom Lucifer locks up in wonted folds
  Till light is quench'd, and Heaven in seas hath flung
  The headlong day : to th' hill the shepherds throng
  And Thirsil now began to end his task and song :

" ' Who now, alas ! shall teach my humble vein,
  That never yet durst peep from covert glade,
  But softly learnt for fear to sigh and plain
  And vent her griefs to silent myrtle's shade ?
  Who now shall teach to change my oaten quill
  For trumpet 'larms, or humble verses fill
  With graceful majesty, and lofty rising skill ?

" ' Ah, thou dread Spirit ! shed thy holy fire,
  Thy holy flame, into my frozen heart ;
  Teach thou my creeping measures to aspire
  And swell in bigger notes, and higher art :
  Teach my low Muse thy fierce alarms to ring,
  And raise my soft strain to high thundering,
  Tune thou my lofty song ; thy battles must I sing.

> " ' Such as thou wert within the sacred breast
>   Of that thrice famous poet, shepherd, king ;
>   And taught'st his heart to frame his cantos best.
>   Of all that e'er thy glorious works did sing ;
>   Or as, those holy fishers once among,
>   Thou flamedst bright with sparkling parted tongues ;
>   And brought'st down Heaven to Earth in those all-conquering songs.' "

But where both fail is first in the adjustment of the harmony of the individual stanza as a verse paragraph, and secondly in the management of their fable. Spenser has everywhere a certain romance-interest both of story and character which carries off in its steady current, where carrying off is needed, both his allegorising and his long descriptions. The Fletchers, unable to impart this interest, or unconscious of the necessity of imparting it, lose themselves in shallow overflowings like a stream that overruns its bank. But Giles was a master of gorgeous colouring in phrase and rhythm, while in *The Purple Island* there are detached passages not quite unworthy of Spenser, when he is not at his very best—that is to say, worthy of almost any English poet. Phineas, moreover, has, to leave *Britain's Ida* alone, a not inconsiderable amount of other work. His Piscatory Eclogues show the influence of *The Shepherd's Calendar* as closely as, perhaps more happily than, *The Purple Island* shows the influence of *The Faërie Queene*, and in his miscellanies there is much musical verse. It is, however, very noticeable that even in these occasional poems his vehicle is usually either the actual stanza of the *Island*, or something equally elaborate, unsuited though such stanzas often are to the purpose. These two poets indeed, though in poetical capacity they surpassed all but one or two veterans of their own generation, seem to have been wholly subdued and carried away by the mighty flood of their master's poetical production. It is probable that, had he not written, they would not have written at all ; yet it is possible that, had he not written, they would have produced something much more original and valuable. It ought to be mentioned that the influence of both upon Milton, directly and as handing on the tradition of Spenser, was evidently very great. The strong Cambridge flavour (not very perceptible in Spenser himself, but of which Milton is, at any rate in his early poems, full) comes out in them, and from *Christ's Victory* at any rate the poet of *Lycidas*, the *Ode on the Nativity*, and *Paradise Regained*, apparently "took up," as the phrase of his own day went, not a few commodities.

The same rich borrower owed something to William Browne, who, in his turn, like the Fletchers, but with a much less extensive indebtedness, levied on Spenser. Browne, however, was free from the *genius loci*, being a Devonshire man born and of Exeter College, Oxford, by education. He was born, they say, in 1591, published the first part of *Britannia's Pastorals* in 1613, made many literary and some noble acquaintances, is thought to have lived for some time at Oxford as a tutor, and either in Surrey or in his native county for the rest of his life, which is (not certainly) said to have ended about 1643. Browne was evidently a man of very wide literary sympathy, which saved him from falling into the mere groove of the Fletchers. He was a personal friend and an enthusiastic devotee of Jonson, Drayton, Chapman. He was a student of Chaucer and Occleve. He was the dear friend and associate of a poet more gifted but more un-equal than himself, George Wither. All this various literary cultivation had the advantage of keeping him from being a mere mocking-bird, though it did not quite provide him with any prevailing or wholly original pipe of his own. *Britannia's Pastorals* (the third book of which remained in MS. for more than two centuries) is a narrative but extremely desultory poem, in fluent and somewhat loose couplets, diversified with lyrics full of local colour, and extremely pleasant to read, though hope-lessly difficult to analyse in any short space, or indeed in any space at all. Browne seems to have meandered on exactly as the fancy took him; and his ardent love for the country, his really artistic though somewhat unchastened gift of poetical de-scription and presentment enabled him to go on just as he

pleased, after a fashion, of which here are two specimens in
different measures :—

" ' May first
(Quoth Marin) swains give lambs to thee ;
And may thy flood have seignory
Of all floods else ; and to thy fame
Meet greater springs, yet keep thy name.
May never newt, nor the toad
Within thy banks make their abode !
Taking thy journey from the sea
May'st thou ne'er happen in thy way
On nitre or on brimstone mine,
To spoil thy taste ! This spring of thine,
Let it of nothing taste but earth,
And salt conceivèd in their birth.
Be ever fresh ! Let no man dare
To spoil thy fish, make lock or wear,
But on thy margent still let dwell
Those flowers which have the sweetest smell.
And let the dust upon thy strand
Become like Tagus' golden sand.
Let as much good betide to thee
As thou hast favour shew'd to me.' "

" Here left the bird the cherry, and anon
Forsook her bosom, and for more is gone,
Making such speedy flights into the thick
That she admir'd he went and came so quick.
Then, lest his many cherries should distaste,
Some other fruit he brings than he brought last.
Sometime of strawberries a little stem
Oft changing colours as he gather'd them,
Some green, some white, some red, on them infus'd,
These lov'd, these fear'd, they blush'd to be so us'd.
The peascod green, oft with no little toil
He'd seek for in the fattest, fertil'st soil
And rend it from the stalk to bring it to her,
And in her bosom for acceptance woo her.
No berry in the grove or forest grew
That fit for nourishment the kind bird knew,
Nor any powerful herb in open field
To serve her brood the teeming earth did yield,

> But with his utmost industry he sought it,
> And to the cave for chaste Marina brought it."

The Shepherd's Pipe, besides reproducing Occleve, is in parts reminiscent of Chaucer, in parts of Spenser, but always characterised by the free and unshackled movement which is Browne's great charm ; and the same characteristics appear in the few minor poems attributed to him. Browne has been compared to Keats, who read and loved him, and there are certainly not a few points of resemblance. Of Keats's higher or more restrained excellences, such as appear in the finest passages of *St. Agnes' Eve*, and *Hyperion*, in the *Ode to a Grecian Urn*, and such minor pieces as *In a Drear-Nighted December*, Browne had nothing. But he, like Keats, had that kind of love of Nature which is really the love of a lover ; and he had, like Keats, a wonderful gift of expression of his love.[1] Nor is he ever prosaic, a praise which certainly cannot be accorded to some men of far greater repute, and perhaps of occasionally higher gifts both in his own time and others. The rarest notes of Apollo he has not, but he is never driven, as the poet and friend of his, to whom we next come, was often driven, to the words of Mercury. This special gift was not very common at the time ; and though that time produced better poets than Browne, it is worth noting in

[1] Something of the same love, but unluckily much less of the same gift, occurs in the poems of a friend of Browne's once hardly known except by some fair verses on Shakespere (" Renowned Spenser," etc.), but made fully accessible by Mr. R. Warwick Bond in 1893. This was William Basse, a retainer of the Wenman family near Thame, the author, probably or certainly, of a quaint defence of retainership, *Sword and Buckler* (1602), and of other poems—*Pastoral Elegies*, *Urania*, *Polyhymnia*, etc.—together with an exceedingly odd piece, *The Metamorphosis of the Walnut-Tree of Boarstall*, which is not quite like anything else of the time. Basse, who seems also to have spelt his name " Bas," and perhaps lived and wrote through the first forty or fifty years of the seventeenth century, is but a moderate poet. Still he is not contemptible, and deserves to rank as a member of the Spenserian family on the pastoral side ; while the *Walnut-Tree*, though it may owe something to *The Oak and the Brere*, has a quaintness which is not in Spenser, and not perhaps exactly anywhere else.

him. He may never reach the highest poetry, but he is always a poet.

The comparative impotence of even the best criticism to force writers on public attention has never been better illustrated than in the case of George Wither himself. The greater part of a century has passed since Charles Lamb's glowing eulogy of him was written, and the terms of that eulogy have never been contested by competent authority. Yet there is no complete collection of his work in existence, and there is no complete collection even of the poems, saving a privately printed one which is inaccessible except in large libraries, and to a few subscribers. His sacred poems, which are not his best, were indeed reprinted in the Library of Old Authors ; and one song of his, the famous "Shall I Wasting in Despair," is universally known. But the long and exquisite poem of *Philarete* was not generally known (if it is generally known now, which may be doubted) till Mr. Arber reprinted it in the fourth volume of his *English Garner.* Nor can *Fidelia* and *The Shepherd's Hunting*, things scarcely inferior, be said to be familiar to the general reader. For this neglect there is but one excuse, and that an insufficient one, considering the immense quantity of very indifferent contemporary work which has had the honour of modern publication. What the excuse is we shall say presently. Wither was born at Brentworth, in the Alresford district of Hampshire (a district afterwards delightfully described by him), on 11th June 1588. His family was respectable ; and though not the eldest son, he had at one time some landed property. He was for two years at Magdalen College, Oxford, of which he speaks with much affection, but was removed before taking his degree. After a distasteful experience of farm work, owing to reverses of fortune in his family he came to London, entered at Lincoln's Inn, and for some years haunted the town and the court. In 1613 he published his *Abuses Stript and Whipt*, one of the general and rather artificial satires not unfashionable at the time. For this, although the book has no direct personal reference that can be discovered, he was im-

prisoned in the Marshalsea ; and there wrote the charming poem
of *The Shepherd's Hunting*, 1615, and probably also *Fidelia*, an
address from a faithful nymph to an inconstant swain, which,
though inferior to *The Shepherd's Hunting* and to *Philarete* in the
highest poetical worth, is a signal example of Wither's copious
and brightly-coloured style. Three years later came the curious
personal poem of the *Motto*, and in 1622 *Philarete* itself, which
was followed in the very next year by the *Hymns and Songs of the
Church*. Although Wither lived until 2d May 1667, and was
constantly active with his pen, his *Hallelujah*, 1641, another
book of sacred verse, is the only production of his that has
received or that deserves much praise. The last thirty years of
his long life were eventful and unfortunate. After being a
somewhat fervent Royalist, he suddenly changed his creed at the
outbreak of the great rebellion, sold his estate to raise men for
the Parliament, and was active in its cause with pen as well as
with sword. Naturally he got into trouble at the Restoration
(as he had previously done with Cromwell), and was imprisoned again, though after a time he was released. At an
earlier period he had been in difficulties with the Stationers'
Company on the subject of a royal patent which he had received
from James, and which was afterwards (though still fruitlessly)
confirmed by Charles, for his *Hymns*. Indeed, Wither, though a
man of very high character, seems to have had all his life what
men of high character not unfrequently have, a certain facility for
getting into what is vulgarly called hot-water.

The defect in his work, which has been referred to above, and
which is somewhat passed over in the criticisms of Lamb and others,
is its amazing inequality. This is the more remarkable in that
evidence exists of not infrequent retouching on his part with
the rather unusual result of improvement—a fact which would
seem to show that he possessed some critical faculty. Such
possession, however, seems on the other hand to be quite incompatible with the production of the hopeless doggerel which he not
infrequently signs. The felicity of language and the command

of rhythmical effect which he constantly displays, are extraordinary, as for instance in the grand opening of his first Canticle :—

> " Come kiss me with those lips of thine,
>   For better are thy loves than wine ;
>   And as the pourèd ointments be
>   Such is the savour of thy name,
>   And for the sweetness of the same
>   The virgins are in love with thee."

Compare the following almost unbelievable rubbish—

> " As we with water wash away
>   Uncleanness from our flesh,
>   And sometimes often in a day
>   Ourselves are fain to wash."

Even in his earlier and purely secular work there is something, though less of this inequality, and its cause is not at all dubious. No poet, certainly no poet of merit, seems to have written with such absolute spontaneity and want of premeditation as Wither. The metre which was his favourite, and which he used with most success—the trochaic dimeter catalectic of seven syllables—lends itself almost as readily as the octosyllable to this frequently fatal fluency ; but in Wither's hands, at least in his youth and early manhood, it is wonderfully successful, as here :—

> " And sometimes, I do admire
>   All men burn not with desire.
>   Nay, I muse her servants are not
>   Pleading love : but O they dare not :
>   And I, therefore, wonder why
>   They do not grow sick and die.
>   Sure they would do so, but that,
>   By the ordinance of Fate,
>   There is some concealèd thing
>   So each gazer limiting,
>   He can see no more of merit
>   Than beseems his worth and spirit.
>   For, in her, a grace there shines
>   That o'erdaring thoughts confines,

Making worthless men despair
To be loved of one so fair.
Yea the Destinies agree
Some good judgments blind should be :
And not gain the power of knowing
Those rare beauties, in her growing.
Reason doth as much imply,
For, if every judging eye
Which beholdeth her should there
Find what excellences are ;
All, o'ercome by those perfections
Would be captive to affections.
So (in happiness unblest)
She for lovers should not rest."

Nor had he at times a less original and happy command of the rhymed decasyllabic couplet, which he sometimes handles after a fashion which makes one almost think of Dryden, and sometimes after a fashion (as in the lovely description of Alresford Pool at the opening of *Philarete*) which makes one think of more modern poets still. Besides this metrical proficiency and gift, Wither at this time (he thought fit to apologise for it later) had a very happy knack of blending the warm amatory enthusiasm of his time with sentiments of virtue and decency. There is in him absolutely nothing loose or obscene, and yet he is entirely free from the milk-and-water propriety which sometimes irritates the reader in such books as Habington's *Castara*. Wither is never mawkish, though he is never loose, and the swing of his verse at its best is only equalled by the rush of thought and feeling which animates it. As it is perhaps necessary to justify this high opinion, we may as well give the "Alresford Pool" above noted. It is like Browne, but it is better than anything Browne ever did ; being like Browne, it is not unlike Keats ; it is also singularly like Mr. William Morris.

" For pleasant was that Pool ; and near it, then,
Was neither rotten marsh nor boggy fen.
It was not overgrown with boisterous sedge,
Nor grew there rudely, then, along the edge

> A bending willow, nor a prickly bush,
> Nor broad-leafed flag, nor reed, nor knotty rush :
> But here, well ordered, was a grove with bowers ;
> There, grassy plots, set round about with flowers.
> Here, you might, through the water, see the land
> Appear, strewed o'er with white or yellow sand.
> Yon, deeper was it ; and the wind, by whiffs,
> Would make it rise, and wash the little cliffs ;
> On which, oft pluming, sate, unfrighted then
> The gagling wild goose, and the snow-white swan,
> With all those flocks of fowl, which, to this day
> Upon those quiet waters breed and play."

When to this gift of description is added a frequent inspiration of pure fancy, it is scarcely surprising that—

> " Such a strain as might befit
> Some brave Tuscan poet's wit,"

to borrow a couplet of his own, often adorns Wither's verse.

Two other poets of considerable interest and merit belong to this period, who are rather Scotch than English, but who have usually been included in histories of English literature—Drummond of Hawthornden, and Sir William Alexander, Earl of Stirling. Both, but especially Drummond, exhibit equally with their English contemporaries the influences which produced the Elizabethan Jacobean poetry ; and though I am not myself disposed to go quite so far, the sonnets of Drummond have sometimes been ranked before all others of the time except Shakespere's.

William Drummond was probably born at the beautiful seat whence he derived his designation, on 13th December 1585. His father was Sir John Drummond, and he was educated in Edinburgh and in France, betaking himself, like almost all young Scotchmen of family, to the study of the law. He came back to Scotland from France in 1610, and resided there for the greater part of his life, though he left it on at least two occasions for long periods, once travelling on the continent for eight years to recover from the grief of losing a lady to whom he was betrothed, and once retiring to avoid the inconveniences of the Civil War. Though a Royalist, Drummond submitted to be requisitioned against the Crown, but as an atonement he is said to have died of grief at Charles I.'s execution in 1649. The most famous incidents of his life are the visit that Ben Jonson paid to him, and the much discussed notes of that visit which Drummond left in manuscript. It would appear, on the whole, that Drummond was an example of a well-known type of cultivated dilettante, rather effeminate, equally unable to appreciate Jonson's boisterous ways and to show open offence at them, and in the same way equally disinclined to take the popular side and to endure risk and loss in defending his principles. He shows better in his verse. His sonnets are of the true Elizabethan mould, exhibiting the Petrarchian grace and romance, informed with a fire and aspiring towards a romantic ideal beyond the Italian. Like the older writers of the sonnet collections generally, Drummond intersperses his quatorzains with madrigals, lyrical pieces of various lengths, and even with what he calls "songs,"—that is to say, long poems in the heroic couplet. He was also a skilled writer of elegies, and two of his on Gustavus Adolphus and on Prince Henry have much merit. Besides the madrigals included in his sonnets he has left another collection entitled "Madrigals and Epigrams," including pieces both sentimental and satirical. As might be expected the former are much better than the latter, which have the coarseness and the lack of point noticeable in most of the similar work of this time from Jonson to Herrick. We have also of his a sacred collection (again very much in accordance with the practice of his models of the preceding generation), entitled *Flowers of Sion*, and consisting, like the sonnets, of poems of various metres. One of these is noticeable as suggesting the metre of Milton's "Nativity," but with an alteration of line number and rhyme order which spoils it. Yet a fourth collection of miscellanies differs not much in constitution from the others, and Drummond's poetical work is completed by some local pieces, such as *Forth Feasting*, some hymns and divine poems, and an attempt in Macaronic called *Polemo-Middenia*, which is perhaps not his He was also a prose writer, and a tract, entitled *The Cypress Grove*, has been not unjustly ranked as a kind of anticipation of Sir Thomas Browne, both in style and substance. Of his verse a sonnet and a madrigal may suffice, the first of which can be compared with the Sleep sonnet given earlier :—

" Sleep, Silence' child, sweet father of soft rest,
    Prince whose approach peace to all mortals brings,
    Indifferent host to shepherds and to kings,
    Sole comforter of minds which are oppressed ;
    Lo, by thy charming rod, all breathing things
    Lie slumb'ring, with forgetfulness possess'd,
    And yet o'er me to spread thy drowsy wings
    Thou spar'st, alas ! who cannot be thy guest.
    Since I am thine, O come, but with that face
    To inward light, which thou art wont to show,
    With feignèd solace ease a true felt woe ;
    Or if, deaf god, thou do deny that grace,
    Come as thou wilt, and what thou wilt bequeath :
    I long to kiss the image of my death."

" To the delightful green
    Of you, fair radiant een,
    Let each black yield, beneath the starry arch.
    Eyes, burnish'd Heavens of love,
    Sinople [1] lamps of Jove,
    Save all those hearts which with your flames you parch
    Two burning suns you prove ;
    All other eyes, compared with you, dear lights
    Are Hells, or if not Hells, yet dumpish nights.
    The heavens (if we their glass
    The sea believe) are green, not perfect blue ;
    They all make fair, whatever fair yet was,
    And they are fair because they look like you."

Sir William Alexander, a friend and countryman of Drummond (who bewailed him in more than one mournful rhyme of great beauty), was born in 1580 of a family which, though it had for some generations borne the quasi-surname Alexander, is said

---

[1] In heraldry (but not English heraldry) = "green."

to have been a branch of the Clan Macdonald.   Alexander early
took to a court life, was much concerned in the proposed planting
of Nova Scotia, now chiefly remembered from its connection with
the Order of Baronets, was Secretary of State for Scotland, and
was raised to the peerage.   He died in 1640.   Professor Masson
has called him " the second-rate Scottish sycophant of an in-
glorious despotism."   He might as well be called " the faithful
servant of monarchy in its struggle with the encroachments of
Republicanism," and one description would be as much question-
begging as the other.   But we are here concerned only with his
literary work, which was considerable in bulk and quality.   It
consists chiefly of a collection of sonnets (varied as usual with
madrigals, etc.), entitled *Aurora;* of a long poem on *Doomsday*
in an eight-lined stanza ; of a *Paraenesis* to Prince Henry ; and
of four "monarchic tragedies" on *Darius, Crœsus, Alexander,*
and *Cæsar,* equipped with choruses and other appliances of the
literary rather than the theatrical tragedy.   It is perhaps in these
choruses that Alexander appears at his best ; for his special forte
was grave and stately declamation, as the second of the following extracts will prove.   The first is a sonnet from *Aurora :*—

> " Let some bewitched with a deceitful show,
> Love earthly things unworthily esteem'd,
> And losing that which cannot be redeemed
> Pay back with pain according as they owe :
> But I disdain to cast my eyes so low,
> That for my thoughts o'er base a subject seem'd,
> Which still the vulgar course too beaten deem'd ;
> And loftier things delighted for to know.
> Though presently this plague me but with pain,
> And vex the world with wondering at my woes :
> Yet having gained that long desired repose
> My mirth may more miraculous remain.
> That for the which long languishing I pine,
> It is a show, but yet a show divine."

> " Those who command above,
> High presidents of Heaven,

By whom all things do move,
As they have order given,
What worldling can arise
Against them to repine?
Whilst castled in the skies
With providence divine ;
They force this peopled round,
Their judgments to confess,
And in their wrath confound
Proud mortals who transgress
The bounds to them assigned
By Nature in their mind.

" Base brood of th' Earth, vain man,
Why brag'st thou of thy might?
The Heavens thy courses scan,
Thou walk'st still in their sight ;
Ere thou wast born, thy deeds
Their registers dilate,
And think that none exceeds
The bounds ordain'd by fate ;
What heavens would have thee to,
Though they thy ways abhor,
That thou of force must do,
And thou canst do no more :
This reason would fulfil,
Their work should serve their will.

" Are we not heirs of death,
In whom there is no trust?
Who, toss'd with restless breath,
Are but a drachm of dust ;
Yet fools whenas we err,
And heavens do wrath contract,
If they a space defer
Just vengeance to exact,
Pride in our bosom creeps,
And misinforms us thus
That love in pleasure sleeps
Or takes no care of us :
' The eye of Heaven beholds
What every heart enfolds.' "

Not a few of his other sonnets are also worth reading, and
the unpromising subject of *Doomsday* (which connects itself in
style partly with Spenser, but perhaps still more with *The Mirror
for Magistrates*), does not prevent it from containing fine passages.   Alexander had indeed more power of sustained versification than his friend Drummond, though he hardly touches the
latter in point of the poetical merit of short isolated passages
and poems.   Both bear perhaps a little too distinctly the complexion of " *Gentlemen* of the Press "—men who are composing
poems because it is the fashion, and because their education,
leisure, and elegant tastes lead them to prefer that form of occupation.   But perhaps what is most interesting about them is the way
in which they reproduce on a smaller scale the phenomenon presented by the Scotch poetical school of the fifteenth century.
That school, as is well known, was a direct offshoot from, or following of the school of Chaucer, though in Dunbar at least it
succeeded in producing work almost, if not quite, original in
form.   In the same way, Drummond and Alexander, while able
to the full to experience directly the foreign, and especially
Italian influences which had been so strong on the Elizabethans,
were still in the main followers of the Elizabethans themselves,
and formed, as it were, a Scottish moon to the English sun of
poetry.   There is little or nothing that is distinctively national
about them, though in their following of the English model they
show talent at least equal to all but the best of the school they
followed.   But this fact, joined to those above noted, helps, no
doubt, to give an air of want of spontaneity to their verse—an air
as of the literary exercise.

    There are other writers who might indifferently come in this
chapter or in that on Caroline poetry, for the reign of James was
as much overlapped in this respect by his son's as by Elizabeth's,
and there are others who need but slight notice, besides yet
others—a great multitude—who can receive no notice at all.
The doggerel of Taylor, the water-poet (not a bad prose writer), received both patronage and attention, which seem to have annoyed

his betters, and he has been resuscitated even in our own times. Francis Beaumont, the coadjutor of Fletcher, has left independent poetical work which, on the whole, confirms the general theory that the chief execution of the joint plays must have been his partner's, but which (as in the *Letter to Ben Jonson* and the fine stoicism of *The Honest Man's Fortune*) contains some very good things. His brother, Sir John Beaumont, who died not so young as Francis, but at the comparatively early age of forty-four, was the author of a historical poem on *Bosworth Field*, as well as of minor pieces of higher merit, including some remarkable critical observations on English verse. Two famous poems, which every one knows by heart, the "You Meaner Beauties of the Night" of Sir Henry Wotton and the "Tell Me no more how fair She is" of Bishop Henry King, are merely perfect examples of a style of verse which was largely if not often quite so perfectly practised by lesser or less known men, as well as by greater ones.[1]

There is, moreover, a class of verse which has been referred to incidentally before, and which may very likely be referred to incidentally again, but which is too abundant, too characteristic, and too charming not to merit a place, if no very large one, to itself. I refer to the delightful songs which are scattered all over the plays of the period, from Greene to Shirley. As far as Shakespere is concerned, these songs are well enough known, and Mr. Palgrave's *Treasury*, with Mr. Bullen's and Bell's *Songs from the Dramatists*, have given an inferior currency, but still a currency, to the best of the remainder. The earlier we have spoken of. But the songs of Greene and his fellows, though charming, cannot compare with those of the more properly Jacobean poets. To name only the

[1] The most interesting collection and selection of verse of this class and time is undoubtedly Dr. Hannah's well-known and charming but rather oddly entitled *Poems of Raleigh, Wotton, and other Courtly Poets* in the Aldine Series. I say oddly entitled, because though Raleigh and Wotton were certainly courtiers, it would be hard to make the name good of some of the minor contributors.

best of each, Ben Jonson gives us the exquisite "Queen and Huntress," which is perhaps the best-known piece of his whole work ; the pleasant " If I freely may discover," and best of all — unsurpassed indeed in any language for rolling majesty of rhythm and romantic charm of tone—" Drink to me only with thine eyes." Again the songs in Beaumont and Fletcher stand very high, perhaps highest of all next to Shakespere's in respect of the "woodnote wild." If the snatch of only half articulate poetry of the " Lay a garland on my hearse," of *The Maid's Tragedy*, is really Fletcher's, he has here equalled Shakespere himself. We may add to it the fantastic and charming " Beauty clear and fair," of *The Elder Brother*, the comic swing of " Let the bells ring," and " The fit's upon me now ;" all the songs without exception in *The Faithful Shepherdess*, which is much less a drama than a miscellany of the most delightful poetry ; the lively war-song in *The Mad Lover*, to which Dryden owed not a little; the catch, " Drink to-day and drown all sorrow ;" the strange song of the dead host in *The Lover's Progress ;* the exquisite "Weep no more," of *The Queen of Corinth ;* the spirited "Let the mill go round," of *The Maid in the Mill;* the " Lovers rejoice," of *Cupid's Revenge ;* the " Roses, their sharp spines being gone," which is one of the most Shakesperean things of *The Two Noble Kinsmen ;* the famous " Hence, all you vain-delights," of *The Nice Valour*, which Milton expanded into *Il Penseroso*, and the laughing song of the same play. This long catalogue only contains a part of the singularly beautiful song work of the great pair of dramatists, and as an example we may give one of the least known from *The Captain :*—

> " Tell me, dearest, what is love ?
> 'Tis a lightning from above ;
> 'Tis an arrow, 'tis a fire,
> 'Tis a boy they call Desire.
>   'Tis a grave,
>   Gapes to have
> Those poor fools that long to prove.

" Tell me more, are women true?
Yes, some are, and some as you.
Some are willing, some are strange
Since you men first taught to change.
          And till troth
          Be in both,
All shall love to love anew.

" Tell me more yet, can they grieve?
Yes, and sicken sore, but live,
And be wise, and delay
When you men are as wise as they.
          Then I see,
          Faith will be
Never till they both believe."

The dirge of *Vittoria Corombona* and the preparation for death
of *The Duchess of Malfi* are Webster's sole but sufficient contributions to the list.   The witch songs of Middleton's *Witch*, and the
gipsy, or rather tramp, songs of *More Dissemblers besides Women*
and *The Spanish Gipsy*, have very high merit.   The songs of *Patient
Grissell*, which are pretty certainly Dekker's, have been noticed
already.   The otherwise worthless play of *The Thracian Wonder*,
attributed to Webster and Rowley, contains an unusual number
of good songs.   Heywood and Massinger were not great at songs,
and the superiority of those in *The Sun's Darling* over the songs
in Ford's other plays, seems to point to the authorship of Dekker.
Finally, James Shirley has the song gift of his greater predecessors.
Every one knows " The glories of our blood and state," but this is
by no means his only good song ; it worthily closes the list of the
kind—a kind which, when brought together and perused separately, exhibits, perhaps, as well as anything else of equal compass, the extraordinary abundance of poetical spirit in the age.
For songs like these are not to be hammered out by the most
diligent ingenuity, not to be spun by the light of the most assidu-
ously fed lamp.   The wind of such inspiration blows where, and
only where, it listeth.

CHAPTER IX

DURING the second and third quarters of the seventeenth century, or (to take literary rather than chronological dates) between the death of Bacon and the publication of *Absalom and Achitophel*, there existed in England a quintet of men of letters, of such extraordinary power and individuality, that it may be doubted whether any other period of our own literature can show a group equal to them; while it is certain that no other literature, except, perhaps, in the age of Pericles, can match them. They were all, except Hobbes (who belonged by birth, though not by date and character of writing, to an earlier generation than the rest), born, and they all died, within a very few years of each other. All were prose writers of the very highest merit; and though only one was a poet, yet he had poetry enough to spare for all the five. Of the others, Clarendon, in some of the greatest characteristics of the historian, has been equalled by no Englishman, and surpassed by few foreigners. Jeremy Taylor has been called the most eloquent of men; and if this is a bold saying, it is scarcely too bold. Hobbes stands with Bacon and Berkeley at the head of English-speaking philosophers, and is, if not in general grasp, in range of ideas, or in literary polish, yet in acuteness of thought and originality of expression, perhaps the superior of both his companions. The excellence of Browne is indeed more purely literary and intensely artistic first of all—a matter of expression rather than of substance,—while he is perhaps more flawed than any of them by the fashionable vices of his time. Yet, as an artist, or rather architect, of words in the composite and florid style, it is vain to look anywhere for his superior.

John Milton—the greatest, no doubt, of the five, if only because of his mastery of either harmony—was born in London on 9th December 1608, was educated at Cambridge, studied at home with unusual intensity and control of his own time and bent; travelled to Italy, returned, and engaged in the somewhat unexpected task of school-keeping; was stimulated, by the outbreak of the disturbances between king and parliament, to take part with extraordinary bitterness in the strife of pamphlets on the republican and anti-prelatical side, defended the execution of the king in his capacity of Latin secretary to the Government (to which he had been appointed in 1649); was struck with blindness, lay hid at the Restoration for some time in order to escape the Royalist vengeance (which does not seem very seriously to have threatened him), composed and published in 1667 the great poem of *Paradise Lost*, followed it with that of *Paradise Regained*, did not a little other work in prose and poetry, and died on 8th November 1674. He had been thrice married, and his first wife had left him within a month of her marriage, thereby occasioning the singular series of pamphlets on divorce, the theories of which, had she not returned, he had, it is said, intended to put into practice on his own responsibility. The general abstinence from all but the barest biographical outline which the scale of this book imposes is perhaps nowhere a greater gain than in the case of Milton. His personal character was, owing to political motives, long treated with excessive rigour. The reaction to Liberal politics early in the nineteenth century substituted for this rigour a somewhat excessive admiration, and even now the balance is hardly restored, as may be seen from the fact that a late biographer of his stigmatises his first wife, the unfortunate Mary Powell, as "a dull and common girl," without a tittle of evidence except the bare fact of her difference with her husband, and some innuendoes (indirect in themselves, and clearly tainted as testimony) in Milton's own divorce tracts. On the whole, Milton's character was not an amiable one, nor even wholly estimable. It is probable that he never in the course of his whole life did anything that he considered wrong ; but unfortunately, examples are not far to seek of the facility with which desire can be made to confound itself with deliberate approval. That he was an exacting, if not a tyrannical husband and father, that he held in the most peremptory and exaggerated fashion the doctrine of the superiority of man to woman, that his egotism in a man who had actually accomplished less would be half ludicrous and half disgusting, that his faculty of appreciation beyond his own immediate tastes and interests was small, that his intolerance surpassed that of an inquisitor, and that his controversial habits and manners outdid the license even of that period of controversial abuse,—these are propositions which I cannot conceive to be disputed by any competent critic aware of the facts. If they have ever been denied, it is merely from the amiable but uncritical point of view which blinks all a man's personal defects in consideration of his literary genius. That we cannot afford to do here, especially as Milton's personal defects had no small influence on his literary character. But having honestly set down his faults, let us now turn to the pleasanter side of the subject without fear of having to revert, except cursorily, to the uglier.

The same prejudice and partisanship, however, which have coloured the estimate of Milton's personal character have a little injured the literary estimate of him. It is agreed on all hands that Johnson's acute but unjust criticism was directed as much by political and religious prejudice as by the operation of narrow and mistaken rules of prosody and poetry ; and all these causes worked together to produce that extraordinary verdict on *Lycidas*, which has been thought unintelligible. But it would be idle to contend that there is not nearly as much bias on the other side in the most glowing of his modern panegyrists—Macaulay and Landor. It is, no doubt, in regard to a champion so formidable, both as ally and as enemy, difficult to write without fear or favour, but it must be attempted.

Milton's periods of literary production were three. In each of them he produced work of the highest literary merit, but at the same time singularly different in kind.   In the first, covering the first thirty years of his life, he wrote no prose worth speaking of, but after juvenile efforts, and besides much Latin poetry of merit, produced the exquisite poems of *L'Allegro* and *Il Penseroso*, the *Hymn on the Nativity*, the incomparable *Lycidas*, the *Comus* (which I have the audacity to think his greatest work, if scale and merit are considered), and the delicious fragments of the *Arcades*.   Then his style abruptly changed, and for another twenty years he devoted himself chiefly to polemical pamphlets, relieved only by a few sonnets, whose strong originality and intensely personal savour are uniform, while their poetical merit varies greatly.   The third period of fifteen years saw the composition of the great epics of *Paradise Lost* and *Paradise Regained*, and of the tragedy of *Samson Agonistes*, together with at least the completion of a good deal of prose, including a curious *History of England*, wherein Milton expatiates with a singular gusto over details which he must have known, and indeed allows that he knew, to be fabulous.   The production of each of these periods may be advantageously dealt with separately and in order.

Milton's Latin compositions both in prose and verse lie rather outside of our scope, though they afford a very interesting subject.   It is perhaps sufficient to say that critics of such different times, tempers, and attitudes towards their subject as Johnson and the late Rector of Lincoln,—critics who agree in nothing except literary competence,—are practically at one as to the remarkable excellence of Milton's Latin verse at its best.   It is little read now, but it is a pity that any one who can read Latin should allow himself to be ignorant of at least the beautiful *Epitaphium Damonis* on the poet's friend, Charles Diodati.

The dates of the few but exquisite poems of the first period are known with some but not complete exactness.   Milton was not an extremely precocious poet, and such early exercises as he has preserved deserve the description of being rather meritorious than remarkable.   But in 1629, his year of discretion, he struck his own note first and firmly with the hymn on the "Nativity." Two years later the beautiful sonnet on his three-and-twentieth year followed.   *L'Allegro* and *Il Penseroso* date not before, but probably not much after, 1632 ; *Comus* dating from 1634, and *Lycidas* from 1637.   All these were written either in the later years at Cambridge, or in the period of independent study at Horton in Buckinghamshire — chiefly in the latter.   Almost every line and word of these poems has been commented on and fought over, and I cannot undertake to summarise the criticism of others.   Among the greater memorabilia of the subject is that wonderful Johnsonism, the description of *Lycidas* as "harsh, the rhymes uncertain, and the numbers unpleasing ; " among the minor, the fact that critics have gravely quarrelled among themselves over the epithet "monumental" applied to the oak in *Il Penseroso*, when Spenser's "Builder Oak" (Milton was a passionate student of Spenser) would have given them the key at once, even if the same phrase had not occurred, as I believe it does, in Chaucer, also a favourite of Milton's.   We have only space here for first-hand criticism.

This body of work, then, is marked by two qualities : an extraordinary degree of poetic merit, and a still more extraordinary originality of poetic kind.   Although Milton is always Milton, it would be difficult to find in another writer five poems, or (taking the *Allegro* and its companion together) four, so different from each other and yet of such high merit.   And it would be still more difficult to find poems so independent in their excellence.   Neither the influence of Jonson nor the influence of Donne—the two poetical influences in the air at the time, and the latter especially strong at Cambridge—produced even the faintest effect on Milton. We know from his own words, and should have known even if he had not mentioned it, that Shakespere and Spenser were his favourite studies in English ; yet, save in mere scattered phrases, none of these poems owes anything to either. He has teachers but no models ; masters, but only in the way of learning how to do, not what to do. The "certain vital marks," of which he somewhat arrogantly speaks, are indeed there. I do not myself see them least in the poem on the "Nativity," which has been the least general favourite. It shows youth in a certain inequality, in a slight overdose of ornament, and especially in a very inartistic conclusion. But nowhere even in Milton does the mastery of harmonies appear better than in the exquisite rhythmical arrange-ment of the piece, in the almost unearthly beauty of the exordium, and in the famous stanzas beginning "The oracles are dumb." It must be remembered that at this time English lyric was in a very rudimentary and ill-organised condition. The exquisite snatches in the dramatists had been snatches merely ; Spenser and his followers had chiefly confined themselves to elaborate stanzas of full length lines, and elsewhere the octo-syllabic couplet, or the quatrain, or the dangerous "eights and sixes," had been chiefly affected. The sestines and canzons and madrigals of the sonnet-eers, for all the beauty of their occasional flashes, have nothing like the gracious and sustained majesty of the "Nativity" piece. For technical perfection in lyric metre, that is not so much to be sung as said, this ode has no precedent rival. As for *L'Allegro* and *Il Penseroso*, who shall praise them fitly ? They are among the few things about which there is no difference of opinion, which are as delightful to childhood as to criticism, to youth as to age. To dwell on their technical excellences (the chief of which is the unerring precision with which the catalectic and acatalectic lines are arranged and interchanged) has a certain air of imper-tinence about it. Even a critical King Alfonso El Sabio could hardly think it possible that Milton might have taken a hint here, although some persons have, it seems, been disturbed because skylarks do not come to the window, just as others are troubled because the flowers in *Lycidas* do not grow at the same time, and because they think they could see stars through the "starproof" trees of the *Arcades*.

The fragments of the masque just mentioned consist only of
three songs and an address in rhymed couplets.   Of the songs,
those ending—

> Such a rural queen,
> All Arcadia hath not seen,

are equal to anything that Milton has done; the first song and
the address, especially the latter, do not fall far below them.
But it is in *Comus* that, if I have any skill of criticism, Milton's
poetical power is at its greatest height.   Those who judge poetry
on the ground of bulk, or of originality of theme, or of anything
else extra-poetical,—much more those (the greater number) who
simply vary transmitted ideas,—may be scandalised at this assertion,
but that will hardly matter much.   And indeed the indebtedness
of *Comus* in point of subject (it is probably limited to the Odyssey,
which is public property, and to George Peele's *Old Wives' Tale*,
which gave little but a few hints of story) is scarcely greater than
that of *Paradise Lost ;* while the form of the drama, a kind nearly
as venerable and majestic as that of the epic, is completely filled.
And in *Comus* there is none of the stiffness, none of the *longueurs*,
none of the almost ludicrous want of humour, which mar the larger
poem.   Humour indeed was what Milton always lacked; had he
had it, Shakespere himself might hardly have been greater.   The
plan is not really more artificial than that of the epic; though in
the latter case it is masked to us by the scale, by the grandeur of
the personages, and by the familiarity of the images to all men
who have been brought up on the Bible.   The versification, as
even Johnson saw, is the versification of *Paradise Lost*, and to my
fancy at any rate it has a spring, a variety, a sweep and rush of
genius, which are but rarely present later.   As for its beauty in
parts, *quis vituperavit ?* It is impossible to single out passages, for
the whole is golden.   The entering address of Comus, the song
" Sweet Echo," the descriptive speech of the Spirit, and the
magnificent eulogy of the " sun-clad power of chastity," would be
the most beautiful things where all is beautiful, if the unapproachable " Sabrina fair " did not come later, and were not sustained

before and after, for nearly two hundred lines of pure nectar. If poetry could be taught by the reading of it, then indeed the critic's advice to a poet might be limited to this : " Give your days and nights to the reading of *Comus*."

The sole excuses for Johnson's amazing verdict on *Lycidas* are that it is not quite so uniformly good, and that in his strictures on its "rhyme" and "numbers" he was evidently speaking from the point of view at which the regular couplet is regarded as the *ne plus ultra* of poetry. There are indeed blotches in it. The speech of Peter, magnificently as it is introduced, and strangely as it has captivated some critics, who seem to think that anything attacking the Church of England must be poetry, is out of place, and in itself is obscure, pedantic, and grotesque. There is some over-classicism, and the scale of the piece does not admit the display of quite such sustained and varied power as in *Comus*. But what there is, is so exquisite that hardly can we find fault with Mr. Pattison's hyperbole when he called *Lycidas* the "high-water mark of English poetry." High-water mark even in the physical world is a variable limit. Shakespere constantly, and some other poets here and there in short passages go beyond Milton. But in the same space we shall nowhere find anything that can outgo the passage beginning " Alas what boots it," down to " head of thine," and the whole conclusion from " Return Alpheus." For melody of versification, for richness of images, for curious felicity of expression, these cannot be surpassed.

" But O the heavy change "—to use an irresistible quotation, the more irresistible that the change is foreshadowed in *Lycidas* itself—from the golden poetry of these early days to the prose of the pamphlets. It is not that Milton's literary faculty is less conspicuous here, or less interesting. There is no English prose before him, none save Taylor's and Browne's in his time, and absolutely none after him that can compare with the finest passages of these singular productions. The often quoted personal descriptions of his aims in life, his early literary studies, his views of poetry and so forth, are almost equal in the " other

harmony of prose" to *Comus* and *Lycidas*. The deservedly famous
Areopagitica is full of the most splendid concerted pieces of prose-
music, and hardly anywhere from the *Tractate of Reformation
Touching Church Discipline* to the *History of Britain*, which he
revised just before his death, is it possible to read a page without
coming across phrases, passages, and even whole paragraphs, which
are instinct with the most splendid life.   But the difference
between Milton's poetry and his prose is, that in verse he is
constantly under the restraint (sometimes, in his later work
especially, too much under the restraint) of the sense of style ;
while in his prose he seems to be wholly emancipated from it.
Even in his finest passages he never seems to know or to care
how a period is going to end.   He piles clause on clause, links
conjunction to conjunction, regardless of breath, or sense, or the
most ordinary laws of grammar.   The second sentence of his first
prose work contains about four hundred words, and is broken in
the course of them like a wounded snake.   In his very highest
flights he will suddenly drop to grotesque and bathos ; and there
is no more difficult task (*haud inexpertus loquor*) than the selection
from Milton of any passage of length which shall not contain
faults of which a modern schoolboy or gutter-journalist would be
ashamed.   Nor is the matter made much better by the consideration that it is not so much ignorance as temper which is the
cause of this deformity.   Lest it be thought that I speak harshly,
let me quote from the late Mr. Mark Pattison, a strong sympathiser
with Milton's politics, in complete agreement if not with his
religious views, yet with his attitude towards dominant ecclesi-
asticism, and almost an idolater of him from the purely literary
point of view.   " In *Eikonoclastes*," Milton's reply to *Eikon
Basilike*, Mr. Pattison says, and I do not care to attempt any
improvement on the words, " Milton is worse than tedious : his
reply is in a tone of rude railing and insolent swagger which
would have been always unbecoming, but which at this moment
was grossly indecent."   Elsewhere (and again I have nothing
to add) Mr. Pattison describes Milton's prose pamphlets as " a

plunge into the depths of vulgar scurrility and libel below the level of average gentility and education." But the Rector of Lincoln has not touched, or has touched very lightly, on the fault above noted, the profound lack of humour that these pamphlets display. Others have been as scurrilous, as libellous, as unfair; others have prostituted literary genius to the composition of paid lampoons; but some at least of them have been saved by the all-saving sense of humour. As any one who remembers the dreadful passage about the guns in *Paradise Lost* must know, the book of humour was to Milton a sealed book. He has flashes of wit, though not many; his indignation of itself sometimes makes him really sarcastic. But humorous he is never.

Destitute of this, the one saving grace of polemical literature, he plunged at the age of thirty-three into pamphlet writing. With a few exceptions his production in this kind may be thrown into four classes,—the *Areopagitica* and the *Letter to Hartlib* (much the best of the whole) standing outside. The first class attacks prelatical government, and by degrees glides, under the guise of apologetics for the famous *Smectymnuus*, into a fierce and indecent controversy with Bishop Hall, containing some of the worst examples of the author's deplorable inability to be jocular. Then comes the divorce series, which, with all its varied learning, is chiefly comic, owing to Milton's unfortunate blindness to the fact that he was trying to make a public question out of private grievances of the particular kind which most of all demand silence. Next rank the pieces composing the Apologia of regicide, the *Eikonoclastes*, the controversy with Salmasius (written in Latin), and the postscript thereto, devoted to the obscure Morus. And lastly come the pamphlets in which, with singular want of understanding of the course of events, Milton tried to argue Monk and the weary nation out of the purpose to shake off the heavy yoke of so-called liberty. The *History of Britain*, the very agreeable fragment on the *History of Muscovy*, the late *Treatise Against Popery*, in which the author holds out a kind of olive branch to the Church of England, in the very act of proclaiming his Arianism, and the

two little masterpieces already referred to, are independent of any
such classification.   Yet even in them sometimes, as always in the
others, *furor arma ministrat;* and supplies them as badly as if he
were supplying by contract.

Nevertheless both Milton's faults and his merits as a prose
writer are of the most remarkable and interesting character.   The
former consist chiefly in the reckless haste with which he con-
structs (or rather altogether neglects the construction of) his
periods and sentences, in an occasional confusion of those rules
of Latin syntax which are only applicable to a fully inflected
language with the rules necessary in a language so destitute of
inflections as English, and in a lavish and sometimes both needless and tasteless adaptation of Latin words.   All these were
faults of the time, but it is true that they are faults which Milton,
like his contemporaries Taylor and Browne, aggravated almost
wilfully.   Of the three Milton, owing no doubt to the fury which
animated him, is by far the most faulty and uncritical.   Taylor
is the least remarkable of the three for classicisms either of
syntax or vocabulary ; and Browne's excesses in this respect are
deliberate.   Milton's are the effect of blind passion.   Yet the
passages which diversify and relieve his prose works are far more
beautiful in their kind than anything to be found elsewhere in
English prose.   Though he never trespasses into purely poetical
rhythm, the solemn music of his own best verse is paralleled in
these ; and the rugged and grandiose vocabulary (it is particularly
characteristic of Milton that he mixes the extremest vernacular
with the most exquisite and scholarly phrasing) is fused and
moulded with an altogether extraordinary power.   Nor can we
notice less the abundance of striking phrase, now quaint, now
grand, now forcible, which in short clauses and "jewels five words
long" occurs constantly, even in the passages least artistically
finished as wholes.   There is no English prose author whose
prose is so constantly racy with such a distinct and varied savour
as Milton's.   It is hardly possible to open him anywhere after
the fashion of the *Sortes Virgilianæ* without lighting on a line

or a couple of lines, which for the special purpose it is impossible
to improve.   And it might be contended with some plausibility
that this abundance of jewels, or purple patches, brings into
rather unfair prominence the slips of grammar and taste, the
inequalities of thought, the deplorable attempts to be funny, the
rude outbursts of bargee invective, which also occur so numerously.
One other peculiarity, or rather one result of these peculiarities,
remains to be noticed ; and that is that Milton's prose is essentially inimitable.   It would be difficult even to caricature or to
parody it ; and to imitate it as his verse, at least his later verse,
has been so often imitated, is simply impossible.

The third and, in popular estimation, the most important
period of Milton's production was again poetical.   The characteristics of the poetry of the three great works which illustrate it
are admittedly uniform, though in *Samson Agonistes* they exhibit
themselves in a harder, drier, more ossified form than in the two
great epics.   This relation is only a repetition of the relation
between *Paradise Lost* and *Paradise Regained* themselves on the
one hand, and the poems of twenty years earlier, especially *Comus*
and *Lycidas*, on the other.   The wonderful Miltonic style, so artificial and yet such a triumph of art, is evident even so early
as the ode on the " Nativity," and it merely developed its own
characteristics up to the *Samson* of forty years later.   That it is
a real style and not merely a trick, like so many others, is best
shown by the fact that it is very hard, if not impossible, to
analyse it finally into elements.   The common opinion charges
Milton with Latinising heavily ; and so he does.   But we open
Paradise Lost at random, and we find a dozen lines, and not the
least beautiful (the Third Day of Creation), without a word in
them that is not perfectly simple English, or if of Latin origin,
naturalised long before Milton's time, while the syntax is also
quite vernacular.   Again it is commonly thought that the habits
of antithesis and parallelism, of omission of articles, of reversing
the position of adjectives and adverbs, are specially Miltonic.
Certainly Milton often indulges in them ; yet in the same way

the most random dipping will find passages (and any number of
them) where no one of these habits is particularly or eminently
present, and yet which every one would recognise as Miltonic.
As far as it is possible to put the finger on one peculiarity which
explains part of the secret of Milton's pre-eminence, I should
myself select his unapproached care and felicity in building what
may be called the verse-paragraph.   The dangers of blank verse
(Milton's preference for which over rhyme was only one of his
numerous will-worships) are many; but the two greatest lie in
easily understood directions.   With the sense generally or frequently ending as the line ends (as may be seen in the early
dramatists and in many bad poets since), it becomes intolerably stiff
and monotonous.   With the process of *enjambement* or overlapping, promiscuously and unskilfully indulged (the commonest
fault during the last two centuries), it is apt to degenerate into
a kind of metrical and barely metrical prose, distinguished from
prose proper by less variety of cadence, and by an occasional
awkward sacrifice of sense and natural arrangement to the
restrictions which the writer accepts, but by which he knows
not how to profit.   Milton has avoided both these dangers by
adhering to what I have ventured to call the verse-paragraph—
that is to say, by arranging the divisions of his sense in divisions
of verse, which, albeit identical and not different in their verse
integers, are constructed with as much internal concerted variety
as the stanzas or strophes of a so-called Pindaric ode.   Of the
apparently uniform and monotonous blank verse he has made an
instrument of almost protean variety by availing himself of the
infinite permutations of cadence, syllabic sound, variety of feet,
and adjustment of sense to verse.   The result is that he has, it
may almost be said, made for himself out of simple blank verse
all the conveniences of the line, the couplet, and the stanza,
punctuating and dividing by cadence, not rhyme.   No device that
is possible within his limits—even to that most dangerous one of
the pause after the first syllable of a line which has " enjambed "
from the previous one—is strange to him, or sparingly used by

him, or used without success.   And it is only necessary to contrast his verse with the blank verse of the next century, especially
in its two chief examples, Thomson and Young,—great verse-smiths
both of them,—to observe his superiority in art.   These two,
especially Thomson, try the verse-paragraph system, but they
do it ostentatiously and clumsily.   Thomson's trick of ending
such paragraphs with such lines as " And Thule bellows through
her utmost isles," often repeated with only verbal substitutions,
is apt to make the reader think with a smile of the breath of
relief which a man draws after a serious effort.   " Thank heaven
that paragraph's done ! " the poet seems to be saying.   Nothing
of the kind is ever to be found in Milton.   It is only on examination that the completeness of these divisions is perceived.   They
are linked one to another with the same incomparably artful
concealment of art which links their several and internal clauses.
And thus it is that Milton is able to carry his readers through
(taking both poems together) sixteen books of epic, without much
narrative interest, with foregone conclusions, with long passages
which are merely versifications of well-known themes, and with
others which the most favourable critics admit to be, if not exactly
dull, yet certainly not lively.   Something the same may be said
of *Samson*, though here a decided stiffening and mannerising of
the verse is to some extent compensated by the pathetic and
human interest of the story.   It is to be observed, however, that
Milton has here abused the redundant syllable (the chief purely
poetical mistake of which he has been guilty in any part of his
work, and which is partly noticeable in *Comus*), and that his
choric odes are but dry sticks in comparison with *Lycidas*.

It may be thought strange that I should say little or nothing
of the subject of these immortal poems.   But, in the first place,
those critics of poetry who tell us that "all depends on the subject " seem to forget that, according to this singular dictum, there
is no difference between poetry and prose—between an epic and
a blue-book.   I prefer—having been brought up at the feet of
Logic—to stick to the genus and differentia of poetry, and not to

its accidents. Moreover, the matter of *Paradise Lost* and its sequel is so universally known that it becomes unnecessary, and has been so much discussed that it seems superfluous, to rediscuss it. The inquiries into Milton's indebtedness to forerunners strike me as among the idlest inquiries of the kind—which is saying a great deal. Italians, Frenchmen, Dutchmen, Englishmen even, had doubtless treated the Creation and the Fall, Adam and Satan, before him. Perhaps he read them ; perhaps he borrowed from them. What then ? Does any one believe that Andreini or Vondel, Sylvester or Du Bartas, could have written, or did in any measurable degree contribute to the writing of *Paradise Lost*? If he does he must be left to his opinion.

Reference may perhaps be made to some remarks in Chapter IV. on the comparative position of Milton in English poetry with the only two writers who can be compared to him, if bulk and majesty of work be taken into consideration, and not merely occasional bursts of poetry. Of his own poetical powers I trust that I shall not be considered a niggard admirer, because, both in the character of its subject (if we are to consider subjects at all) and in its employment of rhyme, that greatest mechanical aid of the poet, *The Faërie Queene* seems to me greater, or because Milton's own earlier work seems to me to rank higher than *Paradise Lost*. The general opinion is, of course, different ; and one critic of no mean repute, Christopher North, has argued that *Paradise Lost* is the only "great poem" in existence. That question need not be argued here. It is sufficient to say that Milton is undoubtedly one of the few great poets in the history of the world, and that if he falls short of Homer, Dante, and Shakespere, it is chiefly because he expresses less of that humanity, both universal and quintessential, which they, and especially the last, put into verse. Narrowness is his fault. But the intense individuality which often accompanies narrowness is his great virtue—a virtue which no poet, which no writer either in verse or prose, has ever had in greater measure than he, and which hardly any has been able to express with more varied and exquisite harmony.

Jeremy Taylor, the ornament and glory of the English pulpit, was born at Cambridge in 1613. He was the son of a barber, but was well educated, and was able to enter Caius College as a sizar at thirteen. He spent seven years there, and took both degrees and orders at an unusually early age. Apparently, however, no solid endowment was offered him in his own university, and he owed such preferment as he had (it was never very great) to a chance opportunity of preaching at St. Paul's and a recommendation to Laud. That prelate — to whom all the infinite malignity of political and sectarian detraction has not been able to deny the title of an encourager, as few men have encouraged them, of learning and piety—took Taylor under his protection, made him his chaplain, and procured him incorporation at Oxford, a fellowship at All Souls, and finally the rectory of Uppingham. To this Taylor was appointed in 1638, and next year he married a lady who bore him several sons, but died young. Taylor early joined the king at Oxford, and is supposed to have followed his fortunes in the field; it is certain that his rectory, lying in a Puritan district, was very soon sequestrated, though not by any form of law. What took him into Wales and caused him to marry his second wife, Joanna Brydges (an heiress on a small scale, and said to have been a natural daughter of Charles I.), is not known. But he sojourned in the principality during the greater part of the Commonwealth period, and was much patronised by the Earl of Carbery, who, while resident at Golden Grove, made him his chaplain. He also made the acquaintance of other persons of interest, the chief of whom were, in London (which he visited not always of his own choice, for he was more than once imprisoned), John Evelyn, and in Wales, Mrs. Katherine Philips, "the matchless Orinda," to whom he dedicated one of the most interesting of his minor works, the *Measure and Offices of Friendship*. Not long before the Restoration he was offered, and strongly pressed to accept, the post of lecturer at

Lisburn, in Ireland. He does not seem to have taken at all kindly to the notion, but was over-persuaded, and crossed the Channel. It was perhaps owing to this false step that, when the Restoration arrived, the preferment which he had in so many ways merited only came to him in the tents of Kedar. He was made Bishop of Down and Connor, held that see for seven years, and died (after much wrestling with Ulster Presbyterians and some domestic misfortune) of fever in 1667.

His work is voluminous and always interesting; but only a small part of it concerns us directly here, as exhibiting him at his best and most peculiar in the management of English prose. He wrote, it should be said, a few verses by no means destitute of merit, but they are so few, in comparison to the bulk of his work, that they may be neglected. Taylor's strong point was not accuracy of statement or logical precision. His longest work, the *Ductor Dubitantium*, an elaborate manual of casuistry, is constantly marred by the author's inability to fix on a single point, and to keep his argumentation close to that. In another, the *Unum Necessarium*, or Discourse on Repentance, his looseness of statement and want of care in driving several horses at once, involved him in a charge of Pelagianism, or something like it, which he wrote much to disprove, but which has so far lasted as to justify modern theologians in regarding his ideas on this and other theological points as, to say the least, confused. All over his work inexact quotation from memory, illicit argumentation, and an abiding inconsistency, mar the intellectual value, affecting not least his famous *Liberty of Prophesying*, or plea for toleration against the new Presbyterian uniformity,—the conformity of which treatise with modern ideas has perhaps made some persons slow to recognise its faults. These shortcomings, however, are not more constant in Taylor's work than his genuine piety, his fervent charity, his freedom from personal arrogance and pretentiousness, and his ardent love for souls; while neither shortcomings nor virtues of this kind concern us here so much as the extraordinary rhetorical merits which distinguish all his work more or

less, and which are chiefly noticeable in his *Sermons*, especially
the Golden Grove course, and the funeral sermon on Lady
Carbery, in his *Contemplations of the State of Man*, and in parts
of his *Life of Christ*, and of the universally popular and admirable
tractates on *Holy Living* and *Holy Dying*.

Jeremy Taylor's style is emphatically and before all things
florid and ornate. It is not so elaborately quaint as Browne's ;
it is not so stiffly splendid as Milton's ; it is distinguished from
both by a much less admixture of Latinisms ; but it is impossible
to call it either verbally chastened or syntactically correct.   Coleridge—an authority always to be differed with cautiously and
under protest—holds indeed a different opinion.   He will have
it that Browne was the corruptor, though a corruptor of the
greatest genius, in point of vocabulary, and that, as far as syntax
is concerned, in Jeremy Taylor the sentences are often extremely
long, and yet are generally so perspicuous in consequence of their
logical structure that they require no reperusal to be understood.
And he will have the same to be true not only of Hooker (which
may pass), but of Milton, in reference to whom admirers not less
strong than Coleridge hold that he sometimes forgets the period
altogether.

It must be remembered that Coleridge in these remarks was
fighting the battle of the recoverers of our great seventeenth
century writers against the devotees of "correctness," and that in
the very same context he makes the unpardonable assertion that
Gibbon's manner is "the worst of all," and that Tacitus "writes
in falsetto as compared to Tully."   This is to "fight a prize" in
the old phrase, not to judge from the catholic and universal
standpoint of impartial criticism ; and in order to reduce Coleridge's assertions to that standard we must abate nearly as much
from his praise of Taylor as from his abuse of Gibbon—an abuse,
by the way, which is strangely contrasted with praise of "Junius."
It is not true that, except by great complaisance of the reader,
Jeremy Taylor's long sentences are at once understandable.   They
may, of course, and generally can be understood *kata to semaino*

menon, as a telegram with half the words left out may at the other end of the scale be understood. But they constantly withstand even a generous parser, even one who is to the fullest extent ready to allow for idiom and individuality. They abuse in particular the conjunction to a most enormous extent—coupling by its means propositions which have no logical connection, which start entirely different trains of thought, and which are only united because carelessness and fashion combined made it unnecessary for the writer to take the little extra trouble necessary for their separation. Taylor will, in the very middle of his finest passages, and with hardly so much as a comma's break, change *oratio obliqua* to *oratio recta*, interrupt the sequence of tenses, make his verbs agree with the nearest noun, irrespective of the connection, and in short, though he was, while in Wales, a schoolmaster for some time, and author of a grammatical treatise, will break Priscian's head with the calmest unconcern. It is quite true that these faults mainly occur in his more rhetorical passages, in his exercises rather of spoken than of written prose. But that, as any critic who is not an advocate must see, is no palliation. The real palliation is that the time had not yet aroused itself to the consciousness of the fact that letting English grammar at one moment go to the winds altogether, and at the next subjecting it to the most inappropriate rules and licenses of Latin, was not the way to secure the establishment of an accomplished and generally useful English prose. No stranger instance of prejudice can be given than that Coleridge, on the point of asking, and justly, from Dryden "a stricter grammar," should exalt to the skies a writer compared to whom Dryden is grammatically impeccable.

But a recognition of the fact that Taylor distinctly belongs to the antinomians of English prose, or at least to those guiltless heathens who lived before the laws of it had been asserted, can not in any competent critic dull the sense of the wonderful beauty of his style. It has been said that this beauty is entirely of the florid and ornate order, lending itself in this way easily enough to the witty and well-worded, though unjust and ungenerous censure which South pronounced on it after the author's death. It may or may not be that the phrases there censured, " The fringes of the north star," and " The dew of angels' wings," and " Thus have I seen a cloud rolling in its airy mansion," are not of that " apostolic plainness " that a Christian minister's speech should have. But they and their likes are extremely beautiful—save that in literature no less than in theology South has justly perstringed Taylor's constant and most unworthy affectation of introducing a simile by " so I have seen." In the next age the phrase was tediously abused, and in the age after, and ever since, it became and has remained mere burlesque ; but it was never good ; and in the two fine specimen passages which follow it is a distinct blot :—

The Prayers of Anger and of Lust.

" Prayer is the peace of our spirit, the stillness of our thoughts, the evenness of recollection, the seat of meditation, the rest of our cares, and the calm of our tempest. Prayer is the issue of a quiet mind, of untroubled thoughts ; it is the daughter of charity and the sister of meekness ; and he that prays to God with an angry—that is a troubled and discomposed—spirit, is like him that retires into a battle to meditate and sets up his closet in the outquarters of an army, and chooses a frontier garrison to be wise in. Anger is a perfect alienation of the mind from prayer, and therefore is contrary to that attention which presents our prayers in a right line to God. For so have I seen a lark rising from his bed of grass, soaring upwards and singing as he rises and hopes to get to Heaven and climb above the clouds ; but the poor bird was beaten back with the loud sighings of an eastern wind and his motion made irregular and inconstant, descending more at every breath of the tempest than it could recover by the vibration and frequent weighing of his wings ; till the little creature was forced to sit down and pant and stay till the storm was over ; and then it made a prosperous flight and did rise and sing as if it had learned music and motion from an angel as he passed sometimes through the air about his ministries here below. So is the prayer of a good man : when his affairs have required business, and his business was matter of discipline, and his discipline was to pass upon a sinning person, or had a design of charity, his duty met with infirmities of a man and anger was its instrument, and the instrument became stronger than the prime agent and raised a tempest and overruled the man ; and then his prayer was broken and his thoughts troubled.

.   .   .   .

" For so an impure vapour—begotten of the slime of the earth by the fevers and adulterous heats of an intemperate summer sun, striving by the ladder of a mountain to climb to heaven and rolling into various figures by an uneasy, unfixed revolution, and stopped at the middle region of the air, being thrown from his pride and attempt of passing towards the seat of the stars— turns into an unwholesome flame and, like the breath of hell, is confined into a prison of darkness and a cloud, till it breaks into diseases, plagues and mildews, stinks and blastings. So is the prayer of an unchaste person. It strives to climb the battlements of heaven, but because it is a flame of sulphur salt and bitumen, and was kindled in the dishonourable regions below, derived from Hell and contrary to God, it cannot pass forth to the element of love ; but ends in barrenness and murmurs, fantastic expectations and trifling imaginative confidences ; and they at last end in sorrows and despair."

Indeed, like all very florid writers, Taylor is liable to eclipses of taste ; yet both the wording of his flights and the occasion of them (they are to be found *passim* in the *Sermons*) are almost wholly admirable. It is always a great and universal idea—never a mere conceit—that fires him. The shortness and dangers of life, the weakness of children, the fragility of women's beauty and men's strength, the change of the seasons, the vicissitudes of empires, the impossibility of satisfying desire, the disgust which follows satiety—these are, if any one chooses, commonplace enough ; yet it is the observation of all who have carefully studied literature, and the experience of all who have observed their own thoughts, that it is always in relation to these commonplaces that the most beautiful expressions and the noblest sentiments arise. The uncommon thought is too likely if not too certain to be an uncommon conceit, and if not worthless, yet of inferior worth. Among prose writers Taylor is unequalled for his touches of this universal material, for the genius with which he makes the common uncommon. For instance, he has the supreme faculty of always making the verbal and the intellectual presentation of the thought alike beautiful, of appealing to the ear and the mind at the same time, of never depriving the apple of gold of its picture of silver. Yet for all this the charge of over-elaboration which may justly be brought against Browne very rarely hits Taylor. He seldom or never has the appearance which ornate writers of all times, and of

his own more especially, so often have, of going back on a thought
or a phrase to try to better it—of being stimulated by actual or
fancied applause to cap the climax.   His most beautiful passages
come quite suddenly and naturally as the subject requires and as
the thought strikes light in his mind.   Nor are they ever, as
Milton's so often are, marred by a descent as rapid as their rise.
He is never below a certain decent level ; he may return to
earth from heaven, but he goes no lower, and reaches even his
lower level by a quiet and equable sinking.   As has been fully
allowed, he has grave defects, the defects of his time.   But from
some of these he was conspicuously free, and on the whole no one
in English prose (unless it be his successor here) has so much
command of the enchanter's wand as Jeremy Taylor.

Sir Thomas Browne was born in the heart of London in 1605,
his father (of whom little is known except one or two anecdotes
corresponding with the character of the son) having been a
merchant of some property, and claiming descent from a good
family in Cheshire.   This father died when he was quite young,
and Browne is said to have been cheated by his guardians ; but
he was evidently at all times of his life in easy circumstances, and
seems to have had no complaint to make of his stepfather, Sir
Thomas Dutton.   This stepfather may at least possibly have
been the hero of the duel with Sir Hatton Cheeke, which Mr.
Carlyle has made famous.   With him Browne visited Ireland,
having previously been brought up at Winchester and at Broadgates Hall, which became, during his own residence, Pembroke
College, at Oxford.   Later he made the usual grand tour.   Then
he took medical degrees ; practised it is said, though on no very
precise evidence, both in Oxfordshire and Yorkshire ; settled, why
is not known, at Norwich ; married in 1641 Dorothy Mileham, a
lady of good family in his adopted county ; was a steady Royalist
through the troubles ; acquired a great name for medical and
scientific knowledge, though he was not a Fellow of the Royal
Society ; was knighted by Charles II. in 1662, and died in 1682.
His first literary appearance had been made forty years earlier in

a way very common in French literary history, but so uncommon
in English as to have drawn from Johnson a rather unwontedly
illiberal sneer.   At a time unknown, but by his own account
before his thirtieth year (therefore before 1635), Browne had
written the *Religio Medici*.   It was, according to the habit of the
time, copied and handed about in MS. (there exist now five MS.
copies showing remarkable differences with each other and the
printed copies), and in 1642 it got into print.   A copy was sent
by Lord Dorset to the famous Sir Kenelm Digby, then under
confinement for his opinions, and the husband of Venetia wrote
certain not very forcible and not wholly complimentary remarks
which, as Browne was informed, were at once put to press.   A
correspondence ensued, and Browne published an authorised
copy, in which perhaps a little "economy" might be noticed.
The book made an extraordinary impression, and was widely
translated and commented on in foreign languages, though its
vogue was purely due to its intrinsic merits, and not at all to the
circumstances which enabled Milton (rather arrogantly and not
with absolute truth) to boast that "Europe rang from side to
side" with his defence of the execution of Charles I.   Four
years later, in 1646, Browne published his largest and in every
sense most popular book, the *Pseudodoxia Epidemica* or *Enquiry
into Vulgar Errors*.   Twelve more years passed before the
greatest, from a literary point of view, of his works, the *Hydrio-
taphia* or *Urn-Burial*,—a magnificent descant on the vanity of
human life, based on the discovery of certain cinerary urns in
Norfolk,—appeared, in company with the quaint *Garden of Cyrus*,
a half-learned, half-fanciful discussion of the mysteries of the
quincunx and the number five.   Nor did he publish anything more
himself; but two collections of posthumous works were issued
after his death, the most important item of which is the *Christian
Morals*, and the total has been swelled since by extracts from his
MSS., which at the death of his grandson and namesake in 1710
were sold by auction.   Most fortunately they were nearly all
bought by Sir Hans Sloane, and are to this day in the British

Museum.   Browne's good luck in this respect was completed by
the devotion of his editor, Simon Wilkin, a Norwich bookseller
of gentle blood and good education, who produced (1835) after
twelve years' labour of love what Southey has justly called the
best edited book in the English language.   Not to mention other
editions, the *Religio Medici*, which exhibits, owing to its history,
an unusual variation of text, has been, together with the *Christian
Morals*, separately edited with great minuteness by Dr. Greenhill.
Nor is it unimportant to notice that Johnson, during his period
of literary hack-work, also edited Sir Thomas Browne, and wrote
what Wilkin's good taste has permitted to be still the standard
text of his Life.

The work of this country doctor is, for personal savour, for
strangeness, and for delight, one of the most notable things in
English literature.   It is not of extraordinary voluminousness,
for though swollen in Wilkin's edition by abundant editorial
matter, it fills but three of the well-known volumes of Bohn's
series, and, printed by itself, it might not much exceed two
ordinary library octavos ; but in character and interest it yields
to the work of no other English prose writer.   It may be
divided, from our point of view, into two unequal parts, the
smaller of which is in truth of the greater interest.   The *Vulgar
Errors*, those of the smaller tracts which deal with subjects of
natural history (as most of them do), many of the commonplace
book entries, the greater part of the *Garden of Cyrus*, and most
of the *Letters*, are mainly distinguished by an interest of matter
constantly increased, it is true, by the display of the author's
racy personality, and diversified here and there by passages also
displaying his style to the full, but in general character not differing from the works of other curious writers in the delightful
period which passed between the childish credulity of mediæval
and classical physics and the arid analysis of the modern
"scientist."   Sir Thomas Browne was of a certain natural
scepticism of temperament (a scepticism which, as displayed in
relation to other matters in the *Religio Medici*, very unjustly

brought upon him the reproach of religious unorthodoxy); he
was a trained and indefatigable observer of facts, and he was by
no means prepared to receive authority as final in any extra-
religious matters. But he had a thoroughly literary, not to say
poetical idiosyncrasy; he was both by nature and education disposed
to seek for something more than that physical explanation which,
as the greatest of all anti-supernatural philosophers has observed,
merely pushes ignorance a little farther back; and he was possessed of an extraordinary fertility of imagination which made
comment, analogy, and amplification both easy and delightful to
him. He was, therefore, much more disposed—except in the face
of absolutely conclusive evidence—to rationalise than to deny a
vulgar error, to bring explanations and saving clauses to its aid,
than to cut it adrift utterly. In this part of his work his distinguishing graces and peculiarities of style appear but sparingly
and not eminently. In the other division, consisting of the
Religio Medici, the *Urn-Burial*, the *Christian Morals*, and the
Letter to a Friend, his strictly literary peculiarities, as being less
hampered by the exposition of matter, have freer scope; and it
must be recollected that these literary peculiarities, independently
of their own interest, have been a main influence in determining
the style of two of the most remarkable writers of English prose in
the two centuries immediately succeeding Browne. It has been
said that Johnson edited him somewhat early; and all the best
authorities are in accord that the Johnsonian Latinisms, differently managed as they are, are in all probability due more to the
following—if only to the unconscious following—of Browne than
to anything else. The second instance is more indubitable still
and more happy. It detracts nothing from the unique charm of
" Elia," and it will be most clearly recognised by those who
know " Elia " best, that Lamb constantly borrows from Browne,
that the mould and shape of his most characteristic phrases is
frequently suggested directly by Sir Thomas, and that though there
seldom can have been a follower who put more of his own in his
following, it may be pronounced with confidence, " no Browne, no

Lamb," at least in the forms in which we know the author of
"Elia" best, and in which all those who know him best, though
they may love him always, love him most. Yet Browne is not a
very easy author to "sample." A few splendid sustained passages, like the famous one in the *Urn-Burial*, are universally
known, but he is best in flashes. The following, from the
Christian Morals, is characteristic enough :—

"Punish not thyself with pleasure ; glut not thy sense with palative delights ; nor revenge the contempt of temperance by the penalty of satiety.
Were there an age of delight or any pleasure durable, who would not honour
Volupia ? but the race of delight is short, and pleasures have mutable faces.
The pleasures of one age are not pleasures in another, and their lives fall short
of our own. Even in our sensual days the strength of delight is in its seldom-
ness or rarity, and sting in its satiety : mediocrity is its life, and immoderacy
its confusion. The luxurious emperors of old inconsiderately satiated themselves with the dainties of sea and land till, wearied through all varieties, their
refections became a study with them, and they were fain to feed by invention :
novices in true epicurism ! which by mediocrity, paucity, quick and healthful
appetite, makes delights smartly acceptable ; whereby Epicurus himself found
Jupiter's brain in a piece of Cytheridian cheese, and the tongues of nightingales
in a dish of onions. Hereby healthful and temperate poverty hath the start of
nauseating luxury ; unto whose clear and naked appetite every meal is a feast,
and in one single dish the first course of Metellus ; who are cheaply hungry,
and never lose their hunger, or advantage of a craving appetite, because obvious
food contents it ; while Nero, half famish'd, could not feed upon a piece of
bread, and, lingering after his snowed water, hardly got down an ordinary cup
of *Calda*. By such circumscriptions of pleasure the contemned philosophers
reserved unto themselves the secret of delight, which the Helluos of those days
lost in their exorbitances. In vain we study delight : it is at the command of
every sober mind, and in every sense born with us ; but Nature, who teacheth
us the rule of pleasure, instructeth also in the bounds thereof and where its line
expireth. And therefore temperate minds, not pressing their pleasures until
the sting appeareth, enjoy their contentations contentedly and without regret,
and so escape the folly of excess, to be pleased unto displacency."

"Bring candid eyes unto the perusal of men's works, and let not Zoilism
or detraction blast well-intended labours. He that endureth no faults in men's
writings must only read his own, wherein for the most part all appeareth white.
Quotation mistakes, inadvertency, expedition and human lapses, may make not
only moles but warts in learned authors, who notwithstanding, being judged by

the capital matter, admit not of disparagement. I should unwillingly affirm that Cicero was but slightly versed in Homer, because in his work *De Gloria* he ascribed those verses unto Ajax which were delivered by Hector. What if Plautus, in the account of Hercules, mistaketh nativity for conception? Who would have mean thoughts of Apollinaris Sidonius, who seems to mistake the river Tigris for Euphrates ; and, though a good historian and learned Bishop of Auvergne, had the misfortune to be out in the story of David, making mention of him when the ark was sent back by the Philistines upon a cart, which was before his time? Though I have no great opinion of Machiavel's learning, yet I shall not presently say that he was but a novice in Roman History, because he was mistaken in placing Commodus after the Emperor Severus. Capital truths are to be narrowly eyed, collateral lapses and circumstantial deliveries not to be too strictly sifted. And if the substantial subject be well forged out, we need not examine the sparks which irregularly fly from it."

Coleridge, as we have seen, charges Browne with corrupting the style of the great age. The charge is not just in regard to either of the two great faults which are urged against the style, strictly speaking ; while it is hardly just in reference to a minor charge which is brought against what is not quite style, namely, the selection and treatment of the thought. The two charges first referred to are Latinising of vocabulary and disorderly syntax of sentence. In regard to the first, Browne Latinises somewhat more than Jeremy Taylor, hardly at all more than Milton, though he does not, like Milton, contrast and relieve his Latinisms by indulgence in vernacular terms of the most idiomatic kind ; and he is conspicuously free from the great fault both of Milton and of Taylor—the clumsy conglomeration of clauses which turns a sentence into a paragraph, and makes a badly ordered paragraph of it after all. Browne's sentences, especially those of the books regularly prepared for the press by him, are by no means long and are usually very perspicuous, being separable in some cases into shorter sentences by a mere mechanical repunctuation which, if tried on Taylor or Milton, would make nonsense. To say that they are sometimes longer than they should be, and often awkwardly co-ordinated, is merely to say that he wrote when he wrote ; but he by no means sins beyond his fellows. In regard to Latinisms his case is not so good. He constantly uses such

words as "clarity" for "clearness," "ferity" for "fierceness" or
"wildness," when nothing is gained by the exotic form.   Dr.
Greenhill's useful glossary to the *Religio* and the *Morals* exhibits
in tabular form not merely such terms as "abbreviatures,"
"æquilibriously," "bivious," "convincible," "exantlation," and
hundreds of others with which there is no need to fill the page,
but also a number only less considerable of those far more objec-
tionable usages which take a word generally understood in one
sense (as, for instance, "equable," "gratitudes," and many others),
and by twisting or translation of its classical equivalents and
etymons give it some quite new sense in English.   It is true
that in some case the usual sense was not then firmly established,
but Browne can hardly be acquitted of wilfully preferring the
obscurer.

Yet this hybrid and bizarre vocabulary is so admirably married
to the substance of the writing that no one of taste can find fault
with it.   For Browne (to come to the third point mentioned
above), though he never descends or diverges—whichever word
may be preferred—to the extravagant and occasionally puerile
conceits which even such writers as Fuller and Glanville cannot
resist, has a quaintness at least equal to theirs.   In no great
writer is the unforeseen so constantly happening.   Every one who
has written on him has quoted the famous termination of the
Garden of Cyrus, where he determines that it is time to go to
bed, because "to keep our eyes open longer were but to act our
antipodes.   The huntsmen are up in America, and they are already past their first sleep in Persia."   A fancy so whimsical as
this, and yet so admirable in its whimsies, requires a style in
accordance ; and the very sentence quoted, though one of the
plainest of Browne's, and showing clearly that he does not always
abuse Latinising, would hardly be what it is without the word
"antipodes."   So again in the *Christian Morals*, "Be not stoically
mistaken in the quality of sins, nor commutatively iniquitous in
the valuation of transgressions."   No expression so terse and yet
so striking could dispense with the classicism and the catachrèsis

of "stoically." And so it is everywhere with Browne. His manner is exactly proportioned to his matter; his exotic and unfamiliar vocabulary to the strangeness and novelty of his thoughts. He can never be really popular; but for the meditative reading of instructed persons he is perhaps the most delightful of English prosemen.

There are probably few English writers in regard to whom the judgment of critics, usually ranked as competent, has varied more than in regard to Edward Hyde, Earl of Clarendon. To some extent this is easily intelligible to any one who, with some equipment, reads any considerable quantity of his work; but it would be idle to pretend that the great stumbling-block of all criticism—the attention to matter rather than to form—has had nothing to do with it. Clarendon, at first not a very zealous Royalist, was the only man of decided literary genius who, with contemporary knowledge, wrote the history of the great debate between king and commonwealth. The effect of his history in deciding the question on the Royalist side was felt in England for more than a century; and since popular judgment has somewhat veered round to the other side, its chief exponents have found it necessary either to say as little as possible about Clarendon or to depreciate him. His interesting political history cannot be detailed here. Of a good Cheshire family, but not originally wealthy, he was educated as a lawyer, was early adopted into the "tribe of Ben," and was among the first to take advantage of the opening which the disputes between king and parliament gave to men of his birth, education, and gifts. At first he was a moderate opponent of the king's attempts to dispense with parliament; but the growing evidence that the House of Commons was seeking to increase its own constitutional power at the expense of the prerogative, and especially the anti-Church tendencies of the parliamentary leaders, converted him at first into a moderate and then into a strong Royalist. One of the chief of the king's constitutional advisers, he was after the Restoration the most distinguished by far of those Cavaliers who had parliamentary and constitutional experience; and with the title and office of Chancellor, he exercised a practical premiership during the first seven years of the Restoration. But ill-fortune, and it must be confessed some unwisdom, marked his government. He has been often and truly said to have been a statesman of Elizabeth, born three-quarters of a century too late. He was thought by the public to be arbitrary, a courtier, and even to some extent corrupt. He seemed to the king to be a tiresome formalist and censor, who was only scrupulous in resisting the royal will. So he was impeached; and, being compelled to quit the kingdom, spent the last seven years of his life in France. His great works, begun during his first exile and completed during his second, are the *History of the Rebellion* and his own *Life*, the former being by much the more important though the latter (divided into a "Life" and a "Continuation," the last of which starts from the Restoration) contains much interesting and important biographical and historical matter. The text of these works was conveyed by his heirs to the University of Oxford, and long remained an exception to the general rule of the terminableness of copyright.

Clarendon is a very striking example of the hackneyed remark, that in some cases at any rate men's merits are their own and their faults those of their time. His literary merits are, looked at by themselves, of nearly the highest kind. He is certainly the best English writer (and may challenge any foreigner without much fear of the result) in the great, difficult, and now almost lost art of character- (or, as it was called in his time, portrait-) drawing— that is to say, sketching in words the physical, moral, and mental, but especially the moral and mental, peculiarities of a given person. Not a few of these characters of his are among the well-known "beauties" justified in selection by the endorsement of half a dozen generations. They are all full of life; and even where it may be thought that prejudice has had something to do with the picture, still the subject lives, and is not a mere bundle of contradictory or even of superficially compatible characteristics. Secondly, Clarendon is at his best an incomparable narrator. Many of his battles, though related with apparent coolness, and without the slightest attempt to be picturesque, may rank as works of art with his portraits, just as the portraits and battle pieces of a great painter may rank together. The sober vivid touches, the little bits of what the French call *reportage* or mere reproduction of the actual words and deeds of the personages, the elaborate and carefully-concealed art of the composition, all deserve the highest praise. Here, for instance, is a fair average passage, showing Clarendon's masterly skill in summary narration and his equally masterly, though, as some hold, rather unscrupulous faculty of insinuating depreciation :—

" Since there will be often occasion to mention this gentleman, Sir Richard Granvil, in the ensuing discourse, and because many men believed that he was hardly dealt with in the next year, where all the proceedings will be set down at large, it will not be unfit in this place to say somewhat of him, and of the manner and merit of his entering into the king's service some months before the time we are now upon. He was of a very ancient and worthy family in Cornwall which had in several ages produced men of great courage, and very signal in their fidelity to and service of the crown ; and was himself younger brother (though in his nature or humour not of kin to him) to the brave Sir Basil Granvil who so courageously lost his life at the battle of Lansdowne. Being a younger brother and a very young man, he went into the Low Countries to learn the profession of a soldier ; to which he had devoted himself under the greatest general of that age, Prince Maurice, and in the regiment of my Lord Vere, who was general of all the English. In that service he was looked upon as a man of courage and a diligent officer, in the quality of a captain, to which he attained after four years' service. About this time, in the end of the reign of King James, the war broke out between England and Spain ; and in the expedition to Cadiz this gentleman served as a major to a regiment of foot, and continued in the same command in the war that shortly after followed against France ; and at the Isle of Rhé insinuated himself into the very good graces of the Duke of Buckingham, who was the general in that mission ; and after the unfortunate retreat from thence was made colonel of a regiment with general approbation and as an officer that well deserved it.

" His credit increased every day with the duke : who, out of the generosity of his nature, as a most generous person he was, resolved to raise his fortune ; towards the beginning of which, by his countenance and solicitation, he prevailed with a rich widow to marry him, who had been a lady of extraordinary beauty, which she had not yet outlived ; and though she had no great dower by her husband, a younger brother of the Earl of Suffolk, yet she inherited a fair fortune of her own near Plymouth, and was besides very rich in a personal estate, and was looked upon as the richest marriage of the West.   This lady, by the duke's credit, Sir Richard Granvil (for he was now made a knight and baronet) obtained, and was thereby possessed of a plentiful estate upon the borders of his own country, and where his own family had great credit and authority.   The war being now at an end and he deprived of his great patron, [he] had nothing to depend upon but the fortune of his wife : which, though ample enough to have supported the expense a person of his quality ought to have made, was not large enough to satisfy his vanity and ambition, nor so great as he upon common reports had possessed himself by her.   By being not enough pleased with her fortune he grew displeased with his wife, who, being a woman of a haughty and imperious nature and of a wit superior to his, quickly resented the disrespect she received from him and in no respect studied to make herself easy to him.   After some years spent together in those domestic un- sociable contestations, in which he possessed himself of all her estate as the sole master of it, without allowing her out of her own any competency for her- self, and indulged to himself all those licenses in her own house which to women are most grievous, she found means to withdraw herself from him ; and was with all kindness received into that family in which she had before been married and was always very much respected."

To superficial observers, or observers who have convinced themselves that high lights and bright colourings are of the essence of the art of the prose writer, Clarendon may seem tame and jejune.   He is in reality just the contrary.   His wood is tough enough and close-grained enough, but there is plenty of sap coursing through it.   In yet a third respect, which is less closely connected with the purely formal aspect of style, Clarendon stands, if not pre-eminent, very high among historians.   This is his union of acute penetration and vigor- ous grasp in the treatment of complicated events.   It has been hinted that he seems to have somewhat lost grasp, if not pene- tration, after the Restoration.   But at the time of his earlier participation in public affairs, and of his composition of the greater part of his historical writings, he was in the very vigour and prime of life ; and though it may be that he was " a Janus of one face," and looked rather backward than forward, even then he was profoundly acquainted with the facts of English history, with the character of his countrymen, and with the relations of events as they happened.   It may even be contended by those who care for might-have-beens, that but for the headlong revolt against Puritanism, which inspired the majority of the nation with a kind of carnival madness for many years after 1660, and the strange deficiency of statesmen of even moderately respectable character on both sides (except Clarendon himself, and the fairly upright though time-serving Temple, there is hardly a respectable man to be found on any side of politics for forty years), Clarendon's post-Restoration policy itself would not have been the failure that it was.   But it is certain that on the events of his own middle age he looked with the keenest discernment, and with the widest comprehension.

Against these great merits must be set a treble portion of the great defect which, as we have said, vitiates all the English prose work of his time, the unconscious or wilful ignoring of the very fundamental principles of sentence- and paragraph-architecture. His mere syntax, in the most restricted sense of that word, is not very bad ; he seldom indulges out of mere *incuria* in false concords or blunders over a relative.   But he is the most offending soul alive at any time in English literature in one grave point. No one has put together, or, to adopt a more expressive phrase, heaped together such enormous paragraphs; no one has linked clause on clause, parenthesis on parenthesis, epexegesis on exegesis, in such a bewildering concatenation of inextricable entanglement. Sometimes, of course, the difficulty is more apparent than real, and by simply substituting full stops and capitals for his colons and conjunctions, one may, to some extent, simplify the chaos.   But it is seldom that this is really effective : it never produces really well balanced sentences and really well constructed paragraphs ; and there are constant instances in which it is not applicable at all.   It is not that the jostling and confused relatives are as a rule grammatically wrong, like the common blunder of putting an "and which" where there is no previous "which"

expressed or implied.   They, simply, put as they are, bewilder
and muddle the reader because the writer has not taken the
trouble to break up his sentence into two or three.   This
is, of course, a very gross abuse, and except when the talents
above noticed either fuse his style into something better, or by
the interest they excite divert the attention of the reader, it constantly makes Clarendon anything but agreeable reading, and
produces an impression of dryness and prolixity with which he is
not quite justly chargeable.   The plain truth is that, as has been
said often before, and may have to be said more than once again,
the sense of proportion and order in prose composition was not
born.   The famous example—the awful example—of Oliver
Cromwell's speeches shows the worst-known instance of this ; but
the best writers of Cromwell's own generation—far better educated
than he, professed men of letters after a fashion, and without the
excuse of impromptu, or of the scurry of unnoted, speech—sometimes came not far behind him.

Against one great writer of the time, however, no such charge
can be justly brought.   Although much attention has recently been
given to the philosophical opinions of Hobbes, since the unjust prejudice against his religious and political ideas wore away, and
since the complete edition of his writings published at last in
1843 by Sir William Molesworth made him accessible, the extraordinary merits of his style have on the whole had rather less than
justice done to them.   He was in many ways a very singular
person.   Born at Malmesbury in the year of the Armada, he was
educated at Oxford, and early in the seventeenth century was
appointed tutor to the eldest son of Lord Hardwick, afterwards
Earl of Devonshire.   For full seventy years he was on and off in
the service of the Cavendish family ; but sometimes acted as
tutor to others, and both in that capacity and for other reasons
lived long abroad.   In his earlier manhood he was much in the
society of Bacon, Jonson, and the literary folk of the English
capital ; and later he was equally familiar with the society (rather
scientific than literary) of Paris.   In 1647 he was appointed

mathematical tutor to the Prince of Wales ; but his mathematics
were not his most fortunate acquirement, and they involved him
in long and acrimonious disputes with Wallis and others—disputes,
it may be said, where Hobbes was quite wrong.   The publication
of his philosophical treatises, and especially of the *Leviathan*,
brought him into very bad odour, not merely on political grounds
(which, so long as the Commonwealth lasted, would not have been
surprising), but for religious reasons ; and during the last years
of his life, and for long afterwards, " Hobbist " was, certainly
with very little warrant from his writings, used as a kind of polite
equivalent for atheist.   He was pensioned after the Restoration,
and the protection of the king and the Earl of Devonshire kept
him scatheless, if ever there was any real danger.   Hobbes, however, was a timid and very much self-centred person, always fancying
that plots were being laid against him.   He died at the great age
of ninety-two.

     This long life was wholly taken up with study, but did not
produce a very large amount of original composition.   It is true
that his collected works fill sixteen volumes ; but they are loosely
printed, and much space is occupied with diagrams, indices, and
such like things, while a very large proportion of the matter
appears twice over, in Latin and in English.   In the latter case
Hobbes usually wrote first in Latin, and was not always his
own translator ; but it would appear that he generally revised
the work, though he neither succeeded in obliterating nor perhaps attempted to obliterate the marks of the original vehicle.
His earliest publication was a singularly vigorous, if not always
scholastically exact, translation of Thucydides into English, which
appeared in 1629.   Thirteen years later he published in Paris
the *De Cive*, which was shortly followed by the treatise on *Human
Nature* and the *De Corpore Politico*.   The latter of these was to a
great extent worked up in the famous *Leviathan*, or the *Matter,
Power, and Form of a Commonwealth*, which appeared in 1651.
The important *De Corpore*, which corresponds to the *Leviathan*
on the philosophical side, appeared in Latin in 1655, in English

next year.   Besides minor works, Hobbes employed his old age
on a translation of Homer into verse, and on a sketch of the
Civil Wars called *Behemoth*.

His verse is a mere curiosity, though a considerable curiosity.
The chief of it (the translation of Homer written in the quatrain,
which his friend Davenant's *Gondibert* had made popular) is completely lacking in poetical quality, of which, perhaps, no man ever
had less than Hobbes ; and it is written on a bad model.   But
it has so much of the nervous bull-dog strength which, in literature
if not in life, was Hobbes's main characteristic, that it is sometimes both a truer and a better representative of the original than
some very mellifluous and elegant renderings.   It is as a prose
writer, however, that Hobbes made, and that he will keep, his
fame.   With his principles in the various branches of philosophy
we have little or nothing to do.   In choosing them he manifested,
no doubt, something of the same defiance of authority, and the same
self-willed preference for his own not too well-educated opinion,
which brought him to grief in his encounter with Wallis.   But
when he had once left his starting points, his sureness of reasoning,
his extreme perspicacity, and the unerring clearness and certainty
with which he kept before him, and expressed exactly what he
meant, made him at once one of the greatest thinkers and one of
the greatest writers of England.   Hobbes never " pays himself
with words," never evades a difficulty by becoming obscure, never
meanders on in the graceful allusive fashion of many philosophers,
—a fashion for which the prevalent faults of style were singularly
convenient in his time.   He has no ornament, he does not seem
to aim at anything more than the simplest and most straightforward presentation of his views.   But this very aim, assisted by
his practice in writing the terse and clear, if not very elegant,
Latin which was the universal language of the literary Europe of
his time, suffices to preserve him from most of the current sins.
Moreover, it is fair to remember that, though the last to die,
he was the first to be born of the authors mentioned in this
chapter, and that he may be supposed, late as he wrote, to have

formed his style before the period of Jacobean and Caroline luxuriance.

Almost any one of Hobbes's books would suffice to illustrate his style; but the short and interesting treatise on *Human Nature*, perhaps, shows it at its best. The author's exceptional clearness may be assisted by his lavish use of italics; but it is not necessary to read far in order to see that it is in reality quite independent of any clumsy mechanical device. The crabbed but sharply outlined style, the terse phrasing, the independence of all after-thoughts and tackings-on, manifest themselves at once to any careful observer. Here for instance is a passage, perhaps his finest, on Love, followed by a political extract from another work :—

" Of love, by which is to be understood the joy man taketh in the fruition of any present good, hath been spoken already in the first section, chapter seven, under which is contained the love men bear to one another or pleasure they take in one another's company : and by which nature men are said to be sociable. But there is another kind of love which the Greeks call "Epωs, and is that which we mean when we say that a man is in love : forasmuch as this passion cannot be without diversity of sex, it cannot be denied but that it participateth of that indefinite love mentioned in the former section. But there is a great difference betwixt the desire of a man indefinite and the same desire limited *ad hunc :* and this is that love which is the great theme of poets : but, notwithstanding their praises, it must be defined by the word need : for it is a conception a man hath of his need of that one person desired. The cause of this passion is not always nor for the most part beauty, or other quality in the beloved, unless there be withal hope in the person that loveth : which may be gathered from this, that in great difference of persons the greater have often fallen in love with the meaner, but not contrary. And from hence it is that for the most part they have much better fortune in love whose hopes are built on something in their person than those that trust to their expressions and service ; and they that care less than they that care more : which not perceiving, many men cast away their services as one arrow after another, till, in the end, together with their hopes, they lose their wits."

" There are some who therefore imagine monarchy to be more grievous than democracy, because there is less liberty in that than in this. If by liberty they mean an exemption from that subjection which is due to the laws, that is, the commands of the people ; neither in democracy nor in any other state of government whatsoever is there any such kind of liberty. If they suppose liberty to consist in this, that there be few laws, few prohibitions, and those too such that, except they were forbidden, there could be no peace ; then I deny that there is more liberty in democracy than in monarchy ; for the one as truly consisteth with such a liberty as the other. For although the word liberty may in large and ample letters be written over the gates of any city whatsoever, yet it is not meant the subjects' but the city's liberty ; neither can that word with better right be inscribed on a city which is governed by the people than that which is ruled by a monarch. But when private men or subjects demand liberty under the name of liberty, they ask not for liberty but domination : which yet for want of understanding they little consider. For if every man would grant the same liberty to another which he desires for himself, as is commanded by the law of nature, that same natural state would return again in which all men may by right do all things ; which if they knew they would abhor, as being worse than all kinds of civil subjection whatsoever. But if any man desire to have his single freedom, the rest being bound, what does he else demand but to have the dominion ?"

It may be observed that Hobbes's sentences are by no means very short as far as actual length goes. He has some on a scale which in strictness is perhaps hardly justifiable. But what may generally be asserted of them is that the author for the most part is true to that great rule, of logic and of style alike, which ordains that a single sentence shall be, as far as possible, the verbal presentation of a single thought, and not the agglomeration and sweeping together of a whole string and tissue of thoughts. It is noticeable, too, that Hobbes is very sparing of the adjective —the great resource and delight of flowery and discursive writers. Sometimes, as in the famous comparison of human life to a race (where, by the way, a slight tendency to conceit manifests itself, and makes him rather force some of his metaphors), his conciseness assumes a distinctly epigrammatic form ; and it is constantly visible also in his more consecutive writings.

In the well-known passage on Laughter as "a passion of sudden glory" the writer may be charged with allowing his fancy too free play ; though I, for my part, am inclined to consider the explanation the most satisfactory yet given of a difficult phenomenon. But the point is the distinctness with which

Hobbes puts this novel and, at first sight, improbable idea, the apt turns and illustrations (standing at the same time far from the excess of illustration and analogy, by which many writers of his time would have spun it out into a chapter if not into a treatise), the succinct, forcible, economical adjustment of the fewest words to the clearest exposition of thought. Perhaps these things strike the more as they are the more unlike the work in juxtaposition with which one finds them ; nor can it be maintained that Hobbes's style is suitable for all purposes. Admirable for argument and exposition, it is apt to become bald in narration, and its abundance of clearness, when translated to less purely intellectual subjects, may even expose it to the charge of being thin. Such a note as that struck in the Love passage above given is rare, and sets one wondering whether the dry-as-dust philosopher of Malmesbury, the man who seems to have had hardly any human frailties except vanity and timidity, had himself felt the bitterness of counting on expressions and services, the madness of throwing away one effort after another to gain the favour of the beloved. But it is very seldom that any such suggestion is provoked by remarks of Hobbes's. His light is almost always dry ; and in one sense, though not in another, a little malignant. Yet nowhere is there to be found a style more absolutely suited, not merely to the author's intentions but to his performances—a form more exactly married to matter. Nor anywhere is there to be found a writer who is more independent of others. He may have owed something to his friend Jonson, in whose *Timber* there are resemblances to Hobbes ; but he certainly owed nothing, and in all probability lent much, to the Drydens, and Tillotsons, and Temples, who in the last twenty years of his own life reformed English prose.

CHAPTER X

THERE are few periods of poetical development in English literary history which display, in a comparatively narrow compass, such well-marked and pervading individuality as the period of Caroline poetry, beginning, it may be, a little before the accession of Charles I., but terminating as a producing period almost before the real accession of his son. The poets of this period, in which but not of which Milton is, are numerous and remarkable, and at the head of them all stands Robert Herrick.

Very little is really known about Herrick's history. That he was of a family which, distinguished above the common, but not exactly reaching nobility, had the credit of producing, besides himself, the indomitable Warden Heyrick of the Collegiate Church of Manchester in his own times, and the mother of Swift in the times immediately succeeding his, is certain. That he was born in London in 1591, that he went to Cambridge, that he had a rather stingy guardian, that he associated to some extent with the tribe of Ben in the literary London of the second decade of the century, is also certain. At last and rather late he was appointed to a living at Dean Prior in Devonshire, on the confines of the South Hams and Dartmoor. He did not like it, being of that class of persons who cannot be happy out of a great town. After the Civil War he was deprived, and his successor had not the decency (the late Dr. Grosart, constant to his own party, made

a very unsuccessful attempt to defend the delinquent) to pay him
the shabby pittance which the intruders were supposed to furnish to the rightful owners of benefices.   At the Restoration he
too was restored, and survived it fifteen years, dying in 1674; but
his whole literary fame rests on work published a quarter of a
century before his death, and pretty certainly in great part written
many years earlier.

The poems which then appeared were divided, in the
published form, into two classes: they may be divided, for
purposes of poetical criticism, into three.   The *Hesperides*
(they are dated 1648, and the *Noble Numbers* or sacred
poems 1647; but both appeared together) consist in the
first place of occasional poems, sometimes amatory, sometimes
not; in the second, of personal epigrams.   Of this second class
no human being who has any faculty of criticism can say any
good.   They are supposed by tradition to have been composed
on parishioners : they may be hoped by charity (which has in this
case the support of literary criticism) to be merely literary exercises—bad imitations of Martial, through Ben Jonson.   They
are nastier than the nastiest work of Swift; they are stupider
than the stupidest attempts of Davies of Hereford; they are
farther from the author's best than the worst parts of Young's
Odes are from the best part of the *Night Thoughts*.   It is
impossible without producing specimens (which God forbid that
any one who has a respect for Herrick, for literature, and for
decency, should do) to show how bad they are.   Let it only be
said that if the worst epigram of Martial were stripped of Martial's
wit, sense, and literary form, it would be a kind of example of
Herrick in this vein.

In his two other veins, but for certain tricks of speech, it is
almost impossible to recognise him for the same man.   The
secular vigour of the *Hesperides*, the spiritual vigour of the *Noble
Numbers*, has rarely been equalled and never surpassed by any
other writer.   I cannot agree with Mr. Gosse that Herrick is in
any sense "a Pagan." ˙ They had in his day shaken off the merely

ascetic temper of the Middle Ages, and had not taken upon them the mere materialism of the *Aufklärung*, or the remorseful and satiated attitude of the late eighteenth and nineteenth century. I believe that the warmest of the Julia poems and the immortal "Litany" were written with the same integrity of feeling. Here was a man who was grateful to the upper powers for the joys of life, or who was sorrowful and repentant towards the upper powers when he felt that he had exceeded in enjoying those joys, but who had no doubt of his gods, and no shame in approaching them. The last—the absolutely last if we take his death-date—of those poets who have relished this life heartily, while heartily believing in another, was Robert Herrick. There is not the slightest reason to suppose that the *Hesperides* were wholly *péchés de jeunesse* and the *Noble Numbers* wholly pious palinodes. Both simply express, and express in a most vivid and distinct manner, the alternate or rather varying moods of a man of strong sensibilities, religious as well as sensual.

Of the religious poems the already-mentioned "Litany," while much the most familiar, is also far the best. There is nothing in English verse to equal it as an expression of religious fear ; while there is also nothing in English verse to equal the "Thanksgiving," also well known, as an expression of religious trust. The crystalline simplicity of Herrick's style deprives his religious poems of that fatal cut-and-dried appearance, that vain repetition of certain phrases and thoughts, which mars the work of sacred poets generally, and which has led to an unjustly strong censure being laid on them by critics, so different from each other as Dr. Johnson and Mr. Matthew Arnold. As the alleged Paganism of some of Herrick's sacred poems exists only in the imagination of readers, so the alleged insincerity is equally hypothetical, and can only be supported by the argument (notoriously false to history and to human nature) that a man who could write the looser *Hesperides* could not sincerely write the *Noble Numbers*. Every student of the lives of other men—every student of his own heart—knows, or should know, that this is an utter mistake.

Undoubtedly, however, Herrick's most beautiful work is to be found in the profane division, despite the admixture of the above-mentioned epigrams, the dull foulness of which soils the most delightful pages to such an extent that, if it were ever allowable to take liberties with an author's disposition of his own work, it would be allowable and desirable to pick these ugly weeds out of the garden and stow them away in a rubbish heap of appendix all to themselves. Some of the best pieces of the *Hesperides* are even better known than the two well-known *Noble Numbers* above quoted. The "Night Piece to Julia," the "Daffodils," the splendid "To Anthea," ("Bid me to live"), "The Mad Maid's Song" (worthy of the greatest of the generation before Herrick), the verses to Ben Jonson, those to Electra ("I dare not ask a kiss"), the wonderful "Burial Piece to Perilla," the "Grace for a Child," the "Corinna Maying" (the chief of a large division of Herrick's poems which celebrate rustic festivals, superstitions, and folklore generally), the epitaph on Prudence Baldwin, and many others, are justly included in nearly all selections of English poetry, and many of them are known by heart to every one who knows any poetry at all. One or two of the least well known of them may perhaps be welcome again :—

> "Good morrow to the day so fair,
>   Good morning, sir, to you ;
> Good morrow to mine own torn hair
>   Bedabbled with the dew.

> "Good morning to this primrose too,
>   Good morrow to each maid ;
> That will with flowers the tomb bestrew
>   Wherein my love is laid.

> "Ah, woe is me, woe, woe is me,
>   Alack and well-a-day !
> For pity, sir, find out that bee
>   That bore my love away.

> "I'll seek him in your bonnet brave ;
>   I'll seek him in your eyes ;

Nay, now I think, they've made his grave
I' th' bed of strawberries.

" I'll seek him there : I know ere this
The cold, cold earth doth shake him ;
But I will go, or send a kiss
By you, sir, to awake him.

" Pray hurt him not ; though he be dead
He knows well who do love him,
And who with green turfs rear his head,
And who do rudely move him.

" He's soft and tender, pray take heed,
With bands of cowslips bind him,
And bring him home ; but 'tis decreed
That I shall never find him."

———

" I dare not ask a kiss ;
I dare not beg a smile ;
Lest having that or this,
I might grow proud the while.

" No, no—the utmost share
Of my desire shall be
Only to kiss that air
That lately kissèd thee."

———

" Here, a little child, I stand
Heaving up my either hand :
Cold as paddocks though they be
Here I lift them up to Thee,
For a benison to fall
On our meat and on us all.
                                    Amen."

But Herrick's charm is everywhere—except in the epigrams.
It is very rare to find one of the hundreds of little poems which
form his book destitute of the peculiar touch of phrasing, the
eternising influence of style, which characterises the poetry of this
particular period so remarkably. The subject may be the merest
trifle, the thought a hackneyed or insignificant one. But the
amber to enshrine the fly is always there in larger or smaller, in

clearer or more clouded, shape. There has often been a certain
contempt (connected no doubt with certain general critical errors
as they seem to me, with which I shall deal at the end of this
chapter) flavouring critical notices of Herrick. I do not think
that any one who judges poetry as poetry, who keeps its several
kinds apart and does not demand epic graces in lyric, dramatic
substance in an anthologia, could ever feel or hint such a contempt. Whatever Herrick may have been as a man (of which
we know very little, and for which we need care less), he was a
most exquisite and complete poet in his own way, neither was
that way one to be lightly spoken of.

Indissolubly connected with Herrick in age, in character, and
in the singularly unjust criticism which has at various times been
bestowed on him, is Thomas Carew. His birth-date has been
very differently given as 1587 and (that now preferred) 1598;
but he died nearly forty years before the author of the *Hesperides*,
and nearly ten before the *Hesperides* themselves were published,
while his own poems were never collected till after his own death.
He was of a Gloucestershire branch of the famous Devonshire family of Carew, Cary, or Cruwys, was of Merton College,
Oxford, and the Temple, travelled, followed the Court, was a
disciple of Ben Jonson, and a member of the learned and
accomplished society of Clarendon's earlier days, obtained a
place .in the household of Charles I., is said by his friend
Hyde to have turned to devotion after a somewhat libertine
life, and died in 1639, before the evil days of triumphant
Puritanism, *felix opportunitate mortis*. He wrote little, and the
scantiness of his production, together with the supposed pains it
cost him, is ridiculed in Suckling's doggerel "Sessions of the
Poets." But this reproach (which Carew shares with Gray, and
with not a few others of the most admirable names in literature),
unjust as it is, is less unjust than the general tone of criticism on
Carew since. The *locus classicus* of depreciation both in regard
to him and to Herrick is to be found, as might be expected, in
one of the greatest, and one of the most wilfully capricious and

untrustworthy of English critics, in Hazlitt.   I am sorry to say
that there can be little hesitation in setting down the extraordinary misjudgment of the passage in question (it occurs in the
sixth Lecture on Elizabethan Literature), in part, at least, to the
fact that Herrick, Carew, and Crashaw, who are summarily damned
in it, were Royalists.   If there were any doubt about the matter,
it would be settled by the encomium bestowed in the very same
passage on Marvell, who is, no doubt, as Hazlitt says, a true poet,
but who as a poet is but seldom at the highest height of the
authors of " The Litany," " The Rapture," and " The Flaming
Heart."   Hazlitt, then, while on his way to tell us that Herrick's
two best pieces are some trivial anacreontics about Cupid and the
Bees—things hackneyed through a dozen literatures, and with no
recommendation but a borrowed prettiness—while about, I say, to
deny Herrick the spirit of love or wine, and in the same breath
with the dismissal of Crashaw as a " hectic enthusiast," informs
us that Carew was " an elegant Court trifler," and describes his
style as a " frequent mixture of the superficial and commonplace, with far-fetched and improbable conceits."

What Carew really is, and what he may be peremptorily
declared to be in opposition even to such a critic as Hazlitt, is
something quite different.   He is one of the most perfect masters
of lyrical form in English poetry.   He possesses a command of
the overlapped heroic couplet, which for sweep and rush of
rhythm cannot be surpassed anywhere.   He has, perhaps in a
greater degree than any poet of that time of conceits, the
knack of modulating the extravagances of fancy by the control of
reason, so that he never falls into the unbelievableness of Donne,
or Crashaw, or Cleveland.   He had a delicacy, when he chose
to be delicate, which is quintessential, and a vigour which is
thoroughly manly.   Best of all, perhaps, he had the intelligence
and the self-restraint to make all his poems wholes, and not
mere congeries of verses.   There is always, both in the scheme
of his meaning and the scheme of his metre, a definite plan of
rise and fall, a concerted effect.   That these great merits were

accompanied by not inconsiderable defects is true.   Carew lacks
the dewy freshness, the unstudied grace of Herrick.   He is even
more frankly and uncontrolledly sensual, and has paid the usual
and inevitable penalty that his best poem, *The Rapture*, is, for
the most part, unquotable, while another, if he carried out its
principles in this present year of grace, would run him the risk of
imprisonment with hard labour.   His largest attempt—the masque
called *Cœlum Britannicum*—is heavy.   His smaller poems, beautiful as they are, suffer somewhat from want of variety of subject.
There is just so much truth in Suckling's impertinence that the
reader of Carew sometimes catches himself repeating the lines of
Carew's master, "Still to be neat, still to be drest," not indeed
in full agreement with them, but not in exact disagreement.   One
misses the "wild civility" of Herrick.   This acknowledgment, I
trust, will save me from any charge of overvaluing Carew.

A man might, however, be easily tempted to overvalue him,
who observes his beauties, and who sees how, preserving the force,
the poetic spell, of the time, he was yet able, without in the least
descending to the correctness of Waller and his followers, to introduce into his work something also preserving it from the weaknesses
and inequalities which deface that of almost all his contemporaries, and which, as we shall see, make much of the dramatic
and poetical work of 1630-1660 a chaos of slipshod deformity to any one who has the sense of poetical form.   It is an un-
wearying delight to read and re-read the second of his poems, the
"Persuasions to Love," addressed to a certain A. L.   That the sentiment is common enough matters little ; the commonest things in
poetry are always the best.   But the delicate interchange of the
catalectic and acatalectic dimeter, the wonderful plays and changes
of cadence, the opening, as it were, of fresh stops at the beginning
of each new paragraph of the verse, so that the music acquires a
new colour, the felicity of the several phrases, the cunning heightening of the passion as the poet comes to "Oh ! love me then, and
now begin it," and the dying fall of the close, make up to me, at least,
most charming pastime.   It is not the same kind of pleasure, no

doubt, as that given by such an outburst as Crashaw's, to be
mentioned presently, or by such pieces as the great soliloquies of
Shakespere. Any one may say, if he likes to use words which
are question-begging, when not strictly meaningless, that it is not
such a " high " kind. But it is a kind, and in that kind perfect.

Carew's best pieces, besides *The Rapture*, are the beautiful
"Ask me no more," the first stanza of which is the weakest ; the
fine couplet poem, " The Cruel Mistress," whose closing distich—

> " Of such a goddess no times leave record,
> That burned the temple where she was adored "—

Dryden conveyed with the wise and unblushing boldness which
great poets use ; the " Deposition from love," written in one of
those combinations of eights and sixes, the melodious charm of
which seems to have died with the seventeenth century ; the
song, " He that loves a rosy cheek," which, by the unusual morality of its sentiments, has perhaps secured a fame not quite due
to its poetical merits ; the epitaph on Lady Mary Villers ; the
song " Would you know what's soft ? " the song to his inconstant
mistress :

> " When thou, poor excommunicate
> From all the joys of love, shalt see
> The full reward, and glorious fate
> Which my strong faith shall purchase me,
> Then curse thine own inconstancy.
>
> " A fairer hand than thine shall cure
> That heart which thy false oaths did wound ;
> And to my soul, a soul more pure
> Than thine, shall by love's hand be bound,
> And both with equal glory crown'd.
>
> " Then shalt thou weep, entreat, complain
> To Love, as I did once to thee ;
> When all thy tears shall be as vain
> As mine were then, for thou shalt be
> Damn'd for thy false apostacy."—

the pleasant pictures of the country houses of Wrest and Sax-
ham ; the charming conceit of " Red and white roses " :

> " Read in these roses the sad story
> Of my hard fate and your own glory :
> In the white you may discover
> The paleness of a fainting lover ;
> In the red, the flames still feeding
> On my heart with fresh wounds bleeding.
> The white will tell you how I languish,
> And the red express my anguish :
> The white my innocence displaying
> The red my martyrdom betraying.
> The frowns that on your brow resided
> Have those roses thus divided ;
> Oh ! let your smiles but clear the weather
> And then they both shall grow together."—

and lastly, though it would be easy to extend this already long list of selections from a by no means extensive collection of poems, the grand elegy on Donne. By this last the reproach of vain and amatorious trifling which has been so often levelled at Carew is at once thrown back and blunted. No poem shows so great an influence on the masculine panegyrics with which Dryden was to enrich the English of the next generation, and few are fuller of noteworthy phrases. The splendid epitaph which closes it—

> " Here lies a king that ruled as he thought fit
> The universal monarchy of wit "—

is only the best passage, not the only good one, and it may be matched with a fine and just description of English, ushered by a touch of acute criticism.

> " Thou shalt yield no precedence, but of time,
> And the blind fate of language, whose tuned chime
> More charms the outward sense : yet thou mayst claim
> From so great disadvantage greater fame.
> Since to the awe of thine imperious wit
> Our troublesome language bends, made only fit
> With her tough thick-ribbed hoops to gird about
> Thy giant fancy, which had proved too stout
> For their soft melting phrases."

And it is the man who could write like this that Hazlitt calls an " elegant Court trifler !"

The third of this great trio of poets, and with them the most remarkable of our whole group, was Richard Crashaw. He completes Carew and Herrick both in his qualities and (if a kind of bull may be permitted) in his defects, after a fashion almost unexampled elsewhere and supremely interesting. Hardly any one of the three could have appeared at any other time, and not one but is distinguished from the others in the most marked way. Herrick, despite his sometimes rather obtrusive learning, is emphatically the natural man. He does not show much sign of the influence of good society, his merits as well as his faults have a singular unpersonal and, if I may so say, *terræfilian* connotation. Carew is a gentleman before all ; but a rather profane gentleman. Crashaw is religious everywhere. Again, Herrick and Carew, despite their strong savour of the fashion of the time, are eminently critics as well as poets. Carew has not let one piece critically unworthy of him pass his censorship : Herrick (if we exclude the filthy and foolish epigrams into which he was led by corrupt following of Ben) has been equally careful. These two bards may have trouble with the *censor morum*,—the *censor literarum* they can brave with perfect confidence. It is otherwise with Crashaw. That he never, as far as can be seen, edited the bulk of his work for press at all matters little or nothing. But there is not in his work the slightest sign of the exercise of any critical faculty before, during, or after production. His masterpiece, one of the most astonishing things in English or any other literature, comes without warning at the end of *The Flaming Heart*. For page after page the poet has been poorly playing on some trifling conceits suggested by the picture of Saint Theresa and a seraph. First he thinks the painter ought to have changed the attributes ; then he doubts whether a lesser change will not do ; and always he treats his subject in a vein of grovelling and grotesque conceit which the boy Dryden in the stage of his elegy on Lord Hastings would have disdained. And then in a moment, in

the twinkling of an eye, without warning of any sort, the
metre changes, the poet's inspiration catches fire, and there
rushes up into the heaven of poetry this marvellous rocket
of song :—

> " Live in these conquering leaves : live all the same ;
> And walk through all tongues one triumphant flame ;
> Live here, great heart ; and love, and die, and kill ;
> And bleed, and wound, and yield, and conquer still.
> Let this immortal life where'er it comes
> Walk in a crowd of loves and martyrdoms.
> Let mystic deaths wait on't ; and wise souls be
> The love-slain witnesses of this life of thee.
> O sweet incendiary ! show here thy art,
> Upon this carcase of a hard cold heart ;
> Let all thy scatter'd shafts of light, that play
> Among the leaves of thy large books of day,
> Combin'd against this breast at once break in,
> And take away from me myself and sin ;
> This gracious robbery shall thy bounty be
> And my best fortunes such fair spoils of me.
> O thou undaunted daughter of desires !
> By all thy pow'r of lights and fires ;
> By all the eagle in thee, all the dove ;
> By all thy lives and deaths of love ;
> By thy large draughts of intellectual day ;
> And by thy thirsts of love more large than they ;
> By all thy brim-fill'd bowls of fierce desire ;
> By thy last morning's draught of liquid fire ;
> By the full kingdom of that final kiss
> That seized thy parting soul, and seal'd thee his ;
> By all the heavens thou hast in him,
> (Fair sister of the seraphim)
> By all of him we have in thee ;
> Leave nothing of myself in me.
> Let me so read thy life, that I
> Unto all life of mine may die."

The contrast is perhaps unique as regards the dead colourless-
ness of the beginning, and the splendid colour of the end.   But
contrasts like it occur all over Crashaw's work.

He was a much younger man than either of the poets with whom we have leashed him, and his birth year used to be put at 1616, though Dr. Grosart has made it probable that it was three years earlier. His father was a stern Anglican clergyman of extremely Protestant leanings, his mother died when Crashaw was young, but his stepmother appears to have been most un-novercal. Crashaw was educated at Charterhouse, and then went to Cambridge, where in 1637 he became a fellow of Peterhouse, and came in for the full tide of high church feeling, to which (under the mixed influence of Laud's policy, of the ascetic practices of the Ferrars of Gidding, and of a great architectural development afterwards defaced if not destroyed by Puritan brutality) Cambridge was even more exposed than Oxford. The outbreak of the civil war may or may not have found Crashaw at Cambridge ; he was at any rate deprived of his fellowship for not taking the covenant in 1643, and driven into exile. Already inclined doctrinally and in matters of practice to the older communion, and despairing of the resurrection of the Church of England after her sufferings at the hands of the Parliament, Crashaw joined the Church of Rome, and journeyed to its metropolis. He was attached to the suit of Cardinal Pallotta, but is said to have been shocked by Italian manners. The cardinal procured him a canonry at Loretto, and this he hastened to take up, but died in 1649 with suspicions of poison, which are not impossibly, but at the same time by no means necessarily true. His poems had already appeared under the double title of *Steps to the Temple* (sacred), and *Delights of the Muses* (profane), but not under his own editorship, or it would seem with his own choice of title. Several other editions followed,—one later than his death, with curious illustrations said to be, in part at least, of his own design. Manuscript sources, as in the case of some other poets of the time, have considerably enlarged the collection since. But a great part of it consists of epigrams (in the wide sense, and almost wholly sacred) in the classical tongues, which were sometimes translated by Crashaw himself. These are not always correct in style or prosody, but are often interesting. The famous line in reference to the miracle of Cana,

> " Vidit et erubuit nympha pudica Deum,"

is assigned to Crashaw as a boy at Cambridge; of his later faculty in the same way the elaborate and, in its way, beautiful poem entitled *Bulla* (the Bubble) is the most remarkable.

Our chief subject, however, is the English poems proper, sacred and profane. In almost all of these there is noticeable an extraordinary inequality, the same in kind, if not in degree, as that on which we have commented in the case of *The Flaming Heart*. Crashaw is never quite so great as there; but he is often quite as small. His exasperating lack of self-criticism has sometimes led selectors to make a cento out of his poems—notably in the case of the exceedingly pretty " Wishes to His Unknown Mistress," beginning, " Whoe'er she be, That not impossible she, That shall command my heart and me "—a poem, let it be added, which excuses this dubious process much less than most, inasmuch as nothing in it is positively bad, though it is rather too long. Here is the opening, preceded by a piece from another poem, " A Hymn to Saint Theresa ":—

> " Those rare works, where thou shalt leave writ
> Love's noble history, with wit
> Taught thee by none but him, while here
> They feed our souls, shall clothe thine there.
> Each heavenly word by whose hid flame
> Our hard hearts shall strike fire, the same
> Shall flourish on thy brows and be
> Both fire to us and flame to thee :
> Whose light shall live bright, in thy face
> By glory, in our hearts by grace.

> " Thou shalt look round about, and see
> Thousands of crown'd souls throng to be
> Themselves thy crown, sons of thy vows :
> The virgin births with which thy spouse
> Made fruitful thy fair soul ; go now
> And with them all about thee, bow

To Him, ' Put on' (He'll say) ' put on,
My rosy love, that thy rich zone,
Sparkling with the sacred flames,
Of thousand souls whose happy names
Heaven heaps upon thy score, thy bright
Life brought them first to kiss the light
That kindled them to stars.'   And so
Thou with the Lamb thy Lord shall go,
And whereso'er He sets His white
Steps, walk with Him those ways of light,
Which who in death would live to see
Must learn in life to die like thee."

———————

" Whoe'er she be,
    That not impossible she,
    That shall command my heart and me ;

" Where'er she lie,
    Lock'd up from mortal eye,
    In shady leaves of destiny ;

" Till that ripe birth
    Of studied Fate stand forth,
    And teach her fair steps to our earth :

" Till that divine
    Idea take a shrine
    Of crystal flesh, through which to shine :

" Meet you her, my wishes
    Bespeak her to my blisses,
    And be ye call'd, my absent kisses."

The first hymn to Saint Theresa, to which *The Flaming Heart*
is a kind of appendix, was written when Crashaw was still an
Anglican (for which he did not fail, later, to make a characteristic
and very pretty, though quite unnecessary, apology).   It has no
passage quite up to the Invocation—Epiphonema, to give it the
technical term—of the later poem.   But it is, on the contrary, good
almost throughout, and is, for uniform exaltation, far the best of
Crashaw's poems.   Yet such uniform exaltation must be seldom
sought in him.   It is in his little bursts, such as that in the
stanza beginning, " O mother turtle dove," that his charm consists.

Often, as in verse after verse of *The Weeper*, it has an unearthly delicacy and witchery which only Blake, in a few snatches, has ever equalled; while at other times the poet seems to invent, in the most casual and unthinking fashion, new metrical effects and new jewelries of diction which the greatest lyric poets since— Coleridge, Shelley, Lord Tennyson, Mr. Swinburne—have rather deliberately imitated than spontaneously recovered. Yet to all this charm there is no small drawback. The very maddest and most methodless of the " Metaphysicals " cannot touch Crashaw in his tasteless use of conceits. When he, in *The Weeper* just above referred to, calls the tears of Magdalene " Wat'ry brothers," and " Simpering sons of those fair eyes," and when, in the most intolerable of all the poet's excesses, the same eyes are called " Two waking baths, two weeping motions, Portable and com- pendious oceans," which follow our Lord about the hills of Galilee, it is almost difficult to know whether to feel most contempt or indignation for a man who could so write. It is fair to say that there are various readings and omissions in the different edi- tions which affect both these passages. Yet :he offence is that Crashaw should ever have written them at all. Amends, however, are sure to be made before the reader has read much farther. Crashaw's longest poems—a version of Marini's *Sospetto d'Herode*, and one of the rather overpraised " Lover and Nightingale " story of Strada—are not his best ; the metre in which both are written, though the poet manages it well, lacks the extraordinary charm of his lyric measures. It does not appear that the " Not impossible she " ever made her appearance, and probably for a full half of his short life Crashaw burnt only with religious fire. But no Englishman has expressed that fire as he has, and none in his expression of any sentiment, sacred and profane, has dropped such notes of ethereal music. At his best he is far above singing, at his worst he is below a very childish prattle. But even then he is never coarse, never offensive, not very often actually dull ; and everywhere he makes amends by flowers of the divinest poetry. Mr. Pope, who borrowed not a little from him, thought, indeed, that you could find nothing of "The real part of poetry" (correct construction and so forth) in Crashaw ; and Mr. Hayley gently rebukes Cowley (after observing that if Pope borrowed from Crashaw, it was "as the sun borrows from the earth ") for his "glow-ing panegyrick." Now, if the real part of poetry is anywhere in Hayley, or quintessentially in Pope, it certainly is not in Crashaw.

The group or school (for it is not easy to decide on either word, and objections might be taken to each) at the head of which Herrick, Carew, and Crashaw must be placed, and which included Herbert and his band of sacred singers, included also not a few minor groups, sufficiently different from each other, but all marked off sharply from the innovating and classical school of Waller and his followers, which it is not proposed to treat in this volume. All, without exception, show the influence in different ways of Ben Jonson and of Donne. But each has its own peculiarity. We find these peculiarities, together with anticipations of post-Reformation characteristics, mixed very curiously in the miscellanies of the time. These are interesting enough, and may be studied with advantage, if not also with pleasure, in the principal of them, *Wit's Recreations* (1640). This, with certain kindred works (*Wit Restored*, and the very unsavoury *Musarum Deliciæ* of Sir John Mennis and Dr. Smith), has been more than once repub-lished. In these curious collections, to mention only one instance, numerous pieces of Herrick's appeared with considerable vari-ants from the text of the *Hesperides ;* and in their pages things old and new, charming pastoral poems, *vers de société* of very unequal merit, ballads, satires, epigrams, and a large quantity of mere scatology and doggerel, are heaped together pell-mell. Songs from the dramatists, especially Fletcher, make their ap-pearance, sometimes with slight variants, and there are forms of the drinking song in *Gammer Gurton's Needle* long after, and of Sir John Suckling's "Ballad on a Wedding," apparently some-what before, their respective publication in their proper places. Here is the joke about the wife and the almanack which reckless tradition has told of Dryden ; printed when Lady Elizabeth

Howard was in the nursery, and Dryden was not yet at Westminster. Here we learn how, probably about the second or third
decade of the century, the favourite authors of learned ladies were
" Wither, Draiton, and Balzack " (Guez de Balzac of the *Letters*),
a very singular trio ; and how some at least loved the " easy
ambling " of Heywood's prose, but thought that he "grovelled on
the stage," which it must be confessed he not uncommonly did.
Wit Restored contains the charming " Phillida flouts Me," with
other real " delights." Even Milton makes his appearance in these
collections, which continued to be popular for more than a century,
and acquired at intervals fresh vogue from the great names of
Dryden and Pope.

Neglecting or returning from these, we may class the minor
Caroline poets under the following heads. There are belated
Elizabethans like Habington, sacred poets of the school of Herbert,
translators like Stanley, Sherburne, and Quarles, philosophico-
theological poets like Joseph Beaumont and More, and poets
of society, such as Lovelace and Suckling, whose class degenerated into a class of boon companion song-writers, such as
Alexander Brome, and, at the extremity of our present period,
Charles Cotton, in whose verse (as for the matter of that in the
famous muses of Lovelace and Suckling themselves) the rapidly
degenerating prosody of the time is sometimes painfully evident.
This is also apparent (though it is compensated by much exquisite
poetry, and on the strictly lyric side rarely offends) in the work of
Randolph, Corbet, Cartwright, Chamberlayne of the *Pharonnida*,
Sidney Godolphin, Shakerley Marmion, Cleveland, Benlowes,
Kynaston, John Hall, the enigmatic Chalkhill, Patrick Carey,
Bishop King. These about exhaust the list of poets who must
be characterised here, though it could be extended. Cowley,
Marvell, and Waller fall outside our limits.

George Herbert, the one popular name, if we except Lovelace
and Suckling, of the last paragraph, was born at Montgomery Castle
in 1593, of the great house now represented in the English peerage
by the holders of the titles of Pembroke, Carnarvon, and Powis.

George was the younger brother of the equally well-known Lord Herbert of Cherbury ; and after being for some years public orator at Cambridge, turned, it is said, on some despite or disappointment, from secular to sacred business, accepted the living of Bemerton, and after holding it for a short time, died in 1633. Walton's *Life* was hardly needed to fix Herbert in the popular mind, for his famous volume of sacred poems, *The Temple*, would have done so, and has done so far more firmly. It was not his only book by any means ; he had displayed much wit as quite a boy in counter-lampooning Andrew Melville's ponderous and impudent *Anti-Tami-Cami-Categoria*, an attack on the English universities ; and afterwards he wrote freely in Greek, Latin, and English, both in prose and verse. Nothing, however, but *The Temple* has held popular estimation, and that has held it firmly, being as much helped by the Tractarian as by the Romantic movement. It may be confessed without shame and without innuendo that Herbert has been on the whole a greater favourite with readers than with critics, and the reason is obvious. He is not prodigal of the finest strokes of poetry. To take only his own contemporaries, and undoubtedly pupils, his gentle moralising and devotion are tame and cold beside the burning glow of Crashaw, commonplace and popular beside the intellectual subtlety and, now and then, the inspired touch of Vaughan. But he never drops into the flatness and the extravagance of both these writers, and his beauties, assuredly not mean in themselves, and very constantly present, are both in kind and in arrangement admirably suited to the average comprehension. He is quaint and conceited ; but his quaintnesses and conceits are never beyond the reach of any tolerably intelligent understanding. He is devout, but his devotion does not transgress into the more fantastic regions of piety. He is a mystic, but of the more exoteric school of mysticism. He expresses common needs, common thoughts, the everyday emotions of the Christian, just sublimated sufficiently to make them attractive. The fashion and his own taste gave him a pleasing quaintness, which his good sense kept from being ever

obscure or offensive or extravagant. The famous "Sweet day so
cool, so calm, so bright," and many short passages which are
known to every one, express Herbert perfectly. The thought is
obvious, usual, in no sense far fetched. The morality is plain and
simple. The expression, with a sufficient touch of the daintiness
of the time, has nothing that is extraordinarily or ravishingly
felicitous whether in phrasing or versing. He is, in short, a poet
whom all must respect; whom those that are in sympathy with his
vein of thought cannot but revere; who did England an inestimable service, by giving to the highest and purest thoughts that
familiar and abiding poetic garb which contributes so much to fix
any thoughts in the mind, and of which, to tell the truth, poetry
has been much more prodigal to other departments of thought by
no means so well deserving. But it is impossible to call him a
great poet even in his own difficult class. The early Latin hymn
writers are there to show what a great religious poet must be like.
Crashaw, if his genius had been less irregular and jaculative, might
have been such. Herbert is not, and could not have been.
With him it is an almost invariable custom to class Vaughan the
"Silurist," and a common one to unite George Sandys, the
traveller, translator of Ovid, and paraphrast of the Psalms and
other parts of the Bible. Sandys, an older man than Herbert by
fifteen, and than Vaughan by more than forty years, published
rather late, so that he came as a sacred poet after Herbert, and
not long before Vaughan. He was son of the Archbishop of York,
and brother of that Edwin Sandys who was a pupil of Hooker,
and who is said to have been present on the melancholy occasion
when the judicious one was "called to rock the cradle." He is
interesting for a singular and early mastery of the couplet, which
the following extract will show :—

> "O Thou, who all things hast of nothing made,
> Whose hand the radiant firmament displayed,
> With such an undiscerned swiftness hurled
> About the steadfast centre of the world ;
> Against whose rapid course the restless sun,
> And wandering flames in varied motions run.

> Which heat, light, life infuse ; time, night, and day
> Distinguish ; in our human bodies sway :
> That hung'st the solid earth in fleeting air
> Veined with clear springs which ambient seas repair.
> In clouds the mountains wrap their hoary heads ;
> Luxurious valleys clothed with flowery meads ;
> Her trees yield fruit and shade ; with liberal breasts
> All creatures she, their common mother, feasts."

Henry Vaughan was born in 1622, published *Poems* in 1646 (for some of which he afterwards expressed a not wholly necessary repentance), *Olor Iscanus* (from Isca Silurum) in 1651, and *Silex Scintillans*, his best-known book, in 1650 and 1655. He also published verses much later, and did not die till 1695, being the latest lived of any man who has a claim to appear in this book, but his aftergrowths were not happy. To say that Vaughan is a poet of one poem would not be true. But the universally known

"They are all gone into the world of light"

is so very much better than anything else that he has done that it would be hardly fair to quote anything else, unless we could quote a great deal. Like Herbert, and in pretty obvious imitation of him, he set himself to bend the prevailing fancy for quips and quaintnesses into sacred uses, to see that the Devil should not have all the best conceits. But he is not so uniformly successful, though he has greater depth and greater originality of thought.

Lovelace and Suckling are inextricably connected together, not merely by their style of poetry, but by their advocacy of the same cause, their date, and their melancholy end. Both (Suckling in 1609, Lovelace nine years later) were born to large fortunes, both spent them, at least partially, in the King's cause, and both died miserably,—Suckling, in 1642, by his own hand, his mind, according to a legend, unhinged by the tortures of the Inquisition ; Lovelace, two years before the Restoration, a needy though not an exiled cavalier, in London purlieus. Both have written songs of quite marvellous and unparalleled exquisiteness, and both have left doggerel which would disgrace a schoolboy. Both, it may be suspected, held the doctrine which Suckling openly champions, that a gentleman should not take too much trouble about his verses. The result, however, was in Lovelace's case more disastrous than in Suckling's. It is not quite true that Lovelace left nothing worth reading but the two immortal songs, "To Lucasta on going to the Wars" and "To Althea from Prison;" and it is only fair to say that the corrupt condition of his text is evidently due, at least in part, to incompetent printing and the absence of revision. "The Grasshopper" is almost worthy of the two better-known pieces, and there are others not far below it. But on the whole any one who knows those two (and who does not?) may neglect Lovelace with safety. Suckling, even putting his dramatic work aside, is not to be thus treated. True, he is often careless in the bad sense as well as in the good, though the doggerel of the "Sessions" and some other pieces is probably intentional. But in his own vein, that of coxcombry that is not quite cynical, and is quite intelligent, he is marvellously happy. The famous song in *Aglaura*, the Allegro to Lovelace's Penseroso, "Why so pale and wan, fond lover?" is scarcely better than "'Tis now since I sat down before That foolish fort a heart," or "Out upon it! I have loved Three whole days together." Nor in more serious veins is the author to be slighted, as in "The Dance;" while as for the "Ballad on a Wedding," the best parts of this are by common consent incomparable. Side by side by these are to be found, as in Lovelace, pieces that will not even scan, and, as *not* in Lovelace (who is not seldom loose but never nasty), pieces of a dull and disgusting obscenity. But we do not go to Suckling for these; we go to him for his easy grace, his agreeable impudence, his scandalous mock-disloyalty (for it is only mock-disloyalty after all) to the "Lord of Terrible Aspect," whom all his elder contemporaries worshipped so piously. Suckling's inconstancy and Lovelace's constancy may or may not be equally poetical,—there is some reason for thinking that the lover of Althea was actually driven to something like despair by the loss of his mistress. But

that matters to us very little.   The songs remain, and remain yet
unsurpassed, as the most perfect celebrations, in one case of
chivalrous devotion, in the other of the coxcomb side of gallantry,
that literature contains or is likely ever to contain.   The song-
writing faculty of the English, which had broken out some half
century before, and had produced so many masterpieces, was near
its death, or at least near the trance from which Burns and Blake
revived it more than a century later, which even Dryden's super-
human faculty of verse could only galvanise.   But at the last it
threw off by the mouths of men, who otherwise seem to have had
very ordinary poetical powers, this little group of triumphs in song,
to which have to be added the raptures—equally strange and sweet,
equally unmatched of their kind, but nobler and more masculine
—of the "Great Marquis," the few and wonderful lines of Mon-
trose.   To quote "My dear and only love, I pray," or "Great,
good, and just, could I but rate," would be almost as much an
insult to the reader as to quote the above-mentioned little masterpieces of the two less heroic English cavaliers.

Quarles, More, and Joseph Beaumont form, as it were, a kind
of appendix to the poetry of Herbert and Vaughan—an appendix
very much less distinguished by poetical power, but very interesting as displaying the character of the time and the fashion (strange
enough to us moderns) in which almost every interest of that time
found its natural way into verse.   The enormous popularity of
Francis Quarles's *Emblems* and *Enchiridion* accounts to some
extent for the very unjust ridicule which has been lavished on
him by men of letters of his own and later times.   But the silly
antithesis of Pope, a writer who, great as he was, was almost as
ignorant of literary history as his model, Boileau, ought to prejudice no one, and it is strictly true that Quarles's enormous
volume hides, to some extent, his merits.   Born in 1592 at
Romford, of a gentle though not very distinguished family, which
enters into that curious literary genealogy of Swift, Dryden, and
Herrick, he was educated at Cambridge, became cup-bearer to
the ill-fated and romantically renowned "Goody Palsgrave," held

the post which Middleton and Jonson had held, of chronologer to
the city of London, followed the King to Oxford to his loss,
having previously had losses in Ireland, and died early in 1644,
leaving his memory to be defended in a rather affecting document
by his widow, Ursula.   Quarles was a kind of journalist to whom
the vehicle of verse came more easily than the vehicle of prose,
and the dangers of that state of things are well known.   A mere
list of his work (the *Enchiridion* is in prose, and a good thing too)
would far exceed any space that can be given to him here.   All
Quarles's work is journey-work, but it is only fair to note the
frequent wealth of fancy, the occasional felicity of expression,
which illustrate this wilderness.

More and Beaumont were not, like Quarles, poetical miscellanists and periodical writers ; but they seem to have shared
with him the delusion that poetry is an instrument of all work.
Henry More, a man well connected and who might have risen,
but who preferred to pass the greater part of a long and studious
life as a fellow of Christ's College, Cambridge, is best known as
a member of the theological school, indifferently called the Cambridge Platonists and the Cambridge Latitudinarians.   His chief
work in verse is a great philosophical poem, entitled the *Song
of the Soul*, with such engaging sub-titles as *Psychozoia, Psycha-
thanasia, Antipsychopannychia*, and *Antimonopsychia*.   I shall not,
I hope, be suspected of being ignorant of Greek, or disinclined to
metaphysics, if I say that the *Song of the Soul* appears to me a
venerable mistake.   A philosophical controversy carried on in
this fashion—

> " But contradiction, can that have place
> In any soul ?   Plato affirms ideas ;
> But Aristotle, with his pugnacious race,
> As idle figments stiffly them denies,"

seems to me to be a signal instance of the wrong thing in the
wrong place.   It is quite true that More has, as Southey says,
" lines and passages of sublime beauty."   A man of his time,
actuated by its noble thought, trained as we know More to have

been in the severest school of Spenser, and thus habituated to the heavenly harmonies of that perfect poet, could hardly fail to produce such.   But his muse is a chaotic not a cosmic one.

Something the same may be said of Joseph Beaumont, a friend of Crashaw, and like him ejected from Peterhouse, son-in-law of Bishop Wren, and, later, head of Jesus College.   Beaumont, a strong cavalier and an orthodox churchman, was a kind of adversary of More's, whose length and quaintness he has exceeded, while he has almost rivalled his learning in *Psyche* or *Love's Mystery*, a religious poem of huge dimensions, first published in 1648 and later in 1702.   Beaumont, as both fragments of this vast thing and his minor poems show, had fancy, taste, and almost genius on opportunity ; but the prevailing mistake of his school, the idea that poetry is a fit vehicle for merely prosaic expression, is painfully apparent in him.

First, for various reasons, among the nondescripts of the Caroline school, deserves to be mentioned William Habington, a Roman Catholic gentleman of good upper middle-class station, whose father was himself a man of letters, and had some trouble in the Gunpowder Plot.   He was born at Hindlip Hall, near Worcester, in the year of the plot itself, courted and married Lucy Herbert, daughter of his neighbour, Lord Powis, and published her charms and virtues in the collection called *Castara*, first issued in 1634.   Habington also wrote a tragic comedy, *The Queen of Aragon*, and some other work, but died in middle life.   It is upon *Castara* that his fame rests.   To tell the truth it is, though, as had been said, an estimable, yet a rather irritating work.   That Habington was a true lover every line of it shows ; that he had a strong infusion of the abundant poetical inspiration then abroad is shown by line after line, though hardly by poem after poem, among its pieces.   His series of poems on the death of his friend Talbot is full of beauty.   His religion is sincere, fervent, and often finely expressed ; though he never rose to Herbert's pure devotion, or to Crashaw's flaming poetry.   One of the later *Castara* poems may be given :—

> "We saw and woo'd each other's eyes,
>   My soul contracted then with thine,
> And both burnt in one sacrifice,
>   By which our marriage grew divine.
>
> " Let wilder youths, whose soul is sense,
>   Profane the temple of delight,
> And purchase endless penitence,
>   With the stolen pleasure of one night.
>
> " Time's ever ours, while we despise
>   The sensual idol of our clay,
> For though the sun do set and rise,
>   We joy one everlasting day.
>
> " Whose light no jealous clouds obscure,
>   While each of us shine innocent,
> The troubled stream is still impure ;
>   With virtue flies away content.
>
> " And though opinions often err,
>   We'll court the modest smile of fame,
> For sin's black danger circles her,
>   Who hath infection in her name.
>
> " Thus when to one dark silent room
>   Death shall our loving coffins thrust :
> Fame will build columns on our tomb,
>   And add a perfume to our dust."

But *Castara* is a real instance of what some foreign critics very unjustly charge on English literature as a whole—a foolish and almost canting prudery.   The poet dins the chastity of his mistress into his readers' heads until the readers in self-defence are driven to say, "Sir, did any one doubt it?"   He protests the freedom of his own passion from any admixture of fleshly influence, till half a suspicion of hypocrisy and more than half a feeling of contempt force themselves on the hearer.   A relentless critic might connect these unpleasant features with the uncharitable and more than orthodox bigotry of his religious poems.   Yet Habington, besides contributing much agreeable verse to the literature of the period, is invaluable as showing the counterside to Milton, the Catholic Puritanism which is no doubt inherent in the English nature, and which, had it not been for the Reformation, would probably have transformed Catholicism in a very strange fashion.

There is no Puritanism of any kind in a group—it would hardly be fair to call them a school—of " Heroic " poets to whom very little attention has been paid in histories of literature hitherto, but who lead up not merely to Davenant's *Gondibert* and Cowley's *Davideis*, but to *Paradise Lost* itself. The " Heroic " poem was a kind generated partly by the precepts of the Italian criticism, including Tasso, partly by the practice of Tasso himself, and endeavouring to combine something of the unity of Epic with something and more of the variety of Romance. It may be represented here by the work of Chalkhill, Chamberlayne, Marmion, and Kynaston. John Chalkhill, the author of *Thealma and Clearchus*, was, with his work, introduced to the public in 1683 by Izaak Walton, who styles him " an acquaintant and friend of Edmund Spenser." If so, he must have been one of the first of English poets to adopt the very loose enjambed decasyllabic couplet in which his work, like that of Marmion and still more Chamberlayne, is written. His poem is unfinished, and the construction and working-up of the story are looser even than the metre ; but it contains a great deal of charming description and some very poetical phrase.

Much the same may be said of the *Cupid and Psyche* (1637) of the dramatist Shakerley Marmion (*v. inf.*), which follows the original of Apuleius with alternate closeness and liberty, but is always best when it is most original. The *Leoline and Sydanis* (1642) of Sir Francis Kynaston is not in couplets but in rhyme-royal—a metre of which the author was so fond that he even translated the *Troilus and Cressida* of Chaucer into Latin, retaining the seven-line stanza and its rhymes. Kynaston, who was a member of both universities and at one time proctor at Cambridge, was a man interested in various kinds of learning, and even started an Academy or *Museum Minervæ* of his own. In *Leoline and Sydanis* he sometimes comes near to the mock heroic, but in his lyrics called *Cynthiades* he comes nearer still to the best Caroline cry. One or two of his pieces have found their way into anthologies, but until the present writer reprinted his works[1] he was almost unknown.

The most important by far, however, of this group is William Chamberlayne, a physician of Shaftesbury, who, before or during the Civil War, began and afterwards finished (publishing it in 1659) the very long heroic romance of *Pharonnida*, a story of the most involved and confused character but with episodes of great vividness and even sustained power : a piece of versification straining the liberties of *enjambement* in line and want of connection in syntax to the utmost ; but a very mine of poetical expression and imagery. Jewels are to be picked up on every page by those who will take the trouble to do so, and who are not offended by the extraordinary nonchalance of the composition.

The *Theophila* of Edward Benlowes (1603 ?-1676) was printed in 1652 with elaborate and numerous engravings by Hollar, which have made it rare, and usually imperfect when met with. Benlowes was a Cambridge man (of St. John's College) by education, but lived latterly and died at Oxford, having been reduced from wealth to poverty by the liberality which made his friends anagrammatise his name into "Benevolus." His work was abused as an awful example of the extravagant style by Butler (*Character of a Small Poet*), and by Warburton in the next century ; but it was never reprinted till the date of the collection just noted. It is a really curious book, displaying the extraordinary *diffusion* of poetical spirit still existing, but in a hectic and decadent condition. Benlowes—a Cleveland with more poetry and less cleverness, or a very much weaker Crashaw—uses a monorhymed triplet made up of a heroic, an octosyllable, and an Alexandrine which is as wilfully odd as the rest of him.

Randolph, the youngest and not the least gifted of the tribe

[1] In *Minor Caroline Poets*, vols. i. and ii. (Oxford, 1905-6). An important addition to the religious verse of the time was made by Mr. Dobell with the *Poems* (London, 1903) of Thomas Traherne, a follower of Herbert, with some strange anticipations of Blake.

of Ben, died before he was thirty, after writing some noteworthy plays, and a certain number of minor poems, which, as it has been well observed, rather show that he might have done anything, than that he did actually do something. Corbet was Bishop first of Oxford and then of Norwich, and died in 1635. Corbet's work is of that peculiar class which is usually, though not always, due to "University Wits," and which only appeals to people with a considerable appreciation of humour, and a large stock of general information. It is always occasional in character, and rarely succeeds so well as when the treatment is one of distinct *persiflage.* Thus the elegy on Donne is infinitely inferior to Carew's, and the mortuary epitaph on Arabella Stuart is, for such a subject and from the pen of a man of great talent, extraordinarily feeble. The burlesque epistle to Lord Mordaunt on his journey to the North is great fun, and the "Journey into France," though, to borrow one of its own jokes, rather "strong," is as good. The "Exhortation to Mr. John Hammond," a ferocious satire on the Puritans, distinguishes itself from almost all precedent work of the kind by the force and directness of its attack, which almost anticipates Dryden. And Corbet had both pathetic and imaginative touches on occasion, as here :—

> "What I shall leave thee none can tell,
> But all shall say I wish thee well,
> I wish thee, Vin, before all wealth,
> Both bodily and ghostly health ;
> Nor too much wealth, nor wit, come to thee,
> So much of either may undo thee.
> I wish thee learning, not for show,
> Enough for to instruct and know ;
> Not such as gentlemen require
> To prate at table, or at fire.
> I wish thee all thy mother's graces,
> Thy father's fortunes, and his places.
> I wish thee friends, and one at court,
> Not to build on, but support
> To keep thee, not in doing many
> Oppressions, but from suffering any.

> I wish thee peace in all thy ways,
> Nor lazy nor contentious days ;
> And when thy soul and body part
> As innocent as now those art."

Cartwright, a short-lived man but a hard student, shows best in his dramas. In his occasional poems, strongly influenced by Donne, he is best at panegyric, worst at burlesque and epigram. In "On a Gentlewoman's Silk Hood" and some other pieces he may challenge comparison with the most futile of the metaphysicals ; but no one who has read his noble elegy on Sir Bevil Grenvil, unequal as it is, will think lightly of Cartwright. Sir Edward Sherburne was chiefly a translator in the fashionable style. His original poems were those of a very inferior Carew (he even copies the name Celia), but they are often pretty. Alexander Brome, of whom very little is known, and who must not be confounded with the dramatist, was a lawyer and a cavalier song-writer, who too frequently wrote mere doggerel ; but on the other hand, he sometimes did not, and when he escaped the evil influence, as in the stanzas "Come, come, let us drink," "The Trooper," and not a few others, he has the right anacreontic vein.

As for Charles Cotton, his "Virgil Travesty" is deader than Scarron's, and deserves to be so. The famous lines which Lamb has made known to every one in the essay on "New Year's Day" are the best thing he did. But there are many excellent things scattered about his work, despite a strong taint of the mere coarseness and nastiness which have been spoken of. And though he was also much tainted with the hopeless indifference to prosody which distinguished all these belated cavaliers, it is noteworthy that he was one of the few Englishmen for centuries to adopt the strict French forms and write rondeaux and the like. On the whole his poetical power has been a little undervalued, while he was also dexterous in prose.

Thomas Stanley has been classed above as a translator because he would probably have liked to have his scholarship thus brought into prominence. It was, both in ancient and modern tongues, very considerable. His *History of Philosophy* was a classic for a very long time ; and his edition of Æschylus had the honour of revision within the nineteenth century by Porson and by Butler. It is not certain that Bentley did not borrow from him ; and his versions of Anacreon, of various other Greek lyrists, of the later Latins, and of modern writers in Spanish and Italian are most remarkable. But he was also an original poet in the best Caroline style of lyric ; and his combination of family (for he was of the great Stanley stock), learning, and genius gave him a high position with men of letters of his day. Sidney Godolphin, who died very young fighting for the King in Hopton's army, had no time to do much ; but he has been magnificently celebrated by no less authorities than Clarendon and Hobbes, and fragments of his work, which has only recently been collected, have long been known. None of it, except a commendatory poem or two, was printed in his own time, and very little later ; while the MSS. are not in very accomplished form, and show few or no signs of revision by the author. Some, however, of Godolphin's lyrics are of great beauty, and a couplet translation of the *Fourth Æneid* has as much firmness as Sandys or Waller. Another precocious poet whose life also was cut short, though less heroically, and on the other side of politics, was John Hall, a Cambridge man, who at barely twenty (1645-6) issued a volume of poems and another, *Horæ Vacivæ*, of prose essays, translated Longinus, did hack-work on the Cromwellian side, and died, it is said, of loose and lazy living. Hall's poems are of mixed kinds—sacred and profane, serious and comic—and the best of them, such as "The Call" and "The Lure," have a slender but most attractive vein of fantastic charm. Patrick Carey, again, a Royalist and brother of the famous Lord Falkland, brought up as a Roman Catholic but afterwards a convert to the Church of England, left manuscript pieces, human and divine, which were printed by Sir Walter Scott in 1819, and are extremely pleasant ; while Bishop King, though not often at the height of his well-known "Tell me no more how fair she is," never falls below a level much above the average.

The satirist John Cleveland, whose poems were extremely popular and exist in numerous editions (much blended with other men's work and hard to disentangle), was made a sort of " metaphysical helot " by a reference in Dryden's *Essay of Dramatic Poesy* and quotations in Johnson's *Life of Cowley*. He partly deserves this, though he has real originality of thought and phrase ; but much of his work is political or occasional, and he does not often rise to the quintessential exquisiteness of some of those who have been mentioned.   A few examples of this class may be given :—

> " Through a low
> Dark vale, where shade-affecting walks did grow
> Eternal strangers to the sun, did lie
> The narrow path frequented only by
> The forest tyrants when they bore their prey
> From open dangers of discovering day.
> Passed through this desert valley, they were now
> Climbing an easy hill, whose every bough
> Maintained a feathered chorister to sing
> Soft panegyrics, and the rude winds bring
> Into a murmuring slumber ; whilst the calm
> Morn on each leaf did hang the liquid balm
> With an intent, before the next sun's birth
> To drop it in those wounds which the cleft earth
> Received from's last day's beams.   The hill's ascent
> Wound up by action, in a large extent
> Of leafy plains, shows them the canopy
> Beneath whose shadow their large way did lie."
>
> CHAMBERLAYNE, *Pharonnida*, iv. 1. 199-216.

It will be observed that these eighteen lines all but *four* are overrun ; and the resemblance to the couplet of Keats's *Endymion* should not be missed.

> " April is past, then do not shed,
>   And do not waste in vain,
>   Upon thy mother's earthy bed
>   Thy tears of silver rain.
>
> " Thou canst not hope that the cold earth
>   By wat'ring will bring forth
>   A flower like thee, or will give birth
>   To one of the like worth.

    " 'Tis true the rain fall'n from the sky
        Or from the clouded air,
     Doth make the earth to fructify,
        And makes the heaven more fair.

   " With thy dear face it is not so,
        Which, if once overcast,
     If thou rain down thy showers of woe,
        They, like the sirens, blast.

   " Therefore, when sorrow shall becloud
        Thy fair serenest day,
     Weep not : thy sighs shall be allow'd
        To chase the storm away.

   " Consider that the teeming vine,
        If cut by chance [it] weep,
     Doth bear no grapes to make the wine,
        But feels eternal sleep."

                       KYNASTON.

   " Be conquer'd by such charms ; there shall
        Not always such enticements fall.
What know we whether that rich spring of light
        Will staunch his streams
        Of golden beams
     Ere the approach of night ?

   " How know we whether't shall not be
        The last to either thee or me ?
He can at will his ancient brightness gain,
        But thou and I
        When we shall die
     Shall still in dust remain."

                       JOHN HALL.

    This group of poets seems to demand a little general criticism. They stand more by themselves than almost any other group in English literary history, marked off in most cases with equal sharpness from predecessors, followers, and contemporaries. The best of them, Herrick and Carew, with Crashaw as a great thirdsman, called themselves " sons " of Ben Jonson, and so in a way they were ; but they were even more sons of Donne.

That great writer's burning passion, his strange and labyrinthine
conceits, the union in him of spiritual and sensual fire, influenced
the idiosyncrasies of each as hardly any other writer's influence
has done in other times; while his technical shortcomings had
unquestionably a fatal effect on the weaker members of the
school.   But there is also noticeable in them a separate and
hardly definable influence which circumscribes their class even
more distinctly.   They were, as I take it, the last set of poets
anywhere in Europe to exhibit, in that most fertile department of
poetry which seeks its inspiration in the love of man for woman,
the frank expression of physical affection united with the spirit
of chivalry, tempered by the consciousness of the fading of all
natural delights, and foreshadowed by that intellectual introspec-
tion which has since developed itself in such great measure—
some think out of all measure—in poetry.   In the best of them
there is no cynicism at all.   Herrick and Carew are only sorry
that the amatory fashion of this world passeth; they do not in
the least undervalue it while it lasts, or sneer at it when it is gone.
There is, at least to my thinking, little coarseness in them (I
must perpetually except Herrick's epigrams), though there is,
according to modern standards, a great deal of very plain speaking.
They have as much frank enjoyment of physical pleasures as
any classic or any mediævalist; but they have what no classic
except Catullus and perhaps Sappho had,—the fine rapture,
the passing but transforming madness which brings merely
physical passion *sub specie æternitatis ;* and they have in addition
a faint preliminary touch of that analytic and self-questioning
spirit which refines even further upon the chivalric rapture and
the classical-renaissance mysticism of the shadow of death, but
which since their time has eaten up the simpler and franker
moods of passion itself.   With them, as a necessary consequence,
the physical is (to anticipate a famous word of which more
presently) always blended with the metaphysical.   It is curious
that, as one result of the change of manner, this should have
even been made a reproach to them—that the ecstasy of their

ecstasies should apparently have become not an excuse but an additional crime.   Yet if any grave and precise person will read Carew's *Rapture*, the most audacious, and of course wilfully audacious expression of the style, and then turn to the archangel's colloquy with Adam in *Paradise Lost*, I should like to ask him on which side, according to his honour and conscience, the coarseness lies.   I have myself no hesitation in saying that it lies with the husband of Mary Powell and the author of *Tetrachordon*, not with the lover of Celia and the author of the lines to " A. L."

There are other matters to be considered in the determination of the critical fortunes of the Caroline school.   Those fortunes have been rather odd.   Confounded at first in the general oblivion which the Restoration threw on all works of "the last age," and which deepened as the school of Dryden passed into the school of Pope, the writers of the Donne-Cowley tradition were first exhumed for the purposes of *post-mortem* examination by and in the remarkable " Life " of Johnson, devoted to the last member of the class.   It is at this time of day alike useless to defend the Metaphysical Poets against much that Johnson said, and to defend Johnson against the charge of confusion, inadequacy, and haste in his generalisations.   The term metaphysical, originating with Dryden, and used by Johnson with a slight difference, may be easily miscomprehended by any one who chooses to forget its legitimate application both etymologically and by usage to that which comes, as it were, behind or after nature.   Still Johnson undoubtedly confounded in one common condemnation writers who have very little in common, and (which was worse) criticised a peculiarity of expression as if it had been a deliberate substitution of alloy for gold.   The best phrases of the metaphysical poets more than justify themselves to any one who looks at poetry with a more catholic appreciation than Johnson's training and associations enabled him to apply ; and even the worst are but mistaken attempts to follow out a very sound principle, that of " making the common as though it were not common."   Towards the end of the eighteenth century some of these poets, especially

Herrick, were revived with taste and success by Headly and other men of letters.   But it so happened that the three great critics of the later Romantic revival, Hazlitt, Lamb, and Coleridge, were all strongly attracted to the bolder and more irregular graces of the great dramatic poets, to the not less quaint but less " mignardised " quaintnesses of prose writers like Burton, Browne, and Taylor, or to the massive splendours of the Elizabethan poets proper.   The poetry of the Caroline age was, therefore, a little slurred, and this mishap of falling between two schools has constantly recurred to it.   Some critics even who have done its separate authors justice, have subsequently indulged in palinodes, have talked about decadence and Alexandrianism and what not. The majority have simply let the Cavalier Poets (as they are sometimes termed by a mere historical coincidence) be something more than the victims of the schools that preceded and followed them.   The lovers of the school of good sense which Waller founded regard the poets of this chapter as extravagant concettists ; the lovers of the Elizabethan school proper regard them as effeminate triflers.   One of Milton's gorgeous but constantly illogical phrases about the poets of his day may perhaps have created a prejudice against these poets.   But Milton was a politician as well as a poet, a fanatic as well as a man of letters of seldom equalled, and never, save in two or three cases, surpassed powers.   He was also a man of a more morose and unamiable private character than any other great poet the world has known except Racine.   The easy *bonhomie* of the Caroline muse repelled his austerity ; its careless good-breeding shocked his middle-class and Puritan Philistinism ; its laxity revolted his principles of morality.   Not improbably the vein of sympathy which discovers itself in the exquisite verse of the *Comus*, of the *Allegro* and *Penseroso*, of *Lycidas* itself, infuriated him (as such veins of sympathy when they are rudely checked and turned from their course will often do) with those who indulged instead of check-ing it.   But because *Lycidas* is magnificent, and *Il Penseroso* charming poetry, we are not to think meanly of " Fair Daffodils," or " Ask me no more," of " Going to the Wars," or " Tell me no more how fair she is."

Let us clear our minds of this cant, and once more admit, as the student of literature always has to remind himself, that a sapphire and diamond ring is not less beautiful because it is not a marble palace, or a bank of wild flowers in a wood because it is not a garden after the fashion of Lenôtre. In the division of English poetry which we have been reviewing, there are to be found some of the most exquisite examples of the gem and flower order of beauty that can be found in all literature. When Herrick bids Perilla

> " Wind me in that very sheet
> Which wrapt thy smooth limbs when thou didst implore
> The gods' protection but the night before :
> Follow me weeping to my turf, and there
> Let fall a primrose and with it a tear ;
> Then lastly, let some weekly strewings be
> Devoted to the memory of me.
> *Then shall my ghost not walk about ; but keep*
> *Still in the cool and silent shades of sleep ;* "

or when he writes that astonishing verse, so unlike his usual style—

> " In this world, *the Isle of Dreams,*
> While we sit by sorrow's streams,
> Tears and terrors are our themes ; "

when Carew, in one of those miraculous closing bursts, carefully led up to, of which he has almost the secret, cries

> " *Oh, love me then, and now begin it,*
> *Let us not lose this present minute ;*
> *For time and age will work that wrack*
> *Which time nor age shall ne'er call back ;* "

when even the sober blood in Habington's decent veins spurts in this splendid sally—

> " So, 'mid the ice of the far northern sea,
> A star about the Arctic circle may
> Than ours yield clearer light ; *yet that but shall*
> *Serve at the frozen pilot's funeral ;* "

when Crashaw writes as if caught by the very fire of which he
speaks,—the fire of the flaming heart of Saint Theresa; when
Lovelace, most careless and unliterary of all men, breaks out as
if by simple instinct into those perfect verses which hardly even
Burns and Shelley have equalled since,—it is impossible for any one
who feels for poetry at all not to feel more than appreciation, not
to feel sheer enthusiasm.   Putting aside the very greatest poets
of all, I hardly know any group of poetical workers who so often
cause this enthusiasm as our present group, with their wonderful
felicity of language; with their command of those lyrical measures
which seem so easy and are so difficult ; with their almost unparalleled blend of a sensuousness that does not make the
intellect sluggish and of the loftiest spirituality.

When we examine what is said against them, a great deal of
it is found to be based on that most treacherous of all founda-
tions, a hard-driven metaphor.   Because they come at the end
of a long and fertile period of literature, because a colder and
harder kind of poetry followed them, they are said to be "decadence," "autumn," "over-ripe fruit," "sunset," and so forth.
These pretty analogies have done much harm in literary history.
Of the Muse it is most strictly and soberly true that "Bocca
bacciata non perde ventura, anzi rinuova come fa la luna." If
there is any meaning about the phrases of decadence, autumn,
and the like, it is derived from the idea of approaching death
and cessation.   There is no death, no cessation, in literature ;
and the sadness and decay of certain periods is mere fiction.
An autumn day would not be sad if the average human being
did not (very properly) take from it a warning of the shortness of
his own life.   But literature is not shortlived.   There was no sign
of poetry dying when Shelley lived two thousand five hundred
years after Sappho, when Shakespere lived as long after Homer.
Periods like the periods of the Greek Anthology or of our Caroline poetry are not periods of decay, but simply periods of difference.   There are no periods of decay in literature so long as
anything good is produced ; and when nothing good is produced,

it is only a sign that the field is taking a healthy turn of fallow. In this time much that was good, with a quite wonderful and charming goodness, was produced. What is more, it was a goodness which had its own distinct characteristics, some of which I have endeavoured to point out, and which the true lover of poetry would be as unwilling to lose as to lose the other goodnesses of all the great periods, and of all but the greatest names in those periods. For the unapproachables, for the first Three, for Homer, for Shakespere, for Dante, I would myself (though I should be very sorry) give up all the poets we have been reviewing. I should not like to have to choose between Herrick and Milton's earlier poems; between the Caroline poets, major and minor, as just reviewed on the one hand, and *The Faërie Queene* on the other. But I certainly would give *Paradise Regained* for some score of poems of the writers just named; and for them altogether I would give all but a few passages (I would not give those) of *Paradise Lost*. And, as I have endeavoured (perhaps to my readers' satiety) to point out, this comparative estimate is after all a radically unsound one. We are not called upon to weigh this kind of poetry against that kind; we are only incidentally, and in an uninvidious manner, called upon to weigh this poet against that even of the same kind. The whole question is, whether each is good in his own kind, and whether the kind is a worthy and delightful one. And in regard of most of the poets just surveyed, both these questions can be answered with an unhesitating affirmative. If we had not these poets, one particular savour, one particular form, of the poetical rapture would be lacking to the poetical expert; just as if what Herrick himself calls "the brave Burgundian wine" were not, no amount of claret and champagne could replace it. For passionate sense of the good things of earth, and at the same time for mystical feeling of their insecurity, for exquisite style without the frigidity and the over-correctness which the more deliberate stylists frequently display, for a blending of Nature and art that seems as if it must have been as simply instinctive in all as it certainly was in some, the poets of the Tribe of Ben, of the Tribe of Donne, who illustrated the period before Puritanism and Republicanism combined had changed England from merriment to sadness, stand alone in letters. We have had as good since, but never the same—never any such blending of classical frankness, of mediæval simplicity and chivalry, of modern reflection and thought.[1]

[1] Since this book first appeared, some persons whose judgment I respect have expressed to me surprise and regret that I have not given a higher and larger place to Henry Vaughan. A higher I cannot give, because I think him, despite the extreme beauty of his thought and (more rarely) of his expression, a most imperfect poet ; nor a larger, because that would involve a critical arguing out of the matter, which would be unsuitable to the plan and scale of this book. Had he oftener written as he wrote in the famous poem referred to in the text, or as in the magnificent opening of " The World "—

> " I saw Eternity the other night,
> *Like a great ring of pure and endless light,*
> All calm as it was bright,"

there would be much more to say of him. But he is not master of the expression suitable to his noble and precious thought except in the briefest bursts—bursts compared to which even Crashaw's are sustained and methodical. His admirers claim for " The Retreat " the germ of Wordsworth's great ode, but if any one will compare the two he will hardly complain that Vaughan has too little space here.

CHAPTER XI

Two great names remain to be noticed in the Elizabethan drama (though neither produced a play till after Elizabeth was dead), some interesting playwrights of third or fourth-rate importance have to be added to them, and in a postscript we shall have to gather up the minor or anonymous work, some of it of very high excellence, of the second division of our whole subject, including plays of the second, third, and fourth periods. But with this fourth period we enter into what may really be called by comparison (remembering always what has been said in the last chapter) a period of decadence, and at its latter end it becomes very decadent indeed. Only in Ford perhaps, of our named and individual authors in this chapter, and in him very rarely, occur the flashes of sheer poetry which, as we have seen in each of the three earlier chapters on the drama, lighten the work of the Elizabethan and Jacobean dramatists proper with extraordinary and lavish brilliance. Not even in Ford are to be found the whole and perfect studies of creative character which, even leaving Shakespere out of the question, are to be found earlier in plays and playwrights of all kinds and strengths, from *The Maid's Tragedy* and *Vittoria Corombona*, to *The Merry Devil of Edmonton* and *A Cure for a Cuckold*. The tragedies have Ben Jonson's labour without his force, the comedies his coarseness and lack of inspiriting life without his keen observation and incisive touch. As the taste indeed turned more and more from tragedy to comedy, we get attempts on the part of playwrights to win it back by a return to the bloody and monstrous conceptions of an earlier time, treated, however, without the redeeming features of that time, though with a little more coherence and art.   Massinger's *Unnatural Combat*, and Ford's *'Tis Pity She's a Whore*, among great plays, are examples of this : the numerous minor examples are hardly worth mentioning.   But the most curious symptom of all was the gradual and, as it were, imperceptible loss of the secret of blank verse itself, which had been the instrument of the great triumphs of the stage from Marlowe to Dekker.   Something of this loss of grasp may have been noticed in the looseness of Fletcher and the over-stiffness of Jonson : it is perceptible distinctly even in Ford and Massinger.   But as the Restoration, or rather the silencing of the theatres by the Commonwealth approaches, it becomes more and more evident until we reach the chaotic and hideous jumble of downright prose and verse that is neither prose nor verse, noticeable even in the early plays of Dryden, and chargeable no doubt with the twenty years' return of the English drama to the comparative bar-barism of the couplet.   This apparent loss of ear and rhythm-sense has been commented on already in reference to Lovelace, Suckling (himself a dramatist), and others of the minor Caro-line poets ; but it is far more noticeable in drama, and resulted in the production, by some of the playwrights of the transition period under Charles I. and Charles II., of some of the most amorphous botches in the way of style that disfigure English literature.

With the earliest and best work of Philip Massinger, however, we are at any rate chronologically still at a distance from the lamentable close of a great period.   He was born in 1583, being the son of Arthur Massinger, a " servant " (pretty certainly in the gentle sense of service) to the Pembroke family.   In 1602 he was entered at St. Alban's Hall in Oxford : he is supposed to have left the university about 1609, and may have begun writing plays

soon.   But the first definite notice of his occupation or indeed
of his life that we have is his participation (about 1614) with
Daborne and Field in a begging letter to the well-known manager
Henslowe for an advance of five pounds on "the new play," nor
was anything of his printed or positively known to be acted till
1622, the date of *The Virgin Martyr.*   From that time onwards
he appears frequently as an author, though many of his plays
were not printed till after his death in 1640.   But nothing is
known of his life.   He was buried on 18th March in St. Saviour's,
Southwark, being designated as a "stranger,"—that is to say, not
a parishioner.

Thirty-seven plays in all, or thirty-eight if we add Mr. Bullen's
conjectural discovery, *Sir John Barneveldt*, are attributed to
Massinger; but of these many have perished, Massinger having
somehow been specially obnoxious to the ravages of Warburton's
cook.   Eighteen survive; twelve of which were printed during
the author's life.   Massinger was thus an industrious and voluminous author, one of many points which make Professor Minto's
comparison of him to Gray a little surprising.   He was, both at
first and later, much given to collaboration,—indeed, there is a
theory, not without colour from contemporary rumour, that he had
nearly if not quite as much to do as Beaumont with Fletcher's
great work.   But oddly enough the plays which he is known to
have written alone do not, as in other cases, supply a very sure
test of what is his share in those which he wrote conjointly.   *The
Old Law*, a singular play founded on a similar conception to
that in the late Mr. Anthony Trollope's *Fixed Period*, is attributed
also to Rowley and Dekker, and has sometimes been thought to
be so early that Massinger, except as a mere boy, could have had no
hand in it.   The contradictions of critics over *The Virgin Martyr*
(by Massinger and Dekker) have been complete; some peremptorily
handing over all the fine scenes to one, and some declaring that
these very scenes could only be written by the other.   It is pretty
certain that the argumentative theological part is Massinger's; for
he had a strong liking for such things, while the passages between

Dorothea and her servant Angelo are at once more delicate than most of his work, and more regular and even than Dekker's. No companion is, however, assigned to him in *The Unnatural Combat*, which is probably a pretty early and certainly a characteristic example of his style. His demerits appear in the exaggerated and crude devilry of the wicked hero, old Malefort (who cheats his friend, makes away with his wife, kills his son in single combat, and conceives an incestuous passion for his daughter), in the jerky alternation and improbable conduct of the plot, and in the merely extraneous connection of the farcical scenes. His merits appear in the stately versification and ethical interest of the debate which precedes the unnatural duel, and in the spirited and well-told apologue (for it is almost that) of the needy soldier, Belgarde, who is bidden not to appear at the governor's table in his shabby clothes, and makes his appearance in full armour. The debate between father and son may be given :—

Malef. sen. " Now we are alone, sir ;
  And thou hast liberty to unload the burthen
  Which thou groan'st under. Speak thy griefs.
Malef. jun. I shall, sir ;
  But in a perplex'd form and method, which
  You only can interpret : Would you had not
  A guilty knowledge in your bosom, of
  The language which you force me to deliver
  So I were nothing ! As you are my father
  I bend my knee, and, uncompell'd profess
  My life, and all that's mine, to be your gift ;
  And that in a son's duty I stand bound
  To lay this head beneath your feet and run
  All desperate hazards for your ease and safety :
  But this confest on my part, I rise up,
  And not as with a father (all respect,
  Love, fear, and reverence cast off) but as
  A wicked man I thus expostulate with you.
  Why have you done that which I dare not speak,
  And in the action changed the humble shape
  Of my obedience, to rebellious rage
  And insolent pride ? and with shut eyes constrain'd me,

I must not see, nor, if I saw it, shun it.
In my wrongs nature suffers, and looks backward,
And mankind trembles to see me pursue
What beasts would fly from.   For when I advance
This sword as I must do, against your head,
Piety will weep, and filial duty mourn,
To see their altars which you built up in me
In a moment razed and ruined.   That you could
(From my grieved soul I wish it) but produce
To qualify, not excuse your deed of horror,
One seeming reason that I might fix here
And move no farther !

Malef. sen.   Have I so far lost
A father's power, that I must give account
Of my actions to my son ? or must I plead
As a fearful prisoner at the bar, while he
That owes his being to me sits a judge
To censure that which only by myself
Ought to be question'd ? mountains sooner fall
Beneath their valleys and the lofty pine
Pay homage to the bramble, or what else is
Preposterous in nature, ere my tongue
In one short syllable yield satisfaction
To any doubt of thine ; nay, though it were
A certainty disdaining argument !
Since though my deeds wore hell's black lining,
To thee they should appear triumphal robes,
Set off with glorious honour, thou being bound,
To see with my eyes, and to hold that reason
That takes or birth or fashion from my will.

Malef. jun.   This sword divides that slavish knot.

Malef. sen.   It cannot :
It cannot, wretch, and if thou but remember
From whom thou had'st this spirit, thou dar'st not hope it.
Who trained thee up in arms but I ?   Who taught thee
Men were men only when they durst look down
With scorn on death and danger, and contemn'd
All opposition till plumed Victory
Had made her constant stand upon their helmets ?
Under my shield thou hast fought as securely
As the young eaglet covered with the wings
Of her fierce dam, learns how and where to prey.

All that is manly in thee I call mine ;
But what is weak and womanish, thine own.
And what I gave, since thou art proud, ungrateful,
Presuming to contend with him to whom
Submission is due, I will take from thee.
Look therefore for extremities and expect not
I will correct thee as a son, but kill thee
As a serpent swollen with poison ; who surviving
A little longer with infectious breath,
Would render all things near him like itself
Contagious.   Nay, now my anger's up,
Ten thousand virgins kneeling at my feet,
And with one general cry howling for mercy,
Shall not redeem thee.

Malef. jun. Thou incensed Power
Awhile forbear thy thunder ! let me have
No aid in my revenge, if from the grave
My mother——

Malef. sen. Thou shalt never name her more."

                              [*They fight.*

The Duke of Milan is sometimes considered Massinger's masterpiece ; and here again there are numerous fine scenes and noble
tirades.   But the irrationality of the *donneé* (Sforza the duke charges
his favourite not to let the duchess survive his own death, and
the abuse of the authority thus given leads to horrible injustice
and the death of both duchess and duke) mars the whole.   The
predilection of the author for sudden turns and twists of situation,
his neglect to make his plots and characters acceptable and conceivable as wholes, appear indeed everywhere, even in what I
have no doubt in calling his real masterpiece by far, the fine
tragi-comedy of *A New Way to Pay Old Debts*.   The revengeful
trick by which a satellite of the great extortioner, Sir Giles Over-
reach, brings about his employer's discomfiture, regardless of his
own ruin, is very like the denouement of the Brass and Quilp part
of the *Old Curiosity Shop*, may have suggested it (for *A New
Way to Pay Old Debts* lasted as an acting play well into Dickens's
time), and, like it, is a little improbable.   But the play is an
admirable one, and Overreach (who, as is well known, was

supposed to be a kind of study of his half namesake, Mompesson, the notorious monopolist) is by far the best single character that Massinger ever drew. He again came close to true comedy in *The City Madam*, another of the best known of his plays, where the trick adopted at once to expose the villainy of the apparently reformed spendthrift Luke, and to abate the ruinous extravagance of Lady Frugal and her daughters, is perhaps not beyond the limits of at least dramatic verisimilitude, and gives occasion to some capital scenes. *The Bondman, The Renegado*, the curious *Parliament of Love*, which, like others of Massinger's plays, is in an almost Æschylean state of text-corruptness, *The Great Duke of Florence, The Maid of Honour* (one of the very doubtful evidences of Massinger's supposed conversion to Roman Catholicism), *The Picture* (containing excellent passages, but for improbability and topsy-turviness of incident ranking with *The Duke of Milan*), *The Emperor of the East, The Guardian, A Very Woman, The Bashful Lover*, are all plays on which, if there were space, it would be interesting to comment ; and they all display their author's strangely mixed merits and defects. *The Roman Actor* and *The Fatal Dowry* must have a little more attention. The first is, I think, Massinger's best tragic effort ; and the scene where Domitian murders Paris, with his tyrannical explanation of the deed, shows a greater conception of tragic poetry—a little cold and stately, a little Racinish or at least Cornelian rather than Shakesperian, but still passionate and worthy of the tragic stage— than anything that Massinger has done. *The Fatal Dowry*, written in concert with Field and unceremoniously pillaged by Rowe in his once famous *Fair Penitent*, is a purely romantic tragedy, injured by the unattractive character of the light-of-love Beaumelle before her repentance (Massinger never could draw a woman), and by not a few of the author's favourite improbabilities and glaring or rather startling non-sequiturs of action, but full also of fine passages, especially of the quasi-forensic kind in which Massinger so much delights.

To sum up, it may seem inconsistent that, after allowing

so many faults in Massinger, I should protest against the rather
low estimate of him which critics from Lamb downwards have
generally given.   Yet I do so protest.   It is true that he has
not the highest flashes either of verbal poetry or of dramatic
character-drawing ; and though Hartley Coleridge's dictum that
he had no humour has been exclaimed against, it is only verbally
wrong.   It is also true that in him perhaps for the first time we
perceive, what is sure to appear towards the close of a period,
a distinct touch of *literary* borrowing—evidence of knowledge
and following of his forerunners.   Yet he had a high, a varied,
and a fertile imagination.   He had, and was the last to have, an
extensive and versatile command of blank verse, never perhaps
reaching the most perfect mastery of Marlowe or of Shakespere,
but singularly free from monotony, and often both harmonious
and dignified.   He could deal, and deal well, with a large range
of subjects ; and if he never ascends to the height of a De Flores
or a Bellafront, he never descends to the depths in which both
Middleton and Dekker too often complacently wallow.   Unless
we are to count by mere flashes, he must, I think, rank after
Shakespere, Fletcher, and Jonson among his fellows ; and this
I say, honestly avowing that I have nothing like the enthusiasm
for him that I have for Webster, or for Dekker, or for Middleton.
We may no doubt allow too much for bulk of work, for sustained
excellence at a certain level, and for general competence as against
momentary excellence.   But we may also allow far too little ; and
this has perhaps been the general tendency of later criticism in
regard to Massinger.   It is unfortunate that he never succeeded
in making as perfect a single expression of his tragic ability as
he did of his comic, for the former was, I incline to think, the
higher of the two.   But many of his plays are lost, and many
of those which remain come near to such excellence.   It is by
no means impossible that Massinger may have lost incomparably
by the misdeeds of the constantly execrated, but never to be
execrated enough, minion of that careless herald.

As in the case of Clarendon, almost absolutely contradictory opinions have been delivered, by critics of great authority, about John Ford. In one of the most famous outbursts of his generous and enthusiastic estimate of the Elizabethan period, Lamb has pronounced Ford to be of the first order of poets. Mr Swinburne, while bringing not a few limitations to this tremendous eulogy, has on the whole supported it in one of the most brilliant of his prose essays ; and critics as a rule have bowed to Lamb's verdict. On the other hand, Hazlitt (who is " gey ill to differ with " when there are, as here, no extra-literary considerations to reckon) has traversed that verdict in one of the most damaging utterances of commonsense, yet not commonplace, criticism anywhere to be found, asking bluntly and pointedly whether the exceptionableness of the subject is not what constitutes the merit of Ford's greatest play, pronouncing the famous last scene of *The Broken Heart* extravagant, and fixing on " a certain perversity of spirit " in Ford generally. It is pretty clear that Hartley Coleridge (who might be paralleled in our own day as a critic, who seldom went wrong except through ignorance, though he had a sublime indifference as to the ignorance that sometimes led him wrong) was of no different opinion. It is not easy to settle such a quarrel. But I had the good fortune to read Ford before I had read anything except Hartley Coleridge's rather enigmatic verdict about him, and in the many years that have passed since I have read him often again. The resulting opinion may not be exceptionally valuable, but it has at least stood the test of frequent re-reading of the original, and of reading of the main authorities among the commentators.

John Ford, like Fletcher and Beaumont, but unlike almost all others of his class, was a person not compelled by need to write tragedies,—comedies of any comic merit he could never have written, were they his neck verse at Hairibee. His father was a man of good family and position at Ilsington in Devon. His mother was of the well-known west-country house of the Pophams. He was born (?) two years before the Armada, and three years after Massinger. He has no university record, but was a member of the

Middle Temple, and takes at least some pains to assure us that he never wrote for money. Nevertheless, for the best part of thirty years he was a playwright, and he is frequently found collaborating with Dekker, the neediest if nearly the most gifted gutter-playwright of the time. Once he worked with Webster in a play (*The Murder of the Son upon the Mother*) which must have given the fullest possible opportunity to the appetite of both for horrors. Once he, Rowley, and Dekker combined to produce the strange masterpiece (for a masterpiece it is in its own undisciplined way) of the *Witch of Edmonton*, where the obvious signs of a play hastily cobbled up to meet a popular demand do not obscure the talents of the cobblers. It must be confessed that there is much less of Ford than of Rowley and Dekker in the piece, except perhaps its comparative regularity and the quite unreasonable and unintelligible bloodiness of the murder of Susan. In *The Sun's Darling*, due to Ford and Dekker, the numerous and charming lyrics are pretty certainly Dekker's ; though we could pronounce on this point with more confidence if we had the two lost plays, *The Fairy Knight* and *The Bristowe Merchant*, in which the same collaborators are known to have been engaged. *The Fancies, Chaste and Noble*, and *The Lady's Trial* which we have, and which are known to be Ford's only, are but third-rate work by common consent, and *Love's Sacrifice* has excited still stronger opinions of condemnation from persons favourable to Ford. This leaves us practically four plays upon which to base our estimate —*'Tis Pity She's a Whore, The Lover's Melancholy, The Broken Heart*, and *Perkin Warbeck*. The last-named I shall take the liberty of dismissing summarily with the same borrowed description as Webster's *Appius and Virginia*. Hartley Coleridge, perhaps willing to make up if he could for a general distaste for Ford, volunteered the strange judgment that it is the best specimen of the historic drama to be found out of Shakespere ; and Hazlitt says nothing savage about it. I shall say nothing more, savage or otherwise. *The Lover's Melancholy* has been to almost all its critics a kind of lute-case for the very pretty version of Strada's fancy about the nightingale, which Crashaw did better ; otherwise it is naught. We are, therefore, left with *'Tis Pity She's a Whore* and *The Broken Heart.* For myself, in respect to the first, after repeated readings and very careful weighings of what has been said, I come back to my first opinion—to wit, that the Annabella and Giovanni scenes, with all their perversity, all their availing themselves of what Hazlitt, with his unerring instinct, called "unfair attractions," are among the very best things of their kind. Of what may be thought unfair in them I shall speak a little later ; but allowing for this, the sheer effects of passion—the "All for love and the world well lost," the shutting out, not instinctively or stupidly, but deliberately, and with full knowledge, of all other considerations except the dictates of desire—have never been so rendered in English except in *Romeo and Juliet* and *Antony and Cleopatra.* The comparison of course brings out Ford's weakness, not merely in execution, but in design ; not merely in accomplishment, but in the choice of means for accomplishment. Shakespere had no need of the *haut goût* of incest, of the unnatural horrors of the heart on the dagger. But Ford had ; and he in a way (I do not say fully) justified his use of these means.

The Broken Heart stands far lower. I own that I am with Hazlitt, not Lamb, on the question of the admired death scene of Calantha. In the first place, it is certainly borrowed from Marston's *Malcontent ;* in the second, it is wholly unnatural ; in the third, the great and crowning point of it is not, as Lamb seemed to think, Calantha's sentimental inconsistency, but the consistent and noble death of Orgilus. There Ford was at home, and long as it is it must be given :—

    Cal. " Bloody relator of thy stains in blood,
           For that thou hast reported him, whose fortunes
           And life by thee are both at once snatch'd from him,
           With honourable mention, make thy choice
           Of what death likes thee best, there's all our bounty.
           But to excuse delays, let me, dear cousin,

        Intreat you and these lords see execution
        Instant before you part.
Near. Your will commands us.
  Org. One suit, just queen, my last : vouchsafe your clemency
        That by no common hand I be divided
        From this my humble frailty.
  Cal. To their wisdoms
        Who are to be spectators of thine end
        I make the reference : those that are dead
        Are dead ; had they not now died, of necessity
        They must have paid the debt they owed to nature,
        One time or other.   Use dispatch, my lords ;
        We'll suddenly prepare our coronation.
                          [Exeunt CAL., PHIL., *and* CHRIS.
Arm. 'Tis strange, these tragedies should never touch on
        Her female pity.
Bass. She has a masculine spirit,
        And wherefore should I pule, and, like a girl,
        Put finger in the eye ?   Let's be all toughness
        Without distinction betwixt sex and sex.
Near. Now, Orgilus, thy choice ?
  Org. To bleed to death.
Arm. The executioner ?
  Org. Myself, no surgeon ;
        I am well skilled in letting blood.   Bind fast
        This arm, that so the pipes may from their conduits
        Convey a full stream ; here's a skilful instrument :
                            [Shows his dagger.
        Only I am a beggar to some charity
        To speed me in this execution
        By lending the other prick to the other arm
        When this is bubbling life out.
Bass. I am for you,
        It most concerns my art, my care, my credit,
        Quick, fillet both his arms.
  Org. Gramercy, friendship !
        Such courtesies are real which flow cheerfully
        Without an expectation of requital.
        Reach me a staff in this hand.   If a proneness
                       [They give him a staff.
        Or custom in my nature, from my cradle
        Had been inclined to fierce and eager bloodshed,

A coward guilt hid in a coward quaking,
Would have betray'd me to ignoble flight
And vagabond pursuit of dreadful safety :
But look upon my steadiness and scorn not
The sickness of my fortune ; which since Bassanes
Was husband to Penthea, had lain bed-rid.
We trifle time in words : thus I show cunning
In opening of a vein too full, too lively.

        [*Pierces the vein with his dagger.*

Arm. Desperate courage !
Near. Honourable infamy !
Hem. I tremble at the sight.
Gron. Would I were loose !
Bass. It sparkles like a lusty wine new broach'd ;
 The vessel must be sound from which it issues.
 Grasp hard this other stick—I'll be as nimble—
 But prithee look not pale—Have at ye ! stretch out
 Thine arm with vigour and unshaken virtue.

          [*Opens the vein.*

 Good ! oh I envy not a rival, fitted
 To conquer in extremities : this pastime
 Appears majestical ; some high-tuned poem
 Hereafter shall deliver to posterity
 The writer's glory, and his subjects triumph.
 How is't man ?—droop not yet.
Org.   I feel no palsies,
 On a pair-royal do I wait in death :
 My sovereign as his liegeman ; on my mistress
 As a devoted servant ; and on Ithocles
 As if no brave, yet no unworthy enemy :
 Nor did I use an engine to entrap
 His life out of a slavish fear to combat
 Youth, strength, or cunning ; but for that I durst not
 Engage the goodness of a cause on fortune
 By which his name might have outfaced my vengeance.
 Oh, Tecnicus, inspired with Phœbus' fire !
 I call to mind thy augury, 'twas perfect ;
 Revenge proves its own executioner.
 When feeble man is lending to his mother
 The dust he was first framed in, thus he totters.
Bass. Life's fountain is dried up.
Org. So falls the standard

Of my prerogative in being a creature,
A mist hangs o'er mine eyes, the sun's bright splendour
Is clouded in an everlasting shadow.
Welcome, thou ice that sit'st about my heart,
No heat can ever thaw thee.

                                                                    [*Dies.*

The perverse absurdity of a man like Orgilus letting Penthea die by the most horrible of deaths must be set aside : his
vengeance (the primary absurdity granted), is exactly and wholly
in character.   But if anything could be decisive against Ford
being "of the first order of poets," even of dramatic poets, it
would be the total lack of interest in the characters of Calantha
and Ithocles.   Fate-disappointed love seems (no doubt from
something in his own history) to have had a singular attraction
for Lamb; and the glorification, or, as it were, apotheosis of it
in Calantha must have appealed to him in one of those curious
and illegitimate ways which every critic knows.   But the mere
introduction of Bassanes would show that Ford is not of the first
order of poets.   He is a purely contemptible character, neither
sublimed by passion of jealousy, nor kept whole by salt of comic
exposition ; a mischievous poisonous idiot who ought to have had
his brains knocked out, and whose brains would assuredly have
been knocked out, by any Orgilus of real life.   He is absolutely
unequal to the place of central personage, and causer of the
harms, of a romantic tragedy such as *The Broken Heart.*

I have said " by any Orgilus of real life," but Ford has little
to do with real life ; and it is in this fact that the insufficiency of
his claim to rank among the first order of poets lies.   He was,
it is evident, a man of the greatest talent, even of great genius,
who, coming at the end of a long literary movement, exemplified
the defects of its decadence.   I could compare him, if there was
here any space for such a comparison, to Baudelaire or Flaubert
with some profit ; except that he never had Baudelaire's perfect
sense of art, and that he does not seem, like Flaubert, to have
laid in, before melancholy marked him for her own, a sufficient
stock of living types to save him from the charge of being a mere

study-student.   There is no Frédéric, no M. Homais, in his
repertory.   Even Giovanni—even Orgilus, his two masterpieces,
are, if not exactly things of shreds and patches, at any rate
artificial persons, young men who have known more of books
than of life, and who persevere in their eccentric courses with
almost more than a half knowledge that they are eccentric.
Annabella is incomplete, though there is nothing, except her love,
unnatural in her.   The strokes which draw her are separate
imaginations of a learned draughtsman, not fresh transcripts from
the living model.   Penthea and Calantha are wholly artificial ;
a live Penthea would never have thought of such a fantastic
martyrdom, unless she had been insane or suffering from green-
sickness, and a live Calantha would have behaved in a perfectly
different fashion, or if she had behaved in the same, would have
been quit for her temporary aberration.   We see (or at least I
think I see) in Ford exactly the signs which are so familiar to us
in our own day, and which repeat themselves regularly at the end
of all periods of distinct literary creativeness—the signs of *excen-
tricité voulue*.   The author imagines that " all is said " in the
ordinary way, and that he must go to the ends of the earth
to fetch something extraordinary.   If he is strong enough, as
Ford was, he fetches it, and it *is* something extraordinary, and
we owe him, with all his extravagance, respect and honour for his
labour.   But we can never put him on the level of the men who,
keeping within ordinary limits, achieve masterpieces there.

    Ford—an Elizabethan in the strict sense for nearly twenty
years—did not suffer from the decay which, as noted above, set in
in regard to versification and language among the men of his own
later day.   He has not the natural trick of verse and phrase
which stamps his greatest contemporaries unmistakably, and even
such lesser ones as his collaborator, Dekker, with a hardly mistak-
able mark ; but his verse is nervous, well proportioned, well
delivered, and at its best a noble medium.   He was by general
consent utterly incapable of humour, and his low-comedy scenes
are among the most loathsome in the English theatre.   His

lyrics are not equal to Shakespere's or Fletcher's, Dekker's or
Shirley's, but they are better than Massinger's.   Although he
frequently condescended to the Fletcherian license of the redundant syllable, he never seems to have dropped (as Fletcher
did sometimes, or at least allowed his collaborators to drop)
floundering into the Serbonian bog of stuff that is neither verse
nor prose.   He showed indeed (and Mr. Swinburne, with his usual
insight, has noticed it, though perhaps he has laid rather too much
stress on it) a tendency towards a severe rule-and-line form both
of tragic scheme and of tragic versification, which may be taken
to correspond in a certain fashion (though Mr. Swinburne does
not notice this) to the " correctness " in ordinary poetry of Waller
and his followers.   Yet he shows no sign of wishing to discard
either the admixture of comedy with tragedy (save in *The Broken
Heart*, which is perhaps a crucial instance), or blank verse, or the
freedom of the English stage in regard to the unities.   In short,
Ford was a person distinctly deficient in initiative and planning
genius, but endowed with a great executive faculty.   He wanted
guidance in all the greater lines of his art, and he had it not ;
the result being that he produced unwholesome and undecided
work, only saved by the unmistakable presence of poetical faculty.
I do not think that Webster could ever have done anything
better than he did : I think that if Ford had been born twenty
years earlier he might have been second to Shakespere, and at
any rate the equal of Ben Jonson and of Fletcher.   But the
flagging genius of the time made its imprint on his own genius,
which was of the second order, not the first.

   The honour of being last in the great succession of
Elizabethan dramatists is usually assigned to James Shirley.[1]
Though last, Shirley is only in part least, and his plays
deserve more reading than has usually fallen to their lot.
Not only in the general character of his plays—a character

[1] There was a contemporary, Henry Shirley, who was also a playwright.
His only extant play, *The Martyred Soldier*, a piece of little merit, has been
reprinted by Mr. Bullen.

hardly definable, but recognisable at once by the reader—but by
the occurrence of such things as the famous song, "The glories
of our blood and state," and not a few speeches and tirades,
Shirley has a right to his place ; as he most unquestionably has
also by date. He was born in London in 1596, was educated
at Merchant Tailors' School, and was a member of both universities, belonging to St. John's College at Oxford, and to Catherine
Hall at Cambridge. Like other dramatists he vacillated in religion,
with such sincerity as to give up a living to which, having been
ordained, he had been presented. He was a schoolmaster for a
time, began to write plays about the date of the accession of
Charles I., continued to do so till the closing of the theatres, then
returned to schoolmastering, and survived the Restoration nearly
seven years, being buried at St. Giles's in 1666. He appears to
have visited Ireland, and at least one monument of his visit
remains in the eccentric play of *St. Patrick for Ireland*. He
is usually credited with thirty-nine plays, to which it is understood that others, now in MS., have to be added, while he
may also have had a hand in some that are printed but
not attributed to him. Shirley was neither a very great nor
a very strong man ; and without originals to follow, it is probable that he would have done nothing. But with Fletcher and
Jonson before him he was able to strike out a certain line of
half-humorous, half-romantic drama, and to follow it with curious
equality through his long list of plays, hardly one of which is
very much better than any other, hardly one of which falls below
a very respectable standard. He has few or no single scenes or
passages of such high and sustained excellence as to be specially
quotable ; and there is throughout him an indefinable flavour as
of study of his elders and betters, an appearance as of a highly
competent and gifted pupil in a school, not as of a master and
leader in a movement. The palm is perhaps generally and rightly
assigned to *The Lady of Pleasure*, 1635, a play bearing some faint
resemblances to Massinger's *City Madam*, and Fletcher's *Noble
Gentleman* (Shirley is known to have finished one or two plays of

Fletcher's), and in its turn the original, or at least the forerunner
of a long line of late seventeenth and eighteenth century plays
on the extravagance and haughtiness and caprice of fine ladies.
Shirley indeed was much acted after the Restoration, and exhibits,
though on the better side, the transition of the older into the
newer school very well.   Of his tragedies *The Traitor* has the
general suffrage, and perhaps justly.   One of Shirley's most
characteristic habits was that not of exactly adapting an old play,
but of writing a new one on similar lines accommodated to the
taste of his own day.   He constantly did this with Fletcher, and
once in *The Cardinal* he was rash enough to endeavour to improve upon Webster.   His excuse may have been that he was
evidently in close contact with the last survivors of the great
school, for besides his work with or on Fletcher, he collaborated
with Chapman in the tragedy of *Chabot* and the comedy of *The
Ball*—the latter said to be one of the earliest *loci* for the use of the
word in the sense of an entertainment.   His versification profited
by this personal or literary familiarity.   It is occasionally lax, and
sins especially by the redundant syllable or syllables, and by the ugly
break between auxiliary verbs and their complements, prepositions
and their nouns, and so forth.   But it never falls into the mere
shapelessness which was so common with his immediate and younger
contemporaries.   Although, as has been said, long passages of high
sustained poetry are not easily producible from him, two short
extracts from *The Traitor* will show his style favourably, but not
too favourably.   Amidea, the heroine, declares her intention—

> " To have my name
> Stand in the ivory register of virgins,
> When I am dead.   Before one factious thought
> Should lurk within me to betray my fame
> To such a blot, my hands shall mutiny
> And boldly with a poniard teach my heart
> To weep out a repentance."

And this of her brother Florio's is better still—

> " Let me look upon my sister now :
> Still she retains her beauty,

> Death has been kind to leave her all this sweetness.
> Thus in a morning have I oft saluted
> My sister in her chamber : sat upon
> Her bed and talked of many harmless passages.
> *But now 'tis night, and a long night with her :*
> *I shall ne'er see these curtains drawn again*
> *Until we meet in heaven."*

Here the touch, a little weakened it may be, but still the touch of the great age, is perceptible, especially in the last lines, where the metaphor of the "curtains," common enough in itself for eyelids, derives freshness and appositeness from the previous mention of the bed.   But Shirley is not often at this high tragic level.   His supposed first play, *Love Tricks*, though it appeared nearly forty years before the Restoration, has a curious touch of post-Restoration comedy in its lively, extravagant, easy farce. Sometimes, as in *The Witty Fair One*, he fell in with the growing habit of writing a play mainly in prose, but dropping into verse here and there, though he was quite as ready to write, as in *The Wedding*, a play in verse with a little prose.   Once he dramatised the *Arcadia* bodily and by name.   At another time he would match a downright interlude like the *Contention for Honour and Riches* with a thinly-veiled morality like *Honoria and Mammon*.   He was a proficient at masques.   *The Grateful Servant*, *The Royal Master*, *The Duke's Mistress*, *The Doubtful Heir*, *The Constant Maid*, *The Humorous Courtier*, are plays whose very titles speak them, though the first is much the best. *The Changes* or *Love in a Maze* was slightly borrowed from by Dryden in *The Maiden Queen*, and *Hyde Park*, a very lively piece, set a fashion of direct comedy of manners which was largely followed, while *The Brothers* and *The Gamester* are other good examples of different styles.   Generally Shirley seems to have been a man of amiable character, and the worst thing on record about him is his very ungenerous gibing dedication of *The Bird in a Cage* to Prynne, then in prison, for his well-known attack on the stage, a piece of retaliation which, if the enemy had not been "down," would have been fair enough.

Perhaps Shirley's comedy deserves as a whole to be better
spoken of than his tragedy.   It is a later variety of the same kind
of comedy which we noted as written so largely by Middleton,—
a comedy of mingled manners, intrigue, and humours, improved
a good deal in coherence and in stage management, but destitute
of the greater and more romantic touches which emerge from
the chaos of the earlier style.   Nearly all the writers whom I
shall now proceed to mention practised this comedy, some better,
some worse ; but no one with quite such success as Shirley at his
best, and no one with anything like his industry, versatility, and
generally high level of accomplishment.   It should perhaps be
said that the above-mentioned song, the one piece of Shirley's
generally known, is not from one of his more characteristic
pieces, but from *The Contention of Ajax and Ulysses*, a work of
quite the author's latest days.

Thomas Randolph, the most gifted (according to general estimate rather than to specific performance) of the Tribe of Ben,
was a much younger man than Shirley, though he died more than
thirty years earlier.   Randolph was born near Daventry in 1605,
his father being a gentleman, and Lord Zouch's steward.   He was
educated at Westminster, and at Trinity College, Cambridge, of
which he became a fellow, and he was also incorporated at Oxford.
His life is supposed to have been merry, and was certainly short,
for he died, of what disease is not known, in his thirtieth year.
He left, however, no inconsiderable literary results ; and if his
dramas are not quite so relatively good as his poems (there is
certainly none of them which is in its own kind the equal of the
fine answer to Ben Jonson's threat to leave the stage and the Ode
to Anthony Stafford), still they are interesting and show a strong
intellect and great literary facility.   The two earliest, *Aristippus*
and *The Conceited Pedlar*, the first a slight dramatic sketch, the
second a monologue, are eminent examples of the class of
university, not to say of undergraduate, wit ; but far stronger and
fuller of promise than most specimens of that class.   *The Jealous
Lovers*, a play with classical nomenclature, and at first seeming

to aim at the Terentian model, drifts off into something like the Jonsonian humour-comedy, of which it gives some good studies, but hardly a complete example. Much better are *The Muses' Looking-Glass* and *Amyntas*, in which Randolph's academic schemes and names do not hide his vivid and fertile imagination. *The Muses' Looking-Glass*, a play vindicating the claim of the drama in general to the title, is a kind of morality, but a morality carried off with infinite spirit, which excuses the frigid nature of the abstractions presented in it, and not seldom rises to the height of real comedy. The scene between Colax and Dyscolus, the professional flatterer and the professional snarler, is really excellent : and others equally good might be picked out. Of the two I am inclined to think that this play shows more natural genius in the writer for its style, than the pretty pastoral of *Amyntas*, which has sometimes been preferred to it. The same penchant for comedy appears in *Down with Knavery*, a very free and lively adaptation of the *Plutus* of Aristophanes. There is no doubt that Randolph's work gives the impression of considerable power. At the same time it is fair to remember that the author's life was one very conducive to precocity, inasmuch as he underwent at once the three stimulating influences of an elaborate literary education, of endowed leisure to devote himself to what literary occupations he pleased, and of the emulation caused by literary society. Jonson's friendship seems to have acted as a forcing-house on the literary faculties of his friends, and it is quite as possible that, if Randolph had lived, he would have become a steady-going soaker or a diligent but not originally productive scholar, as that he would have produced anything of high substantive and permanent value. It is true that many great writers had not at his age done such good work ; but then it must be remembered that they had also produced little or nothing in point of bulk. It may be plausibly argued that, good as what Randolph's first thirty years gave is, it ought to have been better still if it was ever going to be of the best. But these excursions into possibilities are not very profitable, and the chief excuse for indulging in them is that Randolph's critics and editors have generally done the same, and have as a rule perhaps pursued the indulgence in a rather too enthusiastic and sanguine spirit. What is not disputable at all is the example given by Randolph of the powerful influence of Ben on his "tribe."

Very little is known of another of that tribe, Richard Brome. He was once servant to Ben Jonson, who, though in his own old age he was himself an unsuccessful, and Brome a very successful, dramatist, seems always to have regarded him with favour, and not to have been influenced by the rather illiberal attempts of Randolph and others to stir up bad blood between them. Brome deserved this favour, and spoke nobly of his old master even after Ben's death. He himself was certainly dead in 1653, when some of his plays were first collected by his namesake (but it would seem not relation), Alexander Brome. The modern reprint of his dramas takes the liberty, singular in the collection to which it belongs, of not attempting any kind of critical or biographical introduction, and no book of reference that I know is much more fertile, the latest authority—the *Dictionary of National Biography*, in which Brome is dealt with by the very competent hand of the Master of Peterhouse—having little enough to tell. Brome's work, however, speaks for itself and pretty distinctly to all who care to read it. It consists, as printed (for there were others now lost or uncollected), of fifteen plays, all comedies, all bearing a strong family likeness, and all belonging to the class of comedy just referred to—that is to say, a cross between the style of Jonson and that of Fletcher. Of the greater number of these, even if there were space here, there would be very little to say beyond this general description. Not one of them is rubbish ; not one of them is very good ; but all are readable, or would be if they had received the trouble spent on much far inferior work, of a little editing to put the mechanical part of their presentation, such as the division of scenes, stage directions, etc., in a uniform and intelligible condition. Their names (*A Mad Couple well Matched, The Sparagus Garden, The City Wit*, and so forth) tell a good deal about their most common form; while in *The Lovesick Court*, and one or two others, the half-courtly, half-romantic comedy of Fletcher takes the place of urban humours. One or two, such as *The Queen and Concubine*, attempt a statelier and tragi-comic style, but this was not Brome's forte. Sometimes, as in *The Antipodes*, there is an attempt at satire and comedy with a purpose. There are, however, two plays which stand out distinctly above the rest, and which are the only plays of Brome's known to any but diligent students of this class of literature. These are *The Northern Lass* and *A Jovial Crew*. The first differs from its fellows only as being of the same class, but better ; and the dialect of the *ingénue* Constance seems to have been thought interesting and pathetic. *The Jovial Crew*, with its lively pictures of gipsy life, is, though it may have been partly suggested by Fletcher's *Beggar's Bush*, a very pleasant and fresh comedy. It seems to have been one of its author's last works, and he speaks of himself in it as " old."

Our two next figures are of somewhat minor importance. Sir Aston Cokain or Cockaine, of a good Derbyshire family, was born in 1608, and after a long life died just before the accession of James II. He seems (and indeed positively asserts himself) to have been intimate with most of the men of letters of Charles I.'s reign ; and it has been unkindly suggested that posterity would have been much more indebted to him if he had given us the biographical particulars, which in most cases are so much wanted concerning them, instead of wasting his time on translated and original verse of very little value, and on dramatic composition of still less. As it is, we owe to him the knowledge of the not unimportant fact that Massinger was a collaborator of Fletcher. His own plays are distinctly of the lower class, though not quite valueless. *The Obstinate Lady* is an echo of Fletcher and Massinger ; *Trappolin Creduto Principe*, an adaptation of an Italian farce, is a good deal better, and is said, with various stage alterations, to have held the boards till within the present century under the title of *A Duke and no Duke*, or *The Duke and the*

Devil. It is in fact a not unskilful working up of some well-tried theatrical motives, but has no great literary merit. The tragedy of *Ovid*, a regular literary tragedy in careful if not very powerful blank verse, is Cokain's most ambitious effort. Like his other work it is clearly an "echo" in character.

A more interesting and characteristic example of the "decadence" is Henry Glapthorne. When the enthusiasm excited by Lamb's specimens, Hazlitt's, and Coleridge's lectures for the Elizabethan drama, was fresh, and everybody was hunting for new examples of the style, Glapthorne had the doubtful luck to be made the subject of a very laudatory article in the *Retrospective Review*, and two of his plays were reprinted. He was not left in this honourable but comparatively safe seclusion, and many years later, in 1874, all his plays and poems as known were issued by themselves in Mr. Pearson's valuable series of reprints. Since then Glapthorne has become something of a butt; and Mr. Bullen, in conjecturally attributing to him a new play, *The Lady Mother*, takes occasion to speak rather unkindly of him. As usual it is a case of *ni cet excès d'honneur ni cette indignité.* Personally, Glapthorne has some of the interest that attaches to the unknown. Between 1639 and 1643, or for the brief space of four years, it is clear that he was a busy man of letters. He published five plays (six if we admit *The Lady Mother*), which had some vogue, and survived as an acted poet into the Restoration period; he produced a small but not despicable collection of poems of his own; he edited those of his friend Thomas Beedome; he was himself a friend of Cotton and of Lovelace. But of his antecedents and of the life that followed this short period of literary activity we know absolutely nothing. The guess that he was at St. Paul's School is a mere guess; and in the utter and total absence of the least scrap of biographical information about him, his editor has thought it worth while to print in full some not unamusing but perfectly irrelevant documents concerning the peccadillos of a certain *George* Glapthorne of Whittlesea, who was certainly a contemporary and perhaps a relation. Henry Glapthorne as a writer is certainly not great, but he is as certainly not contemptible. His tragedy of *Albertus Wallenstein* is not merely interesting as showing a reversion to the practice, almost dropped in his time (perhaps owing to censorship difficulties), of handling contemporary historical subjects, but contains passages of considerable poetical merit.   His *Argalus and Parthenia*, a dramatisation of part of the *Arcadia*, caught the taste of his day, and, like the *Wallenstein*, is poetical if not dramatic.   The two comedies, *The Hollander* and *Wit in a Constable*, are of the school which has been so frequently described, and not of its strongest, but at the same time not of its weakest specimens.   *Love's Privilege*, sometimes held his best play, is a rather flabby tragi-comedy of the Fletcher-Shirley school.   In short, Glapthorne, without being positively good, is good enough to have made it surprising that he is not better, if the explanation did not present itself pretty clearly.   Though evidently not an old man at the time of writing (he has been guessed, probably enough, to have been a contemporary of Milton, and perhaps a little older or a little younger), his work has the clear defects of age.   It is garrulous and given to self-repetition (so much so that one of Mr. Bullen's reasons for attributing *The Lady Mother* to Glapthorne is the occurrence in it of passages almost literally repeated in his known work) ; it testifies to a relish of, and a habituation to, the great school, coupled with powers insufficient to emulate the work of the great school itself; it is exactly in flavour and character the last *not* sprightly runnings of a generous liquor.   There is nowhere in it the same absolute flatness that occurs in the lesser men of the Restoration school, like the Howards and Boyle ; the ancient gust is still too strong for that.   It does not show the vulgarity which even Davenant (who as a dramatist was ten years Glapthorne's senior) too often displays.   But we feel in reading it that the good wine has gone, that we have come to that which is worse.

I have mentioned Davenant ; and though he is often classed with, and to some extent belongs to the post-Reformation school, he is ours for other purposes than that of mere mention.   His

Shakespere travesties (in one of which he was assisted by a greater than he), and even the operas and "entertainments" with which he not only evaded the prohibition of stage plays under the Commonwealth, but helped to produce a remarkable change in the English drama, do not concern us. But it must be remembered that Davenant's earlier, most dramatic, and most original playmaking was done at a time far within our limits. When the tragedy of *Albovine* (Alboin) was produced, the Restoration was more than thirty years distant, and Jonson, Chapman, Dekker, and Marston—men in the strictest sense of the Elizabethan school—were still living, and, in the case of all but Marston, writing. *The Cruel Brother*, which, though printed after, was licensed before, dates three years earlier; and between this time and the closing of the theatres Davenant had ten plays acted and printed coincidently with the best work of Massinger, Shirley, and Ford. Nor, though his fame is far below theirs, is the actual merit of these pieces (the two above mentioned, *The Wits*, *News from Plymouth*, *The Fair Favourite*, *The Unfortunate Lovers*, etc.), so much inferior as the fame. The chief point in which Davenant fails is in the failing grasp of verse above noted. This is curious and so characteristic that it is worth while to give an example of it, which shall be a fair average specimen and not of the worst :—

> " O noble maid, what expiation can
> Make fit this young and cruel soldier for
> Society of man that hath defiled
> The genius of triumphant glorious war
> With such a rape upon thy liberty !
> Or what less hard than marble of
> The Parian rock can'st thou believe my heart,
> That nurst and bred him my disciple in
> The camp, and yet could teach his valour no
> More tenderness than injured Scytheans' use
> When they are wroth to a revenge ?   But he
> Hath mourned for it : and now Evandra thou
> Art strongly pitiful, that dost so long
> Conceal an anger that would kill us both."

Love and Honour, 1649.

Here we have the very poetical counterpart of the last of Jaques' ages, the big manly voice of the great dramatists sinking into a childish treble that stutters and drivels over the very alphabet of the poetical tongue.

In such a language as this poetry became impossible, and it is still a matter for wonder by what trick of elocution actors can have made it tolerable on the stage. Yet it was certainly tolerated. And not only so, but, when the theatre came to be open again, the discontent with blank verse, which partly at least drove Dryden and others into rhyme, never seems to have noticed the fact that the blank verse to which it objected was execrably bad. When Dryden returned to the more natural medium, he wrote it not indeed with the old many-voiced charm of the best Elizabethans, but with admirable eloquence and finish. Yet he himself in his earliest plays staggered and slipped about with the rest, and I do not remember in his voluminous critical remarks anything going to show that he was consciously aware of the slovenliness into which his master Davenant and others had allowed themselves and their followers to drop.

One more example and we shall have finished at once with those dramatists of our time whose work has been collected, and with the chief names of the decadence. Sir John Suckling, who, in Mr. Swinburne's happy phrase—

> " Stumbled from above
> And reeled in slippery roads of alien art,"

is represented in the English theatre by four plays, *Aglaura*, *Brennoralt*, *The Sad One*, and the comedy of *The Goblins*. Of the tragedies some one, I forget who, has said truly that their names are the best thing about them. Suckling had a fancy for romantic names, rather suggesting sometimes the Minerva press of a later time, but still pretty. His serious plays, however, have all the faults, metrical and other, which have been noticed in Davenant, and in speaking of his own non-dramatic verse ; and they possess as well serious faults as dramas—a combination of extravagance and dulness, a lack of playwright's grasp, an absence in short of the root of the matter.   How far in other directions besides mere versification he and his fellows had slipped from the right way, may be perhaps most pleasantly and quite fully discovered from the perusal, which is not very difficult, of his tragi-comedy or extravaganza, *The Goblins.*   There are several good points about this play—an abundance of not altogether stagey noble sentiment, an agreeable presentment of fresh and gallant youths, still smacking rather of Fletcher's madcap but heart-sound gallants, and not anticipating the heartless crudity of the cubs of the Restoration, a loveable feminine character, and so forth.   But hardly a clever boy at school ever devised anything so extravagantly puerile as the plot, which turns on a set of banished men playing at hell and devils in caverns close to a populous city, and brings into the action a series of the most absurd escapes, duels, chance-meetings, hidings, findings, and all manner of other devices for spinning out an unnatural story.   Many who know nothing more of Suckling's plays know that *Aglaura* enjoys the eccentric possession of two fifth acts, so that it can be made a tragedy or a tragi-comedy at pleasure.   *The Sad One,* which is unfinished, is much better.   The tragedy of *Brennoralt* has some pathos, some pretty scenes, and some charming songs ; but here again we meet with the most inconceivably bad verse, as here   a passage all the more striking because of its attempt, wilful or unconscious, to echo Shakespere :—

> " Sleep is as nice as woman ;
> The more I court it, the more it flies me.
> Thy elder brother will be kinder yet,
> Unsent-for death will come.   To-morrow !
> Well, what can to-morrow do ?
> 'Twill cure the sense of honour lost ;
> I and my discontents shall rest together,
> What hurt is there in this ?   But death against
> The will is but a slovenly kind of potion ;
> And though prescribed by Heaven, it goes against men's stomachs.
> So does it at fourscore too, when the soul's

Mewed up in narrow darkness : neither sees nor hears.
Pish ! 'tis mere fondness in our nature.
A certain clownish cowardice that still
Would stay at home and dares not venture
Into foreign countries, though better than
Its own.   Ha ! what countries? for we receive
Descriptions of th' other world from our divines
As blind men take relations of this from us :
My thoughts lead me into the dark, and there
They'll leave me. I'll no more on it. Within ! "

Such were the last notes of the concert which opened with the music, if not at once of *Hamlet* and *Othello*, at any rate of *Tamburlaine* and *Faustus*.

To complete this sketch of the more famous and fortunate dramatists who have attained to separate presentation, we must give some account of lesser men and of those wholly anonymous works which are still to be found only in collections such as Dodsley's, or in single publications.   As the years pass, the list of independently published authors increases.   Mr. Bullen, who issued the works of Thomas Nabbes and of Davenport, has promised those of W. Rowley.   Nabbes, a member of the Tribe of Ben, and a man of easy talent, was successful in comedy only, though he also attempted tragedy.   *Microcosmus* (1637), his best-known work, is half-masque, half-morality, and has considerable merit in a difficult kind.   *The Bride, Covent Garden, Tottenham Court*, range with the already characterised work of Brome, but somewhat lower.   Davenport's range was wider, and the interesting history of *King John and Matilda*, as well as the lively comedy of *The City Nightcap*, together with other work, deserved, and have now received, collection.   William Rowley was of a higher stamp.   His best work is probably to be found in the plays wherein, as mentioned more than once, he collaborated with Middleton, with Massinger, with Webster, with Fletcher, with Dekker, and in short with most of the best men of his time.   It would appear that he was chiefly resorted to for comic under-plots, in which he brought in a good deal of horse-play, and a power of reporting the low-life humours of the London of his day more accurate than refined, together with not a little stock-stage wit, such as raillery of Welsh and Irish dialect.   But in the plays which are attributed to him alone, such as *A New Wonder*, *a Woman Never Vexed*, and *A Match at Midnight*, he shows not merely this same *vis comica* and rough and ready faculty of hitting off dramatic situations, but an occasional touch of true pathos, and a faculty of knitting the whole action well together.   He has often been confused with a half namesake, Samuel Rowley, of whom very little is known, but who in his chronicle play *When you see Me you know Me*, and his romantic drama of *The Noble Spanish Soldier*, has distinctly outstripped the ordinary dramatists of the time.   Yet another collected drama-tist, who has long had a home in Dodsley, and who figures rather curiously in a later collection of " Dramatists of the Restora-tion," though his dramatic fame was obtained many years before, was Shakerley Marmion, author of the pretty poem of *Cupid and Psyche*, and a " son " of Ben Jonson.   Marmion's three plays, of which the best known is *The Antiquary*, are fair but not exces-sively favourable samples of the favourite play of the time, a rather broad humour-comedy, which sometimes conjoined itself with, and sometimes stood aloof from, either a romantic and tragi-comical story or a downright tragedy.

Among the single plays comparatively few are of the latter kind.   *The Miseries of Enforced Marriage*, a domestic tragi-comedy, connects itself with the wholly tragical *Yorkshire Tragedy*, and is a kind of introduction to it.   These domestic tragedies (of which another is *A Warning to Fair Women*) were very popular at the time, and large numbers now lost seem to have been pro-duced by the dramatisation of notable crimes, past and present. Their class is very curiously mixed up with the remarkable and, in one sense or another, very interesting class of the dramas attri-buted, and in general estimation falsely attributed, to Shakespere. According to the fullest list these pseudo-Shakesperian plays number seventeen.   They are *Fair Em*, *The Merry Devil of*

Edmonton, Edward III., *The Birth of Merlin*, *The Troublesome Reign of King John*, *A Warning to Fair Women*, *The Arraignment of Paris*, *Arden of Feversham*, *Mucedorus*, *George à Green the Pinner of Wakefield*, *The Two Noble Kinsmen*, *The London Prodigal*, *Thomas Lord Cromwell*, *Sir John Oldcastle*, *The Puritan or the Widow of Watling Street*, *The Yorkshire Tragedy*, and *Locrine.* Four of these, *Edward III.*, *The Merry Devil of Edmonton*, *Arden of Feversham*, and *The Two Noble Kinsmen*, are in whole or parts very far superior to the rest.　Of that rest *The Yorkshire Tragedy*, a violent and bloodthirsty little piece showing the frantic cruelty of the ruined gambler, Calverley, to his wife and children, is perhaps the most powerful, though it is not in the least Shakesperian.　But the four have claims, not indeed of a strong, but of a puzzling kind.　In *Edward III.* and *The Two Noble Kinsmen* there are no signs of Shakespere either in plot, character-drawing, or general tone.　But, on the contrary, there are in both certain scenes where the versification and dialogue are so astonishingly Shakesperian that it is almost impossible to account for the writing of them by any one else than Shakespere.　By far the larger majority of critics declare for the part authorship of Shakespere in *The Two Noble Kinsmen;* I avow myself simply puzzled.　On the other hand, I am nearly sure that he did not write any part of *Edward III.*, and I should take it to be a case of a kind not unknown in literature, where some writer of great but not very original faculty was strongly affected by the Shakesperian influence, and wrote this play while under it, but afterwards, either by death or diversion to non-literary employments, left no other monument of himself that can be traced or compared with it.　The difficulty with *Arden of Feversham* and *The Merry Devil* is different.　We shall presently speak of the latter, which, good as it is, has nothing specially Shakesperian about it, except a great superiority in sanity, compactness, pleasant human sentiment, and graceful verse, to the ordinary anonymous or named work of the time.　But *Arden of Feversham* is a very different piece of work.　It is a domestic tragedy of a peculiarly

atrocious kind, Alice Arden, the wife, being led by her passion for a
base paramour, Mosbie, to plot, and at last carry out, the murder of
her husband.   Here it is not that the versification has much
resemblance to Shakespere's, or that single speeches smack of
him, but that the dramatic grasp of character both in principals
and in secondary characters has a distinct touch of his almost
unmistakable hand.   Yet both in the selection and in the treatment of the subject the play definitely transgresses those principles
which have been said to exhibit themselves so uniformly and so
strongly in the whole great body of his undoubted plays.   There
is a perversity and a dash of sordidness which are both wholly
un-Shakesperian.   The only possible hypothesis on which it
could be admitted as Shakespere's would be that of an early
experiment thrown off while he was seeking his way in a
direction where he found no thoroughfare.   But the play is a
remarkable one, and deserves the handsome and exact reproduction which Mr. Bullen has given it.   *The Second Maiden's Tragedy*, licensed 1611, but earlier in type, is one of the gloomy
pity-and-terror pieces which were so much affected in the earlier
part of the period, but which seem to have given way later in
the public taste to comedy.   It is black enough to have been
attributed to Tourneur.   *The Queen of Aragon*, by Habington,
though in a different key, has something of the starchness rather
than strength which characterises *Castara*.   A much higher level
is reached in the fine anonymous tragedy of *Nero*, where at least
one character, that of Petronius, is of great excellence, and where
the verse, if a little declamatory, is of a very high order of declamation.   The strange piece, first published by Mr. Bullen, and
called by him *The Distracted Emperor*, a tragedy based partly on
the legend of Charlemagne and Fastrada, again gives us a specimen of horror-mongering.   *The Return from Parnassus* (see note, p.
81), famous for its personal touches and its contribution to Shakespere literature, is interesting first for the judgments of contemporary writers, of which the Shakespere passages are only the chief;
secondly, for its evidence of the jealousy between the universities

and the players, who after, in earlier times, coming chiefly on the
university wits for their supplies, had latterly taken to provide for
themselves ; and thirdly, for its flashes of light on university and
especially undergraduate life.   The comedy of *Wily Beguiled* has
also a strong university touch, the scholar being made triumphant
in it ; and *Lingua*, sometimes attributed to Anthony Brewer, is
a return, though a lively one, to the system of personification and
allegory.   *The Dumb Knight*, of or partly by Lewis Machin, belongs
to the half-romantic, half-farcical class ; but in *The Merry Devil of
Edmonton*, the authorship of which is quite unknown, though
Shakespere, Drayton, and other great names have been put
forward, a really delightful example of romantic comedy, strictly
English in subject, and combining pathos with wit, appears.   *The
Merry Devil* probably stands highest among all the anonymous
plays of the period on the lighter side, as *Arden of Feversham*
does on the darker.   Second to it as a comedy comes Porter's
Two Angry Women of Abingdon (1599), with less grace and
fancy but almost equal lightness, and a singularly exact picture
of manners.   With *Ram Alley*, attributed to the Irishman
Lodowick Barry, we come back to a much lower level, that of
the bustling comedy, of which something has been said generally
in connection with Middleton.   To the same class belong Haughton's pleasant *Englishmen for my Money*, a good patriot play, where
certain foreigners, despite the father's favour, are ousted from
the courtship of three fair sisters ; *Woman is a Weathercock*, and
Amends for Ladies (invective and palinode), by Nathaniel Field
(first one of the little eyasses who competed with regular actors,
and then himself an actor and playwright) ; "Green's *Tu
Quoque*" or *The City Gallant*, attributed to the actor Cook, and
deriving its odd first title from a well-known comedian of the
time, and the catchword which he had to utter in the play itself ;
The Hog hath Lost his Pearl, a play on the name of a usurer whose
daughter is married against his will, by Taylor ; *The Heir* and *The
Old Couple*, by Thomas May, more famous still for his Latin
versification ; the rather over-praised *Ordinary* of Cartwright, Ben

Jonson's most praised son ; *The City Match* by Dr. Jasper Mayne.
All these figure in the last, and most of them have figured in the
earlier editions of Dodsley, with a few others hardly worth separate notice. Mr. Bullen's delightful volumes of *Old Plays* add
the capital play of *Dick of Devonshire* (see *ante*), the strange
Two Tragedies in One of Robert Yarington, three lively comedies
deriving their names from originals of one kind or another,
Captain Underwit, Sir Giles Goosecap, and *Dr. Dodipoll*, with
one or two more. One single play remains to be mentioned,
both because of its intrinsic merit, and because of the controversy which has arisen respecting the question of priority
between it and Ben Jonson's *Alchemist*. This is *Albumazar*, attributed to one Thomas Tomkis, and in all probability a university
play of about the middle of James's reign. There is nothing in
it equal to the splendid bursts of Sir Epicure Mammon, or the all
but first-rate comedy of Face, Dol, and Subtle, and of Abel
Drugger ; but Gifford, in particular, does injustice to it, and it is
on the whole a very fair specimen of the work of the time.
Nothing indeed is more astonishing than the average goodness
of that work, even when all allowances are made ; and unjust as
such a mere enumeration as these last paragraphs have given
must be, it would be still more unjust to pass over in silence
work so varied and so full of talent.[1]

[1] A note may best serve for the plays of Thomas Goff (1591-1629), acted
at his own college, Christ Church, but not published till after his death.
The three most noteworthy, *The Raging Turk, The Courageous Turk*, and the
Tragedy of Orestes, were republished together in 1656, and a comedy, *The
Careless Shepherdess*, appeared in the same year. The tragedies, and especially *The Raging Turk*, have been a byword for extravagant frigidity, though,
as they have never been printed in modern times, and as the originals are rare,
they have not been widely known at first hand. A perusal justifies the worst
that has been said of them: though Goff wrote early enough to escape the
Caroline dry-rot in dramatic versification. His lines are stiff, but they usually
scan.

CHAPTER XII

THE greatest, beyond all doubt, of the minor writers of the Caroline period in prose is Robert Burton. Less deliberately quaint than Fuller, he is never, as Fuller sometimes is, puerile, and the greater concentration of his thoughts and studies has produced what Fuller never quite produced, a masterpiece. At the same time it must be confessed that Burton's more leisurely life assisted to a great extent in the production of his work. The English collegiate system would have been almost sufficiently justified if it had produced nothing but *The Anatomy of Melancholy;* though there is something ironical, no doubt, in the fact that this ideal fruit of a studious and endowed leisure was the work of one who, being a beneficed clergyman, ought not in strictness to have been a resident member of a college. Yet, elsewhere than in Oxford or Cambridge the book could hardly have grown, and it is as unique as the institutions which produced it.

The author of the *Anatomy* was the son of Ralph Burton of Lindley in Leicestershire, where he was born on the 8th of February 1577. He was educated at Sutton Coldfield School, and thence went to Brasenose College, Oxford. He became a student of Christchurch—the equivalent of a fellow—in 1599, and seems to have passed the whole of the rest of his life there, though he took orders and enjoyed together or successively the living of St. Thomas in Oxford, the vicarage of Walsby in Lincolnshire, and the rectory of Segrave in Leicestershire, at both of which latter places he seems to have kept the minimum of residence, though tradition gives him the character of a good churchman, and though there is certainly nothing inconsistent with that character in the *Anatomy*.   The picture of him which Anthony à Wood gives at a short second hand is very favourable; and the attempts to harmonise his "horrid disorder of melancholy " with his "very merry, facete, and juvenile company," arise evidently from almost ludicrous misunderstanding of what melancholy means and is. As absurd, though more serious, is the traditionary libel obviously founded on the words in his epitaph (*Cui vitam et mortem dedit melancholia*), that having cast his nativity, he, in order not to be out as to the time of his death, committed suicide.   As he was sixty-three (one of the very commonest periods of death) at the time, the want of reason of the suggestion equals its want of charity.

The offspring in English of Burton's sixty-three years of humorous study of men and books is *The Anatomy of Melancholy*, first printed in 1621, and enlarged afterwards by the author. A critical edition of the *Anatomy*, giving these enlargements exactly with other editorial matter, is very much wanted ; but even in the rather inedited condition in which the book, old and new, is usually found, it is wholly acceptable.   Its literary history is rather curious.   Eight editions of it appeared in half a century from the date of the first, and then, with other books of its time, it dropped out of notice except by the learned.   Early in the present century it was revived and reprinted with certain modernisations, and four or five editions succeeded each other at no long interval.   The copies thus circulated seem to have satisfied the demand for many years, and have been followed without much alteration in some later issues.

The book itself has been very variously judged.   Fuller, in one of his least worthy moments, called it "a book of philology." Anthony Wood, hitting on a notion which has often been borrowed since, held that it is a convenient commonplace book of classical quotations, which, with all respect to Anthony's memory (whom

I am more especially bound to honour as a Merton man), is a gross and Philistine error. Johnson, as was to be expected, appreciated it thoroughly. Ferriar in his *Illustrations of Sterne* pointed out the enormous indebtedness of Tristram Shandy to Democritus Junior. Charles Lamb, eloquently praising the "fantastic great old man," exhibited perhaps more perversity than sense in denouncing the modern reprints which, after all, are not like some modern reprints (notably one of Burton's contemporary, Felltham, to be noticed shortly), in any real sense garbled. Since that time Burton has to some extent fallen back to the base uses of a quarry for half-educated journalists ; nevertheless, all fit readers of English literature have loved him.

The book is a sufficiently strange one at first sight ; and it is perhaps no great wonder that uncritical readers should have been bewildered by the bristling quotations from utterly forgotten authorities which, with full and careful reference for the most part, stud its pages, by its elaborate but apparently futile marshalling in " partitions " and " members," in " sections " and " subsections," and by the measureless license of digression which the author allows himself. It opens with a long epistle, filling some hundred pages in the modern editions, from Democritus Junior, as the author calls himself, to the reader—an epistle which gives a true foretaste of the character and style of the text, though, unlike that text, it is not scholastically divided. The division begins with the text itself, and even the laziest reader will find the synopses of Burton's " partitions " a curious study. It is impossible to be, at least in appearance, more methodical, and all the typographical resources of brackets (sub-bracketed even to the seventh or eighth involution) and of reference letters are exhausted in order to draw up a conspectus of the causes, symptoms, nature, effects, and cure of melancholy. This method is not exactly the method of madness, though it is quite possible for a reader to attach more (as also less) importance to it than it deserves. It seems probable on the whole that the author, with the scholastic habits of his time, did actually draw out a

programme for the treatment of his subject in some form not
very different from these wonderful synopses, and did actually
endeavour to keep to it, or at any rate to work on its lines within
the general compass of the scheme. But on each several head
(and reducing them to their lowest terms the heads are legion)
he allowed himself the very widest freedom of digression, not
merely in extracting and applying the fruits of his notebook, but
in developing his own thoughts,—a mine hardly less rich if less
extensive than the treasures of the Bodleian Library which are
said to have been put at his disposal.

The consequence is, that the book is one quite impossible to
describe in brief space. The melancholy of which the author
treats, and of which, no doubt, he was in some sort the victim, is
very far from being the mere Byronic or Wertherian disease which
became so familiar some hundred years ago. On the other hand,
Burton being a practical, and, on the whole, very healthy Englishman, it came something short of "The Melencolia that transcends all wit," the incurable pessimism and quiet despair which
have been thought to be figured or prefigured in Durer's famous
print. Yet it approaches, and that not distantly, to this latter.
It is the Vanity of Vanities of a man who has gone, in thought at
least, over the whole round of human pleasures and interests, and
who, if he has not exactly found all to be vanity, has found each
to be accompanied by some *amari aliquid*. It is at the same
time the frankly expressed hypochondria of a man whose bodily
health was not quite so robust as his mental constitution. It is
the satiety of learning of a man who, nevertheless, knows that
learning, or at least literature, is the only cure for his disease.

In mere style there is perhaps nothing very strongly characteristic in Burton, though there is much that is noteworthy in the
way in which he adapts his style to the peculiar character of his
book. Like Rabelais, he has but rarely occasion to break through
his fantastic habit of stringing others' pearls on a mere string of
his own, and to set seriously to the composition of a paragraph
of wholly original prose. But when he does, the effect is

remarkable, and shows that it was owing to no poverty or awkwardness that he chose to be so much of a borrower. In his usual style, where a mere framework of original may enclose a score or more quotations, translated or not (the modern habit of translating Burton's quotations spoils, among other things, the zest of his own quaint habit of adding, as it were, in the same breath, a kind of summary or paraphrase in English of what he has said in Latin or Greek), he was not superior to his time in the loose construction of sentences ; but the wonder is that his fashion of writing did not make him even inferior to it. One of his peculiar tricks—the only one, perhaps, which he uses to the extent of a mannerism—is the suppression of the conjunctions " or " and " and," which gives a very quaint air to his strings of synonyms. But an example will do more here than much analysis :—

" And why then should baseness of birth be objected to any man ? Who thinks worse of Tully for being *Arpinas*, an upstart ? or Agathocles, that Sicilian King, for being a potter's son ? Iphicrates and Marius were meanly born. What wise man thinks better of any person for his nobility ? as he [1] said in Machiavel, *omnes eodem patre nati*, Adam's sons, conceived all and born in sin, etc. *We are by nature all as one, all alike, if you see us naked ; let us wear theirs, and they our clothes, and what's the difference ?* To speak truth, as Bale did of P. Schalichius, *I more esteem thy worth, learning, honesty, than thy nobility ; honour thee more that thou art a writer, a doctor of divinity, than earl of the Hunnes, baron of Skradine, or hast title to such and such provinces, etc. Thou art more fortunate and great* (so Jovius writes to Cosmus Medices, then Duke of Florence) *for thy virtues than for thy lovely wife and happy children, friends, fortunes, or great Duchy of Tuscany.* So I account thee, and who doth not so indeed ? Abdalonymus was a gardener, and yet by Alexander for his virtues made King of Syria. How much better is it to be born of mean parentage and to excel in worth, to be morally noble, which is preferred before that natural nobility by divines, philosophers, and politicians, to be learned, honest, discreet, well qualified to be fit for any manner of employment in country and commonwealth, war and peace, than to be *degeneres Neoptolemi* as so many brave nobles are, only wise because rich, otherwise idiots, illiterate,

---

[1] Burton, with others of the time, constantly wrote " he " as the equivalent of the classical demonstratives. Modern, but not better, use prefers " the man," or something similar.

unfit for any manner of service? Udalricus, Earl of Cilia, upbraided John Huniades with the baseness of his birth; but he replied, *In te Ciliensis comitatus turpiter exstinguitur, in me gloriose Bistricensis exoritur;* thine earldom is consumed with riot; mine begins with honour and renown. Thou hast had so many noble ancestors; what is that to thee? *Vix ea nostra voco;* when thou art a disard[1] thyself, *quid prodest Pontice longo stemmate censeri?* etc. I conclude, hast thou a sound body and a good soul, good bringing up? Art thou virtuous, honest, learned, well qualified, religious? Are thy conditions good? Thou art a true nobleman, perfectly noble though born of Thersites, *dummodo tu sis Aeacidæ similis non natus sed factus,* noble κατ' ἐξοχὴν, *for neither sword, nor fire, nor water, nor sickness, nor outward violence, nor the devil himself can take thy good parts from thee.* Be not ashamed of thy birth then; thou art a gentleman all the world over, and shalt be honoured, whenas he, strip him of his fine clothes, dispossess him of his wealth, is a funge[2] (which Polynices in his banishment found true by experience, gentry was not esteemed), like a piece of coin in another country, that no man will take, and shall be contemned. Once more, though thou be a barbarian born at Tontonteac, a villain, a slave, a Saldanian negro, or a rude Virginian in Dasamonquepeuc,[3] he a French monsieur, a Spanish don, a seignior of Italy, I care not how descended, of what family, of what order—baron, count, prince—if thou be well qualified and he not but a degenerate Neoptolemus, I tell thee in a word thou art a man and he is a beast."

Such, in his outward aspects, is Burton; but of him, even more than of most writers, it may be said that a brick of the house is no sample. Only by reading him in the proper sense, and that with diligence, can his great learning, his singular wit and fancy, and the general view of life and of things belonging to life, which informs and converts to a whole his learning, his wit, and his fancy alike, be properly conceived. For reading either continuous or desultory, either grave or gay, at all times of life and in all moods of temper, there are few authors who stand the test of practice so well as the author of *The Anatomy of Melancholy.*

Probably, however, among those who can taste old authors, there will always be a friendly but irreconcilable difference as to

---

[1] A "dizzard" = a blockhead. Said to be connected with "dizzy."

[2] Fungus, mushroom.

[3] Saldania is Saldanha Bay. As for Tontonteac and Dasamonquepeuc, I shall imitate the manly frankness of the boy in *Henry V.*, and say, " I do not know what is the French for fer, and ferret, and firk."

the merits of Fuller and Burton, when compared together.   There never can be any among such as to the merits of Fuller, considered in himself.   Like Burton, he was a clerk in orders ; but his literary practice, though more copious than that of the author of *The Anatomy*, divorced him less from the discharge of his professional duties.   He was born, like Dryden, but twenty-two years earlier, in 1608, at Aldwinkle in Northamptonshire, and in a parsonage there, but of the other parish (for there are two close together).   He was educated at Cambridge, and, being made prebendary of Salisbury, and vicar of Broadwindsor, almost as soon as he could take orders, seemed to be in a fair way of preferment.   He worked as a parish priest up to 1640, the year of the beginning of troubles, and the year of his first important book, *The Holy War*.   But he was a staunch Royalist, though by no means a bigot, and he did not, like other men of his time, see his way to play Mr. Facing-both-ways.   For a time he was a preacher in London, then he followed the camp as chaplain to the victorious army of Hopton, in the west, then for a time again he was stationary at Exeter, and after the ruin of the Royal cause he returned to London, where, though he did not recover his benefices, he was leniently treated, and even, in 1655, obtained license to preach.   Nevertheless, the Restoration would probably have brought him promotion, but he lived not long enough to receive it, dying on the 15th of August 1661.   He was an extremely industrious writer, publishing, besides the work already mentioned, and not a few minor pieces (*The Holy and Profane State, Thoughts and Contemplations in Good, Worse, and Better Times, A Pisgah-sight of Palestine*), an extensive *Church History of Britain*, and, after his death, what is perhaps his masterpiece, *The Worthies of England*, an extraordinary miscellany, quartering the ground by counties, filling, in the compactest edition, two mighty quartos, and containing perhaps the greatest account of miscellaneous fact to be found anywhere out of an encyclopedia, conveyed in a style the quaintest and most lively to be found anywhere out of the choicest essayists of the language.

A man of genius who adored Fuller, and who owes to him more
than to any one else except Sir Thomas Browne, has done, in small
compass, a service to his memory which is not easily to be paralleled.
Lamb's specimens from Fuller, most of which are only two or
three lines long, and none a pageful, for once contradict the
axiom quoted above as to a brick and a house.   So perfectly has
the genius of selector and author coincided, that not having myself
gone through the verification of them, I should hardly be surprised to find that Lamb had used his faculty of invention.   Yet
this would not matter, for they are perfectly Fullerian.   Although
Fuller has justly been praised for his method, and although he
never seems to have suffered his fancy to run away with him to
the extent of forgetting or wilfully misrepresenting a fact, the
conceits, which are the chief characteristic of his style, are
comparatively independent of the subject.   Coleridge has asserted
that "Wit was the stuff and substance of his intellect," an assertion which (with all the respect due to Coleridge) would have
been better phrased in some such way as this,—that nearly the
whole force of his intellect concentrated itself upon the witty
presentation of things.   He is illimitably figurative, and though
his figures seldom or never fail to carry illumination of the
subject with them, their peculiar character is sufficiently indicated
by the fact that they can almost always be separated from the
subject and from the context in which they occur without any
damage to their own felicity.   To a thoroughly serious person, to
a person like Lord Chesterfield (who was indeed very serious in
his own way, and abhorred proverbial philosophy), or to one who
cannot away with the introduction of a quip in connection with a
solemn subject, and who thinks that indulgence in a gibe is a clear
proof that the writer has no solid argument to produce, Fuller
must be nothing but a puzzle or a disgust.   That a pious and
earnest divine should, even in that day of quaintness, compare
the gradual familiarisation of Christians with the sacraments of
the Church to the habit of children first taking care of, and then
neglecting a pair of new boots, or should describe a brother clerk

as " pronouncing the word *damn* with such an emphasis as left a
dismal echo in his auditors' ears a good while longer," seems,
no doubt, to some excellent people, unpardonable, and almost
incomprehensible. Yet no one has ever impeached the sincerity
of Fuller's convictions, and the blamelessness of his life. That a
grave historian should intersperse the innumerable trivialities of
the *Worthies* may be only less shocking. But he was an eminent
proof of his own axiom, " That an ounce of mirth, with the same
degree of grace, will serve God farther than a pound of sadness."
Fuller is perhaps the only writer who, voluminous as he is, will
not disappoint the most superficial inquirer for proofs of the
accuracy of the character usually given to him. Nobody perhaps
but himself, in trying to make the best of the Egyptian bondage
of the Commonwealth, would have discovered that the Church,
being unrepresented by any of the four hundred and odd members
of Cromwell's Parliament, was better off than when she had
Archbishops, Bishops, and a convocation all to herself, urging,
" what civil Christian would not plead for a dumb man," and so
enlisting all the four hundred and odd enemies as friends and
representatives. But it is impossible to enter fully on the subject
of Fuller's quips. What may fairly be said of them is, that while
constantly fantastic, and sometimes almost childish, they are never
really silly ; that they are never, or hardly ever in bad taste ; and
that, quaint and far fetched as they are, there is almost always
some application or suggestion which saves them from being mere
intellectual somersaults. The famous one of the " Images of God
cut in ebony," is sufficient of itself to serve as a text. There is
in it all the good side of the emancipation propaganda with an
entire freedom from the extravagance, the vulgarity, the injustice, the bad taste which marked that propaganda a century
and more afterwards, when taken up by persons very different
from Fuller. Perhaps it may be well to give an extract of some
length from him :—

" A lady big with child was condemned to perpetual imprisonment, and in
the dungeon was delivered of a son, who continued with her till a boy of some

bigness. It happened at one time he heard his mother (for see neither of them could, as to decern in so dark a place) bemoan her condition.

" Why, mother (said the child) do you complain, seeing you want nothing you can wish, having clothes, meat, and drink sufficient ? Alas ! child (returned the mother), I lack liberty, converse with Christians, the light of the sun, and many things more, which thou, being prison-born, neither art nor can be sensible of in thy condition.

" The *post-nati*, understand thereby such striplings born in England since the death of monarchy therein, conceive this land, their mother, to be in a good estate. For one fruitful harvest followeth another, commodities are sold at reasonable rates, abundance of brave clothes are worn in the city, though not by such persons whose birth doth best become, but whose purses can best bestow them.

" But their mother, England, doth justly bemoan the sad difference betwixt her present and former condition ; when she enjoyed full and free trade without payment of taxes, save so small they seemed rather an acknowledgment of their allegiance than a burden to their estate ; when she had the court of a king, the House of Lords, yea, and the Lord's house, decently kept, constantly frequented, without falsehood in doctrine, or faction in discipline. God of His goodness restore unto us so much of these things as may consist with His glory and our good."

" I saw a servant maid, at the command of her mistress, make, kindle, and blow a fire. Which done, she was posted away about other business, whilst her mistress enjoyed the benefit of the fire. Yet I observed that this servant, whilst industriously employed in the kindling thereof, got a more general, kindly, and continuing heat than her mistress herself. Her heat was only by her, and not in her, staying with her no longer than she stayed by the chimney ; whilst the warmth of the maid was inlaid, and equally diffused through the whole body.

" An estate suddenly gotten is not so lasting to the owner thereof as what is duly got by industry. The substance of the diligent, saith Solomon, Prov. xii. 27, is precious. He cannot be counted poor that hath so many pearls, precious brown bread, precious small beer, precious plain clothes, etc. A comfortable consideration in this our age, wherein many hands have learned their lesson of labour, who were neither born nor bred with it."

The best judges have admitted that, in contradistinction to this perpetual quipping, which is, as far as it goes, of his time, the general style of Fuller is on the whole rather more modern than the styles of his contemporaries. It does not seem that this is due to deliberate intention of shortening and proportioning his prose; for he is as careless as any one of the whole century about exact grammatical sequence, and seems to have had no objection on any critical grounds to the long disjointed sentence which was the curse of the time. But his own ruling passion insensibly disposed him to a certain brevity. He liked to express his figurative conceits pointedly and antithetically; and point and antithesis are the two things most incompatible with clauses jointed *ad infinitum* in Clarendon's manner, with labyrinths of "whos" and "whiches" such as too frequently content Milton and Taylor. Poles asunder from Hobbes, not merely in his ultimate conclusions but in the general quality of his mind, he perhaps comes nearest to the author of the treatise on *Human Nature* in clear, sensible, unambiguous presentation of the thing that he means to say; and this, joined to his fecundity in illustration of every kind, greatly helps the readableness of his books. No work of his as a working out of an original conception can compete with *The Anatomy of Melancholy;* but he is as superior in minor method to Burton as he is inferior in general grasp.

The remainder of the minor Carolines must be dismissed rapidly. A not unimportant position among the prose writers of this time is occupied by Edward Herbert, Lord Herbert of Cherbury, the elder brother of George Herbert the poet. He was born in 1583, and finished his life ingloriously, and indeed discreditably, during the troubles of the civil war, on the 20th of August 1648. His earlier career is elaborately if not exactly truthfully recorded in his *Autobiography*, and its details have been carefully supplemented by his latest editor, Mr. Lee. His literary activity was various and considerable. His greatest work — a treatise which has been rashly called the foundation of English deism, but which rather expresses the vague and not wholly unorthodox doubt expressed earlier by Montaigne, and by contemporaries of Herbert's own, such as La Mothe le Vayer—was written in Latin, and has never been translated into English. He was an English verse writer of some merit, though inferior to his brother.   His ambitious and academic *History of Henry VIII.* is a regular and not unsuccessful effort in English prose, prompted no doubt by the thorough-going courtiership which ranks with his vanity and want of stability on the most unfavourable aspect of Herbert's character.   But posterity has agreed to take him as an English writer chiefly on the strength of the Autobiography, which remained in manuscript for a century and more, and was published by Horace Walpole, rather against the will of Lord Powis, its possessor and its author's representative. It is difficult to say that Lord Powis was wrong, especially considering that Herbert never published these memoirs, and seems to have written them as much as anything else for his own private satisfaction.   It may be doubted whether there is any more astounding monument of coxcombry in literature.   Herbert is sometimes cited as a model of a modern knight-errant, of an Amadis born too late.   Certainly, according to his own account, all women loved and all men feared him ; but for the former fact we have nothing but his own authority, and in regard to the latter we have counter evidence which renders it exceedingly doubtful.   He was, according to his own account, a desperate duellist.   But even by this account his duels had a curious habit of being interrupted, in the immortal phrase of Mr. Winkle, by " several police constables ; " while in regard to actual war the exploits of his youth seem not to have been great, and those of his age were wholly discreditable, inasmuch as being by profession an ardent Royalist, he took the first opportunity to make, without striking a blow, a profitable composition with the Parliament.   Nevertheless, despite the drawbacks of subject-matter, the autobiography is a very interesting piece of English prose. The narrative style, for all its coxcombry and its insistence on petty details, has a singular vivacity ; the constructions, though sometimes incorrect (" the edict was so severe as they who transgressed were to lose their heads "), are never merely slovenly ; and the writer displays an art, very uncommon in his time, in the alternation of short and long sentences and the general adjustment of the paragraph. Here and there, too, there are passages of more elevated style which give reason for regretting that the *De Veritate* was not written in English. It is very much to be feared that the chief reason for its being written in Latin was a desire on the author's part to escape awkward consequences by an appearance of catering for philosophers and the learned only. It must be admitted that neither of the two great free-thinking Royalists, Hobbes and Herbert, is a wholly pleasant character ; but it may be at least said for the commoner (it cannot be said for the peer) that he was constant to his principles, and that if somewhat careful of his skin, he never seems to have been tempted to barter his conscience for it as Herbert did.

Hardly any other writer among the minor Caroline prosaists is important enough to justify a substantive notice in a work which has already reached and almost exceeded the limits accorded to it. The excellent style of Cowley's *Essays*, which is almost more modern than the work of Dryden and Tillotson, falls in great part actually beyond the limits of our time ; and by character, if not by date, Cowley is left for special treatment in the following volume. He sometimes relapses into what may be called the general qualities with their accompanying defects of Elizabethan prose—a contempt of proportion, clearness, and order ; a reckless readiness to say everything that is in the writer's mind, without considering whether it is appropriate or not ; a confusion of English and classical grammar, and occasionally a very scant attention even to rules which the classical grammars indicate yet more sternly than the vernacular. But as a rule he is distinguished for exactly the opposite of all these things. Much less modern than Cowley, but still of a chaster and less fanciful style than most of his contemporaries, is the famous Protestant apologist, Chillingworth—a man whose orderly mind and freedom from anything like enthusiasm reflected themselves in the easy balance of his style. Sanderson, Pearson, Baxter, the two former luminaries of the Church, the latter one of the chief literary lights of Nonconformity, belong more or less to the period, as does

Bishop Hall.   Baxter is the most colloquial, the most fanciful, and the latest, of the three grouped together ; the other two are nearer to the plainness of Chillingworth than to the ornateness of Jeremy Taylor.   Few English prose writers again are better known than Izaak Walton, though it might be difficult to prove that in matter of pure literature he stands very high.   The engaging character of his subjects, and the still more engaging display of his own temper and mode of thought which he makes in almost every sentence, both of his *Complete Angler* and of his hardly less known *Lives*, account for the survival and constant popularity of books which are neither above nor below the better work of their time in literary form.   Walton was born in 1593 and died ninety years later.   His early manhood was spent in London as a "linen-draper," but in friendly conversation with the best clerical and literary society.   In 1643 he retired from London to avoid the bustle of the Civil War, and the *Complete Angler* appeared in 1653.   Another writer contemporary with Walton, though less long-lived, James Howell, has been the subject of very varying judgments ; his appeal being very much of the same kind as Walton's, but addressed to a different and narrower class of persons.   He was born in 1594(?) of a fair Welsh family, was educated at Jesus College, Oxford, was employed more than once on confidential business errands on the Continent, entered Parliament, was made Clerk of the Council, was imprisoned for years in the Fleet during the Civil War, received at the Restoration the post of Historiographer, and died in 1666. He wrote all manner of things, but has chiefly survived as the author of a large collection of Familiar Letters, which have been great favourites with some excellent judges.   They have something of the agreeable garrulousness of Walton.   But Howell was not only much more of a gossip than Izaak ; he was also a good deal of a coxcomb, while Walton was destitute of even a trace of coxcombry.   In one, however, as in the other, the attraction of matter completely outdoes the purely literary attraction.   The reader is glad to hear at first hand what men thought of Raleigh's execution; how Ben Jonson behaved in his cups; how foreign parts looked to a genuine English traveller early in the seventeenth century, and so forth. Moreover, the book was long a very popular one, and an unusual number of anecdotes and scraps passed from it into the general literary stock of English writers. But Howell's manner of telling his stories is not extraordinarily attractive, and has something self-conscious and artificial about it which detracts from its interest. The *Characters* of Overbury were followed and, no doubt, imitated by John Earle, afterwards Bishop of Salisbury, and a man of some importance. Earle, who was a fellow of Merton, called his sketches *Microcosmography*. Nothing in them approaches the celebrated if perhaps not quite genuine milkmaid of Overbury; but they give evidence of a good deal of direct observation often expressed in a style that is pointed, such as the description of a bowling green as a place fitted for "the expense of time, money, and oaths." The church historian and miscellanist Heylin belongs also to the now fast multiplying class of professional writers who dealt with almost any subject as it might seem likely to hit the taste of the public. The bold and fantastic speculations of Bishop Wilkins and Sir Kenelm Digby, and the *Oceana* or Ideal Republic (last of a long line) of James Harrington (not to be confounded with the earlier Sir John Harington, translator of Ariosto), deserve some notice. The famous *Eikon Basilike* (the authorship of which has perhaps of late years been too confidently ascribed to Dr. Gauden independently, rather than to the king, edited by Gauden) has considerable literary merit. Last of all has to be mentioned a curious book, which made some noise at its appearance, and which, though not much read now, has had two seasons of genuine popularity, and is still highly thought of by a few good judges. This is the *Resolves* of Owen Feltham or Felltham. Not much is known of the author except that he was of a respectable family in East Anglia, a family which seems to have been especially seated in the neighbourhood of Lowestoft. Besides the *Resolves* he wrote some verse, of which the most notable piece is a reply to Ben

Jonson's famous ode to himself ("Come Leave the Loathed Stage ")
—a reply which even such a sworn partisan as Gifford admits to
be at least just if not very kind.   Felltham seems also to have
engaged in controversy with another Johnson, a Jesuit, on theological subjects.   But save for the *Resolves* he would be totally
forgotten.   The estimate of their value will differ very much, as
the liking for not very original discussion of ethical subjects and
sound if not very subtle judgment on them overpowers or not in
the reader a distaste for style that has no particular distinction,
and ideas which, though often wholesome, are seldom other than
obvious.   Wordsworth's well-known description of one of his own
poems, as being " a chain of extremely valuable thoughts," applies
no doubt to the *Resolves*, which, except in elegance, rather resemble the better-known of Cicero's philosophical works.   Moreover, though possessing no great elegance, they are not inelegant ;
though it is difficult to forget how differently Bacon and Browne
treated not dissimilar subjects at much the same time.   So
popular were they that besides the first edition (which is undated,
but must have appeared in or before 1628, the date of the
second), eleven others were called for up to 1709.   But it was not
for a hundred years that they were again printed, and then the
well-meaning but misguided zeal of their resuscitator led him not
merely to modernise their spelling, etc. (a venial sin, if, which
I am not inclined very positively to lay down, it is a sin at all),
but to "improve" their style, sense, and sentiment by omission,
alteration, and other tamperings with the text, so as to give
the reader not what Mr. Felltham wrote early in the seventeenth
century, but what Mr. Cummings thought he ought to have written
early in the nineteenth.

   This chapter might easily be enlarged, and indeed, as Dryden
says, shame must invade the breast of every writer of literary
history on a small scale who is fairly acquainted with his subject,
when he thinks how many worthy men—men much worthier than
he can himself ever pretend to be—he has perforce omitted.   Any
critic inclined to find fault may ask me where is the ever-memor-

able John Hales? Where is Tom Coryat, that most egregious Odcombian? and Barnabee of the unforgotten, though scandalous, Itinerary? Where is Sir Thomas Urquhart, quaintest of cavaliers, and not least admirable of translators, who not only rendered Rabelais in a style worthy of him, who not only wrote in sober seriousness pamphlets with titles, which Master Francis could hardly have bettered in jest, but who composed a pedigree of the Urquhart family *nominatim* up to Noah and Adam, and then improvised chimney pieces in Cromarty Castle, commemorating the prehistoric ancestors whom he had excogitated? Where are the great Bishops from Andrewes and Cosin onwards, and the lesser Theologians who wrangled, and the Latitudinarians who meditated, and the historians with Whitelocke at their head, and the countless writers of countless classes of books who multiplied steadily as time went on? It can only be answered that they are not, and that almost in the nature of things they cannot be here. It is not that they are not intrinsically interesting; it is not merely that, being less intrinsically interesting than some of their forerunners or contemporaries, they must give way when room is limited. It is that even if their individual performance were better than that of earlier men, even if there were room and verge enough for them, they would less concern the literary historian. For to him in all cases the later examples of a style are less important than the earlier, merely because they are late, because they have had forerunners whom, consciously or unconsciously, they have (except in the case of a great genius here and there) imitated, and because as a necessary consequence they fall into the *numerus*—into the gross as they would themselves have said—who must be represented only by choice examples and not enumerated or criticised in detail.

CONCLUSION

A CONCLUSION, like a preface, is perhaps to some extent an old-fashioned thing; and it is sometimes held that a writer does better not to sum up at all, but to leave the facts which he has accumulated to make their own way into the intelligence of his readers. I am not able to accept this view of the matter. In dealing with such a subject as that which has been handled in the foregoing pages, it is at least as necessary that the writer should have something of *ensemble* in his mind as that he should look carefully into facts and dates and names. And he can give no such satisfactory evidence of his having possessed this *ensemble*, as a short summary of what, in his idea, the whole period looks like when taken at a bird's-eye view. For he has (or ought to have) given the details already; and his summary, without in the least compelling readers to accept it, must give them at least some means of judging whether he has been wandering over a plain trackless to him, or has been pursuing with confidence a well-planned and well-laid road.

At the time at which our period begins (and which, though psychological epochs rarely coincide exactly with chronological, is sufficiently coincident with the accession of Elizabeth), it cannot be said with any precision that there was an English *literature* at all. There were eminent English writers, though perhaps one only to whom the first rank could even by the utmost complaisance be opened or allowed. But there was no literature, in the sense of a system of treating all subjects in the vernacular, according to methods more or less decidedly arranged and accepted by a considerable tradition of skilled craftsmen. Something of the kind had partially existed in the case of the Chaucerian poetic ; but it was an altogether isolated something. Efforts, though hardly conscious ones, had been made in the domain of prose by romancers, such as the practically unknown Thomas Mallory, by sacred orators like Latimer, by historians like More, by a few struggling miscellaneous writers. Men like Ascham, Cheke, Wilson, and others had, perhaps with a little touch of patronage, recommended the regular cultivation of the English tongue ; and immediately before the actual accession of Elizabeth the publication of Tottel's *Miscellany* had shown by its collection of the best poetical work of the preceding half century the extraordinary effect which a judicious xenomania (if I may, without scaring the purists of language, borrow that useful word from the late Karl Hillebrand) may produce on English. It is to the exceptional fertilising power of such influences on our stock that we owe all the marvellous accomplishments of the English tongue, which in this respect —itself at the head of the Teutonic tongues by an almost unapproachable distance—stands distinguished with its Teutonic sisters generally from the groups of languages with which it is most likely to be contrasted. Its literary power is originally less conspicuous than that of the Celtic and of the Latin stocks ; the lack, notorious to this day, of one single original English folk-song of really great beauty is a rough and general fact which is perfectly borne out by all other facts. But the exquisite folk-literature of the Celts is absolutely unable either by itself or with the help of foreign admixture to arrive at complete literary perfection. And the profound sense of form which characterises the Latins is apparently accompanied by such a deficiency of originality, that when any foreign model is accepted it receives hardly any colour from the native genius, and remains a cultivated exotic. The less promising soil of Anglo-Saxon idiom waited for the foreign influences, ancient and modern, of the Renaissance to act upon it, and then it produced a crop which has dwarfed all the produce of the modern world, and has nearly, if not quite, equalled in perfection, while it has much exceeded in bulk and length of flowering time, the produce of Greece.

The rush of foreign influences on the England of Elizabeth's time, stimulated alike by the printing press, by religious movements, by the revival of ancient learning, and by the habits of travel and commerce, has not been equalled in force and volume by anything else in history. But the different influences of different languages and countries worked with very different force. To the easier and more generally known of the classical tongues must be assigned by far the largest place. This was only natural at a time when to the inherited and not yet decayed use of colloquial and familiar Latin as the vehicle of business, of literature, and of almost everything that required the committal of written words to paper, was added the scholarly study of its classical period from the strictly humanist point of view. If we could assign marks in the competition, Latin would have to receive nearly as many as all its rivals put together; but Greek would certainly not be second, though it affected, especially in the channel of the Platonic dialogues, many of the highest and most gifted souls. In the latter part of the present period there were probably scholars in England who, whether their merely philological attainments might or might not pass muster now, were far better read in the actual literature of the Greek classics than the very philologists who now disdain them. Not a few of the chief matters in Greek literature—the epical grandeur of Homer, the tragic principles of the three poets, and so forth—made themselves, at first or second hand, deeply felt. But on the whole Greek did not occupy the second place. That place was occupied by Italian. It was Italy which had touched the spring that let loose the poetry of Surrey and Wyatt ; Italy was the chief resort of travelled Englishmen in the susceptible time of youth ; Italy provided in Petrarch (Dante was much less read) and Boccaccio, in Ariosto and Tasso, an inexhaustible supply of models, both in prose and verse. Spain was only less influential because Spanish literature was in a much less finished condition than Italian, and perhaps also because political causes made the following of Spaniards seem almost unpatriotic. Yet the very same causes made the Spanish language itself familiar to far more Englishmen than are familiar with it now, though the direct filiation of euphuism on Spanish originals is no doubt erroneous, and though the English and Spanish dramas evolved themselves in lines rather parallel than connected.

France and Germany were much (indeed infinitely) less influential, and the fact is from some points of view rather curious. Both were much nearer to England than Spain or Italy; there was much more frequent communication with both; there was at no time really serious hostility with either; and the genius of both languages was, the one from one side, the other from the other, closely connected with that of English. Yet in the great productions of our great period, the influence of Germany is only perceptible in some burlesque matter, such as *Eulenspiegel* and *Grobianus*, in the furnishing of a certain amount of supernatural subject-matter like the Faust legend, and in details less important still. French influence is little greater; a few allusions of " E. K." to Marot and Ronsard; a few translations and imitations by Spenser, Watson, and others; the curious sonnets of *Zepheria ;* a slight echo of Rabelais here and there; some adapted songs to music; and a translated play or two on the Senecan model.[1]

But France had already exercised a mighty influence upon England; and Germany had very little influence to exercise for centuries. Putting aside all pre-Chaucerian influence which may be detected, the outside guiding force of literary English literature (which was almost exclusively poetry) had been French from the end of the fourteenth century to the last survivals of the

[1] Some, like my friend Mr. Lee, would demur to this, especially as regards the sonnet. But Desportes, the chief creditor alleged, was himself an infinite borrower from the Italians. Soothern, an early but worthless sonneteer, c. 1584, did certainly imitate the French.

Scoto-Chaucerian school in Hawes, Skelton, and Lindsay. True, France had now something else to give; though it must be remembered that her great school coincided with rather than preceded the great school of England, that the *Défense et Illustration de la Langue Française* was but a few years anterior to Tottel's *Miscellany*, and that, except Marot and Rabelais (neither of whom was neglected, though neither exercised much formal influence), the earlier French writers of the sixteenth century had nothing to teach England. On the other hand, Germany was utterly unable to supply anything in the way of instruction in literary form; and it was instruction in literary form which was needed to set the beanstalk of English literature growing even unto the heavens. Despite the immense advantage which the English adoption of German innovations in religion gave the country of Luther, that country's backwardness made imitation impossible. Luther himself had not elaborated anything like a German style; he had simply cleared the vernacular of some of its grossest stumbling-blocks and started a good plain fashion of sentence. That was not what England wanted or was likely to want, but a far higher literary instruction, which Germany could not give her and (for the matter of that) has never been in a position to give her. The models which she sought had to be sought elsewhere, in Athens, in old Rome, in modern Tuscany.

But it would probably be unwise not to make allowance for a less commonplace and more "metaphysical" explanation. It was precisely because French and German had certain affinities with English, while Italian and Spanish, not to mention the classical tongues, were strange and exotic, that the influence of the latter group was preferred. The craving for something not familiar, for something new and strange, is well known enough in the individual; and nations are, after all, only aggregates of individuals. It was exactly because the models of the south were so utterly divided from the isolated Briton in style and character that he took so kindly to them, and that their study inspired him so well. There were not, indeed, wanting signs of what mischief might have been done if English sense had been less robust and the English genius of a less stubborn idiosyncrasy. Euphuism, the occasional practice of the Senecan drama, the preposterous and almost incredible experiments in classical metre of men not merely like Drant and Harvey, but like Sidney and Spenser, were sufficiently striking symptoms of the ferment which was going on in the literary constitution of the country. But they were only harmless heat-rashes, not malignant distempers, and the spirit of England won through them, with no loss of general health, probably with the result of the healthy excretion of many peccant humours which might have been mischievous if driven in. Even the strongest of all the foreign forces, the just admiration of the masterpieces of classical antiquity, was not in any way hurtful; and it is curious enough that it is only in what may be called the autumn and, comparatively speaking, the decadence of the period that anything that can be called pedantry is observed. It is in Milton and Browne, not in Shakespere and Hooker, that there is an appearance of undue domination and " obsession " by the classics.

The subdivisions of the period in which these purely literary influences worked in combination with those of the domestic and foreign policy of England (on which it is unnecessary here to dilate), can be drawn with tolerable precision. They are both better marked and more important in verse than in prose. For it cannot be too often asserted that the age, in the wide sense, was, despite many notable achievements in the *sermo pedestris*, not an age of prose but an age of poetry. The first period extends (taking literary dates) from the publication of Tottel's *Miscellany* to that of *The Shepherd's Calendar*. It is not distinguished by much production of positive value. In poetry proper the writers pursue and exercise themselves upon the track of Surrey, Wyatt, and the other authors whom Grimoald, or some other, collected; acquiring, no doubt, a certain facility in the adjustment to iambic and other measures of the altered pronunciation since Chaucer's time; practising new combinations in stanza, but inclining too

much to the doggerel Alexandrines and fourteeners (more doggerel still when chance or design divided them into eights and
sixes); repeating, without much variation, images and phrases
directly borrowed from foreign models; and displaying, on the
whole, a singular lack of inspiration which half excuses the mistaken attempt of the younger of them, and of their immediate
successors, to arrive at the desired poetical medium by the use of
classical metres. Among men actually living and writing at this
time Lord Buckhurst alone displays a real poetical faculty. Nor
is the case much better in respect of drama, though here the
restless variety of tentative displays even more clearly the vigorous life which underlay incomplete performance, and which
promised better things shortly. The attempt of *Gorboduc* and
a few other plays to naturalise the artificial tragedy, though a
failure, was one of those failures which, in the great literary " rule
of false," help the way to success; the example of *Ralph Roister
Doister* and *Gammer Gurton's Needle* could not fail to stimulate
the production of genuine native farce which might any day become *la bonne comédie*. And even the continued composition of
Moralities showed signs of the growing desire for life and individuality of character. Moreover, the intense and increasing
liking for the theatre in all classes of society, despite the dis-
couragement of the authorities, the miserable reward offered to
actors and playwrights, and the discredit which rested on the
vocations of both, was certain in the ordinary course of things
to improve the supply. The third division of literature made
slower progress under less powerful stimulants. No emulation,
like that which tempted the individual graduate or templar to
rival Surrey in addressing his mistress's eyebrow, or Sackville in
stately rhyming on English history, acted on the writers of prose.
No public demand, like that which produced the few known and
the hundred forgotten playwrights of the first half of Elizabeth's
reign, served as a hotbed. But it is the great secret of prose
that it can dispense with such stimulants. Everybody who
wished to make his thoughts known began, with the help of the

printing press, to make them known; and the informal use of the vernacular, by dint of this unconscious practice and of the growing scholarship both of writers and readers, tended insensibly to make itself less of a mere written conversation and more of a finished prose style. Preaching in English, the prose pamphlet, and translations into the vernacular were, no doubt, the three great schoolmasters in the disciplining of English prose. But by degrees all classes of subjects were treated in the natural manner, and so the various subdivisions of prose style—oratorical, narrative, expository, and the rest—slowly evolved and separated themselves, though hardly, even at the close of the time, had they attained the condition of finish.

The year 1580 may be fixed on with almost mathematical accuracy as the date at which the great generation of Elizabethan writers first showed its hand with Lyly's *Euphues* in prose and Spenser's *Shepherd's Calendar* in verse. Drama was a little, but not more than a little, later in showing the same signs of rejuvenescence; and from that time forward till the end of the century not a year passed without the appearance of some memorable work or writer; while the total production of the twenty years exceeds in originality and force, if not always in artistic perfection of form, the production of any similar period in the world's history. The group of University Wits, following the example of Lyly (who, however, in drama hardly belongs to the most original school), started the dramas of history, of romance, of domestic life; and, by fashioning through their leader Marlowe the tragic decasyllable, put into the hands of the still greater group who succeeded them an instrument, the power of which it is impossible to exaggerate. Before the close of the century they had themselves all ceased their stormy careers; but Shakespere was in the full swing of his activity; Ben Jonson had achieved the freshest and perhaps capital fruit of his study of humours; Dekker, Webster, Middleton, Chapman, and a crowd of lesser writers had followed in his steps. In poetry proper the magnificent success of *The Faërie Queene* had in one sense no second;

but it was surrounded with a crowd of productions hardly inferior in their own way, the chief being the result of the great and remarkable sonnet outburst of the last decade of the century. The doggerel of the earlier years had almost entirely disappeared, and in its place appeared the perfect concerted music of the stanzas (from the sonnet and the Spenserian downwards), the infinite variety of the decasyllable, and the exquisite lyric snatches of song in the dramatists, pamphleteers, and music-book writers. Following the general law already indicated, the formal advance in prose was less, but an enormous stride was made in the direction of applying it to its various uses. The theologians, with Hooker at their head, produced almost the first examples of the measured and dignified treatment of argument and exposition. Bacon (towards the latter end it is true) produced the earliest specimens of his singular mixture of gravity and fancy, pregnant thought and quaint expression. History in the proper sense was hardly written, but a score of chroniclers, some not deficient in narrative power, paved the way for future historians. In imaginative and miscellaneous literature the fantastic extravagances of Lyly seemed as though they might have an evil effect. In reality they only spurred ingenious souls on to effort in refining prose, and in one particular direction they had a most unlooked for result. The imitation in little by Greene, Lodge, and others, of their long-winded graces, helped to popularise the pamphlet, and the popularisation of the pamphlet led the way to periodical writing—an introduction perhaps of doubtful value in itself, but certainly a matter of no small importance in the history of literature. And so by degrees professional men of letters arose— men of letters, professional in a sense, which had not existed since the days of the travelling Jongleurs of the early Middle Ages. These men, by working for the actors in drama, or by working for the publishers in the prose and verse pamphlet (for the latter form still held its ground), earned a subsistence which would seem sometimes to have been not a mere pittance, and which at any rate, when folly and vice did not dissipate it, kept them alive. Much nonsense no doubt has been talked about the Fourth Estate; but such as it is, for good or for bad, it practically came into existence in these prolific years.

The third period, that of vigorous manhood, may be said to coincide roughly with the reign of James I., though if literary rather than political dates be preferred, it might be made to begin with the death of Spenser in 1599, and to end with the damnation of Ben Jonson's *New Inn* just thirty years later. In the whole of this period till the very last there is no other sign of decadence than the gradual dropping off in the course of nature of the great men of the preceding stage, not a few of whom, however, survived into the next, while the places of those who fell were taken in some cases by others hardly below the greatest, such as Beaumont and Fletcher. Many of the very greatest works of what is generally known as the Elizabethan era—the later dramas of Shakespere, almost the whole work of Ben Jonson, the later poems of Drayton, Daniel, and Chapman, the plays of Webster and Middleton, and the prose of Raleigh, the best work of Bacon, the poetry of Browne and Wither—date from this time, while the astonishingly various and excellent work of the two great dramatists above mentioned is wholly comprised within it. And not only is there no sign of weakening, but there is hardly a sign of change. A slight, though only a slight, depression of the imaginative and moral tone may be noticed or fancied in those who, like Fletcher, are wholly of the period, and a certain improvement in general technical execution testifies to longer practice. But Webster might as well have written years earlier (hardly so well years later) than he actually did; and especially in the case of numerous anonymous or single works, the date of which, or at least of their composition, is obscure, it is very difficult from internal evidence of style and sentiment to assign them to one date rather than to another, to the last part of the strictly Elizabethan or the first part of the strictly Jacobean period. Were it not for the occasional imitation of models, the occasional reference to dated facts, it would be not so much difficult as impossible. If there seems to be less audacity of experiment, less of the fire of youth, less of the unrestrainable restlessness of genius eager to burst its way, that, as has been already remarked of another difference, may not improbably be mainly due to fancy, and to the knowledge that the later efforts actually were later as to anything else. In prose more particularly there is no change whatever. Few new experiments in style were tried, unless the *Characters* of Overbury and Earle may be called such. The miscellaneous pamphlets of the time were written in much the same fashion, and in some cases by the same men, as when, forty years before Jonson summoned himself to "quit the loathed stage," Nash had alternately laughed at Gabriel Harvey, and savagely lashed the Martinists. The graver writers certainly had not improved upon, and had not greatly changed, the style in which Hooker broke his lance with Travers, or descanted on the sanctity of law. The humour-comedy of Jonson, the romantic *drame* of Fletcher, with the marmoreally-finished minor poems of Ben, were the nearest approaches of any product of the time to novelty of general style, and all three were destined to be constantly imitated, though only in the last case with much real success, during the rest of our present period. Yet the post-Restoration comedy is almost as much due to Jonson and Fletcher as to foreign models, and the influence of both, after long failing to produce anything of merit, was not imperceptible even in Congreve and Vanbrugh.

Of the fourth period, which practically covers the reign of Charles I. and the interregnum of the Commonwealth, no one can say that it shows no signs of decadence, when the meaning of that word is calculated according to the cautions given above in noticing its poets. Yet the decadence is not at all of the kind which announces a long literary dead season, but only of that which shows that the old order is changing to a new. Nor if regard be merely had to the great names which adorn the time, may it seem proper to use the word decadence at all. To this period belong not only Milton, but Taylor, Browne, Clarendon, Hobbes (four of the greatest names in English prose), the strange union of learning in matter and quaintness in form which characterises Fuller and Burton, the great dramatic work of Massinger and Ford. To it also belongs the exquisite if sometimes artificial school of poetry which grew up under the joint inspiration of the great personal influence and important printed work of Ben Jonson on the one hand, and the subtler but even more penetrating stimulant of the unpublished poetry of Donne on the other—a school which has produced lyrical work not surpassed by that of any other school or time, and which, in some specially poetical characteristics, may claim to stand alone.

If, then, we speak of decadence, it is necessary to describe with some precision what is meant, and to do so is not difficult, for the signs of it are evident, not merely in the rank and file of writers (though they are naturally most prominent here), but to some extent in the great illustrations of the period themselves. In even the very best work of the time there is a want of the peculiar freshness and spontaneity, as of spring water from the rock, which characterises earlier work. The art is constantly admirable, but it is almost obtrusively art—a proposition which is universally true even of the greatest name of the time, of Milton, and which applies equally to Taylor and to Browne, to Massinger and to Ford, sometimes even to Herrick (extraordinary as is the grace which he manages to impart), and almost always to Carew. The lamp is seldom far off, though its odour may be the reverse of disagreeable. But in the work which is not quite so excellent, other symptoms appear which are as decisive and less tolerable. In the poetry of the time there appear, side by side with much exquisite melody and much priceless thought, the strangest blotches, already more than once noticed, of doggerel, of conceits pushed to the verge of nonsense and over the verge of grotesque, of bad rhyme and bad rhythm which are evidently not the result of mere haste and creative enthusiasm but of absolutely defective ear, of a waning sense of harmony. In the drama things are much worse. Only the two dramatists already mentioned, with the doubtful addition of Shirley, display anything like great or original talent. A few clever playwrights do their journey-work with creditable craftsmanship. But even this characteristic is wanting in the majority. The plots relapse into a chaos almost as great as that of the drama of fifty years earlier, but with none of its excuse of inexperience and of redeeming purple patches. The characters are at once uninteresting and unpleasant ; the measure hobbles and staggers ; the dialogue varies between passages of dull declamation and passages of almost duller repartee. Perhaps, though the prose names of the time are greater than those of its dramatists, or, excluding Milton's, of its poets, the signs of something wrong are clearest in prose. It would be difficult to find in any good prose writer between 1580 and 1625 the shameless anomalies of arrangement, the clumsy distortions of grammar, which the very greatest Caroline writers permit themselves in the intervals, and sometimes in the very course of their splendid eloquence ; while, as for lesser men, the famous incoherences of Cromwell's speeches are hardly more than a caricature of the custom of the day.

Something has yet to be said as to the general characteristics of this time—characteristics which, scarcely discernible in the first period, yet even there to be traced in such work as that of Surrey and Sackville, emerge into full prominence in the next, continue with hardly any loss in the third, and are discernible even in the "decadence" of the fourth. Even yet they are not universally recognised, and it appears to be sometimes thought that because critics speak with enthusiasm of periods in which, save at rare intervals, and as it were by accident, they are not discernible at all, such critics are insensible to them where they occur. Never was there a grosser mistake. It is said that M. Taine, in private conversation, once said to a literary novice who rashly asked him whether he liked this or that, " Monsieur, en littérature j'aime tout." It was a noble and correct sentiment, though it might be a little difficult for the particular critic who formulated it to make good his claim to it as a motto. The ideal critic undoubtedly does like everything in literature, provided that it is good of its kind. He likes the unsophisticated tentatives of the earliest minstrel poetry, and the cultivated perfection of form of Racine and Pope; he likes the massive vigour of the French and English sixteenth centuries, and the alembicated exquisiteness of Catullus and Carew; he does not dislike Webster because he is not Dryden, or Young because he is not Spenser; he does not quarrel with Sophocles because he is not Æschylus, or with Hugo because he is not Heine. But at the same time it is impossible for him not to recognise that there are certain periods where inspiration and accomplishment meet in a fashion which may be sought for in vain at others. These are the great periods of literature, and there are perhaps only five of them, with five others which may be said to be almost level. The five first are the great age of Greek literature from Æschylus to Plato, the great ages of English and French literature in the sixteenth and seventeenth centuries, the whole range of Italian literature from Dante to Ariosto, and the second great age of English from the *Lyrical Ballads* to the death of Coleridge. It is the super-eminent glory of English that it counts twice in the reckoning. The five seconds are the Augustan age of Latin, the short but brilliant period of Spanish literary development, the Romantic era in France, the age of Goethe in Germany, including Heine's earlier and best work, and (with difficulty, and by allowance chiefly of Swift and Dryden) the half century from the appearance of *Absalom and Achitophel* to the appearance of *Gulliver* and *The Dunciad* in England. Out of these there are great men but no great periods, and the first class is distinguished from the second, not so much by the fact that almost all the greatest literary names of the world are found in it, as because it is evident to a careful reader that there was more of the general spirit of poetry and of literature diffused in human brains at these times than at any other. It has been said more than once that English Elizabethan literature may, and not merely in virtue of Shakespere, claim the first place even among the first class. The full justification of this assertion could only be given by actually going through the whole range of the literature, book in hand. The foregoing pages have given it as it were in *précis*, rather than in any fuller fashion. And it has been thought better to devote some of the space permitted to extract as the only possible substitute for this continual book-in-hand exemplification. Many subjects which might properly form the subject of excursus in a larger history have been perforce omitted, the object being to give, not a series of interesting essays on detached points, but a conspectus of the actual literary progress and accomplishment of the century, from 1557 to 1660. Such essays exist already in great numbers, though some no doubt are yet to write. The extraordinary influence of Plato, or at least of a more or less indistinctly understood Platonism, on many of the finer minds of the earlier and middle period, is a very interesting point, and it has been plausibly connected with the fact that Giordano Bruno was for some years a resident in England, and was acquainted with the Greville-Sidney circle at the very time that that circle was almost the cradle of the new English literature. The stimulus given not merely by the popular fancy for rough dramatic entertainments, but by the taste of courts and rich nobles for masques—a taste which favoured the composition of such exquisite literature as Ben Jonson's and Milton's masterpieces—is another side subject of the same kind. I do not know that, much as has been written on the Reformation, the direct influence of the form which the Reformation took in England on the growth of English literature has ever been estimated and summarised fully and yet briefly, so as to show the contrast between the distinctly anti-literary character of most of the foreign Protestant and the English Puritan movement on the one side, and the literary tendencies of Anglicanism on the other. The origins of Euphuism and of that later form of preciousness which is sometimes called Gongorism and sometimes Marinism have been much discussed, but the last word has certainly not been said on them. For these things, however (which are merely quoted as examples of a very numer-

ous class), there could be found no place here without excluding
other things more centrally necessary to the unfolding of the
history. And therefore I may leave what I have written with a
short final indication of what seems to me the distinguishing mark
of Elizabethan literature. That mark is not merely the presence
of individual works of the greatest excellence, but the diffusion
throughout the whole work of the time of a *vivida vis*, of flashes
of beauty in prose and verse, which hardly any other period can
show. Let us open one of the songbooks of the time, Dowland's
Second Book of Airs, published in the central year of our period,
1600, and reprinted by Mr. Arber. Here almost at random we
hit upon this snatch—

> " Come ye heavy states of night,
>   Do my father's spirit right ;
>   Soundings baleful let me borrow,
>   Burthening my song with sorrow :
>   Come sorrow, come ! Her eyes that sings
>   By thee, are turnèd into springs.
>
> " Come you Virgins of the night
>   That in dirges sad delight,
>   Quire my anthems ; I do borrow
>   Gold nor pearl, but sounds of sorrow.
>   Come sorrow, come ! Her eyes that sings
>   By thee, are turnèd into springs."

It does not matter who wrote that—the point is its occurrence in
an ordinary collection of songs to music neither better nor worse
than many others. When we read such verses as this, or as the
still more charming Addiess to Love given on page 122, there is
evident at once the *non so che* which distinguishes this period.
There is a famous story of a good-natured conversation between
Scott and Moore in the latter days of Sir Walter, in which
the two poets agreed that verse which would have made a fortune
in their young days appeared constantly in magazines without
being much regarded in their age. No sensible person will mistake the meaning of the apparent praise. It meant that thirty
years of remarkable original production and of much study of

models had made possible and common a standard of formal merit which was very rare at an earlier time. Now this standard of formal merit undoubtedly did not generally exist in the days of Elizabeth. But what did generally exist was the " wind blowing where it listeth," the presence and the influence of which are least likely to be mistaken or denied by those who are most strenuous in insisting on the importance and the necessity of formal excellence itself. I once undertook for several years the criticism of minor poetry for a literary journal, which gave more room than most to such things, and during the time I think I must have read through or looked over probably not much less than a thousand, certainly not less than five or six hundred volumes. I am speaking with seriousness when I say that nothing like the note of the merely casual pieces quoted or referred to above was to be detected in more than at the outside two or three of these volumes, and that where it seemed to sound faintly some second volume of the same author's almost always came to smother it soon after. There was plenty of quite respectable poetic learning : next to nothing of the poetic spirit. Now in the period dealt with in this volume that spirit is everywhere, and so are its sisters, the spirits of drama and of prose. They may appear in full concentration and lustre, as in *Hamlet* or *The Faërie Queene;* or in fitful and intermittent flashes, as in scores and hundreds of sonneteers, pamphleteers, playwrights, madrigalists, preachers. But they are always not far off. In reading other literatures a man may lose little by obeying the advice of those who tell him only to read the best things : in reading Elizabethan literature by obeying he can only disobey that advice, for the best things are everywhere.[1]

[1] In the twenty years which have passed since this book was first published, monographs on most of the points indicated on p. 459 have appeared, both in England and America.

INDEX

I.—BIBLIOGRAPHICAL

Single plays, poems, etc., not mentioned in this Index will be found in the collections referred to under the headings Arber, Bullen, Farmer, Grosart, Hazlitt, Park, Simpson.

Alexander, Sir William. *See* Stirling.

Arber, E., English Garner, vols. i.-viii., Birmingham and London, 1877-96.
  Also new editions in redistributed volumes by Lee, Collins, and others.

Ascham, Roger, Toxophilus. Ed. Arber, London, 1868.
  The Schoolmaster. Ed. Arber, London, 1870.
  Works. Ed. Giles, 4 vols., London, 1865.

Bacon, Francis, Works of. 3 vols. folio, London, 1753.

Barnabee's Journal. By R. Braithwaite. Ed. Haslewood and Hazlitt, London, 1876.

Barnes, Barnabe, Parthenophil and Parthenophe. In Gosart's Occasional Issues, vol. i.
  The Devil's Charter. Ed. M'Kerrow, Louvain.

Barnfield, Richard, Poems. Ed. Arber, Birmingham, 1882.

Basse, William, Poems of. Ed. Bond, London, 1893.

Beaumont, Francis, Poems of. In Chalmers's British Poets, vol. vi.

Beaumont, Sir John, Poems of. In Chalmers's British Poets, vol. vi.

Beaumont, Joseph, Poems of. Ed. Grosart, 2 vols. Privately printed, 1880.

Beaumont and Fletcher, Dramatic Works of. 10 vols., London, 1750. 2 vols., Ed. Darley, London, 1859. 11 vols., Ed. Dyce, London, 1843. Two new editions in progress now (1907)—one Ed. Bullen, London, the other Ed. Waller, Cambridge.

Benlowes, Edward, Theophila. In Minor Caroline Poets, vol. i., Oxford, 1905.

Bible. The Holy Bible, Authorised Version, Oxford, 1851.
  Revised Version, Oxford, 1885.

Breton, Nicholas, Works of. Ed. Grosart, 2 vols. Privately printed, 1879.

Brome, Alexander, Poems of. In Chalmers's Poets, vol. vi.

Brome, Richard, Plays of. 3 vols., London, 1873.

Brooke, Fulke Greville, Lord, Works of. Ed. Grosart, 4 vols. Privately printed, 1870.

Browne, Sir Thomas, Works of. Ed. Wilkin, 3 vols., London, 1880.
  Religio Medici. Ed. Greenhill, London, 1881.

Browne, William, Poems of. In Chalmers's British Poets, vol. vi.
  Also 2 vols. Ed. Hazlitt, London, 1868.
  Also Ed. Goodwin, 2 vols., London, 1894.

Bullen, A. H., Old Plays, 4 vols., London, 1882-85.
    Ditto, New Series. Vols. i. ii. iii., London, 1887-90.
    Lyrics from Elizabethan Song-books, 2 vols., 1887-88.   Ditto, Romances,
        1890.   Ditto, Dramatists, 1890.
    Speculum Amantis, 1891.
    Davison's Poetical Rhapsody, 2 vols., 1891.
    England's Helicon. London, 1887.
    Arden of Feversham. London, 1887.
Burton, Robert, The Anatomy of Melancholy.   2 vols., London, 1821.

Carey, Patrick.   In Minor Caroline Poets, vol. ii., Oxford, 1906.
Carew, Thomas, Poems of.   Edinburgh, 1824.
    Also in Chalmers's Poets, vol. v.
    Also Ed. Hazlitt, London, 1868.
Cartwright, William, Poems of.   In Chalmers's Poets, vol. vi.
Chalkhill, John, Thealma and Clearchus.   In Minor Caroline Poets, vol. ii.
Chalmers, A., British Poets, 21 vols., London, 1810.
Chamberlayne, William, Pharonnida.   In Minor Caroline Poets, vol. i.
Chapman, George, Works of.   3 vols., London, 1875.
Churchyard, T.   No complete edition.   Some things reprinted by Collier and in
        Heliconia.
Clarendon, Edward Hyde, Earl of.   Works, 1 vol., Oxford, 1843.
Cleveland, John.   Contemporary edd. numerous but puzzling and untrustworthy.
        A recent one by J. M. Berdan, New York, n.d.
Cokain, Sir Aston, Plays of.   Edinburgh, 1874.
Constable, Henry, Diana.   In Arber's English Garner, vol. ii.
Corbet, Bishop, Poems of.   In Chalmers's Poets, vol. v.
Cotton, Charles, Poems of.   In Chalmers's Poets, vol. vi.
Crashaw, Richard, Poems of.   Ed. Grosart, 2 vols.   Privately printed, 1872.
    Also in Chalmers's British Poets, vol. vi.
    Also Ed. Waller, Cambridge, 1904.

Daniel, Samuel, Delia.   In Arber's English Garner, vol. iii.
    Also Works of.   In Chalmers's British Poets, vol. iii.
    Also Works of.   Ed. Grosart, 5 vols.   Privately printed, 1885-96.
Davenant, Sir William, Dramatic Works of.   5 vols., Edinburgh, 1872-73.
    Poems of.   Chalmers's British Poets, vol. iv.
Davies, Sir John, Poems of.   In Chalmers's British Poets, vol. v.
Davies, John, of Hereford, Works.   Ed. Grosart, 2 vols.   Privately printed, 1878.
Day, John, Works of.   Ed. Bullen.   Privately printed, 1881.
Dekker, Thomas, Dramatic Works of.   4 vols., London, 1873.
    Prose Works of.   5 vols.   Ed. Grosart.   Privately printed, 1884-86.
Donne, John, Poems of.   Ed. Grosart, 2 vols.   Privately printed, 1872.
    Also Ed. Chambers, 2 vols., London, 1896.
Drayton, Michael, Idea.   In Arber's English Garner, vol. vi.
    Works of.   In Chalmers's British Poets, vol. iv.
Drummond, William, Poems of.   In Chalmers's British Poets, vol. v.
    Also Published for the Maitland Club.   Edinburgh, 1832.
Dyer, Sir Edward, Poems of.   In Hannah's Courtly Poets.

Early English Dramatists.   Ed. Farmer, vols. i.-ix., London, 1905-6.
Eden, Richard, The First Three English Books on America.   Ed. Arber,
        Birmingham, 1885.
Elizabethan Critical Essays.   Ed. G. Smith, 2 vols., Oxford, 1904.
Elizabethan Sonnets.   Ed. Lee, 2 vols., London, 1904.

Knolles, Richard, History of the Turks.   Third Edition, London, 1621.
Kyd, Thomas, Cornelia.   In Hazlitt's Dodsley, vol. v.
        Jeronimo, (?) in do. vol. iv.
        The Spanish Tragedy, in do. vol. v.
        Works.   Ed. Boas, Oxford, 1900.
Kynaston, Sir Francis, Poems of.   In Minor Caroline Poets, vol. ii.

Lodge, Thomas, Euphues' Golden Legacy *in* Shakespere's Library, vol. ii.,
        London, 1875.
Lovelace, Richard, Poems of.   Ed. Hazlitt, London, 1864.
Lyly, John, Euphues.   Ed. Arber, London, 1868.
        Dramatic Works.   Ed. Fairholt, 2 vols., London, 1858.
        Complete Works.   Ed. Bond, 3 vols., Oxford, 1902.
Lynch, Diella.   In Grosart's Occasional Issues, vol. iv.

Marlowe, Christopher, Works of.   Ed. Dyce, London, 1859.
        Also Ed. Bullen, 3 vols., London, 1887.
Marmion, Shakerley, Plays of.   Edinburgh, 1874.
        Cupid and Psyche.   In Minor Caroline Poets, vol. ii.
Marprelate, Martin, Tracts by and against.   *See* text.
        The Epistle.   Ed. Petheram.
        Also Ed. Arber, The English Scholars' Library.
        Diotrephes, by N. Udall.   Ed. Arber.
        Demonstration of Discipline, by N. Udall.   Ed. Arber.
        An Admonition to the People of England, by T. C.   Ed. Petheram.
        Also Ed. Arber.
        Hay any Work for Cooper.   Ed. Petheram.
        Pap with a Hatchet.   Ed. Petheram.
        An Almond for a Parrot.   Ed. Petheram.
        A Counter-Cuff to Martin Junior, etc., in Works of Nash.   Ed. Grosart.
        Plain Percival, the Peacemaker of England.   Ed. Petheram.
Marston, John, Works of.   Ed. Halliwell, 3 vols., London, 1856.
        Also Ed. Bullen, 3 vols., London, 1885.
        Poems of.   In Grosart's Occasional Issues, vol. xi.
Massinger, Philip.   Ed. Hartley Coleridge, London, 1859.
Middleton, Thomas, Dramatic Works of.   Ed. Bullen, 8 vols., London, 1886.
Milton, John, Poems of.   In Chalmers's British Poets, vol. vii.
        Prose Works of.   2 vols., Philadelphia, 1847.
        Ed. Masson, 3 vols., London, 1890.
Minor Caroline Poets, vols. i. and ii., Oxford, 1905-6.
Mirror for Magistrates, The.   Ed. Hazlewood, 3 vols., London, 1815.
Miscellanies, Seven Poetical.   Ed. Collier, London, 1867.
        Some in Heliconia.
More, Henry, Poems of.   Ed. Grosart.   Privately printed, 1878.
Mulcaster, Richard, Positions.   Ed. Quick, London, 1888.

Nabbes, Thomas, Works of.   In Bullen's Old Plays, New Series, vols. i. and ii.
Nash, Thomas, Works of.   Ed. Grosart, 6 vols.   Privately printed, 1883-85.
        Ed. M'Kerrow, 4 vols., London, 1904.

Park, T., Heliconia.   3 vols., London, 1814.
Peele, George, Works of.   Ed. Dyce, London, 1883.
Percy, W., Cœlia.   In Grosart's Occasional Issues, vol. iv.
Puttenham, George, The Art of English Poesy.   Ed. Arber, London, 1869.
        Also in G. Smith, Elizabethan Critical Essays.

Watson, Thomas, Poems.   Ed. Arber, London, 1870.
Webbe, William, A Discourse of English Poetry.   Ed. Arber, London, 1870.
    Also in G. Smith, Elizabethan Critical Essays.
Webster, John, Works of.   Ed. Dyce, London, 1859.
Wither, George, Hymns and Songs of the Church.   Ed. Farr, London, 1856.
    Hallelujah.   Ed. Farr, London, 1857.
    Philarete, in Arber's English Garner, vol. iv.
    Fidelia, in Arber's English Garner, vol. vi.
    Poems generally in Spenser Society's issues.
Wotton, Sir Henry, Poems of.   In Hannah's Courtly Poets.
Wyatt, Sir Thomas.   *See* Tottel's Miscellany.

II.—GENERAL

THE END